GENERAL THOMAS POSEY
SON OF THE AMERICAN REVOLUTION

GENERAL THOMAS POSEY
SON OF THE AMERICAN REVOLUTION

John Thornton Posey

Michigan State University Press
East Lansing
1992

All Michigan State University Press books are produced on paper which meets the requirements of American National Standard of Information Sciences—Permanence of paper for printed materials ANSI Z23.48-1984

Michigan State University Press
East Lansing, Michigan 48823-5202

Printed in the United States of America

00 99 98 97 96 95 94 93 92 1 2 3 4 5 6 7 8 9 10

Library of Congress Cataloging-in-Publication Data

Posey, John T.
General Thomas Posey: Son Of the American Revolution/ John T. Posey
p. cm.
Includes bibliographical references and index.
ISBN 0-87013-316-0
1. Posey, Thomas, 1750-1818. 2. Generals—United States—Biography. 3.United States. Continental Army—Biography. 4. United States—History—Revolution, 1775-1783—Campaigns. 5. Northwest, Old—History—1775-1865. 6. Southwest, Old—History. I. Title
E207.P74P67 1992
973. 3'092—dc20
[B] 92-50243
CIP

Frontispiece photograph reproduced with permission from The Society of the Cincinnati Library.

CONTENTS

INTRODUCTION

Next let us praise illustrious men. . . .
Some of them left a name behind them,
  so that their praises are still sung,
While others have left no memory,
  and disappeared as though they had not existed,
They are now as though they had never been. . . .

Ecclesiasticus, 44:1, 8-9*

A casual browser, coming upon this volume in a library or bookstore, might well wonder who Thomas Posey was and why a book would be written about his life. Widely known and respected in his own time, his name is unfamiliar to recent generations, and his memory has all but disappeared, as though he had never existed.

Posey was a brave soldier and an outstanding public statesman. His lifetime spanned one of the most exciting and meaningful periods of modern history—the creation and early formative years of the United States. He was by birth a member, and by achievement a notable representative, of what must surely be regarded as the most remarkable and prolific generation to grace this nation. This generation, born between 1725 and 1760, was courageous enough to fight and win the "glorious cause" of freedom and independence, wise enough to create a durable system of democratic government, and enterprising enough to launch a flourishing new society on the unsettled western frontier. In all these grand endeavors Thomas Posey played an active and constructive role. While admittedly not in the first rank of the founding fathers, the cumulative total of his many contributions to the historic events of his era stands out as a truly exceptional and productive life's work.

A life of such proportions has significance and deserves recall and recognition, not only on its own merits, but also as a prototype of many other uncelebrated yet dedicated patriots of Posey's generation, whose worthy but obscure lives adorned their singular era in time. Clearly there were countless other such now-forgotten men

***The Jerusalem Bible,* (Garden City, NY: Doubleday, 1966), 442-443.

who, after fighting for a cause even before there was a country, went on to help establish a government and forge a nation—men who, like Thomas Posey, up to this time have had no biographers. Yet, but for their aggregate efforts and sacrifices history strongly suggests that the revolutionary dream of a democratic society would have failed and life as we know it today in our world would be altered beyond all imagination.

Although Posey's origin is uncertain and his early life and upbringing are not fully documented, he is generally believed to have spent his formative years on the Potomac River adjacent to George Washington's Mount Vernon estate in Fairfax County, Virginia. At an early age and with a limited education, he was forced by financial and family adversity to strike out on his own to the sparsely settled Virginia frontier, where he emerged as a young entrepreneur in the saddlery trade. His first military experience—with an expedition of frontier militiamen sent against the warlike Shawnee Indians beyond the towering Appalachian range—culminated in a bloody, day-long battle along the banks of the Ohio River at Point Pleasant, (now West Virginia).

Posey was an early, eager, and valiant fighter in the American Revolution. His seven years of continuous service in the Virginia Continental line took him from the frozen Great Lakes in the north to the malaria-ridden swamps of south Georgia. His outstanding war record contains documented evidence of repeated acts of personal bravery and resourceful leadership in many military engagements. He fought in, among other battles, the decisive American victories at Saratoga and Yorktown and was wounded in an heroic assault upon the British stronghold of Stony Point on New York's Hudson River, emerging from the conflict a renowned and respected lieutenant-colonel.

In the peaceful interlude following the war Posey married into a patrician family and settled into a new role as a gentleman-planter in his native Virginia, raising a large family while remaining active in national, state and local civic affairs. Posey interrupted this comfortable country lifestyle only once, to serve a tour of duty as brigadier-general in a major expedition against a hostile Native American federation in the Northwest Territory. Soon thereafter, seeking new challenges and following a course pursued by many of his fellow Revolutionary War veterans, he moved his household to the primitive but rapidly expanding western frontier. There, in the last decades of his life, he made many significant contributions in high public office to the formation and development of four new states—as Lieutenant-Governor of Kentucky, United States

Senator from Louisiana, Governor of Indiana Territory, and finally as U.S. Agent for Indian Affairs in Illinois Territory.

The first half-century of Thomas Posey's life was repeatedly and inextricably linked to that of his childhood neighbor and later military and governmental mentor, George Washington. This association, along with personal relationships of varying closeness with Thomas Jefferson, James Madison, James Monroe, John Marshall, Henry Lee and other influential Virginians, launched Posey's postwar civic activities in his native state and enhanced his wide-ranging public career on the western frontier. But as time and distance diminished the influence of national gentry leadership in these emerging states, and a new generation of young, state-oriented populist leaders rose to power, his political fortunes waned. At a time when Federalist extremists in the eastern states were reviled as aristocratic and monarchistic, Posey's fierce nationalism and dedication to a strong central government were perceived as anti-republican. As a result, he lost as many electoral contests in the west as he won, and some of his highest posts came through political appointment, including his crowning achievement as an effective and unifying governor of faction-torn Indiana Territory.

Thomas Posey had his faults and human frailties. Personal vanity, as much as an outraged sense of honor, impelled him, as a young major, to complain directly to commander-in-chief George Washington when General Anthony ("Mad Anthony") Wayne denied him special commendation after the storming of Stony Point. Later, along with other Virginia officers, he threatened to resign his commission after being ordered to embark upon a distant winter campaign without adequate clothing or supplies. In both instances he withdrew his complaints after learning that they had caused acute discomfort and embarrassment to General Washington. Once, in the heat of battle, Posey struck down with his sword one of his own men after mistaking him for an enemy in the darkness; he apologized profusely to the badly wounded sergeant the next day. In his later public career, his retention of two former slaves as indentured servants lent an ambivalent cast to his public position on the politically-explosive issue of slavery in Indiana Territory.

A man of generally meticulous personal integrity and probity, Thomas was not always a good or discerning judge of the characters or motives of others. Several times during his adult life he was financially victimized by unscrupulous or irresponsible men. During the Northwest campaign he felt himself compelled to resign his prized brigadier-general's commission after finding himself caught in a ruthless power struggle between two higher-ranked generals, both of whom considered him a friend and supporter. A single, ill-advised public appearance with the charismatic but delusive former vice-president, Aaron Burr, probably cost Posey the governorship of Kentucky. Finally, he unaccountably chose to maintain an old wartime friendship with the machiavellian General James Wilkinson, long after that "tarnished warrior," a longtime secret agent of Spain, had fallen into disrepute.

Never wealthy, Thomas struggled throughout his life to give his numerous children the educational advantages, stable home environment, and positive paternal role model that he himself had been denied. Although in the end he perceived himself to have failed in many of these cherished goals, it is perhaps a mark of his success as a husband and father that numbered among his ten adult children were a doctor, a lawyer, a pioneering woman educator, a legendary army colonel, and several successful merchants and businessmen. One or more of his issue settled permanently in each of the four frontier states in which he served to become leaders of their communities and founders of local educational or religious institutions.

Some years after his death, an undocumented but persistent tradition arose. It was widely disseminated and accepted as fact throughout the Midwest and seriously addressed in many reputable publications that Thomas Posey had actually been the natural son of George Washington. Although the evidence of such a paternal relationship is circumstantial and speculative, it has never been conclusively refuted, but Posey's importance and claim to fame do not rest upon this unproven mythic folklore. Nevertheless, a strong case can be made that Washington was truly the spiritual, if not the biological, father of Thomas Posey.

The subject of this biography was in his own right an illustrious man well worth remembering. He was arguably the very archetype of a generation of entirely dissimilar individuals who were forged by the unifying crucible of the revolutionary struggle into a dynamic, irresistible force. Some of these same men and women, not content with the laurels won in founding and nurturing a new nation, then turned westward to lend their considerable energies and talents to the expansion and development of that nation. Thomas Posey, a true son of the American Revolution, was one of those productive pioneers, typifying the best and brightest of his extraordinary times. In recounting and documenting the impact of his life upon those times this book aspires to memorialize the first and to illuminate the latter.

CHAPTER ONE

(1750-1774)

". . . born of respectable parentage. . . ."

> He was born of respectable parentage near the Potomack in Virginia in the year 1750 9th of July. In the year 1769 being a young man without fortune, but of tolerable english education he set out in quest of a situation in life that would better his fortune, and settled in the back parts of Virginia near the frontiers. . . .[1]

When Indiana territorial governor Thomas Posey sat down at his desk near the end of his life to compose a detailed autobiographical sketch he chose, for whatever reasons, to devote only eighteen words to his birth, parentage, and his first nineteen years of life. Nowhere in his many surviving letters and other writings is any reference made to the existence or identity of his forebears, parents, brothers or sisters, nor to the circumstances and conditions of his childhood or youthful upbringing. No known birth, marriage, church, death or burial records provide any clue to this missing data, and his name never appears in the contemporary writings or official records of this early period of his life. The very totality of this void has itself become the basis of much speculation and conjecture. In short, his origin and family background constitute the least-known aspects of Posey's long and otherwise well-documented life.

The great weight of scholarly authority holds that Thomas was a member of the household of one Captain John Posey, a colorful if somewhat irresponsible neighbor of George Washington. Captain Posey's home, called "Rover's Delight," was sited on land overlooking the Potomac River, directly adjacent to Washington's Mount Vernon estate in Fairfax County, Virginia. The capricious captain's twenty-five-year social and financial relationship with George Washington has exposed him and his family to unusually-close scrutiny by generations of historians, researchers and biographers of his more renowned neighbor and friend. The considered judgment of many highly respected scholars—among them Dr. J. M. Toner, John C. Fitzpatrick, Rupert Hughes, Nathaniel Wright Stephenson and Waldo Hilary Dunn, Charles W. Stetson, Elswyth Thane, and James Thomas Flexner—places young Thomas within the troubled Posey family circle at Rover's Delight for the first nineteen years of his life.[2] Since, however, no authority has ever cited any documented evidence to support this view, it must still be considered a presumptive, if probable, hypothesis.

An objective examination of what is actually known of Thomas Posey discloses many similarities to George Washington in character, personality and temperament. Perhaps it was these shared qualities that led these scholars and other observers to conclude that the young man's formative years were indeed spent in near proximity to Mount Vernon, where he would have been exposed almost daily to the outstanding example and benign influence of its high-principled squire. In Posey's mature years, the many interactions between the two men arguably support, and certainly do nothing to contradict, the presumption of a close early relationship. Furthermore, there is no known record of any other Posey family, fitting Thomas' autobiographical time and place specifics, from which he could have sprung. Accordingly, the consensus of the cited authorities that Rover's Delight was the household in which Thomas Posey was nurtured and grew to manhood, though admittedly conjectural, is too unanimous and credible to be seriously challenged.

Infinitely more speculative, however, are stories which began to circulate more than a half-century after his death claiming that Posey had really been George Washington's son. These reports were based not only on the known contiguity of the Washington and Posey families in Fairfax County but also on real or perceived similarities in their physical appearance, personal attributes, characters, and achievements. Such startling assertions were unfailingly advanced with fanciful but plausible scenarios, usually supported by totally circumstantial evidence. This basic premise appears to have originated in the Midwest and later became imbedded in the oral tradition or folklore of many of the states where Posey held high public offices in his later career. Such rumors spread throughout the nation and persisted for many decades in newspaper feature articles as well as in the biographical sketches of reputable publications. They were seriously discussed in at least three leading biographies of Washington.[3] The sources, substance and evaluation of these widespread accounts of a paternal relationship between George Washington and Thomas Posey are extensively addressed in Appendix A of this volume.

After more than two centuries, it is highly unlikely that Posey's real parentage or lineage will ever be established with absolute historical certitude. The absence of this basic but critical genetic data lends added significance to the environmental influences that shaped his character and demands closer examination of the particular circumstances and conditions of his upbringing. Thus, from his birth in 1750 to his departure in 1769, young Thomas' life story is inextricably linked to the sorry saga of Captain John Posey—a man characterized by one eminent biographer of Washington, perhaps unfairly, as "that prince of scapegraces."[4] A more balanced and charitable assessment might adjudge the captain to have been a tragi-comic figure, whose obvious flaws and human failings seem even more glaring in the reflected light of his illustrious neighbor's nobility. These two disparate men—John Posey and George Washington—were the role models of Thomas Posey, the child and youth. Their unlikely and uneasy relationship during his maturation is the backdrop to his experience of growing up in an unstable and deteriorating domestic setting, next door to the dignified and disciplined household at Mount Vernon.

The precise time of the arrival in Fairfax County of John Posey, a native Marylander, [5] is uncertain. His first recorded presence there was his appointment as "processioner" of Truro Parish in May 1751,[6] and the earliest confirmation of his marriage to Martha Price Harrison was on 27 June 1752.[7] Martha, the widow of George Harrison who died on or about 21 March 1749,[8] was a substantial freeholder in the county. A record defining her status as a widow dated 26 June 1750,[9] just two weeks before Thomas Posey's known birth date, strongly indicates that she was not his natural mother. Thus, Thomas must have been John Posey's son by an earlier marriage or an unsanctioned union—or he might have been brought later into the household of John and Martha Posey as an adopted or foster child.

During the first decade of their marriage—that of the 1750s—the Poseys' family and fortunes grew and flourished. In addition to substantial Harrison lands Martha brought to the marriage, John won from the Virginia House of Burgesses a coveted license to operate a public ferry across the Potomac River to Maryland.[10] He operated the Virginia side of the franchise from six acres of riverfront land initially leased and later purchased from Thomas Hanson Marshall, owner of Marshall Hall, the Maryland terminus of the ferry.[11] There, on a high bluff overlooking the stately river below, he built for himself and his family a fine home he chose to call "Rover's Delight." The name implies that Posey's past life had been restless or unsettled—a trait that was to continue to characterize him throughout his life.

The structure not only accommodated his growing family, but was large enough to house and feed transient ferry passengers; although not a publicly licensed inn, his ferry advertisements proudly boasted "Private Entertainment kept at the Subscriber's House for Man and Horse." [12] Thus, through the hospitable doors of Rover's Delight, before the alert eyes of the young and impressionable Thomas Posey, passed a panorama of travelers of every class and level of colonial society—from the aristocratic Fairfaxes and eminent gentry like the Washingtons and the George Masons, to the humblest tradesmen, artisans, laborers and slaves. Posey added to his Harrison farms by purchasing from George Washington's youngest brother, Charles, 200 acres of land on the estuary of Dogue Run, a stream flowing into the Potomac just below the ferry landing.[13] There he built a fishing landing and curing sheds, in which he processed for local sale and consumption plentiful catches of shad, herring, bass, carp, perch and sturgeon, all seined and prepared by his slaves from the waters where the creek emptied into the river.[14]

During this decade of material growth, several younger siblings joined Thomas in the Posey household. Martha Posey bore at least four children, John Price, Amelia (Milly), Hanson and St. Lawrence,[15] and possibly a fifth, William.[16] The family was not wealthy enough to afford a resident tutor, but the older children at least received a good basic schooling—the "tolerable english education" mentioned in Thomas' autobiography. Until the family fragmented in 1769, the children probably studied intermittently at one of the Free Schools attended by the offspring of other freeholders of rural Fairfax County, but none of them appear to have advanced beyond the secondary level of education.

John Posey was a frequent and often involuntary party to litigation in the local Fairfax County courts. His most serious legal dispute, extending over most of a decade, was a running battle over land boundaries with John West, Jr. West was both the Executor of George Harrison's will, and as his nephew was the sole residuary devisee of all of Harrison's lands when death terminated Martha's dower life interest in those properties.[17] The case eventually transcended legal issues and became a bitter personal feud between West and Posey, a factor which was to contribute to the latter's eventual financial collapse.

In the spring of 1758, Posey left his young family to pursue a brief soldierly career, during which he acquired the military title by which he was thereafter known by his contemporaries, and later by historians. As a militia captain, he capably led a company of "artificers," serving under George Washington in the French and Indian War. In a six-month campaign to drive the enemy from the strategic frontier post at Fort Duquesne (now Pittsburgh), General John Forbes' combined British-colonial force advanced over the formidable Appalachian range. The job of the artificers, the combat engineers of their day, was to cut a trail through the thick forests, to construct bridges across numerous streams, and to clear and fortify advance camp sites for the main army following some distance behind.[18] Posey and his men were later awarded special compensation for their service, often performed while exposed to sniping and harassment from Indian and French raiding parties.[19]

It is not difficult to envision how eight-year-old Thomas' imagination could be galvanized as Captain Posey related his "war stories" (perhaps embellished by time and distance) to his wife and children around the family fireside. The boy was probably a spellbound audience as the captain re-lived campaign experiences with Washington over a glass of wine during one of the colonel's frequent visits to Rover's Delight while making his daily ride around his beloved Mount Vernon farms. These occasions would have inspired many boyhood games and fantasies; perhaps they sowed seeds that were to flower fifteen years later at another wilderness confrontation along the Ohio with the Indian enemy, at the battle of Point Pleasant. The military influence at Rover's Delight did not end with the Forbes expedition. Captain Posey maintained his militia connections for another four years, with occasional active service on the frontier, notably during Colonel William Byrd's campaign against the Cherokee Indians in south western Virginia. He later collected £137 in bounty money and subsistence pay for recruiting, housing, and training militiamen on his Dogue Run tract during this period.[20]

Tragically, the decade of the 1760s was to bring the financial and personal ruin of Captain John Posey, with devastating impact upon himself and his family. Driven into heavy debt by excessive land acquisitions and improvements, he was unable to control his mounting obligations despite substantial fishery and ferry revenues and farm operations. Some of Washington's biographers judged the captain harshly, others tolerantly. They describe him variously as kindly but unfortunate,[21] shiftless,[22] careless and lazy,[23] improvident, cheerful and lighthearted,[24] amiable, irresolute and "Macawber-like,"[25] happy-go-lucky and unpenitent,[26] and as a "miscreant" and "deadbeat."[27] Captain John might well have been all of this and more, but there was some undefined element in his character that held George Washington's steadfast loyalty and friendship through all the years of their turbulent relationship. One respected scholar attributed Posey's financial distress less to personal shortcomings than to Virginia's "unstable agricultural economy,"[28] but the captain obviously lacked the frugality and prudence of his sagacious Mount Vernon neighbor.

In any event Posey, after exhausting his credit from all other available sources, was forced to turn to Washington for economic support. From small sums borrowed as early as 1755, as time passed the captain began to lean more and more heavily upon his neighbor for cash and services, including the construction of a large barn, outbuildings and barracks on his Dogue Run property. By 1763, after Washington had redeemed several of Posey's overdue notes and relieved him of sizable debts due other creditors, the balance owed had soared to the enormous total of £700. The increasingly uneasy master of Mount Vernon then belatedly secured the debt by taking a first mortgage on Posey's land, slaves and personal property. But two years later, the obligation had grown to £750 when the captain failed to pay even the £35 annual interest charges on the account.[29]

Given this background, Washington's shock can be easily understood when, in 1767, Captain Posey, rather than reducing his debt, sought an additional £500 loan to pay claims other creditors had filed against him in the courts. Not having cash of that magnitude, Washington had to decline the request. But he seized the occasion to offer his struggling friend "the same advice I would give my Bror; were he under the same circumstances." With rare eloquence, he urged Posey to sell off his Fairfax properties, pay all his debts, and move his family to the western frontier, "where an enterprising Man with very little Money may lay the foundation of a Noble Estate."[30] But Captain John was less enterprising than resourceful. A few weeks later, with the sheriff figuratively if not literally at his heels, he was back at Mount Vernon with a new plan—one that would not require any immediate cash outlay by Washington. George Mason, their canny neighbor at nearby Gunston Hall, would loan Posey £300, but only if he could get a responsible surety to co-sign his note. Would the Colonel please oblige? Washington was torn between friendship and sound business judgment, and verbally agonized over what he felt was the inadequate and diminishing value of his collateral. But he finally put aside all his dire misgivings and agreed to sign, although "I dread the consequences of joining you in such a Bond."[31]

Oddly, although Mount Vernon and Rover's Delight were only minutes apart by horseback, Washington invariably chose to express all his strongly-felt views on the alarming state of their financial relationship in the form of letters written to his desperate neighbor. It was almost as though he was too embarrassed or reserved to engage in face-to-face discussions on such a painful topic. He particularly stressed that he was putting his friendship for Captain John and his regard for the Poseys above his fiscal misgivings. He emphasized that none of his past favors to Posey had been granted in the role of moneylender or for the purpose of financial gain or advantage, but on the contrary, "Twas done to serve your family and if possible to save your Estate from dispersion."[32] It is clear that Washington was fond of John and Martha Posey, and was deeply concerned for their children, whom he realized would face almost insurmountable obstacles in life if they were pauperized by the captain's folly.

A decade of declining material fortune does not appear to have diminished Captain Posey's personal prestige or status as one of the most respected gentrymen of Fairfax County. In 1765 he was one of the twelve "most able and discreet persons" elected to the vestry of Truro Parish, receiving the third-highest total of votes, equaling the number cast for Washington himself.[33] Four years later, as his personal world was collapsing about him, his fellow-vestrymen elected him churchwarden, a financial post of the highest trust.[34] He was equally well-regarded by the voters of Fairfax County, coming within a few votes in 1765 of winning one of its two seats in the Virginia House of Burgesses.[35] Throughout this period of economic distress, John Posey, his wife and children continued to be welcome guests of George and Martha Washington at Mount Vernon.[36] Both men were particularly fond of fox hunting, and the captain often joined Washington in daylong gallops over the rolling hills and fields of Fairfax. They rode together to the hounds at least eight times in February of 1768 alone,[37] a frolic prompting Pultzer Prize-winning biographer Douglas Southall Freeman to observe, "Captain Posey had ample hours for the chase and apparently for anything else not connected with paying his debts."[38]

Sadly, the bleak future so grimly foreseen by Washington for the Posey family arrived in the fateful year 1769. Sometime in the months prior, Martha Posey had died, leaving a motherless family of at least five children in the care of her increasingly distracted husband. Upon her death, title to all the lands in which she held a life estate from her first husband reverted to John West, Jr. This event only exacerbated the already bitter dispute between West and Posey over the true land boundaries of the Harrison properties, and West was now also claiming legal title to the six-acre tract upon which Rover's Delight stood. The captain was spending long periods in Maryland, seeking ways to repair his rapidly-dwindling fortunes. In his absence, responsibility for day-to-day operations fell largely upon the family's oldest sibling, 18-year-old Thomas Posey. He must have had to turn frequently to his concerned neighbors, the Washingtons, for advice and aid in coping with worsening conditions at home. In one revealing note, Captain Posey wrote Washington on 28 January 1769 to ask if his wife could spare any winter clothes for his daughter Amelia, explaining that he himself did not expect to return from Maryland for at least another month.[39]

Less than four months later, after a brief visit home, the captain had again left his struggling family and returned to Maryland. Finding his creditors there as persistent as those in Virginia, he resorted to a desperate but typically flamboyant gesture—a public notice in the weekly Maryland Gazette that he would meet them all in one of three designated towns in August, "where they will thankfully be paid." For his part, Captain John solemnly asserted, "nothing but Death will prevent his Attendance."[40] A fortnight later, for those creditors who remained skeptical of his intent or ability to pay, he ran two additional notices, one announcing that on 25 May 1769 Captain John Posey, Esq. had married one Miss Elizabeth Adair,

> . . . a Person of good Family, considerable Education, and large Fortune. Captain Posey's Oeconomy, Honour and Spirit must have been great. It is said that the Lady, the morning before she married, made her estate, real and personal, over to Captain Posey, tho' she has a Sister, and courted by many.[41]

The second notice, placed just below the first, asserted that "one of Captain John Posey's House Wenches . . . had Three Sons at a Birth, February, 1766; August, 1767, Two Girls; March, 1769, one Son and a Daughter; there was but Two Hours between the Two, the Boy is black with Wool, the Girl is White with white Hair, like a white Child. All the children is living."[42]

Whatever effect this series of three bizarre public advertisements had on his other creditors, Posey got an immediate reaction from his principal patron George Washington, an avid scanner of the weekly journals. After first wishing him "joy" in his new marriage, the squire of Mount Vernon had nothing but bad tidings for the new bridegroom—his neglected affairs back in Fairfax County had "now come to a Crisis." George Mason was demanding immediate payment on Posey's now-defaulted £300 note and bond, and a group of Virginia creditors had sued in Chancery court to compel an immediate public sale of the captain's estate. At Rover's Delight itself, conditions were deplorable—the horses had nothing to eat, and the slaves had only a few days' supply of bread left on hand. Left unspoken was how the hapless Posey children were faring in these dire circumstances.[43]

Captain John hurried home with his new bride but soon found himself engulfed in a sea of troubles. On 10 July Posey's attorney, Philip Alexander, came to Rover's Delight with John West, Jr. to make a joint survey of the six-acre tract preliminary to an approaching hearing on West's pending eviction suit. Washington stopped by, as he often did when out inspecting his outlying farms, and happened to overhear the captain openly boasting to other well-wishers of the great wealth he had acquired by his recent marriage.[44] Washington had good reason to believe that Posey was bluffing, but said nothing. Later, after getting Captain John's fervid assurance that George Mason's insistent demands for repayment of his loan would be fully satisfied from Mrs. Posey's holdings by mid-October, he retorted candidly: "I shall tell you what I have heard, and that is, that your Wife not only denies having conveyed her Estate, or any part of it, to you but has also declared that She will never do it."[45] Washington's information on the mindset of that feisty lady would soon be proved to have been only too accurate.

The luckless head of the Posey family reached new depths of ignominy on 21 August when he was haled before the Fairfax County Court by his bondsmen to answer the complaint of several individual creditors and was committed to jail when he was unable to pay their outstanding claims.[46] Washington, who probably would have stepped in to spare his friend this crowning indignity, was unfortunately far away at this time in Berkeley Springs, taking the waters with his family.[47] The captain was not released until 18 September, and then only when two other compassionate neighbors posted a special security bond on his behalf.[48]

Upon his return to Mount Vernon, Washington rode repeatedly to Rover's Delight to discuss with Posey the approaching Chancery Court lawsuit but discovered to his dismay that it was "no easy matter to find the Captn. at home and still more difficult to take him in a trim capable of business."[49] Having seen with his own eyes that the distraught captain was drinking heavily, he soon learned from a reliable source that Posey was also experiencing serious domestic strife with his new wife, Elizabeth. During the Washingtons' absence, one of these altercations had become so heated that Mrs. Posey had to flee for her life, with the captain in hot pursuit, across Dogue Run to the nearest available neighbors, the patrician George William Fairfaxes of Belvoir. There, the angry couple resumed their quarrel in the presence of their embarrassed hosts. The Fairfaxes later told Washington that the captain's wife accused him of planning to secretly ship both his and her slaves to be sold at the Florida slave market. When the alarmed Washington, visualizing the disappearance of a major part of his loan collateral, confronted the captain on the truth of this accusation, Posey denied that he actually had any such plan, "but acknowledged that he had made use of such expressions to his Wife in Order to plague her."[50]

But the incident had sown seeds of suspicion in Washington's mind, and he began to fear that all his trust and confidence in his friend's integrity might well have been misplaced. His emotions were understandably mixed when one day soon thereafter Posey rode up to Mount Vernon's small, rounded front entrance "perfectly Sober and proposed of his own voluntary action to sell his Estate finding it in vain to struggle on longer against the Terms of Debt that oppresses him."[51] He had some lingering doubts that the captain was only stalling for time, and that his proposed plan to sell off his properties was "only a finess to bespeak Security."[52] But Posey was as good as his word. He posted in several nearby towns formal notices that on 23 October there would be a public sale of:

> A TRACT of valuable LAND . . . adjoining to the land on which the subscriber now keeps ferry . . . On the premises is a large barn . . . eight framed barracks . . . a large corn-house . . . with a good fishery appertaining . . . about twenty-five choice SLAVES, consisting of men, women and children. Also sundry horses, cattle, sheep, and hogs; together with various kinds of household furniture, and implements of husbandry . . . .[53]

The notice, which Posey also published in the Virginia Gazette, stipulated that "the money arising from the sales to be paid into the hands of George Washington, Esq." Washington warned creditors who threatened court action to delay the voluntary sale that Posey was unreliable, citing "the Mad and distracted manner in which he lives." Recommending discretion, he added that "if Captn. Poseys Intentions are honest and upright, I shall be sorry even for my Suspicions of him, but should be more so if any thing was propagated through my means that should cast any unjust odium on His Character."[54] The creditors accordingly had the court simply confirm the 23 October sale date, providing that its initial proceeds be applied to satisfy Washington's first lien, with any excess going to the secondary creditors.[55]

The three-day public auction at Posey's premises attracted most of the gentry of the area, as well as large crowds of curious spectators and idle busybodies. When the auctioneer's hammer fell for the last time, all of the captain's lands, slaves, horses, livestock, farm implements and household furniture had been sold. The only property of value spared was the six-acre homesite and Potomac ferry landing, the legal title to which was tied up in the John West litigation. As a welcome addition to the Mount Vernon estate, Washington bid in for himself the 200-acre Dogue Run tract once owned by his brother, Charles, containing the fishery and other buildings his craftsmen and slaves had built on credit for Captain Posey. The total sales receipts were sufficient to satisfy all of Washington's claims against the captain, including the £300 bond to George Mason, except a £70 open account not subject to lien and thus not included in the Chancery Court's order allocating the proceeds of sale.[56]

The children of John Posey were forlorn witnesses to the destruction of their father's dream of a handsome estate for himself and the irretrievable loss of their own fortunes and future prospects. But the worst was yet to come. Within a few weeks after enduring this public humiliation, Elizabeth Adair Posey, the captain's ill-fated wife of less than six months, suddenly died of unknown causes.[57] It would take still later personal and financial reverses to finally crush the "Micawber-like" spirit of Captain John Posey. But the devastating effect of the events of 1769 upon his helpless family can only be imagined, as the year's end left them in a house stripped of most of its furnishings and personal possessions, virtually landless, and without any adequate means of support or sustenance.

Only two years had passed since George Washington, in what a biographer termed "one of the longest and most eloquent letters he ever wrote,"[58] had strongly advised his friend, Captain Posey to salvage what he could from his Fairfax holdings and make a new start on the frontier. Such a move, he declaimed in glowing terms, surely offered "the moral certainty of laying the foundation of good Estates to yr. childn . . . many good families are retiring into the Interior parts of the Country for the benefit of their Children."[59] The captain, to his children's disadvantage and his own discredit, chose to ignore Washington's wise counsel. But sometime late in the traumatic year 1769, probably soon after the public sale, nineteen-year-old Thomas Posey, having witnessed the ruin of his family and any prospects for himself in Fairfax County, set out to pursue for himself the vision so vividly portrayed to the captain by the master of Mount Vernon.

When young Posey rode out alone for the last time from decimated Rover's Delight an impenetrable and immutable curtain of time seemingly dropped, either by choice or chance, between his past life and all that was to come in the future. If, after his departure, there was any further contact or association by or between Thomas and any other member of the Rover's Delight family, no record remains today. What else is known of the further fortunes and ultimate fate of his siblings, and of the improvident Captain John Posey, is described in Appendix B of this volume.

There is every reason to believe that Thomas consulted with George Washington before setting his sights on a promising area in the west to go "in quest of a situation in life that would better his fortune."[60] No one, after all, had a more intimate knowledge of frontier conditions. A decade before, as commander of colonial militia, Washington had spent many months beyond the Blue Ridge mountains, establishing and maintaining a string of military outposts throughout the Shenandoah Valley.[61] His duties had taken him often to the vast reaches of Augusta County, composing the southern portion of the Valley. In the intervening years, Staunton, its county seat, had grown from a little frontier settlement to a key crossroads center—a final destination for many settlers, a major point of departure for other, more daring, pioneers preparing to venture across the towering Appalachian range to the immense wilderness beyond.

It was to this vibrant community that Thomas came in pursuit of his own personal dream of a successful and fulfilling life. Robert Mitchell, in his scholarly study of the socio-economic structure of the early Shenandoah Valley, has painstakingly described the world into which young Posey rode in the year 1769. The early development of Augusta County grew from huge land grants held by such noted Virginia proprietors as William Beverley, whose descendant and namesake was to marry Thomas Posey's youngest daughter, Sarah Ann. The area was soon attracting a swarm of German and Scotch-Irish immigrants, funneled down the Valley floor from Pennsylvania and Maryland on the Great Wagon Road. Other arriving land-seekers were displaced freeholders and recent European immigrants from eastern Virginia. Some of the newcomers stayed in the lush dale, farming small plots on which they paid annual quit-rents to the proprietors, while others pushed on into the Carolinas and Georgia, and later into Kentucky and Tennessee. In this period, living conditions in the Valley were, at best, primitive—in stark and pervasive contrast to the more affluent and comfortable society of Tidewater Virginia into which Thomas Posey had been born and raised.[62]

Posey's first two years in Staunton are not documented by any public or private record, but they clearly epitomize a period of great hardship and adjustment, an unremitting struggle to overcome want and to rise above obscurity. Virtually penniless, he did not have the means to buy or lease land. His only marketable skills were whatever knowledge of farming and any hands-on experience in the related trades of husbandry that he might have acquired while growing up in the slave-supported economy of Fairfax County. He chose (or perhaps was reduced) to apprentice at one of those trades—saddlery. With his good basic education and innate intelligence, familiarity with commercial dealings observed at Rover Delight's ferry and fishery, and undoubtedly with much toil and sweat, he first emerges into documented history in the year 1771 as a trained craftsman and budding entrepreneur.[63]

In most colonial towns of the era, the local inn was the center of social and commercial intercourse, providing food, drink and shelter for weary travelers, as well as a lively gathering place for local townspeople of all classes and persuasions. That vital function in Staunton was served by Mathews' Ordinary. Its proprietors were Sampson Mathews and his younger brother George, who rose to be a general in the Revolution, and later served as governor of Georgia.[64] The brothers were the most important merchants in Staunton. In addition to their central inn-store-residence on the town's Main Street, they operated two other outlying stores, owned several town lots and nearby farms, and were community leaders in most civic and military enterprises.[65] Their parents, John and Ann Archer Mathews, who were among the first settlers in the Valley, had had two other sons.[66] John Mathews, Jr., along with his wife and all six of their children, had been massacred and burned in their farm homestead during one of the random Indian raids to which all outlying residents in the area were exposed. The fourth son, Joshua, and his wife had also died young, possibly at the hands of marauders, but they had left surviving them two daughters, the younger of whom, Martha, was the legal ward of her uncle Sampson Mathews.[67]

That convivial and peripatetic rover, Captain John Posey, had spent considerable time in Augusta County while serving under Colonel William Byrd in the Cherokee expedition of the early 1760s. During his stopovers in Staunton, he had certainly become well acquainted with the accommodations of Mathews' Ordinary and also with its hospitable proprietors. Accordingly, it is highly likely that Thomas Posey carried with him to Staunton a letter of introduction from the captain to the well-connected innkeepers and merchants, Sampson and George Mathews. There is no reason to doubt that they extended a cordial welcome and perhaps some early financial or moral support to the well-mannered and hard-working young man from Fairfax County. It is equally likely that Thomas appeared to be, at least in the estimation of Sampson Mathews, an ideal match for his eligible young ward. Under these circumstances, the record not surprisingly shows that, by late 1772, Posey had wooed and won the hand of eighteen-year-old Martha Mathews.[68] Within months thereafter, young Thomas had opened his own saddlery shop in Fincastle, the tiny county seat of the newly created Shenandoah Valley county of Botetourt, about fifty miles south of Staunton.[69]

The curing and tanning of animal hides and the manufacture of leather goods was one of the most important small-craft industries in the Valley. Raw materials for the laborious process were provided by local hunters and Indian traders, who brought in bear and deer skins, as well as the hides and skins of cattle, sheep and hogs from local farmers. In this early period, most of the finished products of this industry were sold and consumed in the immediate area, but after 1800 leather goods were produced in such quantities that they became a major export. Augusta County eventually became the leading saddlewear manufacturer in the state.[70]

From all appearances, Thomas' marriage and business both seem to have flourished. The new Posey household soon acquired the services of its first servant, an indentured female maid,[71] doubtless to assist Martha Posey in caring for the young couple's first child, Thomas, born in 1773.[72] That same year, one James Gray, age 22 and late of Augusta County, entered into an "Indenture of Apprenticeship" with Thomas Posey, Saddler, of Botetourt County, "to be taught the art and mystery of a saddler."[73] A second child, born to the Poseys on 19 September 1774, was named John, honoring either Captain Posey of Rover's Delight, or possibly Martha's late grandfather or uncle.[74] But the rising young craftsman was not at his wife's bedside to welcome the arrival of his new son. He was in the wilderness beyond the massive mountain range that towered just west of the little frontier town—on a perilous venture that was to write the opening chapter of Thomas Posey's long and wide-ranging military career.

The dozen or so years immediately preceding 1774 had brought events of portentous historical significance—a series of increasingly serious and hostile occurrences that had driven a deep wedge between Great Britain and its restive American colonies. Repressive legislation, beginning with the Stamp Act (1765) and the 1767 Townshend Acts, designed to curb growing colonial disaffection, had only produced growing and more organized opposition, culminating in the dramatically symbolic "Boston Tea Party" in late 1773. The British reacted to this latest overt demonstration of American resistance with a series of punitive laws known in the colonies as the "Coercive and Intolerable Acts." The implementation of these laws virtually blockaded the city of Boston, and led directly to the convening of the first colonial Continental Congress in Philadelphia on 5 September 1774.

This sequence of events was being closely followed throughout Virginia. But of more immediate concern to frontier Virginians were the after-effects of the royal Proclamation Line of 1763, which had reserved for the resident Indian tribes all ground west of the Appalachian mountains. This unwelcome delineation had been more honored in breach than in observance by the land-hungry Virginians, who continued to straggle over the mountains to stake out homesteads along the Great Kanawha and other southern tributaries of the Ohio River, in what is now West Virginia. Here, they were exposed to repeated and deadly raids by the war-like Shawnee Indians, whose main villages were located just north of the Ohio. In a move intended to discourage further white migration into the troubled area, the British government enacted the Quebec Act of 1774. It provided for the annexation to Quebec Province of all territory north of the Ohio River—land which Virginia (as well as Pennsylvania) claimed as its own.[75]

Meanwhile John Murray, Earl of Dunmore, the colonial governor of Virginia, was under great pressure to respond to frantic appeals from the beleaguered frontier settlers south of the Ohio. He moved to organize an expeditionary force of volunteer militia to secure the lives and homes in the settled area by quelling further Shawnee incursions. Lord Dunmore's strategy called for separate columns to advance into the region from two different directions. Three regiments of frontiersmen recruited solely in Augusta, Botetourt and Fincastle counties, commanded by an experienced Indian-fighter, Colonel Andrew Lewis,[76] were to move across the Allegheny range and follow the Great Kanawha River to its confluence with the Ohio. Meanwhile, another force made up of militia from the northern Shenandoah counties plus some British regulars, under Dunmore's personal command, was to move by water down the Ohio from Fort Duquesne (present-day Pittsburgh). Dunmore's column was to link up with Lewis' at the Great Kanawha, and the combined force would then cross the Ohio and advance together against the Shawnees to the north.

Eight hundred stalwart frontiersmen flocked to Lewis' banner. Most who survived the campaign would later fight in the American revolution, and of their number seven became generals, and another six regimental commanders. After the War of Independence, many of this little army would also go on to posts of distinction in civil life, as governors, senators and congressmen, and dozens of counties, cities and towns would honor their names.[77] It was Thomas Posey's unique destiny to be numbered in each of these categories of distinguished service. He, along with his wife Martha's two uncles, Sampson and George Mathews, signed on to this risky venture.[78] At age twenty-four, Posey was commissioned Commissary General, or quartermaster, of Lewis' brigade, a post of heavy responsibility for the inexperienced young saddler. It was his duty to procure, transport and distribute all food, supplies and equipment required by the troops, as they plodded along their line of march farther and farther from Camp Union, their supply base near what is today's Lewisburg, West Virginia.[79]

In his later autobiographical sketch, Posey attributes his selection to the commissariat post to "being a young man pretty well acquainted with business, and very active in all his transactions."[80] It is apparent that in the short time he had operated his saddlery, he had already acquired a reputation for honesty and efficiency in his commercial dealings. Campaign dispatches confirm that he was indeed quite "active" in bringing up packhorses laden with ammunition, flour, salt and other necessities along newly cut trails too narrow to accommodate wagons and in driving small herds of beef cattle along those same trails. For nineteen arduous days the little army struggled for 160 miles through high mountains and thick forests, crossing many rivers and streams, and constantly exposed to the threat of ambush by the always watchful but unseen Indian enemy.[81] On 1 October, Lewis' brigade reached the southern bank of the broad Ohio River at Point Pleasant, the agreed rendezvous point, but waited there in vain for the arrival of Lord Dunmore's column. The governor, instead of moving on down the river to join Lewis according to plan, had unaccountably landed many miles upstream in what is now southern Ohio, and marched northward. He halted before reaching the nearest Shawnee village, to receive and consider peace overtures from the enemy tribes.

Contextually, it is noteworthy that at this very time, Virginia's delegation to the first Continental Congress, numbering among its members George Washington and Patrick Henry, was convening with its counterparts in Philadelphia. Even at this early date, most knowledgeable observers felt that an armed struggle with the mother country was inevitable. In retrospect, although not yet realized by the isolated frontiersmen waiting uneasily along the banks of the Ohio River, the American Revolution had already begun. There has been much subsequent speculation that Dunmore, callously anticipating the approaching conflict, had not only unnecessarily initiated the Indian war,[82] but had devised his two-pronged strategy and his later deviation from it to "set up" Lewis' force for annihilation.[83] The loss of eight hundred of Virginia's best fighting men would certainly have depleted the future manpower pool of the state's revolutionary forces. Furthermore, a Dunmore-contrived or sanctioned victory by the Indians over the hated frontiersmen would arguably have reinforced the inclination of these interior tribes to ally themselves with the British in the coming war—as indeed most of them subsequently did.

The hypothesis remains unproven, but the fact is that, in the first light of dawn on 10 October, while Dunmore's parleys with Indian peace emissaries were proceeding a hundred miles away, a large force of Shawnee, Delaware, Mingo, Wynadot and Cayuga warriors, led by the able war chief Cornstalk, attacked Lewis' riverbank encampment at Point Pleasant. The battle lasted for many hours—one of the few engagements in American history when Indians mounted a sustained, mass assault upon a fortified white position. Throughout the attack, Chief Cornstalk's deep voice could be heard above the gunfire and cries of the combatants, exhorting his warriors to "be strong, be strong!" After repeated waves of attackers failed to breach the last barricade protecting the main camp, the Indians retired with heavy but uncounted losses, while the Virginians counted 75 killed and 140 wounded.[84] The defeated

Cornstalk skillfully withdrew the remnants of his war party across the river and, with Lewis' force in hot pursuit, retreated rapidly toward Chillicothe, the site of the peace talks between Lord Dunmore and tribal chiefs. The Native Americans so feared and hated Lewis' "Long Knives" that they prevailed upon the governor to exclude the Virginians from the conference—they were ordered to return across the Ohio while he finalized the terms of the peace treaty.[85]

Thomas Posey's personal role in the Point Pleasant fighting is unknown. It may be safely assumed, on the basis of his later behavior in combat, that he did not flinch from his first exposure to hostile fire and imminent peril—the ordeal may indeed have laid the foundation for future battle exploits. Perhaps, like George Washington in his first military engagement in this same wilderness setting, he heard the musket balls whistling past his head and found "something charming in the sound."[86]

Posey had proved himself to be a good soldier in Dunmore's War. The experience gained in fighting American Indians would serve him well in years to come, and he had earned the respect of his peers—always of much importance to him. Late in 1774, the victorious frontiersmen marched back to their homes to the cheers of their friends and families and the acclaim of all Virginia. But, having prevailed over a menacing presence in the west, they were immediately confronted by an even greater challenge looming over the eastern horizon. Thomas hardly had time to get settled down with his wife and two young sons in Fincastle and start to rebuild his neglected saddlery trade when he was caught up in the irresistible tide of history now rapidly engulfing the continent.

NOTES

1. "A Short Biography of the Life of Governor Thomas Posey," Thomas Posey Papers, Indiana Historical Society Library, Indianapolis, IN (hereafter cited as IHS).
2. J.M. Toner, ed., *Diary of Col. George Washington, 1771* (Washington, DC: American Historical Society, 1892), 123n.37; John C. Fitzpatrick, "The George Washington Scandals," *Scribner's Magazine*, 81 (April 1927): 389-95; in John C. Fitzpatrick, *The George Washington Scandals* (Alexandria, VA: *Scribner's Magazine*, 1929), 5; Rupert Hughes, *George Washington: The Rebel and the Patriot, 1762-1777* (New York: William Morrow & Co., 1927), 655; Nathaniel Wright Stephenson and Waldo Hilary Dunn, *George Washington* (New York, London, and Toronto: Oxford University Press, 1940), 1:269n.46; Charles W. Stetson, *Washington and His Neighbors*

(Richmond: Garrett & Massies, 1956), 143; Elswyth Thane, *Potomac Squire* (Mount Vernon, VA: Mount Vernon Ladies Association, 1953), 83; James Thomas Flexner, *George Washington: The Forge of Experience, 1732-1775* (Boston: Little, Brown & Co., 1965), 253; see also: Kate Mason Rowland, *The Life of George Mason* (New York and London: Oxford University Press, 1892), 118-19; Christopher B. Coleman, "George Washington and the West," *Indiana Magazine of History*, 28(1932): 159.

3. John C. Fitzpatrick, *George Washington Himself* (Indianapolis: Bobs Merrill, 1933), 155; Hughes, *Washington*, 655-56; Stephenson and Dunn, *Washington*, 1:269n.46.
4. Flexner, *Washington*, 252. Flexner inadvertently refers to Captain John Posey as "Captain Thomas Posey."
5. James Wade Emison Jr., T*he Emison Families: Final Supplement* (Vincennes, IN: James Wade Emison, Jr., 1969), 220.
6. Rev. Philip Slaughter, *The History of Truro Parish in Virginia*, ed. Edward L. Goodwin (Philadelphia: George W. Jacobs & Co., 1908), 28-29.
7. W.W. Abbot and Dorothy Twohig, eds., *The Papers of George Washington, Colonial Series,* 6 vols. to date (Charlottesville, VA: The University Press of Virginia, 1982-), 1:51-52.
8. George Harrison's will was filed 21 March 1749, Will Book "A," 260-62, Fairfax County Court Archives, Judicial Center, Fairfax County, Fairfax, VA (hereafter cited as FXCOVA).
9. A court order dated 26 June 1750 refers to the "widow and relict of George Harrison" as Martha Harrison. Court Order Book 1749, FXCOVA, 78-79.
10. William Waller Hening, ed., *The Statutes at Large: Being a Collection of all the Laws of Virginia . . .* Session of November 1753, Vol. 6, 375-76.
11. Thomas Marshall to John Posey, 21 September 1757, deed of conveyance, Deed Book D-1, FXCOVA, 477-78.
12. *The Maryland Gazette*, 1 July 1762; Donald Jackson and Dorothy Twohig, eds., *The Diaries of George Washington*, 7 vols. (Charlottesville, VA: The University Press of Virginia, 1976-79), 1:211.
13. Jackson and Twohig, eds., *The Diaries of Washington*, 1:235-36.
14. Hughes, *Washington*, 651; Stetson, *Washington*, 105-6.
15. Jackson and Twohig, eds., *The Diaries of Washington*, 1:231.
16. Wilfred Jordan, ed., *Colonial and Revolutionary Families*, (Pennsylvania), new ser., part 2, vol 4. (New York: Genealogical Publishing Co., 1932), 4:494-97.
17. Court Order Book 1754, 37, 67; Court Order Book 1756, FXCOVA, 85, 109.
18. Murtie Jane Clark, *Colonial Soldiers of the South, 1732- 1774* (Baltimore: Genealogical Publishing Co., 1986), 503, 505-6, 520, 522-25, 528, 534, 538-40; Abbot and Twohig, eds., *Papers of Washington, Colonial Series*, 5:258n.1, 5:268n.1, 5:287n.3, 5:364n.5, 5:383n.2, 6:32n.1, 6:127n.1.
19. Douglas Southall Freeman, *George Washington: A Biography.* 7 vols. (New York: Charles Scribner's Sons, 1948-57), 3:99.
20. Ibid.; F.B. Kegley, *Virginia Frontier* (Roanoke, VA: Southwest Virginia Historical Society, 1938), 269.
21. Paul Wilstach, *Mount Vernon: Washington's Home and the Nation's Shrine* (New York: Doubleday,1916), 77.

22. Hughes, *Washington,* 656.
23. Paul Van Dyke, *George Washington: The Son of His Country* (New York and London: Charles Scribner's Sons, 1931), 209.
24. Stephenson and Dunn, *Washington,* 1:269, 272-73.
25. Stetson, *Washington,* 139.
26. Thane, *Potomac Squire*, 55
27. Flexner, *Washington*, 252.
28. Freeman, *Washington*, 3:234n.23. Dr. Freeman suggested that a scholarly monograph on the decline and fall of Captain John Posey might provide an interesting study of the economic distress of rural colonial Virginia.
29. *Ledger A of George Washington,* 3 vols. (Boston: Massachusetts Historical Society, 1922), 1:14, 92; 2:168, 3:256, The Newberry Library, Chicago, IL.
30. Washington to John Posey, 24 June 1767, *The Writings of George Washington,* ed. John C. Fitzpatrick, 39 vols. (Washington, DC: U.S. Government Printing Office, 1931-44), 2:455-60.
31. Ibid., 24 September 1767, 2:477.
32. Ibid.
33. Freeman, *Washington*, 3:142.
34. Court order dated 22 March 1769, Court Order Book 1768, FXCOVA, 107.
35. Freeman, *Washington*, 3:141.
36. John C. Fitzpatrick, ed., *The Diaries of George Washington*, 4 vols. (Boston and New York: Houghton Mifflin Co., 1925), 1:119-20, 124, 139, 142, 252, 265, 333, 348-49, 373-74; 2:6, 23, 45, 64, 66, 71-72, 75, 83, 120-21, 138-39, 147, 183.
37. Ibid., 1:251-54.
38. Freeman, *Washington*, 3:196.
39. John Posey to Washington, 28 January 1769, *Letters to Washington and Accompanying Papers*, ed. Stanislaus M. Hamilton, 5 vols. (Boston and New York: Houghton Mifflin Co., 1898-1902), 3:341.
40. *The Maryland Gazette,* 15 May 1769.
41. Ibid., "The two following being paid for as Advertisements, we insert them as such," 1 June 1769.
42. Ibid.
43. Washington to John Posey, 11 June 1769, *Writings of Washington*, ed. Fitzpatrick, 2:507-11.
44. Jackson and Twohig, eds., *Diaries of Washington*, 2:166.
45. Washington to John Posey, 26 July 1769, *Writings of Washington*, ed. Fitzpatrick, 2:517-21.
46. Court Order Book 1768, FXCOVA, 212.
47. Freeman, *Washington*, 3:231.
48. Court Order Book 1768, FXCOVA, 234.
49. Washington to Robert Hanson Harrison, 7 October 1769, *Writings of Washington*, ed. Fitzpatrick, 2:523-25.
50. Ibid., Washington to Hector Ross, 9 October 1769, 2:525-27.
51. Ibid., Washington to Robert Hanson Harrison, 7 October 1769, 2:523-25.
52. Ibid., Washington to Hector Ross, 9 October 1769, 2:525-27.
53. "To be SOLD for ready money, at Rover's Delight, in Fairfax County, on Monday the 23rd inst. (October)," *Virginia Gazette*, 19 October 1769.

54. Washington to Hector Ross, 9 October 1769, *Writings of Washington*, ed. Fitzpatrick, 2:525-27.
55. Jackson and Twohig, eds., *Diaries of Washington*, 2:188.
56. Ibid., 2:189; Freeman, *Washington*, 3:231-33.
57. Daniel McCarty to Washington, 6 December 1869, *Letters to Washington*, ed. Hamilton, 3:365-66, .
58. Hughes, *Washington*, 652.
59. Washington to John Posey, 24 June 1767, *Writings of Washington*, ed. Fitzpatrick, 2:455-60.
60. "A Short Biography of the Life of Governor Thomas Posey," Thomas Posey Papers, IHS.
61. Freeman, *Washington*, 2:120, 170, 208.
62. Robert Mitchell, *Commercialism and the Frontier: Perspectives on the Early Shenandoah Valley* (Charlottesville, VA: The University Press of Virginia, 1977), 56, 58, 64, 230.
63. Lyman Chalkley, ed., *Records of Augusta County, Virginia, 1745-1800*, 3 vols. (Baltimore: Genealogical Publishing Co., 1966), 3:524.
64. Joseph A. Waddell, *Annals of Augusta County, Virginia* (Staunton, VA: C.R. Caldwell, 1902), 310.
65. Mitchell, *Commercialism and the Frontier*, 216-18.
66. Gladys B. Clem, *It Happened Around Staunton in Virginia* (Berryville, VA: Gladys B. Clem, 2nd ed., 1976), 21-22.
67. Chalkley, ed. *Records of Augusta County*, 1:149, 168, 357.
68. Ibid., 1:42; William A. Crozier, ed. *Virginia County Records* (Richmond, VA: Genealogical Publishing, Co, 1986), 4:88.
69. Robert Douthat Stoner, *A Seed Bed of the Republic* (Radford, VA: Commonwealth Press, Inc.,1962), 311.
70. Mitchell, *Commercialism and the Frontier*, 206.
71. Stoner, *A Seed Bed of the Republic*, 311.
72. Emison, *Emison Families—Final Supplement*, 220.
73. Chalkley, ed. *Records of Augusta County*, 1:372.
74. Emison, *Emison Families—Final Supplement*, 220.
75. Curtis P. Nettles, "Washington on the Eve of the Revolution," *George Washington: A Profile*, ed. James Morton Smith (New York: Hill & Wang, 1969), 77; Virginius Dabney, *Virginia—The New Dominion* (Garden City, NY: University Press of Virginia,1971), 123-25.
76. The Irish-born Lewis had fought alongside Washington in three earlier campaigns: Fort Necessity, Braddock's expedition, and (along with Captain John Posey) the Forbes campaign. *Dictionary of American Biography,* 1963 ed. s.v. "Lewis, Andrew," 6:206.
77. Dabney, *Virginia,* 124.
78. Clem, *It Happened Around Staunton,* 22.
79. William A. Crozier, *Virginia Colonial Militia, 1651-1776* (Baltimore: Genealogical Publishing Co.,1954), 89-90.
80. "A Short Biography of the Life of Governor Thomas Posey," Thomas Posey Papers, IHS.

81. Reuben G. Twaites et al., eds. *Documentary History of Dunmore's War* (Madison, WI: Heritage Books, 1905), 196, 314-16, 350.
82. Nettles, "Washington," *Washington: A Profile,* ed., Smith, 77.
83. J. Lewis Peyton, *History of Augusta County, Va.*, 2d ed. (Bridgewater, VA: Heritage Books,1953), 155-56; Charles Campbell. *History of the Colony and Ancient Dominion of Virginia* (Philadelphia: Lippincott, 1860), 588, 594; James Hall, "Memoir of Thomas Posey, Major General and Governor of Indiana," in *The Library of American Biography*, ed. Jared Sparks, ser. 2 (Boston: Little, Brown & Co., 1846), 9:366, 370.
84. Hall, "Memoir," *Library of American Biography,* ed. Sparks, 369; Campbell, *History of the Colony and Ancient Dominion*, 586-87.
85. For detailed accounts of the battle of Point Pleasant and its immediate aftermath, see generally: Virgil A. Lewis, *History of the Battle of Point Pleasant* (Charleston, WV: N.p., 1909); Livia Nye Simpson-Poffenbarger, *The Battle of Point Pleasant.* (Point Pleasant, WV: *The State Gazette*, 1909). It was to this conference that the Cayuga chief, Logan, sent his emotional and eloquent address (later immortalized by Thomas Jefferson in his "Notes on Virginia"), lamenting the massacre of his entire family by drunken white settlers. Campbell, *History of the Colony and Ancient Dominion*, 590-593.
86. Flexner, *Washington*, 89.

CHAPTER TWO

(1775-1778)

"The glorious cause"

The new year of 1775 brought word to Fincastle of the unfolding of one momentous event after another in the northeastern colonies. The first serious skirmishes between British regular troops and American minutemen at Lexington and Concord in faraway Massachusetts were followed by the patriots' siege of the king's forces in Boston and the decisive sessions of the Second Continental Congress in Philadelphia. Historians have ably identified and analyzed the improbable bond, transcending distance and disparate economic, social and cultural values, that drew together all classes and strata of American colonial society in a great common undertaking. But to the young frontier saddler, Thomas Posey, one single occurrence in the fast-moving chain of events must have overshadowed all others: the Congress' selection of George Washington,[1] the generous neighbor of his youth and the continued benefactor of his Fairfax County family,[2] as commander-in-chief of the Continental army.

It is eminently plausible to surmise that Posey's complete and steadfast dedication to the revolutionary movement was conceived on the day and at the hour he learned that the mantle of American leadership had been draped over the broad shoulders of his revered Mount Vernon mentor. Point Pleasant had tested Thomas' mettle in a fight to preserve the lives of himself and his fellow frontiersmen. Now he was imbued with an even higher purpose, the attainment of national independence—a quest which Washington, in humbly accepting his military command, had aptly called "the glorious cause."[3] Swept up in the fervor that was spreading like wildfire from the eastern cities to the most remote frontier hamlets, Posey did not hesitate to declare his allegiance to that cause and its leader, or to act upon his resolve. He was soon serving on the Botetourt County Committee of Correspondence, a body of leading citizens formed in each Virginia county to organize local revolutionary efforts and to coordinate them with the state's oversight Committee of Safety.[4] But as reports of massive mobilization and sharp military engagements with the enemy filtered from the east to Fincastle, he could not be content long with a civilian role in the great adventure.

Charles Royster's insightful treatise on the basic elements of character that motivated the revolutionary movement generally, and the soldiers of the Continental army in particular, defines the unique sense of duty that drove America's first freedom fighters. Apart from the higher goals of independence and freedom, the revolutionaries' fealty ran, not only to themselves and their comrades, but to their children and posterity also. To these intrepid soldiers, the concept of "fame" was not limited to gaining the esteem and respect of their contemporaries—it extended to the achievement through their exploits on the field of battle of a kind of timeless immortality extending far beyond their own life spans. "The participants often felt the presence of tens of millions more and looked at their own conduct through the eyes of the unborn."[5] This acute consciousness of their role in history, the feeling that future generations were constantly peering over their shoulders and judging their every action in combat, may account for the dogged tenacity of the revolutionaries' eight-year struggle against staggering odds.

From all that is known of Thomas Posey's character and values, he may well be regarded as a paradigmatic representative of his revolutionary generation. As if to validate Royster's core thesis, Posey throughout his life displayed an almost-obsessive sensitivity to his role in recorded history, as well as a compelling and sometimes self-conscious concern for the welfare and regard of his children and their progeny. Both in his military career and his later public offices, he seemed to live his life as though always aware that uncounted future generations of descendants—whose vast numbers and identities he could not possibly have envisioned—would someday critically examine and judge his actions through the convoluted but inexorable prism of the intervening centuries.

Mindful of these faceless generations, and confronting the greatest challenge of his time, Posey went for a soldier in the Revolution.

On 12 January 1776 his fellows on the Botetourt Committee of Correspondence authorized him to raise a company of recruits pledged to serve in the national (Continental) army for the duration of the conflict. The area around Fincastle boasted many veterans of the Point Pleasant expedition, so it is not surprising that Thomas could later write that "no material difficulty attended the raising and completing the compy."[6] Pursuant to accepted practice, the young saddler paid the new enlistees their stipulated recruiting bonuses out of his own funds. Including other costs incidental to assembling the soldiers, his out-of pocket expenses came to the considerable total of £144, for which he was reimbursed on 31 January by the Virginia Committee of Safety.[7] Posey's formal commission as a captain came through from that same body effective 20 March. The intervening weeks had been devoted to drilling and military exercises on Fincastle's broad public commons. He and his company were officially assigned to the 7th Virginia Regiment of the Continental army, and were ordered to immediate duty on the state's eastern seaboard.[8]

From 12 January 1776 to 24 May 1777, Captain Thomas Posey kept a written record of his activities in a bound, ledger-like book, of the type probably used to list accounts in his saddlery business.[9] The journal has happily survived to provide a direct eyewitness narrative of the military and personal experiences of the young company commander and his men, at a place and time not extensively researched or reported by historians. The entries vividly reflect the enthusiasm as well as the innocence of those heady early days of the Revolution, when the complete success of the glorious cause seemed imminent, and the long years of adversity, hardship and struggle that lay ahead could not even be imagined.

All along the long trek from Fincastle to the shores of Chesapeake Bay, Posey's rugged and homespun-clad frontiersmen were welcomed and cheered by local patriots. Thomas wrote proudly that the march "was performed with great regularity and much good behavior shown by the soldiers; their conduct was the occasion of a good deal of respect paid by the inhabitants."[10] Arriving at their regimental headquarters near Gloucester County Courthouse, the men pitched camp while Captain Posey rode over to state army headquarters in nearby Williamsburg to draw £233 in cash to cover his company's pay and subsistence allowances through 1 April.[11]

The revolutionary cause had not been universally embraced by Virginians; many remained loyal to the Crown. Although most adult male loyalists had left their homes and rallied to Governor Dunmore's call for armed resistance to the rebels, a few stubbornly refused to conceal either their presence or sympathies from their neighbors. The provisional state government regarded these recalcitrants as security risks or worse. Posey was ordered to lead a detachment of his men on a brief sortie to Urbanna, in Middlesex County, to apprehend Ralph Wormley, one of the most notorious Tories in Virginia. Shortly after completing this successful mission, the company was moved to New Point Comfort, on the tip of a narrow peninsula overlooking the broad entrance to Chesapeake Bay, "to guard against any alarm or surprize made by the enemy upon the troops stationed at the courthouse, or to prevent depredations being committed upon the inhabitants." At this scenic station, Posey soon discovered that even active military duty had its lighter side: "This being rather a pleasant situation than otherwise, I spent my time very agreeably, meeting with frequent invitations."[12]

The warm and friendly hospitality extended by Tidewater Virginians to the officer from the frontier did not abate with time. A platoon of Posey's men was detached from the main company and posted about fifteen miles up the peninsula at Burton's Point, near the mouth of the Piankantank River, facing Gwynn's Island a few hundred yards offshore in the Bay. He inspected this detachment periodically, and on one such visit in mid-May he mentions in his journal that one evening he "recreated at Maj'r. Smiths, where I dined in company with some very agreeable young ladies."[13] The visiting captain might well have made more than one girlish heart flutter that evening at Major Smith's soiree. In the full bloom of his young manhood, Thomas was, by all accounts, an imposing physical specimen—a powerfully built but athletic and graceful six feet two inches.[14] His light brown hair set off a "remarkably handsome" face, with features "high, fine and prominent." Yet there was "a softness in his fine blue eyes, a spirit and intelligence mingled with a calm and benevolent expression which pervaded the whole countenance, that at once attracted the admiration and won the affections of the beholder."[15]

Nor could even the most refined and cultivated eastern Virginia belle fault the deportment of the young frontier officer. One word-portrait avers that Posey's "appearance united dignity and gracefulness, and in his manners were blended in a remarkable degree the stately and gallant bearing of a soldier, with the ease and suavity of the polished gentleman."[16] Another contemporary of later years describes him as "a man of noble appearance and courtly manners."[17] Elsewhere it was said of him that "in his manners the bearing of the soldier was harmoniously blended with the ease of the refined gentleman."[18] Clearly, Thomas' seven-year sojourn in the rustic west had not eroded the civility, decorum and social graces acquired and indelibly ingrained in his personality and character through long association with the Washingtons, Fairfaxes, Masons and other gentry neighbors of his youthful Fairfax County upbringing.

But it is doubtful if Thomas allowed himself to be beguiled by the coquettish eyes or admiring glances of the "very agreeable young ladies" seated with him around the dinner table at Major Smith's home near Burton's Point. Three days later, after having crossed over to Gwynn's Island to reconnoiter the terrain and having been "very politely treated by the inhabitants," he returned to his company encampment at New Point Comfort. There, he reports with the undisguised delight and pleasure felt by every soldier ever stationed far from his loved ones, he found awaiting him "a letter from home"—in all likelihood, a warm and tender missive from his affectionate wife Martha, with endearing passages and eagerly-read reports on the growth and accomplishments of his two young sons.[19]

The mission of Posey's two outposts was to watch for the expected appearance of a sizable host of British troops and loyalist recruits under the personal command of Lord Dunmore. The rapid deployment of the Virginia revolutionary forces had compelled the enemy to withdraw from the mainland, but they were known to be aboard vessels now standing somewhere off the coast. On 26 May, while Thomas was at Gloucester Courthouse picking up supplies for his company, a courier informed him that Dunmore's fleet had just been observed dropping anchor off Gwynn's Island. Hastily notifying his regimental commander, Colonel William Daingerfield, of the sighting, Captain Posey returned to his company at New Point Comfort, and marched with them to join his detached platoon and other elements of the 7th Regiment assembling at Burton's Point. The arriving units came under immediate heavy fire from British warships anchored off Gwynn's Island. Although the local militia panicked and ran after taking a few casualties, Posey's company and the other regular troops stood fast and dug in. During a pelting rainstorm, they observed Dunmore's troops disembarking onto the island.[20]

During the next six weeks, each side fortified its positions against possible amphibious assault by the other. Posey's soldiers, posted as picket guards or sentries along the shoreline facing the island, came under almost daily fire from British tenders and smaller warships patrolling the offshore channel. In early July Brigadier General Andrew Lewis, Thomas' recent Point Pleasant commander and now leader of American forces in Virginia, arrived with two fresh regiments. Under cover of darkness, they covertly emplaced several artillery pieces, including two huge eighteen-pounders, trained on the island. At precisely 10:00 on the morning of 8 July, the well-concealed American batteries opened a sudden and sustained two-hour barrage, sinking or damaging several nearby enemy ships and severely damaging British positions on the island, including several of their land batteries. Only a shortage of powder and the scarcity of small landing craft precluded the mounting of an immediate all-out assault upon the island. But Dunmore's tactical position had become so precarious that the next day he evacuated his remaining forces by sea from Gwynn's Island.[21]

Captain Posey and his company comprised part of the 200 American troops sent across the channel in rowboats and small barges to engage the British rear guard and to take possession of the island. While only a few parting shots were exchanged between the two sides, the arrival of the revolutionaries forced the enemy to leave behind many valuable supplies in their haste to depart. But a shocking sight awaited the Americans as they advanced across the island. Thomas' journal movingly describes the grisly end met by hundreds of runaway slaves Lord Dunmore had induced to join his ranks as recruits before leaving the Virginia mainland:

> I cannot help observing that I never saw more distress in my life, than what I found among some of the poor deluded negroes which they could not take time, or did not chuse to carry off with them, they being sick . . . some were dying, and many calling out for help . . . and throughout the whole Island we found them strew'd about, many of them torn to pieces by wild beasts—great numbers of the bodies having never been buried.[22]

The grim fate of these unfortunates deserves more than a footnote in history. As early as the spring of 1775, following the second session of the openly-rebellious Virginia Convention, Dunmore had "made known his intention of arming his own slaves to protect himself, and of emancipating all slaves who would fight with him" against the gathering revolutionary forces.[23] After the governor later issued a formal proclamation to that effect, hundreds of freedom-seeking slaves from around the state flocked to his side, and were loosely organized into military units. But freedom for these brave black troops proved to be illusory and short-lived. They apparently were never given the respect or status accorded to the white Tory volunteers in Dunmore's force, and as Posey's journal relates, most were cruelly abandoned by the British when Gwynn's Island was evacuated. Thomas estimated that at least 400 to 500 of the black soldiers perished there (most succumbing to smallpox) along with about 150 British and loyalist troops. The Americans had only one serious battle casualty.[24]

In strictly military terms, the Gwynn's Island action does not compare in scope or integral importance to the engagements fought by the main revolutionary army to the north in the year 1776. But the ouster of Lord Dunmore and his forces had strategic significance belying the numbers involved and might well have averted an early damaging blow to the overall American cause. Had the governor been able to retain his beachhead in Virginia long enough to receive heavy reinforcements from the British army in New York City, the colonies would have been virtually split into two halves. Further, the indispensable human and material resources of the Union's most populous state would have been largely denied to the revolutionary effort.[25] The irony of Lewis, Posey, and other Point Pleasant veterans driving Lord Dunmore from Virginia (less than two years after fighting under his command against the western Indian tribes) could not have been lost upon the haughty governor, and surely not on the Virginians themselves. But Thomas Posey chose not to comment in his journal on this curious and remarkable role reversal.

Posey was put in command of a two-company garrison left to hold Gwynn's Island, but the decimated enemy force made no further attempts to land there or elsewhere on Virginia soil. Soon, though, the summer's relative tranquility was shattered by disturbing news from the western counties, reports that the frontier settlements were facing imminent attack from nearby Indian tribes incited by British agents. Fearing for the safety of his little family, Thomas sought and obtained emergency leave from General Lewis. He arrived back in Fincastle on 15 September, only to find that the frontier was relatively secure and in no immediate peril from the enemy's Native American allies. Bidding farewell to his wife and children on 15 October, he rejoined his company and regiment, now in winter quarters near Williamsburg. Of the time spent in the old colonial capital, Thomas noted in his journal only that its citizens "endeavored to make it pass as agreeable as possible." But he chafed under inactivity, and was delighted to note on 9 January that "the whole of the regular troops received orders to march with all imaginable expedition to the Jerseys to join Genl. Washington."[26] The young captain was clearly looking forward with eager anticipation to serving under the direct command of his former Mount Vernon role model.

The northward march began on 16 January, and Thomas took advantage of the move to obtain "leave to go by home, and join the regiment in Baltimore, or Philadelphia." After enjoying an eleven-day stay in Fincastle, he hastened up the Shenandoah Valley and arrived in Frederickstown, Maryland on 18 February, where he voluntarily "went under inoculation for the smallpox," the dreaded camp pestilence of the Revolutionary army. The three-week ordeal, spent in quarantine in the boarding house of a certain Mrs. Charleton, was not an entirely unpleasant experience:

> A number of other gentlemen being inoculated in the same house, rendered it much more agreeable to me. Mrs. Charleton and her daughters were very polite to the boarders, and rendered every thing as agreeable to them as possible. Doctor Thomas who performed the inoculation was very attentive.[27]

Captain Posey, now immunized against the greatest single source of casualties in the Revolutionary War, rejoined his company in Philadelphia on 15 March, "where I found the greatest part of the regt. just recovering from the smallpox. Here we were taken up some time in clothing the regt. and preparing for our march to the main army." But the regiment saw its first action of the year sooner than it expected. Hurrying to join General Benjamin Lincoln's brigade near Boundbrook, New Jersey on 13 April, it heard gunfire in the distance, and soon learned from panicky American soldiers fleeing from the scene "that they had met with a defeat":

> Our regt. was under arms from the first discovery of the action, and proceeded on towards the place, to afford what relief we could, but before we could reach the ground saw Genl. Lincoln who gave orders to cover the broken troops. This was accordingly done, and in a very little time the enemy began to retreat.[28]

On 24 May 1777 Posey's 7th Virginia Regiment became a part of General George Washington's main Continental army, then encamped at a "very formidable" position between the Jersey mountains at Middlebrook. Here, regrettably, Thomas' war diary ends, with the comment, "My intention was only to keep a journal until we joined the main body of the army under the command of Genl. Washington."[29] Had he continued his narrative throughout the many campaigns of his succeeding six years of service, it would have provided fascinating and invaluable eyewitness accounts of many of the major battles of the Revolution.

In describing the siege of Gwynn's Island, Posey's journal had taken particular note of how effectively the American forces used the frontier hunting rifle.[30] This gun, in the hands of a skilled marksman, was deadly accurate at twice the range of the smoothbore musket, which at the time was the standard infantry weapon used by both the British and American armies. The rifle could not be fired and reloaded as fast as the musket, making it ill-suited to the massed attack and defense formations then prescribed by prevailing military tenets. But General Washington, veteran of many a frontier skirmish, was well aware of the rifle's range and accuracy, and was convinced that its unique qualities, if properly employed, would give his forces a tactical advantage over the enemy's conventionally armed troops.

The Virginia regiments were generously endowed with frontiersmen from the state's western regions, and not long after their arrival at the Middlebrook encampment, Washington directed that a special regiment-sized corps of marksmen proficient in the use of the rifle be selected from the ranks of the main army. These picked men, mostly roughhewn natives of the western frontiers of Pennsylvania and Virginia, were put under the command of Colonel Daniel Morgan, a grizzled, hulking Virginian survivor of Braddock's campaign, Lord Dunmore's War and General Benedict Arnold's ill-fated invasion of Canada.[31] Colonel Morgan, in turn, selected Captain Thomas Posey as one of his eight company commanders in what became known as the Rifle Regiment or Rifle Corps.

The riflemen wore distinctive attire: long buckskin hunting shirts, extending over their trousers to mid-thigh. Since the rifle, unlike the musket, did not have a muzzle socket collar-and-ring assembly to lock on a bayonet, riflemen wore long scalping knives in leather sheathes attached to their belts. Most also tucked into their belts a wicked-looking tomahawk or hatchet as a secondary sidearm for use in hand-to-hand combat. Even so, General Washington feared that the absence of bayonets would expose the riflemen to the saber thrusts and slashes of enemy cavalrymen. He accordingly ordered Morgan to provide his men with 13-foot-long spears, "as a defense against Horse; till you are furnished with these, take care not to be caught in such Situation as to give them any advantage over you." The commanding general was also concerned that Rifle Corps officers, who wore only conventional infantry swords and pistols as sidearms, would be vulnerable to enemy cavalry. He directed that they carry a shorter, six-foot spear or pike, called a "spontoon," which he hoped would offset the reach advantage of British mounted troops, and would also be effective in close encounters with the bayonet-tipped muskets of enemy infantry.[32]

The initial tactical rôle of the riflemen in the summer of 1777 was to snipe at enemy sentries and picket guards from cover beyond the range of their muskets, and to waylay and harass British foraging and scouting parties. Such skirmishes occurred almost daily in the Jersey countryside outside the Middlebrook encampment. But when British General Charles Cornwallis chose to withdraw his army back toward New York City, Morgan's regiment received a more challenging assignment: to interdict and cut off the enemy rear guard. Posey's autobiography contains a brief account of a harrowing moment in that engagement. His company, moving along a narrow causeway across a swamp, became separated from the rest of the Corps and found itself sandwiched between the British main army and rear guard:

> . . . a sharp conflict took place, but the light infantry of the enemy surrounded his company, and was near cutting him off, he perceiving his situation order'd a well directed fire upon a particular spot of the enemy, which open'd a passage for him to retreat through.[33]

It is clear from his performance in this skirmish, as well as his earlier role in the siege and occupation of Gwynn's Island, that Posey was emerging as a competent and resourceful company commander. One of the most remarkable achievements of the revolutionary army was its development, within a very limited time span, of a corps of young officers of near-professional caliber. Thomas, apart from his short tour of duty in Dunmore's War, had no known military background or experience. The Continental army was too busily engaged in fighting for its very existence to provide its newly-commissioned junior officers with any formal training in military tactics or theory. The young men who suddenly found themselves leading platoons or companies of inexperienced soldiers against a highly trained, professional European army could draw only upon their own innate resources for leadership, coolness under fire and tactical proficiency. The military success of the Revolution surely owes as much to the existence and emergence of these latent attributes in men such as Posey and his contemporaries as to the powerful cultural and political stimuli that drew them from their shops and farms onto the battlefields of America.

Nor was this unlikely but propitious metamorphosis in character confined to the officer class of the revolutionary forces. History stands in awe that a single human generation could simultaneously produce both the formidable array of political and intellectual giants—the founding fathers—with the vision and moral genius to conceive the revolutionary ideal, and the military leaders with the vigor and conviction to assure its realization. From that same generation also came the thousands of citizen-soldiers, the stalwart rank-and-filers, who actually fought and won the decisive battles. But in the hindsight of historical perspective, the final victory was not achieved solely by a few dozen prodigious leaders, a few hundred gallant officers, or even by these thousands of intrepid soldiers. The glorious cause was the synergetic accomplishment of an entire generation of individual men and women, swept up and lifted in the high tide of history by an idea—an ideal—whose time had finally come.

In August, Colonel Morgan's new corps was detached from the main army and sent by forced march to reinforce General Horatio Gates' Northern Army in upstate New York. Gates' difficult mission was to somehow block the advance of an enemy army of some 10,000 British, Hessian and Canadian troops under the command of General John Burgoyne. This massive force was accompanied by a large number of allied Indian warriors, and it was against these Native American auxiliaries that Washington felt the riflemen's special talents could be most effectively used, as he informed General Gates:

> I am forwarding . . . Colonel Morgan's corps of riflemen, amounting to about 500. These are all chosen men, selected from the army at large, well acquainted with the use of rifles, and with that mode of fighting which is necessary to make them a good counterpoise to the Indian . . . .[34]

It was critical to the revolutionary cause to stop Burgoyne before he could join forces with General Cornwallis' army, which was expected to move northward out of New York City to meet the British troops advancing from Canada. Their juncture, if successfully executed, would split New England from its sister states to the south, with dire consequences to the struggling new nation. This may have weighed heavily on General Washington's mind as he sent Morgan on his way to Gates with this vote of confidence: "I know of no corps so likely to check their (the enemy's) progress, in proportion to its number, as that under your command. I have great dependence on you, your officers and men."[35] A few weeks later, Morgan's deadeye marksmen would more than meet Washington's high expectations. They were destined to play a role even greater than that envisaged by the anxious commander-in-chief, in the two battles which forced "Gentleman Johnny" Burgoyne to surrender to Gates at Saratoga on 17 October 1777.

In the first engagement, at Freeman's Farm on 19 September, the Rifle Corps was in the thick of the daylong conflict, which ended in a standoff and an orderly withdrawal by American forces from a battlefield littered with the dead and wounded of the extremely heavy British casualties. At the second and decisive battle of Bemis Heights on 7 October, as the enemy advanced on a broad front, Morgan's sharpshooters were skillfully deployed in and behind a stand of trees on a rise overlooking the British right flank. From this natural cover, the riflemen poured such a devastating fire into the massed enemy ranks that they halted in confusion, with all or most of their mounted officers hit and fallen. When the gallant General Simon Fraser, Burgoyne's second-in-command, rode along the faltering line trying to spur on his demoralized troops, he was struck down and mortally wounded by a single shot from a marksman's rifle. Morgan's men beat back every enemy charge aimed at dislodging them from their position. Then, electrified by the unexpected arrival in their sector of the fiery Brigadier General Benedict Arnold, who had been relieved of his regular American command by Gates, the Corpsmen threw aside their rifles and, brandishing their spears, scalping knives and tomahawks, joined other units in an all-out charge. The enemy right flank collapsed, and the British position, both on the battlefield and in the campaign itself, became untenable.[36]

While no account of Posey's personal role in these battles exists, there can be no doubt that he bravely led and was in the forefront of his company of frontiersmen in both engagements. What is known and duly recorded is that he was a proud eyewitness to the resultant surrender of Burgoyne's entire army at Saratoga. True to his acquired instincts as a meticulous tradesman, he entered on one of the back pages of his war journal an exact count and breakdown of the capitulating troops: 2,419 British, 2,198 Hessians, and 1,100 Canadians—all that remained of an original invading force of 9,713 men.[37] At the customary formal reception given by the victorious Gates for top British officers immediately following the surrender ceremony, General Burgoyne shook Colonel Morgan's hand, saying, "Sir, you command the finest regiment in the world."[38] The enemy rank-and-file shared their commander's high opinion of the riflemen's fighting prowess. When General Gates was told that wounded and hospitalized British troops were fearful that they would be attacked and scalped by their erstwhile Indian allies while lying helpless in the darkness, he allayed their concerns by sending a message that their hospital area would be patrolled and guarded by a contingent of Morgan's men, "whom the Indians feared worse than the devil."[39]

The outcome at Saratoga is generally considered to have been a crucial turning point in the Revolution. Apart from its obvious military and strategic importance, the performance of American troops in this major battle clearly demonstrated the dedication and will to win of the revolutionary movement, and was thus a decisive factor in bringing France into the war.[40] Its immediate effect upon the citizens of the new nation, hungry for any kind of victory, was galvanizing. The honor of taking the official report of this great triumph to the Continental Congress at Philadelphia was awarded by Gates to his twenty-year-old adjutant, Colonel James Wilkinson, a devious and complex man who was to play a significant and recurrent role in the later military and public careers of young Captain Thomas Posey.

Morgan's regiment was immediately ordered to rejoin the main army. Although badly weakened by battle casualties and camp diseases, the Rifle Corps arrived back in Middlebrook on 18 November after an arduous forced march. All of its officers and men still fit for duty were placed in the eastern New Jersey command of General Lafayette, where they were engaged in constant skirmishes with British and Hessian patrols on the periphery of the enemy's New York City fortifications. The young marquis, himself the personification of military ardor and elan, was so impressed by the spirit and determination of Morgan's riflemen that he singled them out for special commendation in several of his field reports to General Washington.[41]

In December the American forces retired into winter quarters at Valley Forge, but the singular skills of the riflemen denied them the seasonal surcease from combat accorded to most foot soldiers of both armies. Throughout that long, cold winter, the Corps was posted at Radnor, Pennsylvania in a forward area outside the main encampment. There, on the west bank of the deep but narrow Schuylkill River, the regiment was arrayed eyeball-to-eyeball with forward units of the enemy on the opposite shore, just outside British-held Philadelphia. In this exposed position the riflemen, along with a wide-ranging cavalry unit led by Major Henry ("Lighthorse Harry") Lee, skirmished almost daily with heavily armed scouting and foraging parties.[42] Thomas Posey's only respite from the fighting was a brief home leave taken early in March of 1778. Arriving back in Fincastle, he finalized the purchase of two adjoining half-acre lots on the town's Main Street,[43] and moved his wife and two sons into a large frame house, dominated by a massive stone chimney, which stood on one of the properties.[44] The furlough reunion ended all too quickly. Sadly, on the day he bade farewell to his little family and rode north to rejoin his regiment, it was the last time he would ever again see his devoted young wife.

Arriving back at Radnor, Posey, as senior captain, (all other officers of higher rank having been killed or transferred), took over temporary command of the Rifle Corps while Colonel Morgan left for Virginia on home leave.[45] Perhaps in recognition of these increased responsibilities, Thomas was promoted to the rank of major on 30 April 1778.[46] As welcome as that advancement was, the date of his promotion was made even more auspicious by the arrival of the momentous news that France had formally recognized American independence, and had pledged to dispatch land and sea forces to support the revolutionary cause. Every survivor of the bitterly cold Valley Forge ordeal realized the significance of this pivotal historical event. Six days later, General Washington hosted a celebratory reception at his headquarters for all commissioned officers of the main army.[47] The occasion afforded Posey, proudly wearing his new major's insignia, an opportunity to personally thank his commander-in-chief for his promotion. Mrs. Martha Washington presided over the buffet of cold meats laid out for the attending officers, and it is not unlikely that she gave an especially warm greeting to the strapping young man she had seen grow up in the family of her friend and nearest Fairfax County neighbor, the late Martha Price Harrison Posey.[48]

Despite all the well-known and very real hardships and deprivations borne by the revolutionary soldiers during the harsh winter, the mood and outlook at Washington's Valley Forge reception was bright and decidedly upbeat. After an initial few weeks of seeming indifference and apathy to their plight, the American people had responded generously with food, clothing and supplies to alleviate the troops' sufferings. Word of French backing gave new promise of the ultimate success of the glorious cause, and a spirit of renewed dedication was manifest within all ranks of the Continental forces. Their now-proven ability to withstand the most extreme adversities had bolstered lagging self-confidence, while General von Steuben's winter-long training program of intensive mass drills and systematic battlefield maneuvers had produced a growing sense of professional pride and discipline throughout the regular army.[49] These were essential qualities that would be repeatedly drawn upon on the long, difficult road that lay ahead before the final victory.

Colonel Daniel Morgan had returned from Virginia and resumed command of his regiment just in time to attend Washington's soiree, and to oversee the integration into its depleted ranks of twenty-five picked marksmen from each brigade of the main army. When the British executed a planned withdrawal from Philadelphia on 18 June, the Rifle Corps was the first unit sent in to occupy the city and secure it against looting and lawlessness.[50] As the enemy army proceeded along its line of march through New Jersey toward New York City, the regiment moved parallel to its right flank, keeping up a harassing fire on outlying light infantry and cavalry units.[51]

Confident in the new martial skills of his men, Washington had ordered a general attack to be mounted upon the main British forces at Monmouth on 28 June, but General Charles Lee, commanding the first wave of American troops, unaccountably withdrew without pressing the assault. Only General Washington's timely arrival on the scene and prompt support from several subordinate commanders prevented a retreat from becoming a rout. Lee's failure to relay Washington's battle orders to Colonel Morgan delayed the Rifle Corps' arrival at the scene of the intended attack until too late to be a factor in the battle. The Americans' opportunity to strike a major blow had been lost, but when the enemy army resumed its march, the riflemen continued to harass its flanks until the British neared their fortified positions on the outskirts of New York City.[52]

The major shift in the strategic posture of the two main armies required some restructuring of American forces, and caused another change of scenery for Thomas Posey. Shortly after the battle of Monmouth, the Rifle Corps was partially disbanded, and its two senior officers, Morgan and Lieutenant Colonel William Butler, were re-assigned to their original state regiments. The three companies of riflemen remaining intact were formed into a battalion under the command of Major Posey, and on 18 July the unit was ordered to march immediately to Albany in upstate New York, which now faced a new peril on its western frontier.[53] Large war parties from the six nations of the militant Iroquois League, incited by British officers operating out of Fort Niagara on Lake Ontario, were making devastating raids on American settlements in western New York and Pennsylvania. In the Wyoming Valley area of the latter state, the warriors, accompanied by a troop of irregular Tory

"Rangers" led by Colonel John Butler, had ambushed a 450-man colonial militia force on 3 July. Over 300 men were killed and many were horribly tortured to death after being captured.[54]

On the New York frontier to the north, the major threat to Americans was posed by the warriors of the Mohawk Nation, led by its able and well-educated war chief, Joseph Brant. A mixed band of Mohawks and Rangers had attacked and destroyed the small settlement of Andrustown on 18 July, killing eleven settlers. Three weeks later, the larger nearby village of German Flats was totally wiped out, although Brant mercifully allowed most of its inhabitants to find safety in flight before the attack.[55] Local militia forces and the few regular troops posted in the area clearly could not handle the problem, and New York Governor George Clinton appealed to Washington for assistance. In dispatching Posey's battalion of riflemen to the region, the commander-in-chief obviously felt that their marksmanship and frontier experience in Indian fighting could be put to good use in quelling these continued Native American incursions.

The first of six known letters Thomas Posey wrote to General Washington during the Revolution was a simple acknowledgment of urgent orders to march his unit northward, along with elements of the 4th Pennsylvania Regiment under Lieutenant Colonel William Butler, Thomas' recent superior in the old Rifle Corps. His second letter of 31 August was directed from Fort Defiance, his new post near the town of Schoharie, located about twenty-five miles west of the state capital of Albany. It confirmed the arrival from army headquarters of a $2,500 warrant drawn on the fort's military paymaster, to cover his battalion's accumulated pay and subsistence allowances. In this letter, Major Posey apologized to the commander-in-chief for not yet having converted the warrant into cash for distribution to his men, "as my time has been much taken up with Duty."[56]

Although not further explained in Thomas' letter, that risky "Duty" had been to lead a scouting expedition southward along the east branch of the Delaware River, deep into territory dominated by the hostile Mohawks. Along the way, Posey's party of about 150 men entered a settlement of known Tory sympathies, only to find that all of its inhabitants had fled, except for a group of uneasy women gathered in one house. Nearby, however, two armed men were apprehended. Under questioning, they admitted that they were loyal to the Crown, and had provided beef cattle and other supplies to foraging parties sent into the area by Tory Colonel John Butler and Chief Joseph Brant. Soon after this interrogation, one of the two loyalist prisoners, by the name of Demond, tried to escape from his three-man militia guard, but was fatally shot. When his family later complained to Governor Clinton of brutality by the troops, the governor ordered the army to surrender the three guards to civil authority for inquiry and possible criminal trial.[57]

Military protocol required that Major Posey, the commander of the mission, and other officers in the scouting party submit sworn affidavits describing the circumstances surrounding the incident. But Thomas, obviously concerned that General Washington not form an unfavorable opinion of his young former neighbor's soldierly conduct, was not content to let his formal affidavit speak for itself. He wrote a detailed personal letter of explanation directly to the commander-in-chief, "knowing that some of the People . . . who are friends of this Demond have been endeavouring to Paint this matter in a very Black Light to the Governor & sundry other People."[58] Meanwhile, Lieutenant Colonel William Butler, Posey's immediate superior, had forwarded the affidavits of all the officers to Washington, informing him that the guards would be turned over to Governor Clinton, "altho I think the men not the least blamable, but rather deserve commendation for doing their duty so well."[59] There is no record of what, if any, action was taken by the civil authorities against the three militia guards.

An interesting sidelight on the problem of maintaining military professionalism and discipline among the citizen-soldiers of the Revolutionary army is provided in the affidavit of one of the junior officers who witnessed the Demond incident. He reported that after the scouting party had left the Tory settlement Major Posey halted the column and directed that all the men be searched. When some were found to be in possession of various articles of clothing and other items taken from the empty homes of the inhabitants, Thomas ordered that all such property be collected and immediately returned to the women left in the settlement.[60] The abandoned loyalist village had apparently proved to be too much of a temptation for some of the rank-and-file Continental and militia soldiers in Posey's task force. One can assume that General Washington read the affidavit detailing this occurrence with a gleam of approval in his eye for the young major's vigilant and astute handling of such unmilitary conduct.

Within a few weeks, a larger force of 260 men, in which Posey's full rifle battalion was the largest single component, left Fort Defiance on 2 October. Its mission was to seek out and engage the elusive enemy raiders. Moving swiftly southward along the Schoharie and Susquehanna rivers, the column penetrated through the heart of Mohawk country all the way to Chief Joseph Brant's home village, Oquaqa. Brant and his 600 warriors were at that time far to the south, pillaging settlements along the lower Delaware River—an unwelcome but possibly fortunate circumstance for the smaller American force. The soldiers burned Oquaqa and several other nearby deserted Mohawk villages, as well as a Scotch Tory settlement in the vicinity, and destroyed all the growing crops in the area. But the troops returned to Schoharie on 16 October after a 300-mile sweep of Mohawk territory, without having met any significant resistance.[61]

The Americans at first appeared to have accomplished their main objective of halting further raids on their settlements. Chief Brant and his followers, returning to their ruined villages and facing the approaching winter without food or shelter, began a long trek northwest toward the British outpost of Fort Niagara. Along the way, however, they encountered a large outbound raiding party of 200 Tory Rangers and 350 Seneca warriors, under the command of Captain Walter Butler, (son of the Ranger commander, Colonel John), moving toward the populous American towns in the Mohawk River valley. Brant and 250 of his Mohawks, eager to exact retaliation for the destruction of their villages, decided to join the raiding party. Their target of opportunity was the large settlement of Cherry Valley, located less than thirty miles west of Schoharie itself.[62]

Colonel Ichabod Alden, commanding 300 regular and militia soldiers stationed at Cherry Valley, had ample advance warning of a possible impending raid. But he was inexplicably derelict in deploying his troops for the proper defense of the settlement and its inhabitants. When the Indian-Tory forces attacked on 11 November, most of the garrison's regular troops were huddled within the walls of the small fort at the center of the village, leaving defenseless in their homes outside the fort most of the settlers of Cherry Valley. Thirty-two civilians, nearly all women and children, and forty-two local militia were brutally killed and scalped, mostly by the Senecas, while many others were spared and taken prisoner only through the intercession of Brant's Mohawks. The raiders did not sustain a single casualty. Every structure standing outside the walls of the small fort was looted and then burned to the ground, as the soldiers inside watched helplessly.[63]

As soon as word of the attack reached Fort Defiance, a relief force led by Posey and his rifle battalion immediately rushed to the scene. When it arrived at the smoking ruins of Cherry Valley, the enemy forces had long since withdrawn toward Fort Niagara with their prisoners and plunder.[64] As he rode at the head of his troops into the ruined settlement, Posey's horror at viewing the mutilated bodies of women, young boys and girls, and even infants, can only be imagined. But the young major's shock and grief that day were soon to be matched by the belated arrival of news of an even more intimate tragedy which, unknown to him, had already played itself out in yet another small frontier town, in faraway Virginia.

Nature, in those times, could often be as senseless and cruel as man's inhumanity to man, and life itself was, at best, precarious and uncertain. On 4 August 1778, Posey's wife Martha had given birth to their third child, a son whom she named Sampson, after her uncle and former guardian Sampson Mathews. But her time had come prematurely, and the difficult birthing process went badly. Martha contracted the dread puerperal fever, and died three days later, at age 24. Baby Sampson did not long survive his mother, dying on 30 August.[65] His two older brothers, five-year-old Thomas and John, age four, were taken in by the grieving women of the Mathews family in Staunton, there to await their father's return from the war—a war that was not to end for another four years and more.

NOTES

1. James Thomas Flexner, *George Washington: The Forge of Experience, 1732-1775* (Boston: Little, Brown & Co., 1965), 339.
2. Washington's moving letter to his wife informing her of his appointment expressly asked that he be remembered to Milly Posey, then a member of the Mount Vernon household. W.W. Abbot and Dorothy Twohig, eds., *The Papers of George Washington, Revolutionary Series*, 3 vols. to date (Charlottesville, VA: The University Press of Virginia, 1982-), 1:5, 6n.8.
3. Flexner, *Washington*, 341.
4. "A Short Biography of the Life of Governor Thomas Posey," Thomas Posey Papers, Indiana Historical Society Library, Indianapolis, IN (hereafter cited as IHS).
5. Charles Royster, *A Revolutionary People at War: The Continental Army and American Character, 1775-1783* (Chapel Hill, NC: The University of North Carolina Press, 1979), 8.
6. 12 January 1776, MS Memorandum Book of Thomas Posey, Thomas Posey Papers, IHS.
7. Robert L. Scribner and Brent Tarter, eds., *Revolutionary Virginia: The Road to Independence* (Charlottesville, VA: The University Press of Virginia, 1983), 6:39.
8. Ibid., 388; 1 March 1776, MS Memorandum Book; MS Appointment of Thomas Posey as Captain in the Seventh Regiment, Committee of Safety for the Colony of Virginia, 20 March 1776, Thomas Posey Papers, IHS.

9. MS Memorandum Book, Thomas Posey Papers, IHS.
10. Ibid., 1 March 1776.
11. Ibid.; 1 April 1776; Scribner and Tarter, eds., *Revolutionary Virginia,* 6:388.
12. 15 April 1776 and 7 May 1776, MS Memorandum Book, Thomas Posey Papers, IHS.
13. Ibid., 19 May 1776.
14. Rupert Hughes, *George Washington: The Rebel and the Patriot, 1762-1777* (New York: William Morrow & Co., 1927), 655.
15. "General Thomas Posey," Memoirs of Eminent Persons, *Port Folio* (Philadelphia: Harrison Hall, 1827). From unpaginated transcript copy, Henderson County Public Library, Henderson, KY; excerpt quoted verbatim in: "The Posey Romance," St. Louis (MO) *Daily Globe-Democrat*, 6 November 1898.
16. Ibid.
17. James W. Alexander, *The Life of Archibald Alexander* (New York: Charles Scribner, 1854), 34.
18. James Hall, "Memoir of Thomas Posey, Major General and Governor of Indiana," *The Library of American Biography*, ed. Jared Sparks, ser. 2 (Boston: Little, Brown & Co., 1846), 9:403.
19. 22 May 1776, MS Memorandum Book,Thomas Posey Papers, IHS.
20. 26 May 1776 and 27 May 1776, MS Memorandum Book, Thomas Posey Papers, IHS.
21. 9 July 1776, MS Memorandum Book, Thomas Posey Papers, IHS; John E. Selby, *The Revolution in Virginia, 1775-1783* (Williamsburg, VA: The Colonial Williamsburg Foundation, 1988), 124-26.
22. 10 July 1776, MS Memorandum Book, Thomas Posey Papers, IHS.
23. Richard E. Beeman, *Patrick Henry: A Biography* (New York: McGraw-Hill, 1974), 69, 75.
24. Ibid.; Selby, *Revolution in Virginia*, 126.
25. Selby, *Revolution in Virginia*, 124.
26. 9 January 1777, MS Memorandum Book, Thomas Posey Papers, IHS.
27. Ibid., 19 February 1777.
28. Ibid., 15 March 1777 and 13 April 1777.
29. Ibid., 24 May 1777.
30. Ibid., 28 May 1777.
31. *Dictionary of American Biography,* 1963 ed. s.v. "Morgan, Daniel," 7:166.
32. Harold L. Peterson, *The Book of the Continental Soldier* (Harrisburg, PA: Stackpole Books, 1968), 38-44, 100-7.
33. "A Short Biography of the Life of Governor Thomas Posey," Thomas Posey Papers, IHS.
34. Peterson, *Continental Soldier*, 44.
35. North Callahan, *Daniel Morgan: Ranger of the Revolution* (New York: Holt, Rinehart & Winston, 1961), 128.
36. "A Short Biography of the Life of Governor Thomas Posey," Thomas Posey Papers, IHS. For detailed accounts of both battles, see generally: Callahan, *Morgan*, 132-48.

37. Undated entry, MS Memorandum Book, Thomas Posey Papers, IHS. Posey's count included no Indians. Presumably they had fled Burgoyne's camp after the battles, but before the surrender ceremony.
38. Callahan, *Morgan*, 149.
39. Ibid.
40. Ibid., 151.
41. Ibid., 152-54.
42. Ibid., 156-57.
43. The transaction was recorded 11 March 1778. F.B. Kegley, ed., *Virginia Frontier* (Roanoke, VA: Southwest Virginia Historical Society, 1938), 406.
44. Robert Douthat Stoner, *A Seed Bed of the Republic* (Radford, VA: Commonwealth Press, Inc.,1962), 235.
45. Callahan, *Morgan*, 157.
46. Francis B. Heitman, ed., *Historical Register of Officers of the Continental Army, 1775-1783* (Washington, DC: Lowdermilk & Co., 1893), 333-34.
47. Douglas Southall Freeman, *George Washington: A Biography*, 7 vols. (New York: Charles Scribner's Sons, 1948-57), 5:1.
48. Royster, *Revolutionary People at War*, 250-54.
49. Ibid., 194-95.
50. Callahan, *Morgan*, 162.
51. Freeman, *Washington*, 5:14.
52. Ibid., 5:24-38; Callahan, *Morgan*, 165-66.
53. Tench Tilghman to Thomas Posey, 18 July 1778, *The George Washington Papers* (Washington, DC: Library of Congress, 1964, text-fiche), reel 50, (Hereafter cited as *GW Papers—text-fiche—LC*).
54. Allan W. Eckert, *The Wilderness War* (Boston and Toronto: Little, Brown & Co., 1978), 203-25.
55. Ibid., 227-29, 237.
56. Thomas Posey to Washington, 24 July 1778; Washington to Thomas Posey, 5 August 1778; Thomas Posey to Washington, 31 August 1778, *GW Papers—text-fiche—LC*, reel 51.
57. Ibid., Affidavit of Major Thomas Posey, 18 September 1778, reel 52.
58. Ibid., Thomas Posey to Washington, 23 September 1778.
59. Ibid., William Butler to Washington, 27 September 1778.
60. Ibid., Affidavit of Lieutenant Alexander Ramsel, 16 September 1778.
61. Eckert, *Wilderness War*, 238-39; "A Short Biography of the Life of Governor Thomas Posey," Thomas Posey Papers, IHS.
62. Eckert, *Wilderness War*, 244-45.
63. Ibid., 253-77.
64. Ibid.
65. Obituary of Captain John Posey, Thornton and Posey Bible, The Presbyterian Study Center Library, Montreat, NC; reprinted in John Frederick Dorman, ed., *The Virginia Genealogist*, 9:161; Lloyd Franklin Posey and Betty Sue Drake Posey, *The Posey Family in America* (Hattiesburg, MS: University of Southern Mississippi Press, 1971), 155.

CHAPTER THREE

(1778-1779)

"The fort's our own!"

The bloody attack on Cherry Valley was the last engagement on the northwest frontier in 1778. Both sides retired to winter quarters, the Indian warriors and Tory Rangers to the safety and sustenance of British Fort Niagara, the American regulars to Schoharie and nearby forts. The year's flurry of raids had, however, convinced General George Washington that the sector could be made secure only by a major, all-out invasion of Iroquois country and the total destruction of all its villages and crops. Such a campaign, under the able command of Major General John Sullivan, was successfully mounted in 1779, but Thomas Posey was not destined to serve in that expedition. Washington had other plans for the young major. Less than six weeks after the Cherry Valley massacre, Posey received orders from army headquarters that "your presence with the Regt. to which you belong is now necessary." He was told to "lose no time in coming" back to the main army, then in winter quarters at Middlebrook, New Jersey.[1] The three-company rifle battalion remained at Fort Defiance. Under its senior captain, James Parr, who succeeded Posey as its commander, it went on to distinguish itself the following summer in the Sullivan campaign against the Iroquois Nation.[2]

Doubtlessly still grieving over the recent loss of his wife and infant son in Virginia, the major hurried back to Middlebrook, where he was given temporary command of the newly formed and incomplete 11th Virginia Regiment.[3] He was, however, under consideration for a new and even more challenging military assignment. A pivotal and defining event awaited him, one that would demand every fiber of courage and leadership he possessed. It would, incidentally, also provide a rare insight into the principles of honor, conduct and justice that so strongly motivated and guided Posey and the entire officer class of the Revolutionary army.

General Sir Henry Clinton, commander-in-chief of British forces in America, had been directed by his government to strike a decisive and, hopefully, fatal blow against the main rebel army during the 1779 campaign season. Land and sea reinforcements for that purpose had already been dispatched to his base of operations in occupied New York City. In May, as a prelude to his planned general offensive, Clinton sent a sizable force up the Hudson to occupy and fortify two natural river bastions, Stony Point and Verplanck's Point. These lightly held colonial outposts guarded the opposite shores of a major ferry crossing. They were located about fifteen miles below West Point, the American strategic stronghold which blocked further access up the Hudson River to British land and sea forces. The fall of West Point would open up to the enemy the New York Highlands and the northern states beyond. General Washington realized that the seizure of the two downstream outposts signaled the objective and route of the expected British offensive. He promptly moved his main army from Middlebrook to the network of fortifications around West Point.[4] The decisive battle of the American Revolution appeared imminent.

When Clinton unaccountably failed to immediately follow up his preliminary advance, Washington conceived a bold plan to throw the enemy off balance—a surprise night attack on the two recently fortified river outposts. His major target, Stony Point, was a 150-foot-high rocky promontory jutting half a mile into the Hudson from its western bank. Its land side was surrounded by virtually impassable swamps, through which the only access was over a narrow, easily defended causeway. The adjacent marshes extended to the river bank on both sides of the steep cliff, where they merged into thin strips of beaches or sandbars, usually covered by one to three feet of water. The enemy, after occupying this natural strongpoint practically unopposed, had wasted no time in transforming it into an awesome fortress.

On the steep rocky slopes of the hill, which rose at a sharp angle from the marshes, skilled British engineers constructed two high breastworks or "abatis" of logs and earth fill, completely girding the hillside beyond its north and south river banks. The areas in front, between, and behind these shoulder-high barriers were cleared of all trees and natural cover. Along the crest of the hill a more sturdy and solid walled redoubt was constructed, with embrasures carved out for fifteen large brass cannons, expertly positioned so as to sweep and enfilade the slopes below. Alongside and between the big guns the engineers cut protective firing posts for use by infantrymen supporting the artillery batteries. Within the fortress itself, over 600 veteran British regulars were garrisoned, led by a seasoned commander, Lieutenant Colonel Henry Johnson, and amply provided with ammunition, food and supplies. Only the river side of the position was less heavily fortified, but it was well protected by the heavy guns of the British sloop-of-war, *Vulture*, and smaller warships anchored in the deep channel of the Hudson. The enemy had complete and unchallenged control of the river from New York City to the Stony Point/Verplanck's Point ferry crossing.[5]

An attack on this formidable fortress was clearly the kind of dangerous mission General Washington had in mind when, a few months earlier, he had directed the creation of a special light infantry division. Crossing the customary strict state lines, the new unit was to be composed of the most experienced and battle-tested officers and men in the American army. His choice to command this elite corps was Brigadier General Anthony Wayne, a brusque and dynamic Pennsylvanian whose fiery and impetuous nature had earned him the nickname "Mad Anthony." But Wayne had proved his valor and leadership at Quebec and Brandywine, and most particularly at Monmouth.[6] Colonel Daniel Morgan, Posey's old commander in the Rifle Regiment, was so disappointed at not getting this coveted command that he resigned his commission and returned home to Virginia.[7]

The rosters of all forty-six infantry battalions in the main army were combed to fill the ranks of the four select regiments of the Light Infantry—every man had previously served from one to three years in the Continental line. These rank-and-file soldiers were issued the best available weapons and equipment. They were given a short but intensive combat training course personally directed by the ex-Prussian martinet, General Baron Friedrich von Steuben, one of the few general officers in the army with any appreciable experience in classic European military drill and tactics. Every officer in the new division, from ensign to colonel, was personally selected by Wayne and Washington himself, solely on the basis of proven performance and leadership in past combat. It speaks eloquently of his soldierly credentials that Major Thomas Posey was chosen to command one of the eight battalions in Wayne's Light Infantry Corps.[8]

Although the overall composition of the division was multiregional, its internal structure followed traditional state lines. The First Regiment of the new Corps was headed by Colonel Christian ("Old Denmark") Febiger, a doughty Danish-born Virginian who had fought at Bunker Hill, Quebec, Brandywine, Germantown and Monmouth. Of the two battalions under Febiger, one, composed of four companies of picked Virginians, was led by Major Thomas Posey. The other, made up of two Virginia and two Pennsylvania companies, was headed by Lieutenant Colonel François Louis de Fleury, an early and valiant French volunteer officer who had joined the revolutionary cause for glory and advancement of his military career.[9]

Of the other three regiments, the Second was commanded by Pennsylvania's Colonel Richard Butler, under whom Posey had served both in the Rifle Regiment and in the recent upstate New York Indian-Tory campaign. It consisted of a battalion of four Pennsylvania companies under Lieutenant Colonel Samuel Hay, and another of four Maryland companies led by Major John ("Crazy Jack") Steward. The all-Connecticut Third Regiment was headed by Colonel Return Jonathan Meigs, with battalion commanders Lieutenant Colonel Isaac Sherman and acting-Major Henry Champion. The Fourth Regiment's designated commander, Colonel Rufus Putnam of Massachusetts, had not yet assumed his post due to illness. In his absence, Major William Hull led a battalion of four Massachusetts companies, and Major Hardy Murfree (Murphy) a battalion of two Massachusetts and two North Carolina companies.[10]

General Washington assigned his two top scouting units to the mission. Mounted troops called "partizens," commanded by Major Henry ("Lighthorse Harry") Lee and Captain Allen McLane, charted the general area, and on 6 July the commander-in-chief personally reconnoitered the approaches to the fort itself.[11] Major Lee, whose troop escorted Washington on this foray, made an unusual request of him as they rode back to headquarters. Lee's earlier patrols had apprehended three American army deserters, and he now asked the general for authority to summarily execute and decapitate one of these prisoners, as an example and warning to other would-be deserters. Three days later, after considering the request, Washington approved the proposed execution, but expressly forbade decapitation. Later that same day Lee oversaw the public execution, by firing squad, of an unnamed corporal. The next day, his severed head was stuck on top of a gallows at Smith's Clove, New York, where another deserter, Private Neil Magonigle, was being hanged pursuant to a sentence imposed earlier by a formal army court martial.[12]

When the report of this grisly scene reached Washington, he was both angered and horrified. He ordered the immediate secret burial of the head and body of the unfortunate corporal, so that the British would not learn of the atrocity and publicize it. Major Lee, far from being abashed by Washington's stern rebuke for having exceeded orders, reported to him on 11 July that the summary execution and decapitation "had a very immediate effect for the better on both troops and inhabitants."[13] Although, by modern standards, military discipline was harsh and punishment severe in the revolutionary army, most deserters did not suffer the extreme penalty. Death sentences were usually commuted—sometimes literally at the last moment—by higher authority. The most common punishment for major disciplinary offenses was flogging, typically, 100 lashes with a cat-o'-nine tails, laid on by the most robust drummer-boy in the unit's fife-and-drum corps.[14]

Shortly after making his personal inspection of the Stony Point fortifications, General Washington carefully wrote out in his own hand a detailed plan of attack. He stressed that absolute secrecy, surprise and precision of execution were essential to the success of his scenario. The assault was to be made under cover of darkness. He chose midnight, noting in passing that the more conventional pre-dawn hour—"the usual time for exploits of this kind"—would be more likely to find an experienced garrison alert and prepared for any surprise onslaught. In the hours preceding the actual attack, every sentry and any other nearby person suspected of Tory sympathies or otherwise likely to sound an alarm had to be seized and silenced as the troops approached the fort.[15]

The main assault was to be made along a narrow sandy beach on the river's edge south of the target, while a secondary force would strike simultaneously from the opposite sandbar north of the promontory. As soon as the approach was detected, a diversionary unit would mount a feint attack upon the British guard holding the narrow causeway leading through the swamp to the citadel's landside entrance. To assure against any premature or inadvertent alarm, no officer or man in the two attack columns was to load or fire a weapon—thus, the entire assault was to be carried at the point of bayonet, spear and sword. Wayne was given complete discretion in setting the specific battle order of the forces at his disposal, and in making any last-minute changes in the plan deemed necessary at the time of the attack.[16]

General Washington went over the plan in detail with Wayne, pointing out its difficulties and dangers, and then asked the younger man if he was prepared to accept the challenge. "Mad

Anthony" replied, characteristically, "General, if you give me permission, I'll storm Hell itself for you."[17] A few nights later, it is not hard to imagine that the men of the Light Infantry must have felt that the commander-in-chief had indeed ordered them to mount that ultimate infernal charge—as they sloshed with unloaded muskets through the murky marshes toward the silent but menacing guns bearing down on them from the pinnacle of Stony Point, looming high above them in the midnight darkness of 17 July 1779.

At precisely 11:00 a.m. on the morning before the assault, the entire Corps was drawn up in ranks on the parade grounds outside Fort Montgomery near West Point. Every man was "fresh shaved and powdered," fully equipped and rationed, as he stood at rigid attention for a dress review by Generals Washington and Baron von Steuben. Each officer wore a sword at his side, and bore a short spear or pike called a spontoon; each rank-and-file soldier carried a well-cleaned and oiled musket, and wore attached to his belt a well-honed bayonet. After a few encouraging words from Washington the corpsmen, led by the resplendently-uniformed Anthony Wayne astride his horse, filed off the parade grounds to the measured cadence of fifes and drums. But instead of returning to their camp, as most expected, they plunged into the surrounding heavily wooded and mountainous terrain on a fifteen-mile trek southward—all but the top officers still unaware of their dangerous mission.[18]

Major Thomas Posey was not in the lead column of his battalion of Virginians during the march. General Wayne had sent him ahead with the mounted partizens on a scouting mission, in the company of Major Henry Lee and Captain Allen McLane. At the very hour of the Corps' dress review, the three officers were crouched in waist-high swamp water, reconnoitering the enemy's actions and armaments from a hidden vantage point just outside Stony Point.[19] During the bitter winter at Valley Forge, an unlikely but warm and lasting friendship had developed between Posey, the plebian frontier saddler, and Harry Lee, the well-born scion of the aristocratic and powerful Lee family of Virginia. As dusk began to obscure the harsh outlines of the target fortress, Posey, Lee and McLane withdrew from their observation post and joined General Wayne and advance elements of his force at Springsteel's Farm, the designated assembly area some 1½ miles west of Stony Point. They reported to the commander that they had seen no apparent signs of alarm or heightened defensive preparations at the British stronghold.[20]

All during the day and early evening, partizan detachments had scoured the area surrounding the Light Infantry's line of march, detaining anyone who might alert the enemy to the troop movements. Among those turned aside were two elderly widows of Tory persuasion who were en route to the fort with fresh provisions to sell to the garrison officers' mess. Even stray dogs found within earshot of British sentries were pursued and bayoneted, to forestall their giving away the presence of passing troops.[21] By the time full darkness had fallen at 8:00 p.m., the last unit of the Corps had reached the staging area, and partizens had been deployed along the causeway leading toward the fort, to intercept any incoming British couriers or American deserters who might possibly have strayed from the ranks during the march.[22] General Washington had been bluntly explicit on the need for absolute surprise: "Knowledge of your intention, ten minutes previously obtained, blasts all your hopes."[23]

Now, for the first time, Wayne revealed all the details of his tactical plan to his senior officers. In the battle order of the main column approaching the fort from the south, Febiger's First Regiment would lead, followed by Meigs' Third, then six companies of the Fourth Regiment under Major Hull. Colonel Butler's Second Regiment would compose the secondary column attacking from the north sandbar. Major Murfree, with the two remaining companies of the Fourth regiment, would make the diversionary feint at the fort's causeway entrance, while the partizan cavalry would continue to patrol the surrounding area. If things went badly, Washington had posted a separate reserve force under General John Peter Gabriel Muhlenberg a few miles away, to cover retreating Light Infantrymen in the event they were repulsed and forced to flee an enemy counterattack.

The date of the assault had purposely been set for a dark, moonless night. As the evening progressed, each man was told to attach a small strip of white paper or cloth to his hat or cap, for identification in the darkness and confusion of battle. Strict orders were passed down the line to every man that under no circumstances was anyone permitted to carry a loaded weapon—any man seen loading a musket or sidearm during the approach to the fort was to be immediately put to death by the nearest officer.[24] Using the discretion granted him by Washington, General Wayne announced that the first five men to reach and scale the highest parapet of Stony Point would receive generous cash awards.

Since Febiger's First Regiment was first in the battle order of the main column, Wayne called upon it for volunteers to act as a vanguard of shock troops to lead the assault. Fleury and Posey immediately stepped forward with 150 of their men. From this group, a special 20-man squad—designated, appropriately, the "Forlorn

Hope"—led by Lieutenant George Knox, was selected to precede the vanguard with axes and long spiked poles. It was their task to dismantle and open gaps in the two rows of abatis barring access to the summit.

Wayne used the same process in organizing the battle order of Colonel Butler's Pennsylvanians and Marylanders composing the north assault column. Major John Steward (Stewart) was to command its smaller 100-man vanguard, and Lieutenant James Gibbons was designated leader of its Forlorn Hope. As for himself, General "Mad Anthony" Wayne, never a man to shrink from combat or to ask others to take risks he was not prepared to accept personally, chose to march alongside Colonel Febiger at the head of the First Regiment, just behind the vanguard of the main assault force.[25]

After the corpsmen had been arranged in the proper groupings and marching order, and all final preparations were completed, nearly an hour remained before the time set to advance into the marshes surrounding Stony Point. A profound silence descended upon the 1,300 soldiers of the Light Infantry, as they sat or knelt in the damp darkness of Springsteel's pasture. Countless times in the long history of human warfare, men had waited in this way, silently undergoing an intensely personal experience common to all about to go into deadly combat, and utterly foreign and incomprehensible to all others. Each man's thoughts turned inwardly upon himself, reliving his life's most meaningful moments, recalling his loved ones, wondering if the next few hours would be his last, and feeling, although surrounded by comrades, an almost unbearable loneliness. It has been well said that nothing so concentrates and clarifies the mind as the prospect of imminent death.

Wayne himself was sure that he would not survive the desperate charge up the rocky slope. He used this quiet time to write a letter to his closest friend, imploring him to "attend to the education of my little son and Daughter." As for himself, "I am called to Sup, but where to breakfast, either within the enemy's lines in triumph, or in the other World."[26] Colonel Febiger had a similar premonition, expressed almost facetiously in an informal will written in the form of a letter addressed to his trusted friend and subordinate, Thomas Posey: "As there is a probability of my going on a very hazardous expedition in which there is some danger of my taking a place among the deceased heroes of America. . . ."[27]

As the hour set to storm Stony Point rapidly drew near, most, if not all, of the soldiers of the Light Infantry shared some such dark foreboding during this time of painful introspection. But if Posey was one of those who reduced his innermost feelings to pen and paper, no such writing has survived. Possibly, as a recent and still-grieving widower, with his two sons much too young to grasp the significance or gravity of the moment, he kept his deepest thoughts to himself, and chose simply to accept for safekeeping such parting messages as Febiger and others in his regiment might have entrusted to him. But he must have felt fear, the fear known by every man who has ever faced mortal combat.

At the agreed signal, the two assault columns moved out, slogging through the swampy approaches as planned, but upon reaching the sandbars along the river, their progress was slowed by waist-high water, a depth greater than anticipated. Striding forward as quickly as possible through the impeding current, bayonets fixed on muskets held high above the water, the main column enjoyed the element of surprise until it neared the enemy's outer picket line. There, the startled British sentries hastily fired a few warning shots before retreating up the hill into the fort. Lieutenant Knox's Forlorn Hope rushed forward to the lower abatis, but had only partially dismantled it when Fleury and Posey arrived with their vanguard. As sounds of alarm began to be heard from the heights, Thomas seized an axe from an exhausted soldier and hacked desperately at the remaining logs impeding passage through the barrier. After climbing and stumbling in the darkness over and through the broken limbs and mounds of dirt, he and Fleury paused only long enough to assemble and re-form their ranks on the other side. Then they again followed Knox and his men upward to the second abatis.

In the meantime, within the fort the full garrison, alerted by the pickets' shots, had been called to arms with drum rolls and the shouts of watch officers. The gunners ran to their assigned artillery pieces and worked frantically to put them into action. Hundreds of infantrymen rushed to the walls, loading their muskets as they ran. Within minutes they stood shoulder to shoulder, ringing the parapet from one side of the enclosure to the other. When the advancing line of the assaulting vanguard reached the upper abatis, it was met by a furious barrage of grapeshot from the six cannons commanding the southern slope, and a deadly hail of musket balls fired down at them from above. In the darkness below, the attackers could see only the blinding explosions of flame from the artillery blasts, and the smaller but more numerous and repeated flashes of light from the muzzles of hundreds of muskets trained down upon them. Many Americans were hit, some fatally, but Knox, Fleury and Posey, shouting encouragement to their men, led them through and over the second barrier, and in the teeth of a murderous fire, raced upward toward the summit.[28]

Surprised by the rapid progress of the forward units, General Wayne had sent Colonel Febiger back to bring up the lagging rear ranks of his troops and the regiments following. Marching at the head of the First Regiment's front line, the general was brought down in the first volley by a musket ball that grazed his head as he picked his way over the lower abatis. Momentarily dazed, and fearing that he was mortally wounded, he raised himself on one elbow and, motioning forward with a spontoon, exhorted the men behind him to press ahead. Febiger, who had also sustained a slight face wound, took over Wayne's position, leading his regiment up the slope. They were quickly followed by Meigs' regiment and Hull's detachment.

Major Murfree's two companies of North Carolinians had been silently deployed in the swamp a few dozen yards away from the enemy force guarding the causeway entrance to Stony Point. The only American troops authorized to fire their weapons, when they heard the first sounds of alarm within the fort, they promptly mounted a feint attack. Their gunfire and loud shouts drew the immediate attention of the British commander, Lieutenant Colonel Johnson. Never imagining that the Americans would seriously try to breach the impregnable sides of his stronghold, he was persuaded that the main assault was directed at the causeway entrance. He quickly pulled six companies of his infantrymen from their firing positions on the parapet, and led them in battle order down the front slope. There, they engaged in a lively but largely harmless fire fight with Murfree's well-concealed soldiers. When some of the British defenders taunted the hidden Americans, daring them to come out and fight, from the darkness of the surrounding swamp came a laconic reply in a deep Carolinian drawl: "Take your time, my lads, we'll be there soon."[29]

Meanwhile, Colonel Richard Butler's north assault column had been slowed by cloying mud in the marshes and swirling high water on the sandbar. When they arrived at the base of the rocky promontory, the assault on the other side of the fort was already well underway, while the artillery pieces and gun ports above them were fully manned by British defenders loaded and poised to fire. Faced with this opposition, Lieutenant Gibbons' Forlorn Hope was understandably hampered in cutting through the sharpened tree trunks pointed downward at them from the two abatis. Major John Steward's vanguard was pinned down by a withering fire from the summit, inching slowly forward behind any available debris until it reached and paused for cover under the base of the parapet itself.

On the south wall, the Americans would not be denied. If the initial charge faltered, there would be no second chance—the entire operation would end in disastrous failure. Fleury was the first man to reach and vault over the parapet, followed immediately by Lieutenant Knox and three intrepid sergeants of his Forlorn Hope, each bleeding from at least two wounds. Posey was next—he paused halfway over the wall, turned, and shouted out the prearranged watchword, "The fort's our own!"[30] This was the signal to the main body of the assault column that the vanguard had breached the top bastion. As the rest of Fleury's and Posey's shock troops followed them over the wall, Febiger, Meigs and Hull quickly brought up their regiments to the summit, where they poured into the fort at a dozen points.

Once within the central enclosure Fleury, with unerring Gallic instincts, headed straight for the nearby British standard and struck it down with his sword. Posey, sword in one hand and a spontoon in the other, drove the closest defenders away from their gun ports. He then formed a group of his Virginians into a phalanx and led them in a relentless bayonet charge that carried across the entire width of the fort to its north wall. There, they silenced the two large 24-pounders pinning down Colonel Butler's column, which then began surging over the parapet. While his men busied themselves disarming a number of enemy soldiers retreating before their advance, Posey reached down through a gun embrasure and helped Major Steward, leader of Butler's vanguard, climb into the fort.[31]

At some point during the vicious hand-to-hand combat within the fort, Thomas had overcome and captured an unnamed British officer—probably another major. He accepted as a token of surrender a handsome pair of silver-mounted, ivory-handled pistols, prize spoils of war that he cherished throughout his life, and referred to in his will as "the Stony Point pistols."[32] Sometime during the fray, he acquired also a less welcome souvenir of the battle, a wound in his lower leg. The laceration was minor enough to be ignored during the heat of battle, but it never completely healed, and partially disabled him from time to time in his last years.[33]

The outnumbered enemy defenders within the enclosure had been overwhelmed by the bayonet-wielding Americans pouring over both sides of the fort. Lieutenant Colonel Henry Johnson, the British commander, realized too late that he had been outflanked and overrun on both sides. He rushed back up to the summit, only to find it in the attackers' hands. He surrendered his sword to Colonel Febiger, the highest-ranking American officer then on the scene.

The remaining British defenders threw down their arms and pleaded for mercy, after which not a single man was harmed. This gesture of humanitarian compassion, rarely exhibited before or after by either side in this bitter war, was still a point of great personal pride to Thomas Posey nearly four decades later.[34]

As General Wayne, bleeding profusely from a deep two-inch scalp wound and supported on either side by aides, entered the fort, the fury and tumult of battle had ended, and the clear night air rang and rang again with the cheers of the Light Infantry. Stony Point, the impregnable fortress, had been overrun and captured in less than one hour's time, without a single shot having been fired by the unstoppable American assault columns. Wayne scratched out a hasty note, and an aide sped it fifteen miles northward into the hand of the sleepless and anxiously waiting Washington. It read, simply, "The fort and garrison with Col. Johnston are ours. Our officers and men behaved like men who are determined to be free."[35]

In a single hurried sentence, the bloodied general had summarized the core dynamic of the entire revolutionary generation—the ultimate and intrinsic truth of its "glorious cause." Clearly freedom was not just a trite buzzword or an abstract philosophical concept to any man who would willingly—almost eagerly—risk death and oblivion in a hailstorm of musket balls and cannon fire. A man so fiercely "determined to be free" must surely have been pursuing a very real and tangible goal, one attainable only at a very great price, perhaps life itself. But even if he might not personally survive to enjoy freedom's hard-gained benefits, his contemporaries and descendants would still esteem his sacrifice and honor his memory. Whether he lived or died, he would have fulfilled his solemn and binding social contract with future generations. It was truly what Charles Royster called "the American character"—that complex bundle of attitudes and emotions fueling the revolutionary movement—that drove men hellbent to be free up the lethal slopes and over the blazing walls of Stony Point.[36]

Within hours of the battle, Colonel Christian Febiger also found the time and opportunity to write a more endearing, if less historic, note to his wife Elizabeth:

> My Dear Girl: . . . at 12 o'clock last night we stormed this Confounded place, and, with the loss of about fourteen killed forty or fifty wounded, we carried it. I can give you no particulars as yet. A musquet ball scraped my nose. No other damage to "Old Denmark." God bless you. Farewell, FEBIGER [37]

Most of the American fatalities occurred during the charge up the outer slopes, while the British loss of sixty-three dead within the fort itself attests to the ferocity of the Americans' attack there. The Corps captured 543 of the enemy, plus 15 precious and badly needed cannons, several mortars, and much ammunition, equipment and supplies. The total value of the booty, later calculated at $180,655, was distributed among all the troops participating in the action, as had been agreed to beforehand by Washington and Wayne. The cash bonuses promised by Wayne to the first five men over the wall were properly awarded to Fleury, Knox and the three valiant sergeants, Baker, Spencer and Donlop. However, the two officers, following tradition, distributed their awards equally among their enlisted men.[38]

The immediate aftermath of the battle was anti-climactic. General Washington rode down to the fort early the next morning to personally congratulate the Light Infantry, inspect the site, and appraise the strategic situation. A poorly conceived and badly executed secondary effort to capture Verplanck's Point across the river had failed, and word soon arrived that the British were sending a large land and sea force up the Hudson to regain the lost position. The surrounding area did not offer favorable terrain for a major military engagement, and Stony Point itself was vulnerable to bombardment from British warships which had temporarily moved downstream after the assault. Washington wisely ordered that the captured fort be stripped of all armaments and supplies, and three days later, after all its buildings and fortifications had been destroyed, it was evacuated.

The immediate military significance of the Stony Point assault was over-shadowed by its psychological and moral effects. The fragile American cause and sagging public morale badly needed bolstering—there had been no clear-cut victory over the enemy since Saratoga. Washington himself predicted that "the event will have a good effect upon the minds of the people, give our troops greater confidence in themselves, and depress the spirits of the enemy proportionately."[39] As published reports of the battle spread throughout the Union and abroad, all these favorable results became apparent. The heterogeneous composition of the Light Infantry gave nearly every state its own contingent of local heroes to extol—some states, including New York, declared that the battle's anniversary date would be observed as a public holiday. The Americans' fighting prowess, and particularly their restraint and mercy toward the enemy soldiers after the victory, earned the begrudging admiration and respect of the British themselves.

These citizen-rebels had, after all, bested professional European soldiers at their own game, in hand-to-hand combat.[40] As Washington clearly foresaw, General Clinton's "spirits" were perhaps the most depressed of all—he abandoned all his carefully laid plans to launch a decisive Hudson River valley offensive against the main American army in 1779.[41]

A grateful Congress promptly ordered that a special gold medal be struck and presented to General Wayne. It also voted, on the basis of Wayne's first full battle report, to award silver medals to Lieutenant Colonel Fleury and Major Steward, while lieutenants Knox and Gibbons, and Wayne aide Mr. Archer, (a civilian volunteer), were rewarded with brevet captaincies. But it was precisely this Wayne battle report, and its treatment of some officers who had played major roles in the victory, that was to incite a storm of controversy within the Light Infantry itself. A close study of the flurry of correspondence it provoked provides some revealing insights into the unique code of conduct that prevailed in the officer corps of the revolutionary army, and more particularly, into the character and mindset of young Major Thomas Posey.

Anthony Wayne's formal report of 17 July, written while he was still at Stony Point and suffering considerable weakness and discomfort from his head wound, was promptly endorsed and sent forward to Congress by General Washington. It was soon published verbatim in leading public journals throughout the land. It accurately depicted events as they happened up to the moment Wayne fell wounded at the lower abatis. Thereafter, he necessarily relied upon others in relating the main column's final thrust up the slope and the fighting at the parapet and within the fortress itself. His knowledge of the performance of the north secondary column probably came from its commander, Colonel Butler, Wayne's close friend and protege. These circumstances may partially explain, but can in no way excuse, the sins of commission and omission in the battle scenario that was soon being eagerly devoured by the citizens of a young nation hungry for heroes.

Wayne was profuse in his praise for the officers and men of his Corps as a group, but he chose to single out by name for special commendation and honors only twelve specific individuals. Military protocol dictated his first naming the senior regimental commanders, Colonels Febiger, Butler and Meigs—inexplicably omitting Major Hull, de facto commander of the Fourth Regiment. Next, he expressly commended—without delineating in any way their vastly differing roles in the actual fighting—the ranking officers of the two vanguards, Fleury and Steward, and the leaders of the two Forlorn Hopes, Knox and Gibbons. He then singled out three fellow-Pennsylvanians: his two personal aides, Archer and Fishbourne, (whose only role had been to assist the general into the fort after it had fallen), and Lieutenant Colonel Hay of Butler's regiment, whose performance in the battle, other than sustaining a serious wound, was not particularly noteworthy. Finally, two noncombatants, General Muhlenburg, commander of the reserve force, and Major Henry Lee of the partizan cavalry, were named. Conspicuous by their absence were the names of Major Hull, Major Hardy Murfree, (whose diversionary attack at the fort's entrance played a key role in the victory), and Major Thomas Posey, co-commander of the main vanguard, first to sound the critical watchword, and the effective leader of the assault forces in the decisive hand-to-hand encounters within the fort itself.[42]

Major Hull was so incensed at his omission from the honors list of regimental commanders that he stormed up to Wayne and demanded immediate transfer out of the elite Light Infantry Corps. Only after a personal meeting with General George Washington was the offended Massachusetts officer mollified and he eventually withdrew his application for re-assignment out of Wayne's command.[43]

Hull was not the only New Englander affronted by Wayne's account. Others shared his suspicions that the general had shown marked favoritism toward his six fellow-Pennsylvanians, (Butler, Hay, Gibbons, Knox, Fishbourne and Archer), in handing out battle honors.[44] On 22 August Wayne received scorching letters from the two highest-ranking officers of the all-Connecticut Third Regiment—Colonel Meigs and Lieutenant Colonel Sherman. Meigs, who had been named in the report, spoke not for himself, but for "many Officers in the Brigade" who, after reading Wayne's report, had expressed a conviction that "there is the appearance of partiality, in not mentioning any wounded Officer except L't Colonel Hay." Meigs strongly suggested that, since Hay had already been singled out solely because of his wound, Wayne should issue a supplemental report listing the names of all other wounded officers. That report, Colonel Meigs urged, should also expressly honor "two or three others who enter'd the Fort nearly at the same instant with Col'o Fleury."[45] Meigs clearly felt that Thomas Posey, whom he knew had vaulted over the ramparts right behind Fleury, and who had also been wounded, should have been accorded honors second only to those bestowed upon the intrepid French officer.

Sherman's letter to Wayne was much more emotional and bitterly personal than his superior Meigs' had been. He asserted that "your letter to Gen'l Washington on the reduction of Stony Point, in the minds of many judicious persons, has in some measure tarnished the lustre of your character." He charged that "there appears in the account you have given evident marks of State partiality." Sherman carefully stressed that "I am not writing for myself, but I feel for those officers under my command as well as others who merit as much as those most distinguished by you."[46]

Wayne did not immediately answer Sherman's diatribe, but he promptly fired off a lengthy response to Meigs, in which he vehemently denied harboring any state or regional partiality: "I detest Local Prejudices, as much as I pity the man who would unjustly suspect me of them." Almost as an afterthought, Wayne then added an ominous postscript. "I have rec'd a letter . . . from Lieu't Col'o Sherman, of a very extraordinary Nature—which at a Proper Season will require a very Serious & particular explanation—for altho' I don't wish to incur any Gentlemans displeasure, yet, I put up with no man's Insults."[47]

Sherman was apparently warned by Meigs of General Wayne's clear intention to challenge him to a duel. He hastened to write the general a second letter, assuring him that "to insult you, I declare upon my honor, never was my intention; my view was to acquaint you there was an uneasiness among the officers of your command, and the cause." His purpose in writing, Sherman vehemently declared, was "so far from thinking to make use of compulsive measures to gain redress that I can assure you: it never entered my mind." The Connecticut officer then apologized for the "warmth" of his expressions, and Wayne's honor was presumably appeased.[48]

Colonel Christian Febiger, unlike Hull, Meigs and Sherman, did not directly confront Wayne, but he also felt strongly that the general's first report had slighted his Virginians generally, and Thomas Posey in particular. In an unpublished account of the battle, he related how "the gallant Major Posey, whose name has not even been mentioned, at the head of Febiger's Regiment pressing close upon him, threw away his axes and took to the Bayonet and followed Fleury and Knox into the works." Febiger flatly denied the statement in Wayne's report that both assault columns had entered the fort at the same time. He asserted that Steward's north vanguard had been unable to enter until after Posey had silenced the two cannons impeding their advance, and "of course the right column led by Posey had full possession of the Fort previous to even a single man of the left being in."[49]

In a private letter to Colonel Henry Heth of Virginia, Febiger reaffirmed this sequence of events, stating that "the gallant Posey, a most valuable Posey, helped Major Stewart, who commanded the advance on the left, into the works."[50] The casualty lists lend credence to Febiger's scenario. Of the fifteen Americans killed in the assault, twelve were in the main south column, of whom seven were from Febiger's own lead regiment. [51]

Major Thomas Posey was not, however, a man to let others plead his cause. On 10 August he had written his own letter of protest—addressing it, not to Wayne, but directly to his commander-in-chief and former neighbor, General George Washington. It was only two days later that he sent a copy of his letter to General Wayne, attached to this cryptic note: "I have enclosed you a copy of a letter which I wrote to his Excellency, General Washington."[52]

Thomas told Washington that he felt "a most sensible mortification, and am most feelingly hurt, by finding myself totally neglected" in Wayne's battle report. He detailed his role in the engagement—commander of one of the two battalions at the front of the main assault column, the second field officer into the enemy works, first to sound the watchword, extensive hand-to-hand fighting inside the fort, the silencing of the two heavy guns on the north parapet, and his assisting Major Steward over the wall. But the young major stressed that he claimed no particular merit and wanted no reward for doing his duty, "farther than being mentioned as a field officer, who had made use of all his endeavors . . . to promote the success of the enterprise: *This* I have certainly a just claim to, but even this has been denied me."[53]

Reminding his commander-in-chief that he had fought in "as many engagements with the enemy as any officer who has not been longer in the service of the Continental Army," Posey closed his letter with an appeal to Washington's sense of fair play:

> . . . as I have had an equal share in the danger and the fatigue attending the reduction of Stony Point, I expected an equal share of the honor resulting from the success of the enterprise. I expected to have been mentioned to my countrymen; this is all I ask, all I want, and all I wish to receive . . . To be utterly forgotten would give uneasiness to a man of the least sensibility, and would induce the most modest being that ever had an existence to speak his complaints.[54]

There is no written record of any reply made by Washington to any of the complaining officers. But there are clear signs that he moved behind the scenes to calm the widespread unrest in the Light Infantry's officer corps. Perhaps, as in the case of Major Hull, he quietly spoke to and reassured the other offended men. But almost certainly he took up the issue directly with Anthony Wayne. This is best evidenced by a second, supplementary report Wayne prepared and submitted to John Jay, then President of the Continental Congress. Significantly, it is dated 10 August—the same day Washington received Posey's impassioned letter, but two days before Wayne received a written copy of that letter, and well before he received the complaints sent to him by Meigs and Sherman.

Wayne thanked the governing body for the honors it had bestowed upon him, but then, after expressing satisfaction that he had used his best efforts in carrying out General Washington's orders, conceded that,

> . . . I feel very hurt that I did not in my letter to him of the 17th of July, mention (among other brave and worthy officers), the names of Lieut. Col. SHERMAN, Majors HULL, MURPHY and POSEY, whose good conduct and intrepedity justly entitled them to that attention . . . Permit me, therefore, thro your Excellency, to do them that justice now which the state of my wound diverted me from in the first instance. . . . [55]

There is no evidence that Wayne back-dated or otherwise falsified the time when he wrote this letter to John Jay. Thus, on the record, he appears to have acted to remedy the grievances of the three officers named therein, (as well as the injustice done to the uncomplaining Murfree), before receiving any of their formal protestations. Accordingly, in later responding to these complaints, he had the considerable advantage of being able to point convincingly to his prior corrective action, even while (in the case of Meigs and Sherman) denying their accusations of partiality to his fellow-Pennsylvanians.

Posey's letter to Washington had not raised, or even hinted at, the issue of state bias. But it seems to have inadvertently touched an even more sensitive nerve of the splenetic Wayne—his vaunted and well-deserved reputation for valor in combat. Thomas, in relating his own role in leading the assault of the vanguard up the slope of Stony Point, had casually referred in passing to that point in the battle "where Gen. Wayne left the head of the column." But he negligently failed to mention the general's head wound as the cause of that absence, probably assuming that Washington was well aware of the circumstances.[56]

Although Wayne uncharacteristically waited more than two weeks before responding to Posey's "very Laconic" note of 12 August enclosing his letter to Washington, he did not let this perceived slur go unchallenged. But first he addressed the issue of Thomas' role in the battle. He pointed out (correctly) that, besides himself, there were several other officers of higher rank than Posey in the main assault column—Fleury in the vanguard, and Febiger, Meigs and Sherman leading the nearest backup regiments. Wayne then stressed that, even after falling wounded, he continued to direct with his spear "the greater part of the Column over the Abbatis and into the Works." But he did not denigrate Posey's performance, readily acknowledging that he had indeed done his duty well. He averred that he "highly approved of your Conduct," and to clinch his point, he enclosed a copy of his supplementary letter to Congress as proof that he had already done "further Justice to your Merit which I thought you entitled to."[57]

Having refuted to his own satisfaction the young major's charge of unfairness, Wayne then turned forcefully to what had bothered him even more about Posey's letter to Washington: "some expressions made use of tending to hold up an Idea of want of Prowess in me." If that really was what Posey meant, "Mad Anthony" stated ominously, he had better be prepared to acknowledge it, "not to me as your Superior Officer, but to me as a Private Gentleman very tenacious of my Honor,—which honor is now plighted to meet you on that ground only." But, the general concluded, if Posey had not intended to impugn his courage in combat, he should "as a Gentleman of those nice feelings which I believe you to possess . . . place that matter in a proper point of View."[58]

Thomas was probably as surprised and chagrined as Lieutenant Colonel Sherman had been to learn that he had offended Wayne's feelings to the point of his demanding satisfaction. His reply, hastily written and hand-delivered on the same day that Wayne wrote him, was short and very much to the point:

> . . . You imagine I have cast some reflections on your courage or conduct in your military character. I can aver to you upon the word of a man of honor, of a gentleman, that I had no intention . . . to cast any reflection upon your military character, or your character in any manner whatsoever. . . .
>
> I am as far to attack any man's reputation, as I am to endure the least ground for mine to be questioned. You had (consistent with my ideas) injured me, my reputation was at stake; I called for redress, your sense of honor and justice has induced you to give me satisfaction; your letter to Congress is a sufficient one, and I hope that this will be a sufficient one to you.[59]

Although Wayne's sense of honor was appeased, he understandably would not let Thomas have the last word. He promptly sent back a note pointing out that his supplementary report to Congress commending Posey had been issued before he had received a copy of Posey's letter to Washington. Therefore, Wayne asserted, the major's demand for redress was not, (and could not have been), the cause that "induced" him to do the right thing, as Thomas' last letter had inferred.[60]

At some point in the exchange of these elegantly-worded messages, Thomas had solicited the thoughts of a legally trained comrade from Virginia, Captain John Marshall, on the adequacy of Wayne's supplementary report to Congress. The future Chief Justice of the United States Supreme Court, who was to remain a lifelong friend of Posey's, had been in General Muhlenburg's unneeded reserve force outside Stony Point, and had come in to inspect the fort personally on the morning of its capture. Marshall responded with a typically lawyerlike and appropriately-judicious opinion. He reminded Posey that he had complained to Washington only of not being "mentioned" in Wayne's report. "You are now mentioned . . . & you cannot, in my opinion, without acting inconsistently demand anything farther." But Marshall was less than impressed with Wayne's remedial gesture:

> . . . I think Genl. Wayne ought to have done more . . . he ought I think to have said more for his own sake . . . The Man who has seen with what a liberal hand the Genl. has, in his first letter, dealt out praises to Men who could not have deserved much more than yourself will confess that he has been rather sparing in his encomiums on Major Posey . . . you can ask nothing farther but Genl. Wayne might & ought to have done more . . . [61]

Both Wayne and Posey had referred to their "honor" in deferential, almost reverent terms. In the hindsight of two centuries, the Revolutionary War concept of military honor might appear to be archaic and specious. But among the army officers of that generation it was, next to devotion to freedom itself, the single most compelling element in their hierarchy of values and self-esteem. An officer was, by definition, a gentleman. He was always conscious of his rank, duty and code of conduct, forever cultivating a keen sensitivity, (or "sensibility," as it was then called), that set him far apart from the rank-and-file. As Charles Royster has pointed out, "the slightest indignity or affront struck him as an attack on his rights as a gentleman."[62]

Furthermore, public recognition of military prowess was just as important to the revolutionary officer as the actual performance of the battle exploits themselves. "Officers expected to be mentioned by name in official records, to distinguish themselves for promotion, to be remembered always by a grateful posterity through histories of the revolution . . . the proper accompaniment and reward of military value."[63] Personal self-knowledge of one's own worth did not suffice. As Royster notes, "to have honor and to be honored were very close . . . officers were keen to detect attacks on their honor in other people's offhand remarks, criticisms, or even silence. Failing to mention an officer's name in the report of a battle . . . might so mortify him that he would construe the silence as a declaration that he was unfit for his post."[64]

Thomas Posey shared the concept of fame or glory prevalent among officers of the revolutionary generation. It was important to him that his achievements in battle be made known to and acknowledged by his peers. But of equal or greater import was the assurance that his contributions to the glorious cause would be recognized by posterity. For all he knew in the summer of 1779, Stony Point might be his last chance to attain that special kind of immortality that he and his contemporaries aspired to so avidly. The next battle could be his last. Denial of a hard-earned and well-deserved claim to fame, by omission of his name from the official report of the engagement, deprived him of the one "encomium" he sought above all others—the respect, regard and gratitude of his descendants, and indeed all future generations, for his bravura performance in the storming of Stony Point.

Accordingly, Thomas' seeming overreaction to Wayne's slight must be judged in the context of these prevailing notions of military virtue and honor, fame and immortality. But a close reading of the Stony Point letters also tells us much about the underlying nature and character of the young major from the Virginia frontier—about who and what Thomas Posey really was. Neither he nor the other protesting officers objected to the commendation of any of those named in Wayne's first report. It is clear, however, that much more raw courage and valor was displayed on those rocky slopes than the commander chose to communicate to General Washington, Congress and the eager nation. Certainly no participant could (or did) take exception to the high honors given Fleury, the gallant French officer. Perhaps the naming of John Steward, his counterpart in the opposite column, was dictated by military protocol or practice, although his true role in the engagement was demonstrably less significant than Fleury's. But the inclusion of Steward's name made all the more glaring the omission of other officers of equal rank who had borne far more visibly the burden and the hazards of actual fighting both outside and within the fort.

It was this disparity between honors bestowed purely on the basis of command position, as opposed to combat performance, that seemingly moved Posey to the extraordinary step of protesting directly to the commander-in-chief. He had been almost literally at Fleury's heels going over the parapet; had fought his way with sword and spear across the entire works to silence the guns pinning down the opposite column; and then had reached down to help Steward climb into the fort after most of its defenders had laid down their arms. A silver Congressional medal and nationwide acclaim for Major Steward, and not even an honorable mention in the official record for Major Posey—this was the egregious injustice that provoked the indignant letter to the man Thomas had known from his earliest days at Rover's Delight as the very embodiment of fairness and honor, and a commander whose respect and approval he ever sought to gain.

Washington, for his part, surely disapproved of the young major's disregard of command channels, but he must have read his letter with mixed emotions. It reflected to a remarkable degree one of his own most notable characteristics—an almost obsessive insistence that the historical record reflect meritorious performance of duty. Twenty-five years before, the same trait had moved young militia Colonel George Washington, after a desultory encounter with the French enemy on the frontier, to offer a detailed written defense of his conduct to Virginia Governor Dinwiddie.[65] Now the same shared quality suddenly sprang from the pages of the letter he held in his hand from his former neighbor.

Barry Schwartz, in his recent brilliant analysis of Washington's character, identifies what he called the general's "deep yearning for public recognition . . . an intense and deep-seated vanity." But he could not separate Washington's "adult egotism from his commitment to his country's ideals. Both traits, egotism and patriotism, fed off yet reinforced the other." According to Schwartz, the great man and his generation distinguished between vanity, or self-love, and the pursuit of fame. "Fame was regarded as a kind of moral brass, minted to drive out the immoral currency of ambition. A love of fame, and a readiness to bestow it, were necessary safeguards against tyranny . . . when Washington announced to the world that he was motivated solely by the desire for 'reputation,' he was not only confessing to his egotism but also conforming to his culture's code of honor." Washington openly prized his countrymen's good opinions of him, and "he defined those opinions as the primary source of his motivation and reward."[66]

The vanity of Thomas Posey cannot be denied, but it clearly found expression in this purified form of egotism that he equated with devotion to the revolutionary cause, and the quest for fame and immortality through military prowess, just as Washington sought his highest reward in the esteem and respect of his contemporaries. Posey's appeal for just recognition of his achievements must have struck a responsive chord in the commander-in-chief. It must also have stirred, at the very least, a sense of irony, exposing as it did the character of the young officer Washington had seen growing to manhood in the family of Captain John Posey—a man whose legacy of written discourse does not display the slightest sensitivity to the judgments of history. Thus, it is entirely plausible to believe that the commander-in-chief played more than a minor role in General Wayne's decision to issue a second report commending the officers he unfairly omitted in his first.

It is to the resounding credit of both Wayne and Posey that this contentious aftermath to the Stony Point triumph left no lasting trace of bitterness or animosity between them. The young major whom General Wayne, "as a Private Gentleman very tenacious of my Honor," was prepared to challenge on the field of honor, was fated to see extensive service with the fiery Pennsylvanian in two later major campaigns. As lieutenant colonel in the backwaters of south Georgia, and as brigadier general in the wilderness of the Northwest Territory, Thomas was destined not only to serve under this same Anthony Wayne, but to fight shoulder-to-shoulder alongside him, with every display of mutual respect, admiration and genuine affection for one another.

NOTES

1. Washington to Major Thomas Posey, 20 December 1778, *The Writings of George Washington*, ed. John C. Fitzpatrick, 39 vols. (Washington, DC: U.S. Government Printing Office, 1931-44), 13:439.
2. For an excellent account of the Sullivan expedition, see generally: Allan W. Eckert, *The Wilderness War* (Boston and Toronto: Little, Brown & Co., 1978).
3. "A Short Biography of the Life of Governor Thomas Posey," Thomas Posey Papers, Indiana Historical Society Library, Indianapolis, IN (Hereafter cited as IHS).
4. Henry P. Johnston, *The Storming of Stony Point on the Hudson, Midnight, July 15, 1779* (New York: Da Capo Press, 1900, reprint 1971), 26-29, 44-47.
5. Ibid., 63-65.

6. Ibid., 71.
7. Douglas Southall Freeman, *George Washington: A Biography*, 7 vols. (New York: Charles Scribner's Sons, 1948-57), 5:111.
8. Johnston, *Stony Point*, 69, 71; Bruce Lancaster, *From Lexington to Liberty* (Garden City, NY: Doubleday, 1955), 371-72; Harry Emerson Wildes, *Anthony Wayne—Trouble Shooter of the American Revolution* (Westport, CT: Greenwood Press, 1970), 180-81.
9. As he took up his new post, Posey served as conciliator in resolving a misunderstanding between Fleury and Colonel Daniel Morgan, who heard that the French officer had questioned his military judgment in a prior campaign. Thomas Posey to Col. Daniel Morgan, 22 June 1779, Myers Collection no. 1013, New York Public Library, New York, NY.
10. Johnston, *Stony Point*, 215-16.
11. Henry Steele Commanger and Richard B. Morris, eds., *The Spirit of Seventy Six* (New York: Harper & Row, 1958), 722-23; Noel B. Gerson, *Lighthorse Harry* (Garden City, NY: Doubleday, 1966), 65.
12. Charles Royster, *A Revolutionary People at War: The Continental Army and American Character, 1775-1783* (Chapel Hill, NC: The University of North Carolina Press, 1979), 80-82.
13. Ibid.
14. Ibid., 77-79.
15. Johnston, *Stony Point*, 65-67.
16. Ibid.
17. Wildes, *Wayne*, 191.
18. Lancaster, *Lexington to Liberty*, 371-72.
19. Commanger and Morris, eds., *Spirit of Seventy Six*, 723.
20. Ibid.; Lancaster, *Lexington to Liberty*, 373.
21. Wildes, *Wayne*, 191.
22. Commanger and Morris, eds., *Spirit of Seventy Six*, 723.
23. Lancaster, *Lexington to Liberty*, 373.
24. Wildes, *Wayne*, 191. One account, possibly apocryphal, has it that an unfortunate soldier in Hull's detachment did panic, stopped to load his musket, and was immediately run through by the sword of a lieutenant in his company. Johnston, *Stony Point*, 192-93.
25. Wildes, *Wayne*, 192; Johnston, *Stony Point*, 77-78.
26. Wildes, *Wayne*, 192-93.
27. Freeman, *Washington*, 5:118n.64.
28. For detailed accounts of the battle, see: Johnston, *Stony Point*, 78-87; Wildes, *Wayne*, 193-96; Lancaster, *Lexington to Liberty*, 373-74; Paul David Nelson, *Anthony Wayne: Soldier of the Early Republic* (Bloomington, IN: Indiana University Press, 1985), 94-114.
29. Wildes, *Wayne*, 194.
30. John Marshall, *The Life of Washington*, 5 vols. (Philadelphia: AMS Press, 1832 ed.), 3:128-29; Washington Irving, *The Life of Washington*, 5 vols. (New York: G. P. Putnam, 1859); "A Short Biography," Thomas Posey Papers, IHS.
31. Johnston, *Stony Point*, 83, 184, 189.
32. Last will and testament of Thomas Posey, 6 April 1816, Will Record Book A, 96, Office of the Clerk of the Circuit Court, Knox County, Vincennes, IN.

33. Thomas Posey (the younger) to Lewis I. Gratz, 4 December 1854, Gratz Collection, Alpha Section, Historical Society of Pennsylvania Library, Philadelphia, PA (hereafter cited as HSP).
34. "A Short Biography," Thomas Posey Papers, IHS. Then-prevailing rules of war would have allowed the Americans to kill every man of the garrison found to be under arms when they entered the fort—a grim privilege mercilessly exercised by the British when they overran Wayne's camp in a surprise night attack at Paoli (PA) in 1777. Richard K. Showman, ed., *The Papers of Nathanael Greene*, 4 vols. to date (Chapel Hill, NC: The University of North Carolina Press, 1986-), 4:236-39, 239n.3.
35. Johnston, *Stony Point*, 85.
36. Royster, *Revolutionary People at War*, vii-xi.
37. Johnston, *Stony Point*, 186.
38. Ibid., 207; Freeman, *Washington*, 5:119n.2; Charles Janaway Stille, *Major-General Anthony Wayne and the Pennsylvania Line* (Port Washington, NY: Kennikat Press, 1893), 403.
39. Fitzpatrick, ed., *Writings of Washington*, 15:451.
40. Freeman, *Washington*, 5:120-21; Johnston, *Stony Point*, 3-4, 88-89, 95-96; Stille, *Wayne*, 197; Wildes, *Wayne*, 198.
41. Showman, ed. *Papers of Greene*, 4:236-239, 239n.4; William B. Willcox, *Portrait of a General: Sir Henry Clinton in the War of Independence* (New York: Alfred A. Knopf, 1964), 278; Freeman, *Washington*, 5:140.
42. Stille, *Wayne*, 208-10.
43. Ibid., 413-14.
44. Wayne's bias in favor of the officers of his native Pennsylvania is readily acknowledged by one of his recent biographers. Nelson, *Wayne*, 101.
45. Stille, *Wayne*, 407-408.
46. Ibid., 408-10.
47. Ibid., 410-12.
48. Ibid., 412-13.
49. Johnston, *Stony Point*, 182-86.
50. Ibid., 189.
51. Ibid., 206.
52. Thomas Posey to Anthony Wayne, 12 August 1779, Anthony Wayne Papers, HSP, 7:101.
53. Thomas Posey to George Washington, 10 August 1779, Anthony Wayne Papers, HSP, 7:102.
54. Ibid.
55. Stille, *Wayne*, 403-4.
56. Thomas Posey to George Washington, 10 August 1779, Anthony Wayne Papers, HSP, 7:102.
57. Stille, *Wayne*, 414-16.
58. Ibid.
59. Thomas Posey to Anthony Wayne, 28 August 1779, Anthony Wayne Papers, HSP, 7:104.
60. Anthony Wayne to Thomas Posey, 2 September 1779, Anthony Wayne Papers, HSP, 7:105.

61. John Marshall to Thomas Posey, 2 September 1779, Thomas Posey Papers, IHS. In an eyebrow-lifting reference to the more seamy side of camp life in the Revolution, the future Chief Justice mentions observing "a scene of lewdness . . . at the venerable Mrs. Sydmon's." The behavior of the young ladies there was so scandalous, Marshall declared facetiously, as to make the comparative virtue of "our Camp Ladies" seem almost exemplary enough to consider them as desirable marriage partners. The letter is reproduced in Charles T. Cullen, ed. *The Papers of John Marshall*, 6 vols. to date (Chapel Hill, NC: The University of North Carolina Press, 1974-), 1:32-34.
62. Royster, *Revolutionary People at War*, 88-89.
63. Ibid., 204.
64. Ibid., 207. Nearly four decades after Posey's death, one of his sons still vividly recalled his father stating that his greatest mortification during the Revolution had been the omission of his name from General Wayne's first Stony Point battle report. Thomas Posey (the younger) to Lewis I. Gratz, 4 December 1854, Gratz Collection, Alpha Section, HSP.
65. Freeman, *Washington*, 1:403n.118; 1:540-55, App. I-9. This trait of Washington's character is also noted in Virginius Dabney, *Virginia: The New Dominion* (Garden City, NY: The University Press of Virginia, 1971), 183.
66. Barry Schwartz, *George Washington: The Making of an American Symbol* (New York and London: Free Press/Macmillan,1987), 188-89.

CHAPTER FOUR

(1780-1782)

"The veracity of Posey was as unquestioned as his courage."

Stony Point was the major encounter between the two opposing main armies during the 1779 campaign season. General Clinton did not venture in force beyond his well-fortified outposts in and around New York City, while Washington's only hope of striking a decisive blow against him there was totally dependent upon the promised arrival of a French fleet from the West Indies. That force, commanded by Admiral Comte d'Estaing, was expected to bring troop reinforcements with siege proficiency. But even more vital to American military strategy, the French men-of-war would hopefully overcome or neutralize British sea power, and thus deny the enemy the ability to evacuate its army from any threat of a successful siege or onslaught, as at Boston. The French admiral, however, instead of sailing to New York, chose to land in Georgia and make a brief attempt to capture british-held Savannah. That feeble effort failed, and in early October the French re-embarked and returned to the West Indies for the winter. In December, the disappointed Washington moved his army into winter quarters at Morristown, New Jersey.[1]

During these months, General Anthony Wayne, his recent achievements having whetted his appetite for further glory, submitted a new plan to storm Stony Point a second time, but Washington wisely rejected it as too risky. The Light Infantry was instead posted along the Jersey shore of the Hudson River, with orders to intercept British sorties and foraging parties operating out of New York City, and to scout enemy movements into and out of its port. Early in December, Wayne notified Washington that over 5,000 British troops had loaded onto 130 transport vessels and sailed out of the harbor. The commander-in-chief correctly surmised that it was Clinton's purpose to initiate a major winter offensive against the American Southern Army under General Benjamin Lincoln, then headquartered in Charleston, South Carolina. In order to counter that threat, Washington directed a restructuring of his forces. Wayne's elite Corps was disbanded, and its officers and men were returned to their original state regiments. Then, virtually the entire Virginia Continental line was ordered to march south with all deliberate speed to reinforce General Lincoln's small and untried army.[2]

In the months preceding the dissolution of the Light Infantry, Major Thomas Posey's name appears frequently in the Orderly Book kept by Captain Robert Gamble, aide-de-camp to Colonel Christian Febiger. That surviving record provides some interesting insights into day-to-day camp life in the Revolutionary army. Thomas drew periodic duty as regimental officer of the day, and as night picket guard field officer. On 28 August—coincidentally, the very day General Wayne and Posey exchanged letters resolving their Stony Point differences—the entire Corps was ordered out on dress parade to witness a disciplinary "Troop Beating." Such formal events called for the playing of appropriate military airs as the ranks of soldiers entered and left the parade grounds, and it appears that on this occasion the renditions of the First Regiment's marching band left a great deal to be desired. Colonel Febiger, who had a keen ear for properly-played martial music, noted that "the Drums & Fifes in Stead of Improving themselves since they have been on this Detachment have Grone a Great Deal worse." He issued stern orders that the offending bandsmen be taken out to practice two hours every afternoon, "Sundays and Rainy Day(s) excepted." It is doubtful, however, if their performance could have been much better five days later, when deserter William Matlock was executed by firing squad before the full corps drawn up in dress parade formation.[3]

Reading between the lines of Captain Gamble's Orderly Book, it is clear that the high morale and rigid discipline so evident at Stony Point was rapidly disintegrating, as it often does in any army experiencing protracted inactivity and idleness. Major Posey's last official duty with the Light Infantry, beginning 7 November, was as presiding officer in several courts-martial. Nine days later he reported to Wayne that a number of pending cases had been disposed of, and "the court proceeds to the trial of John Dobbs tomorrow who is charged by Col. Putnam with making and spreading a false alarm among the inhabitants near a place called the liberty pole . . . as a spie to serve the purpose and designes of the enemy."[4]

A month later, Thomas was back in his state regiment, the 7th Virginia, in command of a battalion at Bordentown, New Jersey, near Trenton. There, he received a friendly letter and invitation from his recent superior, Colonel Febiger, who had been detached from his 2nd Virginia Regiment and assigned to staff work for the Board of War in Philadelphia, the nation's capital. "Old Denmark" spoke approvingly of Posey's diligence in providing for the needs of his new battalion:

> I am highly pleased with your Conduct in procuring provisions, too much cannot be done for our brave fellows . . . if possible come to Town yourself as myself and some of your friends are very desirous to see you. Mrs. Febiger has brought you a pair of neat Epauletts and lace to sett off your new Suit . . . .[5]

Posey probably did visit with his friends in Philadelphia, but within a few weeks the Virginia regiments moved southward toward Lincoln's army in Charleston. As they marched through their native state, Thomas' regimental commander, Lieutenant Colonel Samuel Cabell, allowed him to ride over to Staunton for a few days to visit his two sons, still being cared for by the Mathews family. Doubtlessly looking splendid in his new uniform with its gold epaulets and offsetting lace trim, he had a happy if poignant reunion with his boys, whom he had not seen since leaving them with their late mother, Martha, two years before.[6]

The Virginia reinforcements arrived in Charleston ahead of Thomas. But even as he was hurrying south to rejoin his comrades, they, along with the rest of the Southern Army, were becoming enmeshed in the very trap Washington had feared and expressly warned General Lincoln against. Clinton's British army had disembarked near the city, and was soon laying siege to this key American base by land and sea. By the time Posey arrived in the area, the city was completely encircled and cut off from outside access. He stayed in the vicinity for several weeks, avoiding capture while seeking an opportunity to slip into Charleston. But as the British expertly tightened their vise, Lincoln's position became indefensible, and he was forced to surrender his entire army and the city itself to the enemy on 12 May 1780.[7]

From occupied Charleston, the British dispatched strong detachments throughout the South Carolina countryside, establishing formidable fortified outposts. Left without a command, Posey put himself at the disposal of the state governor, John Rutledge, who had barely escaped the city before it was cut off. But the governor, who would have welcomed the veteran officer's aid and expertise, informed him that "the militia could not be collected, the inhabitants flying in all directions."[8] Since he obviously could be of no military value in the Carolinas, Thomas notified army headquarters of his availability, as one of the few uncaptured officers of the entire Virginia Continental line. He was ordered to return to his native state, and since there were no Virginian soldiers left to command, he was sent to Staunton to assist in recruiting a new regiment of regulars from the western frontier counties.[9]

Given a choice, Thomas would surely have preferred a field command had it been available, but his new assignment undeniably offered some welcome advantages to the young major. First and foremost, it afforded close proximity to his two sons, of whom he had seen little since their infancy. After more than four years of continuous service in the field, often enduring hardship and deprivation, he undoubtedly welcomed an opportunity to maintain more stable and comfortable living conditions in Augusta County, his main base of recruiting operations. Finally, he gained some respite from the constant exposure to camp epidemics and the intermittent perils of combat—although, given his past apparent disregard for his own life in battle, he might have regarded the relative safety of his new post as, at most, a mixed blessing.

On the negative side, Posey's new duties turned out to be both difficult and frustrating. By late 1780, Virginia was far from being fertile ground for the raising of new recruits. After his conquest of Charleston, Clinton had returned to New York, but he left a sizable army under General Charles Cornwallis to solidify and enlarge British domination over the southern theater of war. Cornwallis was spectacularly successful in his mission. On 10 August at Camden, South Carolina, he soundly defeated and routed the only organized American force remaining in the south, under the command of General Horatio Gates, the erstwhile hero of Saratoga.[10]

Left virtually undefended, Virginia then increasingly became the target of British strategy. In October and November 2,200 enemy troops under General Alexander Leslie occupied and sacked coastal areas around Portsmouth and Hampton Roads for several weeks before moving on to Charleston. A month later another expedition under the turncoat Benedict Arnold (now a

British brigadier general) penetrated as far as Richmond, the state capital, and Petersburg, a major supply base.[11] When Cornwallis' force, moving up from the Carolinas, joined Arnold's contingent on 20 May 1781, the combined size of British troops in eastern Virginia had risen to over 7,000 men.[12]

Striking out repeatedly with lightning speed from that formidable army, the mounted dragoons of Lieutenant Colonel Banastre Tarleton, a daring and ruthless British cavalryman, pursued the fleeing state government all the way to the provisional capital at Charlottesville and beyond. After nearly capturing Governor Thomas Jefferson at his Monticello home during their sweep of the area, Tarleton's raiders forced the state legislators and other government officials to flee over the Blue Ridge mountains to frontier Staunton, Thomas Posey's recruiting station.[13]

Posey's assignment in the western counties had not entirely insulated him from the military action erupting elsewhere in Virginia. Early in January of 1781, he led a detachment of 250 Augusta County militiamen across the state to Smithfield, on the lower James River. There he turned them over to the command of Colonel Sampson Mathews, Thomas' old innkeeper friend from Staunton, and uncle of his late wife, Martha. Governor Jefferson had ordered Mathews to march his augmented forces north to Fredericksburg, but bitter cold and torrential rains, "the wett and the badness of the boats" had frustrated his efforts to cross the James.[14] On 13 January he reported to the governor that "I have Prevailed with Major Posey to go with me who will be of great service."[15]

Thus, for a brief period at least, Thomas served with Colonel Mathews in the Piedmont area, but there is no record of any other personal participation in the frantic skirmishes and troop movements in that region for the next few months. It may be noted in passing that Virginia militia Major George Thornton, first husband of Posey's future wife Mary, met his death on the hot spring day of 30 April 1781 after pausing to drink cold spring water while on a forced march with his command from Fredericksburg to Williamsburg to confront an enemy threat.[16]

Virginia's frontier counties were in a similar state of utter turmoil, beset on the west by the ever-present danger of hostile Indian raids, and on the east by the threat of new incursions by Tarleton's dragoons and other British forces. The manpower pool had been depleted over the past year by repeated militia levies called out to defend against the enemy advance through the Carolinas into Virginia. Returning survivors who had served out their six-month terms were far from tempted by Posey's efforts to recruit them into the regular army for the duration of the war. They were openly hostile to a new 18-month draft law recently enacted by the desperate state government. Arriving back in Staunton from his temporary service with Colonel Sampson Mathews, Thomas indignantly reported to Inspector-General von Steuben (now stationed in Virginia) that in his absence nothing had been done by the local authorities to enforce the draft law. "Nay instead of exhorting themselves to raise the men, they have demonstrated at the assembly against the measure of drafting for eighteen months, but instead think to Draft for three."[17]

In a wistful but revealing postscript in his letter to the Baron, Thomas added: "I hope by this time you have Arnold in your possession."[18] One of the highest priorities of all the American units then in action in Virginia was the capture and punishment of the traitor Benedict Arnold. Posey had been among the brave soldiers in Daniel Morgan's Rifle Regiment who had willingly followed Arnold's bold lead in the courageous charge against the right flank of General Burgoyne's British army at the battle of Bemis Heights in 1777. Four years later, Thomas clearly had nothing but contempt for the once-admired turncoat, who had not only betrayed the revolutionary cause, but had accepted a brigadier's commission in the enemy army and was now leading an invasion force against his own countrymen in eastern Virginia.

Posey's frustration over his lack of recruiting success in the western counties was beginning to show in his correspondence. He complained to Governor Jefferson that part of the problem was the army's 5' 4" minimum height requirement, which was being rigidly enforced by the height-conscious ex-Prussian, von Steuben. This regulation, he insisted, was directly responsible for the exclusion from military service of many potential fighting men of smaller stature, but otherwise willing and able to serve.[19] Thomas was also alarmed by news of Tory uprisings in the northern Shenandoah Valley, and even closer to home, the forcible seizure and destruction of the state draft lists by armed bodies of men in several western counties including Augusta itself.[20] When Major Posey, who had not personally witnessed the last incident, later reported it to his state Adjutant General, Colonel William Davies, he exclaimed angrily: "I don't know where this may stop, if there is not a timeous check, in Hanging a few, for examples to the rest."[21]

As time passed, lower-ranking Virginia officers who had been captured at Charleston, but had since been exchanged or paroled, began to filter back into the state. On 12 February 1781 a special board of senior officers met at Chesterfield Court House to reorganize the decimated Virginia Continental line. It placed all such officers into a temporary battalion under the leadership of Major Thomas Posey.[22] Although popular resistance to the 18-month draft continued, Posey's vigorous efforts to raise soldiers for these officers to command met with at least moderate success. In mid-May he was ordered by General von Steuben to bring forward all available men to a central rendezvous station in Albemarle County.[23] Within a few weeks, Posey marched the troops to Cumberland Old Court House in central Powhatan County, where he was reunited with his old Light Infantry commander and friend, Colonel Christian Febiger, recently returned from his staff duties in Philadelphia. Febiger, technically the commander of the 2nd Virginia Regiment, (then only a paper organization), had been given overall responsibility for mobilizing and training Virginia's new Continental troops, with Posey acting as his deputy and second-in-command.[24]

As the rank-and-file soldiers arrived at Cumberland, many were so poorly clothed as to even exceed the bounds of decency. "Old Denmark" Febiger, a graphic as well as prolific letter writer, after conducting his first review of the newly arrived troops, reported to Colonel Davies that his men were so "literally naked" that "a modest army of Women on examining Any Thing lower than the navel, would instantly take to their Scrapers." For the sake of modesty as well as health, he urgently pleaded for "a sufficiency of shoes, Overalls and Hatts"; otherwise the troops would, "from real nakedness, be compelled to quitt the Feild."[25]

The recurrent problem of clothing, feeding and arming the new levies would soon jeopardize Virginia's continued military role in the Revolution. A recent restructuring of the regular army's supply system had shifted from the national authorities to each state government full responsibility for the maintenance and upkeep of its own Continental regiments. But the economy and monetary system of Virginia had been totally devastated by the enemy's repeated incursions and the continued occupation of its most productive regions. Tax revenues were almost non-existent, and the paper currency printed by the state to pay its obligations was virtually worthless. Officers as well as enlisted men were affected. Febiger protested to new Virginia Governor Thomas Nelson that, because he had been stationed in Philadelphia, a delay in receiving four months' pay (already calculated at 100-to-1 to allow for inflation) had undergone another 400 percent devaluation. He returned the money to Richmond with a request that it not be charged to his military account if it could not be increased to its original equivalent in buying power.[26] In mid-August he asked Colonel Davies, "What in the name of God will become of our paper money in a very little time—it certainly must, and will sink in the hands of the holders." But he added philosophically, "I have no fears on this head, as my Pockets are pretty empty. I, as well as the poor Devils that are with me, must have a little of the Trash."[27]

Febiger was already planning an early return to Philadelphia to escort his wife Elizabeth back to Virginia. But he assured Davies that the troops stationed at Cumberland Old Court House would be in good hands during his absence, since affairs were "so regulated here, that Major Posey, who is with me, can with propriety transact the Business of the Post."[28] As it turned out, while "Old Denmark" was away, Posey's promotion to lieutenant colonel came through.[29] But this timely recognition was soon crowned by an even more gratifying experience. His temporary command responsibilities in handling the "Business of the Post" included an active role in what was to be perhaps the single most glorious day in American history, and certainly the most memorable day in the life of Thomas Posey.

Events of historic proportions had intervened just when the revolutionary cause in Virginia had sunk to its lowest ebb. George Washington sent two of his best generals, Lafayette and Wayne, to join von Steuben in carrying out a deliberate policy to contain the activities and movements of General Cornwallis' 7,000-man army. Operating under strict orders not to commit their outnumbered troops to a direct confrontation with the enemy, the plan was skillfully executed by the American generals. By 1 August, their tactics had induced the British commander to re-position his forces near a convenient port of exit—the harbor at the mouth of the York River—and to fortify the towns of York and Gloucester Point on either side of the river estuary. Meanwhile, a British fleet stood by to cover and execute their withdrawal, if necessary, by way of Chesapeake Bay. This land-sea capability had precluded any major defeat of British armies on American soil since Burgoyne's landlocked debacle at Saratoga in 1777.

But after four years, a new and different scenario prevailed. Anticipating the imminent arrival of a new French fleet, General Washington on 19 August began covertly moving to Virginia the combined American-French army then stationed outside New York City. The French armada, under Admiral Comte de Grasse, arrived off Jamestown on schedule, disembarked 3,000 additional French troops, and then on 5 September fought a naval action with the enemy fleet. Although the result was militarily inconclusive, the British ships were forced to retire to New York harbor, leaving Chesapeake Bay in control of the French. Washington and his

French army counterpoint, General Comte de Rochambeau, after a two-day rest stop at Mount Vernon,[30] arrived at Williamsburg on 14 September. Within a few days, they were joined by the last elements of their combined armies. The long-planned trap had finally been sprung. It closed, not on Clinton's army in the big city of New York, as originally visualized by Washington, but in his own native state, on the forces of Lord Cornwallis, now encircled on all sides in the little coastal town of York, Virginia.[31]

An urgent call went out for every available man to join in the decisive confrontation. Lieutenant Colonel Thomas Posey hurriedly marched his battalion-sized detachment across Virginia to the main army encampment, where it was reviewed by General Washington, who made due note in his official report of the men's dire need for clothing.[32] The unit then took its place in General Lafayette's right wing of the siege lines. Every day the front trenches were systematically extended closer and closer toward the enemy, exposing first the outer redoubts, and then the main body of British troops, to devastating artillery fire. Cornwallis' position soon became untenable. On 19 October 1781 his forces capitulated in an historic ceremony that epitomized victory and ultimate independence for the American nation.

Sitting astride his horse in front of his ragged battalion, Thomas Posey was a proud eyewitness to the formal surrender ritual. There had been no entries in his battered war journal since his enumeration of British forces he had seen yield at Saratoga four years before. Now, just below that accounting, he carefully entered a detailed breakdown of "Prisoners taken at York Towne," ranging from "1 Lt. Gen." to "3,273 rank and file"—a grand total of 7,416 men, including 1,875 sick and wounded. Below this second list, in handwriting as large and as exultant as his own spirit must have been on this day of victory, Thomas wrote: "I had the happiness to see the two foregoing armies (Burgoin and Cornwallace) defeated and lay down their arms. Th. Posey."[33]

The Virginians had little time to bask in the euphoria of Yorktown. Four days later, General Washington ordered that the battalion "be marched to Cumberland Old Court House, there to be cloathed, together with those now at that place . . . from thence they will march Southward."[34] Despite the popular perception that the recent victory had won the war and ended the fighting, peace negotiations to end the conflict were not to be concluded for another eighteen months. In the meantime, hostilities continued. Cornwallis' surrender had left fully three-fourths of the British expeditionary forces still intact, and they continued to pose a major threat to the revolutionary cause. The enemy still controlled several major American cities, including Charleston and Savannah to the south, where the able General Nathanael Greene's badly outnumbered Southern army needed immediate reinforcement.

It was Washington's strong desire that every able-bodied soldier at Cumberland join Greene's forces as soon as possible. He was well aware, from his own personal observation, that the Continental soldiers from his own state were in rags, that their officers had not received pay or subsistence allowances for several years, and that the insolvency of the state government had made the current supply system completely ineffective. But he still had a war to win, and could only tell General von Steuben helplessly that "I wish the means in my power, for their relief, were equal to my inclinations, but as I am divested of them, I can do (no) more than recommend them, with others, to Congress and their own State in particular."[35]

Colonel Febiger, with wife in tow, had returned from Philadelphia just in time to join his troops at the Yorktown surrender ceremony and to march them back to Cumberland. There he sought to resolve the critical issue of back pay by suggesting to Colonel Davies that "a memorial or a Petition be drawn up in Behalf of the Line" for presentation to the Virginia legislature. The proposed supplication would seek "a final and conclusive settlement with each Individual Officer and Soldier of the Line for what sums of Pay and Depreciation or Pay and Subsistence may be due to each."[36]

On the pressing need for clothing, Febiger spoke feelingly of "the shameful and unmilitary appearance of this sd. Detachment whom I believe you saw at York." He was, nonetheless, making preparations to comply with General Washington's marching orders, reporting that "I have now gott the men properly arrang'd and a tolerable Officer putt at the head of each company, and Posey at the head of the whole." But a serious reason to delay the march had arisen: "the Small Pox is brought up from York." While "General Washington seemed anxious that these men should be immediately sent to the Southward . . . what can I do—to send them unequip'd and with the small pox breaking out among them daily, I thought would be madness."[37]

Rather than risk spreading the infection among citizens all along the line of march, Febiger delayed their departure and ordered a general inoculation of all the men at Cumberland. That procedure, he stated, required the use of molasses, vinegar and rice, as well as strong drink. "It is shameful that the poor naked men are working here every day in the cold, and not a Drop of Liquor of any kind—in short we are Destitute of everything."[38] But the inoculation was bitterly opposed by the nearby inhabitants of Powhatan County, and had to be stopped before it was completed. An unnamed but leading local notable, acting on behalf of his fellow citizens, presented a memorial of protest to Colonel Febiger, stating that "If we inoculated, they would withhold all Supplies and cease all communication with us. He spoke also of loaded guns, and in Fact made use of some very imprudent Expressions."[39] To add to his quandary, Febiger told Davies that his immediate army superior, General Arthur St. Clair, had again "positively ordered all the well men to march immediately."[40]

But despite all Febiger's efforts, the state of Virginia with its economy in chaos, would or could do nothing to relieve the distress or satisfy the grievances of its tattered Continental soldiers. Finally, on 17 November the senior officers of the detachment designated to join the Southern Army took matters into their own hands. They presented Colonel Febiger with a written memorial stating their unwillingness to march until they and their men were adequately supplied. "We are truly destitute of cloathing, having barely sufficient to support us against the inclemencies of a Winter Campaign, nor has each officer a Blanket . . . we are destitute of Cash (and . . . have had none for two and some for three years past, except some small sums of State money, which from its depreciated State, was of very little account or advantage)." The officers emphasized, however, that "we wish to render our Country every service in our power. We have done it, tho with the loss of health and fortune, and are still agreed and ready to march upon the shortest notice to any the most distant post, for her releif and advantage, if supply'd in any Suitable manner."[41]

The memorial complained bitterly that no state in the Union had abused its officers so badly as Virginia. "Observe to our Rulers, how ungenerously, nay how inhumanely they have treated us . . . the Ballance of ill usage and neglect has fallen with unmerciful weight on the shoulders of the Officers of the Continental Line of this State." After expressing high regard for Colonel Febiger, and regret for any pain the protest might cause him, the officers flatly declared their unanimous determination to resign their commissions if their minimal needs for the upcoming march were not met. "Independence is so firmly fixed," they reasoned, "that we can retire without doing any essential injury to our Country." The memorial was signed by the battalion's five highest-ranking and most battle-tested veterans: Captains Alexander Parker and Joseph Scott,

Majors Samuel Finley and John Poulson, and Lieutenant Colonel Thomas Posey.[42]

Febiger forwarded the protest to General St. Clair, who immediately cancelled his order to march, and sent the original document to General Washington, with the comment, "It is too true that they have reason for complaint, but it pains me that they should take such means and such an occasion to express it, and I was much surprised to see Colonel Posey's name to the memorial."[43] The commander-in-chief was undoubtedly just as surprised, and quite likely deeply disappointed as well. Posey had compiled, at great risk, a long and honorable military record. To join in what appeared to be, on its face, an emotional protest against valid but largely irremediable grievances, backed by a reckless and irresponsible threat to resign his commission, seemed to be totally out of character for his young former neighbor.

Washington's immediate reaction to the memorial was probably influenced to some extent by prior suspicions he had harbored of possible malingering among the rank-and-file of the Virginia battalion. Commenting earlier on a progressively-diminishing number of able-bodied troops in Febiger's command attributed to desertions and illness, he expressed fear that "a Dislike to the Service to the South, or some other Reasons have operated to lessen the Numbers beyond what ought to be."[44]

Although such qualms were obviously rekindled by the timing of the officers' petition, he waited nearly two months to respond to what he called "a positive refusal to march except certain terms were complied with by the State." Labeling such a stand clearly improper, he wrote Febiger on 12 January 1782 to ask, "What can they expect from their soldiers, when they themselves strike at the Root of Authority and discipline?" He did not contest the credibility of the officers' grievances, but denied that the Virginians had fared any worse than their counterparts in other states. He stated he was asking Governor Benjamin Harrison "to use every exertion, so to provide for and equip the detachment which is ready, that both Officers and Men may be enabled to go upon service with some tolerable degree of comfort. This I hope he will do, after which," the general firmly stressed, "I expect and insist, in the most positive Manner, that the detachment shall march."[45]

Washington scathingly dismissed the smug view, "which I am sorry to see given by Officers and those too of my own Country, that they look upon our independence as established . . . Do they think the remaining force of the enemy is to be crushed by words or Blows? I should suppose by the former, or they would never have started an Idea not only ridiculous but of dangerous tendency." After Yorktown, the general had found it increasingly necessary to refute such complacency, in and out of the army, and throughout the Union. He closed his letter with two appeals that he well knew would strike to the heart of every true Virginia officer—honor, and devotion to the commander-in-chief. "The Officers must and do very well know that it is not in the power of the State to pay them up in good Money. If therefore they continue to make that a plea, I shall take it for granted that disinclination to the service upon which they are going is the real motive." Finally, the most telling point of all: "you must suppose my feelings are particularly wounded on the occasion. When asked whether any and what reinforcements have marched from Virginia, I shall blush when I say none, and more so when I assign the cause."[46]

Washington had already sent a plea to Governor Harrison for his assistance in resolving the problem. Commenting on the issue of back pay and subsistence, he conceded that "the Officers have reason to complain of the great arrearages," but declared that they were not justified in "prescribing terms to their Country at a very critical moment." He closed by expressing to the governor his earnest hope that "the State will make every possible exertion to equip and provide for the Officers and Men going upon service, That they will have no reasonable ground of complaint."[47]

In the meantime, Lieutenant Colonel Thomas Posey had carried the officers' memorial to the state capital at Richmond, and personally presented it to the governor and the state legislature for consideration. He appears to have received a very cordial and sympathetic reception from the government leaders—and in the process, to have perhaps demonstrated latent political skills that foreshadowed his later success in public affairs. Governor Harrison informed Washington that the petition had been "laid before the Assembly at their last Setting and every relief given to them that it was in their power to give. They (the officers) seemed so sensible of this that I had no Doubt of their marching immediately."[48] To partially cover the officers' arrearage in pay and subsistence, the legislature authorized the issuance of state certificates of warrant, which the merchants in Powhatan County were more likely to accept than paper currency.[49]

The governor himself had given every cooperation to Thomas during his stay in Richmond. He assured Washington that "The little that it was in the Power of the Executive to do to quiet them has been done, and I am told by Colo. Posey who left us yesterday that he expects they will now march." But Harrison, like Washington, was fearful that the officers' openly expressed discontent might have spread to the enlisted men at Cumberland. He was prepared to take drastic action if the measures taken by the state to clothe and equip the troops failed to head off a threatened mutiny among the rank-and-file. A detachment of cavalry from General de Rochambeau's French army remained stationed in eastern Virginia after the British surrender at Yorktown. Harrison fully intended to use that unit, if necessary, to force his recalcitrant fellow-Virginians to march: "It is a lucky Circumstance that the French Legion is marching that Way."[50]

So far as Posey and the other protesting officers were concerned, that draconian step would certainly not be needed. They had been both surprised and abashed that General Washington had interpreted their memorial as a flat ultimatum to resign their commissions unless they received full payment of their back pay in "good money." Furthermore, they were completely won over by the commander-in-chief's shrewd appeal to their personal honor and loyalty. They were more than satisfied with the actions taken in their behalf by the state government. Colonel Febiger was therefore able to assure Washington with complete confidence on 10 February that, despite continued deficiencies in clothing and equipment, "as they are, they shall march on Wednesday." Febiger also had a favorable word about his subordinate to pass along to Washington—his letter had made Lieutenant Colonel Posey "extremely uneasy, and I am inclined to think that he was more urg'd by the Importunitys of other Officers than by his own inclination to sign the Representations."[51]

The term "uneasy" is hardly adequate to describe Thomas' reaction when, upon his return from Richmond, he learned for the first time of Washington's harsh assessment of the officers' memorial. He was so upset at having incurred the disapproval of his Mount Vernon mentor that he was moved to write a personal letter of explanation directly to the general—just as he had done after the shooting incident at the Tory settlement in upstate New York, and again after he had been slighted in Anthony Wayne's Stony Point battle report. In another ten years, he would do so once again when, as a perplexed father in a mid-life career crisis, he turned to his old neighbor for counsel and assistance. Now, he frankly admitted to the commander-in-chief that the conduct of himself and his fellow officers had indeed been "blamable." Their grievances could and should have been expressed "in a more eligible Mode, for it was only to make known our Situation that induced the officers to write to Colonel Febiger in hopes that it might be a means of procuring some small Supplies to subsist us in our march to the Southern army . . . As to the officers having the most distant idea of not marching without the whole of their pay from the country, such was not intended."[52]

Posey's greatest concern was that Washington not construe their actions as indifference to or abandonment of their revolutionary ideals. "I hope you have a better opinion of the most of us than to think it is for the sake of pay altogether that has induced or induces us to take on the character of Soldiers." Nor was there any reluctance on their part to continuing the struggle against the enemy: "However distressing the Situation of the Officers is or may have been," he assured the commander, "there is not one, to my knowledge . . . but has always expressed a desire to march to the assistance of General Green as soon as the men could be properly equipt for that purpose." As for himself, Thomas ruefully confessed to his exemplar, "I wish that I had not been one that signed the letter without having more maturely considered many parts of it, for I am affraid it may have a tendency to injure my Character which I hold exceedingly dear."[53] Posey should not have signed the memorial. He knew it and, to his credit, was not above admitting his mistake.

The officers were now ready and willing to march, but word of their protest had spread among their men,[54] and as Washington had so eloquently predicted, had struck at the very root of authority and discipline. The rank-and-file's morale was further eroded by appalling deprivation and physical hardship. After recently having gone twelve straight days without meat of any kind, a wagon load of spoiled, rotten beef arrived at the Cumberland encampment. Febiger himself admitted that its stench was so overpowering that it was "dangerous to be near it." When the putrid meat was nonetheless rationed out to the men, some of them protested so loudly that they had to be arrested and confined to the camp prison. This step caused such indignation, Febiger reported, that about 150 men "rose in arms to rescue them. But by the Vigilance of the officers they were dispers'd." Inflammatory notes advocating open insurrection began circulating among the enlisted ranks. One such circular was found by an officer and brought to Febiger. He reported to Colonel Davies that he was trying "to prevent an open Rupture," but feared "the men might attempt something to morrow."[55]

The colonel had informed General Washington that about 400 officers and men in his command were fit enough to begin the march southward. "Colo. Posey commands the Detachment, it's well officered and, I hope when it gets into the field it will in part retrieve the sinking character of the Va. Line."[56] He delayed the scheduled departure one day to allow for the delivery of "a few stores which Col. Posey has procured in Richmond."[57] But as the critical day approached, tensions within the camp mounted. On 8 February, a general court martial had found Joseph Hawkins, a mulatto soldier in Posey's detachment, guilty of the theft of military stores. Two days later, he was hanged, "with great Solemnity," before the full complement of the base, drawn up in company formation facing the gallows on the courthouse lawn.[58] Febiger intended this sobering ceremony to suppress if not dispel the rising discontent among his troops, but it probably only exacerbated the disciplinary disarray in the camp.

In the early morning mist of Thursday, 14 February 1782, the detachment of soldiers designated as reinforcements for Nathanael Greene's Southern Army was assembled outside Cumberland Old Court House. Muted talk of defiance and rebellion passed through the ranks as Lieutenant Colonel Thomas Posey, facing his men, read aloud General Washington's marching orders. When Posey gave the command to prepare to depart, most of the hungry and ill-clad men refused to break ranks, stubbornly remaining in place in the face of their company officers' shouted orders and the strident curses of their sergeants. Colonel Febiger's later description of the unruly scene to Washington was brief and discreet: "the men very uneasy about Pay and other necessaries, when ordered by Colo. Posey to strike their tents refused, saying they would not march without money. I was on the spot with a little Threatening, some Provisions and an excellent band of Musick to play them off all was quieted."[59]

To Governor Harrison, Febiger reported, also with uncharacteristic restraint that "the Detachment under Lt. Col. Posey marched on the 14th inst: the men leaving with considerable reluctance, for want of money and cloathing; the latter exceeding bad Quality especially the Linnen over-alls."[60] But to his friend and confidant Colonel Davies, Febiger was considerably more graphic about what he had termed "a little Threatening" in his report to Washington. He noted that, "on the 14th inst. I gott rid of the said Detachment after hanging one and whipping 73 of them, and they are well officer'd & Posey informs me behave well on their march. I dismounted the Officers, which has a good Effect."[61]

The reality behind these brief glimpses into the tumultuous scene at Cumberland Old Court House represented a major crisis in the lives of both Christian Febiger and Thomas Posey. Had the disorder confronting them outside the ancient court building grown into open mutiny and a continued refusal to march, the proud record of the Virginia Continental line would have been stained, and the military reputations of the two veteran officers forever damaged. But it was not necessary to call upon the French Legion to quell the disturbance. The disgruntled battalion did march out of Cumberland, with their dismounted commander, Lieutenant Colonel Posey, striding along with his men to the martial music of a military band. The means employed to move the soldiers off the field may be judged harsh and extreme in these more enlightened times. Subsequent events were to show, however, that all the threats, whippings and hangings did not weaken their will to fight, or their devotion to the revolutionary cause. In reconstructing the circumstances leading up to and following this dramatic confrontation at an old Virginia courthouse on 14 February 1782, one can only wonder and marvel at the intensity and persistence of that dedication.

The morale of the marching detachment soon began to rebound from its Cumberland nadir. Two days along the way, Posey informed Febiger that "the Spirit, which seem'd to provoke them just before our March is in a great manner subsided and cheerfullness appears in the mens Countenances."[62] Perhaps that cheerful glow was at least partly derived from the timely arrival of a barrel of bay rum that caught up to the unit at Prince Edward Court House. Posey immediately "issued a Gill to every man; but not haveing had any so long, some of them gott very Tipsey on their Gill, though none acted out of caracter except one or two . . . I have not a Doubt of marching every man now with the Detachment to General Greene's army."[63] Along with the mellow warming brew, Posey reported that music played a positive role in soothing "the turbulent Spirit which seemed to agitate the Soldiers the Day we left you . . . they seem satisfied and many of them ashamed of their Conduct there . . . your Band has been of infinite service. I don't know that I have ever seen men more delighted with it, than on the March. I esteem Sheldon much."[64]

The part played by military music in the dreary lives of Revolutionary soldiers has not been well appreciated. Fife Major Peter Sheldon, the detachment's bandmaster, had been a prized recruit of Colonel Febiger, who was a firm believer in the lyric art. The colonel had informed General Washington that his regimental band exerted "more influence on the minds and motions of the militia last summer in the State than would the oratory of a Cicero, and in the recruiting business they are at least as useful as a well spoken recruiting Sergeant."[65] Posey seems to have shared Febiger's love of music. Farther along the march, he again speaks highly of

Sheldon, but now as the leader of "my Band." He noted that the esteemed bandmaster had been in the Revolutionary army since 1775, and had gained early fame "for playing an excellent Fife."[66] Posey's troop return of 18 February confirms that the roster of his detachment included a marching band of "22 Drums and Fifes."[67] They appear to have been extensively used to raise the spirits of the weary marchers at evening bivouacs and all along the rugged southward journey.

This battalion-sized unit of 29 commissioned and 51 noncommissioned officers and 356 rank-and-file enlisted men was the largest command entrusted to Posey during the Revolution. The sole responsibility for their well-being during the difficult conditions encountered along the long march seems to have weighed heavily on the shoulders of the young lieutenant colonel. On the eighth day, he proudly reported to Colonel Davies that "not a man has deserted me since I set out from Prince Edward Court House." At Peytonsburg, he gave the exhausted men a day's rest, "which will be a means of healing their feet a little and haveing their cloaths washed."[68]

But a serious and potentially deadly threat to his men was of greater immediate concern to Thomas—a new outbreak of smallpox. Three soldiers had recently come down with that most dreaded of all camp diseases; they had been "provided for" and left at Cub's Creek, thirty-five miles north of Peytonsburg. But the epidemic was spreading, and the inability of Febiger to complete the general inoculation he had tried to conduct at Cumberland now seemed about to imperil the entire expedition. Concern for the lives and welfare of his men, and frustration over the indifference, (if not hostility), of local authorities to their plight drove the young battalion commander to a rare emotional outburst, bordering on panic:

> My heavens! what am I to do about the men breaking out with the Small pox, another man has this moment discovered that he has it, and God knows what I shall do with him, for the inhabitants every where upon the route we march, is frightened, and I am really afraid that some of the men will perish; was this the last man to break out with it, I should be happy, but you may rely upon it I shall be plagu'd the whole march. I have applied to the magistrates for some provision to be made for these poor unhappy mortals, but damn them I can get nothing done.[69]

As Posey's unit left Virginia and moved through the Carolinas, he reported regularly on the location and condition of his troops, not only to Colonels Febiger and Davies, but to his new commander, General Nathanael Greene. The rigors of the road took a heavy toll on the men's poorly made footwear and clothing—halfway through the march, many of them were again barefoot and half-naked. Feeding the men and horses proved to be an unexpected problem, as caches of food and fodder supposedly stockpiled along the line of march turned out to be non-existent. Thomas reluctantly found it necessary to send out details of men to "impress" these staples from local farmers and merchants. Although he paid for these provisions with army warrants, the process caused considerable delay to the detachment, as well as understandable resentment among the inhabitants. Movement was often hampered by bad weather and breakdowns of wagons and dray-horses. Apart from smallpox casualties, and contrary to his earlier high hopes, Posey did lose a few of his men to desertion as the hardships of the trail took their toll.[70]

Despite all these adversities, the battalion was largely intact as it drew close to Greene's army, encamped near Charleston. But within two day's march of his destination, Posey received new orders from the general. He was to proceed still further southward, into Georgia, and there join a small American force stationed outside British-held Savannah. Those troops were under the command of Thomas' old nemesis in the Light Infantry Corps, General Anthony Wayne.[71]

The two officers appear to have welcomed their new association. Written exchanges between them display no trace or hint of any rancor from their prior differences over the awarding of battle honors after the assault on Stony Point three years before. Wayne warmly assured Thomas that he was looking forward to having his former subordinate serve under him again, because "I know your military abilities so well." Even before the Virginians reached Wayne's camp, he gave them an urgent assignment—to intercept a reported British sortie in their immediate area. In his dispatch, the general stated that, "as I have the honor of knowing the troops and the officer who commands them; I am confident that no exertion will be wanting to make the enemy suffer for their temerity."[72]

Even before receiving Wayne's supportive message, Thomas had already written ahead to the general that he would "gladly serve under you, knowing you to be an experienced officer." Summarizing the many problems that had plagued his battalion on its long march, he proudly assured Wayne that it was "composed of good men . . . I am persuaded the whole both officers and soldiers can be depended upon." He added that, "I have endeavored to instill such a degree of pride in the soldiers as to make them cut the best appearance possible in the indifferent cloathing drawn from Virginia."[73] The enemy troop movement the battalion had been sent to confront proved to have been a "false alarm."[74] On 7 April Posey's footsore Virginians, indifferent clothing and all, marched into Wayne's encampment at Ebenezer, Georgia, stepping smartly to the military airs and martial beat of their fife-and-drum corps.

The comfortable relationship with Anthony Wayne at his new post made it easier for Posey to handle both his field and routine staff duties. Other detachments of fresh recruits from Virginia were expected to be sent forward by Colonel Febiger in the coming months. On 9 May Thomas proposed to General Greene that his battalion be designated to form the nucleus of a new regiment to receive those levies as they arrived. To underscore that his proposal was not meant as a self-serving device to gain his own promotion to the full colonelcy of a regimental commander, he assured Greene that, "Certainly I should think myself happy to have the command, but should I be ordered at any time to give place to an older officer, either by acting under him in the same regt., or being removed to any other, I would cheerfully submit to the orders."[75] Although not confirmed by official army records, Greene appears to have tentatively agreed to the proposed conformation, as in future dispatches Posey refers to his unit as a regiment.

On 11 May, Colonel Davies in Virginia raised an issue as to the use and disposition of property issued to the detachment since its service at Yorktown. Much of this material had not been properly accounted for in army records. Posey readily assumed responsibility for all the clothing and supplies drawn by the unit since he officially took over its command at Cumberland, but asserted somewhat indignantly that he could and should not be held answerable for property charged to the battalion before that time.[76]

These less than exciting administrative duties were soon overshadowed by events much more appealing to Posey's martial ardor. The arrival of the Virginia battalion had nearly doubled Wayne's motley force of regulars, Georgia militia partisans, ex-Tories and friendly Indians. Even so, it was still outnumbered more than three to one by the well-armed professional British garrison in Savannah. Wayne was accordingly under strict order from General Greene to confine the scope of his operations to the harassment of enemy foraging parties and supply trains sent into the city by Tory supporters, and by the Creek and other regional Indian tribes allied with the British. These constraints had afforded little opportunity to gain the military glory and laurels coveted by the ambitious Wayne. Furthermore the British, anticipating the imminent arrival of orders to leave the city by sea, showed little inclination to come out and fight in force, as the American general so ardently wished.

Emboldened by his recent Virginian reinforcements, "Mad Anthony" drew up and submitted a daring plan "to dig the caitiffs out" by an all-out attack on the city itself, but General Greene wisely restrained the bellicose Pennsylvanian.[77] Late in May, however, an unexpected opportunity arose when the British, under cover of darkness, sent out a strong party of 450 cavalry and infantrymen to meet and escort into the city an approaching Creek supply train. The enemy force eluded the Americans on its outward passage, but when it failed to find the Indians at the agreed rendezvous and started back toward Savannah, it ran into an ambush along a narrow causeway through deep marshes. Troops personally led by Wayne and Posey attacked the front of the column, throwing the following ranks into disorder. Most of the British soldiers escaped by jumping into the surrounding swamps and straggling back into the city. But when the trailing Indian supply train approached soon afterward without escort, it was halted by Wayne and turned back with a rude admonition to return home forthwith, and in the future not set foot in the area.[78]

The Creek Indian Nation was a proud and fiercely independent tribe, with a long history of boldness and prowess in battle. Its chiefs regarded Wayne's behavior as insulting, and they vowed to avenge the shame and humiliation cast upon them by his treatment of their emissaries. From their main villages deep in the interior of what is now Alabama, they assembled a heavily armed party of 300 picked warriors under the leadership of Guristersigo, their foremost war chief. Traveling only at night, and carefully avoiding any contact with settlements or individual homesteads along the way, the Creek war party moved completely undetected across the entire width of Georgia to the vicinity of Savannah.

In the meantime General Wayne, craving further encounters with the British, had moved his camp from Ebenezer to Sharon, a swamp-surrounded crossroads settlement less than five miles from the fortified outskirts of Savannah. Captain Alexander Parker's company of Virginia light infantry, just relieved from arduous front line duty opposite the enemy's picket lines, had retired to the rear section of the new camp—regarded as its most secure area—to rest and recuperate. On a dark, moonless night, at three o'clock in the morning of 24 June, the Creek warriors emerged from the nearby swamps and fell upon the sleeping Virginians with guns, spears, knives and tomahawks.

Thomas Posey was not with his battalion when the attack began. Two weeks earlier, stricken with "camp fever" (malaria), he had moved temporarily to the house of a local settler near the camp to recover his strength. In notifying Wayne of his absence, he emphasized: "In the meantime, dear General, should any move or any operations against the enemy take place, pray inform me, as it will give me pleasure to be with you, and great uneasiness to be from my regiment at such a time."[79] Early on the evening of the attack, Posey had returned to camp to confer with Wayne over a planned operation. When the hour grew late, possibly because Thomas was still weak from malaria, the general told him to remain overnight in his more comfortable headquarters building rather than return to his own camp billet.

Three eyewitness accounts of the ensuing battle are available. Wayne sent a field report to General Greene immediately after the attack;[80] Captain Parker's later recollections were summarized in Henry Lee's 1812 treatise on the Southern Army;[81] and Posey submitted a supplementary report, (verified by Parker), to Lee after his book appeared, but not published until Lee's son, Robert E. Lee, put out a new edition in 1869.[82] The versions vary more in emphasis and perspective than in fact. But together they graphically portray brave men fighting for their lives in desperate hand-to-hand combat, in total darkness pierced only by war whoops, battle cries, shouted commands and curses, the clash of weapons, and the groans of pain and fear from the wounded and the dying.

The Creeks' first assault penetrated the perimeter of Parker's company—extolled by Wayne as "that little gallant Corps"—and overran two artillery pieces parked nearby. A futile attempt by the Indians to put the cannons into action momentarily slowed the initial onrush of many of the warriors, allowing most of Parker's men to awaken and escape certain death. They hastily withdrew with their captain deeper into the encampment, closely pursued by the attackers. There the fleeing Virginians were met by Wayne and Posey who, hearing the alarm, had awakened, seized their swords, and rushed out to organize a counterattack. Posey and Parker, rallying a few of their demoralized comrades around them, fought their way back through the onrushing Creeks toward the main body of the Virginia battalion. That force, under the immediate command of Major Samuel Finley, had formed ranks and started to move toward the scene of the action.

During his advance through the Indian attackers, Posey personally killed or wounded several of the warriors. Another who fell under the frantic thrusts of his sword, as he later ruefully related, was one of his own men, a Sergeant Thompson, who, contrary to standing orders, had in the heat of battle removed his coat and tied a handkerchief around his head, and was thus mistaken for an Indian in the darkness. Thirty years later Thomas, still troubled and guilt-ridden over the incident, wrote that "he greatly lamented the circumstances when he visited the hospital the next morning, and learned from the brave but incautious sergeant the particulars of his wounds."[83] Finally struggling through to Major Finley's troops, Posey quickly stepped to the front of a double assault line and, as at Stony Point, led a fierce bayonet charge against the left flank of the attacking Indian forces.

In the meantime, General Wayne had somehow found a horse in the darkness, and quickly assembled a group of mounted troopers led by army dragoon Captain James Gunn and Georgia partisan Lieutenant Colonel James Jackson. With Wayne out in front waving his sword and shouting orders, the horsemen formed a skirmish line and mounted a spirited cavalry charge into the center and right flank of the Indians, driving them back to the rear of the camp, and regaining the two cannons. It was here that the courageous Guristersigo, refusing to retreat farther, made his last stand. Shooting Wayne's horse from beneath him,[84] the valiant Creek leader, "after receiving an espontoon and three bayonets in his body, encouraging his warriors all the while, retired a few paces, composedly laid himself down, and died without a groan or struggle." Parker described the fallen war chief as "the largest and bravest of the warriors—six feet, three inches high—weighing about two hundred and twenty pounds—of a manly and expressive countenance, and thirty years of age." Of this worthy enemy, all but forgotten in history, Henry Lee wrote admiringly: "Guristersigo died as he had lived, the renowned warrior of the Overhill Creeks." [85]

While Wayne and his cavalry were driving the surviving Indians back into the swamps at the rear of the contested area, Posey reformed his Virginia battalion of infantry and led it at quick time back through the camp and beyond, toward the city of Savannah. At any moment they fully expected to encounter a massive attack by the British garrison forces supporting their Indian allies. Approaching within less than a mile of the enemy picket lines, Thomas observed no sign of any hostile activity. A trooper from his rear guard then reported that a body of unidentified men was arrayed between the battalion and the American camp. Hurrying back with most of his soldiers, he came across a large group of Creek Indians who, in the first light of dawn, mistook the Virginians for British forces advancing to their aid from Savannah. Posey halted his men, and motioned with his sword for the Indians to come forward. After some hesitation, twelve subchiefs approached, and were surrounded and captured without a struggle, while the rest of the dismayed warriors fled back into the nearby swamp.[86]

Soon thereafter General Wayne, also expecting an imminent attack from the enemy garrison, arrived on the scene with the remainder of his troops. He was exhilarated by his victory over the Indians, and despite his zest for combat, was probably relieved to learn from Posey that the British were showing no signs of leaving their fortifications. But the mood of the mercurial general quickly changed, as related in Thomas' later account of this incident:

> The general appeared in a good humor until he discovered the Indian prisoners, his countenance then changed, and he asked Posey in a very peremptory manner, how he could think of taking those savages prisoners. Posey related the circumstances of the manner in which they were decoyed, and observed that he thought it wrong to put them to death after they became prisoners; he said they should not live, and they were accordingly put to death.[87]

Wayne's field dispatch sent to General Greene shortly after the battle reported the brutal fate of the twelve Creek subchiefs in a somewhat different context. He related that after his troops joined forces with Posey's battalion not far from the British lines, the enemy was showing positive signs of mounting an attack, and thus "caused some Indians captured by (Posey) to experience the bayonet to free us from incumbrance. The British after sustaining some loss were drove back to their work by a small detachment of Infantry and Cavalry."[88] But neither Posey nor Parker, who later rose to colonel, in their later accounts reported any such threatened or actual attack by the British.

The aftermath of the Creek Indian attack provides keen insight into the character of Thomas Posey. In furnishing his version of this vivid scene to Henry Lee more than thirty years later, Thomas clearly felt a need to contrast his attitude toward the Indian prisoners to that of Wayne, and to establish for the record who was actually responsible for their deaths. Moreover, consistent with the constant concern of the revolutionary soldier over how he would be judged by future generations, Posey was equally determined to correct an inaccurate portrayal of his personal combat role during the engagement. For once again, as at Stony Point, Anthony Wayne had minimized, if not misrepresented, his Virginia subordinate's exploits on the field of battle. He had reported to General Greene only that, "Col. Posey & Major Finley hearing the fire came up about the same time charged the Indians in flank."[89]

Posey's later account emphasized that it was due to Wayne's direct order that he was not with his battalion when the attack began, a fact surely well known by that general. It then detailed the extraordinary and perilous effort required to rejoin his troops—a feat possibly unknown to Wayne—before leading them against the attackers. Posey's determination that history duly record and recognize his outstanding performance in action was a trait that had almost led to a duel with Wayne after the earlier engagement. Then, George Washington had intervened to obtain fair play for his young former neighbor. Now, no less a judge of character and military honor that Robert E. Lee did the same, albeit posthumously. Long after Posey's death, General Lee reissued his father Henry's work, and inserted Thomas' account of the battle word for word, with the simple observation: "The veracity of Posey was as unquestioned as his courage, and it is satisfactory to be able to render him justice in his own words."[90]

The Creek assault upon the American camp at Sharon was the last significant military engagement of the Revolution. Less than three weeks later, the British occupation army peacefully evacuated Savannah by sea. Wayne's polyglot little force marched jubilantly into the city, symbolically led by Lieutenant Colonel Jackson's mounted Georgia partisans. But as at Yorktown, the Virginia battalion was given little time to savor the victory. General Greene wanted these battle-tested veterans to join his Southern Army, and although nearly half of the detachment was hospitalized with malaria, on 5 August all the able-bodied men in Posey's unit marched north toward Charleston.[91] Thomas was proud of the way his men had performed since leaving Virginia, and wanted his remaining troopers to cut as good a figure as possible when they marched into Greene's camp. He turned to the stylish Wayne to help add a touch of panache to their threadbare and ragged uniforms:

> Pray my dear General is there a possibility of procure 30 or 40 yards of red (shaloon rouge) or in short any thing red to finish the mens coats, as there is a deficient, you'll very much

> oblige the poor fellows of my corps. If the state will not include it among what has already been purchased, I will be answerable.[92]

Prior to his triumphant entry into Savannah, Wayne had met with a group of its British and Tory merchants, who wished to remain in the city and continue to do business after their army's departure. They were particularly concerned for their lives and safety from Wayne's Georgia militia and partisans, who had fought many bloody and merciless engagements with British regular and Tory forces before coming under direct Continental army command. The general allayed the merchants' fears on this score, and further assured them that their property and business interests would be protected to the extent allowed by his military orders.

That Wayne was as good as his word is established by one transaction with a British merchant in Savannah, one which incidentally was destined later to cause considerable anxiety to Thomas Posey. During their brief stay in the city, some junior officers of the Virginia battalion entered into a contract with a Patrick Crookshank for the purchase of certain necessities for themselves and their men. The officers (later described by Posey as half-starved and naked) who had still not received their back pay and subsistence allowances, agreed that tobacco valued at £1415 would be delivered to Crookshank's agent in Virginia before the end of 1782. Neither the officers nor the state of Virginia ever paid for the merchandise, and thirty years later Crookshank sued Posey and the heirs of Anthony Wayne for the balance due.

Thomas, then residing in Louisiana, strongly resisted the claim, and urged Wayne's son to do the same, and the matter was eventually dropped without further incident. But the correspondence with Isaac Wayne is interesting for Posey's comment on the true place of the senior Wayne in the hierarchy of American revolutionary generals: "I consider him worthy to be rank'd as third, if not second, to the great Washington."[93] Despite repeated slights and other indignities suffered at the hands of the brusque Pennsylvanian, Thomas Posey was not a man to hold a personal grudge, or to deny "Mad Anthony" his rightful place in military annals. Wayne, indeed, in personal style and military achievements, may well be considered to have been the Revolutionary counterpart of World War II's General George Patton.

Within days, Wayne and his troops followed Posey's battalion to Greene's encampment outside British-held Charleston, South Carolina, but the Virginians were soon transferred out of the Pennsylvania general's direct line of command. Their parting was cordial and mutually deferential. On 30 August Posey and his second-in-command, Major Samuel Finley, in the name of all "the officers of the Virginia detachment who had the honor to serve under you in Georgia," paid lavish tribute to Wayne for his "military abilities, for which they all entertain the highest esteem." They extended "their warmest thanks, for the generous & polite manner in which you always and at all times treated them."[94]

Wayne, never at a loss for words in responding to either praise or criticism, promptly replied that "the unanimous approbation of myself so politely expressed this Day by Gentlemen of such distinguished abilities & appearance as the Officers of the Virginia Detachment" moved him "to acknowledge: that by their unparalled fortitude & example, added to the steady bravery of the troops which composed that small but gallant army: I was enabled . . . to defeat a much more numerous foe."[95] While an element of perfunctory military etiquette (and perhaps just a hint of sarcasm?) might be detected on both sides of this effusive exchange, it must be largely taken as a genuine expression of mutual respect and professional regard. Anthony Wayne, unlike George Washington, did not inspire personal affection in his subordinates, but his military credentials are unimpeachable—and there is no bond stronger than that shared by men who have stood and fought beside each other, shoulder to shoulder, as had Wayne and the Virginians in the terror and panic of the recent Creek Indian night attack.

During the eventful year which had elapsed since Yorktown, progress in the peace negotiations underway in Europe had been agonizingly slow. But the end of the war now finally appeared to be in prospect, and Congress was contemplating a major reduction in the size of the standing army, with increased reliance upon militia forces for postwar defensive purposes. On 7 August it passed a resolution mandating a survey of regular army officers seeking voluntary retirement. General Greene assigned Posey to canvass all the officers of the Virginia Continental line then in active service with the Southern Army. It is remarkable that, with all the hardships endured and grievances over back pay and subsistence still unresolved, Thomas reported to Greene that, of the twenty-six officers he interviewed, only three indicated a desire to resign their commissions and retire as of 18 September.[96]

As it turned out, the Virginia battalion had fought its last battle. But it is altogether fitting that most of its officers opted to remain in Greene's disease-ridden camp, if only to experience a final day of glory and vindication of their state's military reputation and honor.

On 14 December the British occupation forces evacuated Charleston by sea. The opposing commanders, Nathanael Greene and Alexander Leslie, both feared that during the transition the city might be looted or vandalized. They reached an agreement that, as the British troops withdrew toward the docks to board their ships, a reliable and disciplined American advance guard would follow at a distance of 200 yards, to maintain order while the last enemy soldiers departed. Greene delegated all the details of the operation to Anthony Wayne. Well aware that the city had been the scene of Virginia's greatest humiliation when virtually its entire line surrendered there in 1780, he chose Posey's Virginians to lead the American army into Charleston. As Thomas described the assignment, "he was ordered with his Battalion to march into Charleston to prevent the enemy from committing any depredations, as soldiers are apt to do upon evacuating any post where they have been stationed."[97]

Perhaps it was only poetic justice that one of the units assigned to follow Thomas and his men into the city was headed up by Lieutenant Colonel John Steward (Stewart), commander of the First Maryland Regiment. This was the same Steward who, as a major leading the secondary assault column at Stony Point, was helped into the fort by Major Thomas Posey, but was later awarded a congressional silver medal for his valor in the engagement. So Posey entered Charleston, just as he had Stony Point, well ahead of "Crazy Jack" Steward. Sadly for the unfortunate Maryland officer, Steward did not long survive that event, dying in a riding accident only three months after the liberation of the city.[98]

Charleston's inhabitants were fearful and uncertain of what might happen during the transfer of military forces—rape and pillage were not uncommon in such circumstances. Its streets were deserted and eerily quiet as the back ranks of the British rear guard hastily marched down King's Street to Gadsden's Wharf, where the last transport vessel awaited them. Looking back nervously over their shoulders, they called out repeatedly to the eagerly advancing Americans, warning them to maintain the agreed 200-yard interval.[99]

Thomas Posey's emotions can only be imagined as he rode proudly through the silent streets at the head of his troops. Their shabby clothing and tattered footwear contrasted sharply with the enemy's bright red coats, shiny boots, and elegant accoutrements. But surely no British band ever produced sweeter or more triumphant music than Fife Major Peter Sheldon's little drum-and-fife corps as the Virginians stepped smartly to its spirited cadence down the cobblestone streets of Charleston. Their pride was well earned. From a most inauspicious beginning at Cumberland Old Court House, the discontented officers and rebellious soldiers had more than fulfilled Colonel Febiger's pledge to George Washington that, once in the field, they would indeed redeem "the sinking character of the Va. Line."[100]

Once rid of its enemy occupiers, the gracious old city of Charleston rediscovered its traditional southern hospitality. Within a week its foremost citizens hosted a gala reception and ball for the officers of the Southern Army. As each officer entered the crowded ballroom, he was personally greeted by General Greene and his pretty and vivacious wife, Kitty. According to contemporary accounts, the celebratory occasion was attended by most of the leading ladies of the city, bedecked in their most stylish gowns. For one memorable evening, at least, the war-weary Posey and his fellow Virginians enjoyed a brief respite from the grime, filth, and disease of army camp life.[101]

On 1 January 1783, Posey's battalion, along with other scattered units of Virginia regulars, was incorporated into a reconstituted First Virginia Regiment, under the command of Colonel James Wood. The new unit was not disbanded until July.[102] But it took an unconscionably longer period before justice was finally rendered to some of the new nation's bravest and longest-suffering soldiers. Six years later, in 1789, Alexander Hamilton's Treasury Department still listed, as unsatisfied obligations in the federal government's national debt, subsistence allowances due the officers of the Virginia line for the entire year 1782—as well as back pay due the noncommissioned officers and privates of "Col. Posey's detachment" for four months' additional service in 1783.[103]

Posey himself was not officially assigned to the newly-created Virginia regiment. It appears that in the early months of 1783 he returned to his home state, either alone or with a few other detached fellow officers. The war itself, for all practical purposes, had ended on 30 November 1782, when preliminary articles of peace were signed in Paris between the warring powers, but news of this event did not reach the new nation until the following February. The full text of the pact only became available on 19 March, and ratification of the final treaty was officially observed in Richmond ten days later. It is likely that these solemn ceremonies were attended by the recently-arrived Posey.[104] He had formally resigned his commission on 10 March 1783, having devoted seven full years of his life to the glorious cause of American freedom and independence.[105]

What kind of soldier was Thomas Posey? His personal bravery in battle, demonstrated many times over, cannot be questioned, and his record attests to his dedication and steadfastness in the noble quest pursued by his revolutionary generation. As an officer and leader, without any military background or training other than by example and experience, he was competent and technically proficient. As a commander, he was caring and solicitous of his men, active in procuring their provisions and clothing, heedful of their health and well-being, and deeply concerned when they fell ill or wounded in the field. As a human being, he was compassionate to his defeated British and Indian enemies. He was perhaps self-centered, too absorbed in having his exploits duly recognized, and overly preoccupied with his place in history, but these were qualities shared by many, if not most, of the revolutionary army's officer class. On balance, he may be fairly assessed as a good and courageous fighter in the best of causes.

Charles Royster, the astute chronicler of the Continental army, provokingly speculated upon the effect wrought by the war on the lives and characters of the warriors of the revolutionary generation. "Soldiers who had rarely left their own localities before the war changed under the influence of their army travels. . . . Many 'self-made industrious men' who, in ordinary times, would have made a respectable local reputation, found their abilities fit for wider scope. 'It seemed as if the war not only required but created talents.' "[106] It is interesting to ponder what kind of life Thomas Posey would have made for himself in frontier Botetourt County, Virginia, had there been no War of Independence. It seems likely that his natural abilities might eventually have raised him to some position of local, perhaps even state, prominence. But it appears unlikely that any such limited success would have reached the level of achievement Posey actually attained in his lifetime. The forge of a remarkable seven years in the American Revolution unquestionably shaped a man of greatly enhanced character and talents, which he would in time employ effectively in the further service of his country, giving back, in effect, something of what he had been given.

Shortly after celebrating in Richmond the successful conclusion of the long struggle for freedom, Posey hurried westward to the frontier counties. Pausing in Staunton just long enough to reclaim his two sons, Thomas and John, (now nine and eight, respectively), he returned home with them to Fincastle. There he faced a challenging and uncertain future as he began the difficult process of picking up the scattered pieces of his young life.

NOTES

1. John S. Pancake, *This Destructive War: The British Campaign in the Carolinas, 1780-1782* (Tuscaloosa, AL: University of Alabama Press,1985), 34-35; Douglas Southall Freeman, *George Washington: A Biography*, 7 vols. (New York: Charles Scribner's Sons, 1948-57), 5:138-39.
2. Paul David Nelson, *Anthony Wayne: Soldier of the Early Republic* (Bloomington, IN: Indiana University Press, 1985), 202-3; Freeman, *Washington*, 5:141.
3. *Virginia Historical Society Collections*, vol. 9, new ser. (Richmond, VA: Proceedings of 1891), Historical Papers, Chap. 12, 231, 233-34, 236, 241, 243, 246, 248, 256-57, 260-62.
4. Thomas Posey to Anthony Wayne, 16 November 1779, Anthony Wayne Papers, 9:22, Historical Society of Pennsylvania, Philadelphia, PA (hereafter cited as HSP).
5. Christian Febiger to Thomas Posey, 22 December 1779, Dreer Collection, Generals of the Revolution, HSP. Febiger's wife was the former Elizabeth Carson of Philadelphia. *Dictionary of American Biography*, 1963 ed., s.v. "Febiger, Christian," 3:309.
6. Fred Anderson Berg, *Encyclopedia of Continental Army Units* (Harrisburg, PA: Stackpole Books, 1974), 128; "A Short Biography of the Life of Governor Thomas Posey," Thomas Posey Papers, Indiana Historical Society Library, Indianapolis, IN (hereafter cited as IHS).
7. Pancake, *Destructive War*, 62-67; "A Short Biography of the Life of Governor Thomas Posey," Thomas Posey Papers, IHS.
8. "A Short Biography of the Life of Governor Thomas Posey," Thomas Posey Papers, IHS.
9. Ibid.
10. Pancake, *Destructive War*, 103-7.
11. John E. Selby, *The Revolution in Virginia, 1775-1783* (Williamsburg, VA: The University Press of Virginia, 1988), 216-25, 265-74.
12. Ibid., 275.
13. Ibid., 281-85. Thomas Posey's ill-fated sibling, John Price Posey, represented New Kent County in the Virginia Assembly at this time, but he does not appear to have attended its sessions in Staunton. Gladys B. Clem, *It Happened Around Staunton in Virginia* (Berryville, VA: Gladys B. Clem, 2nd ed. 1976), 24. (See Appendix B).
14. Clem, *It Happened Around Staunton*, 23.
15. Julian P. Boyd et al., eds. *The Papers of Thomas Jefferson*, 22 vols. to date (Princeton, NJ: Princeton University Press, 1950-), 4:350.
16. George B. Goode, *Virginia Cousins* (Harrisonburg, VA: C. J. Carrier Co., 1974), 213.
17. Thomas Posey to General Baron von Steuben, 8 March 1781, New York Historical Society Library, New York, NY.
18. Ibid.
19. Joseph A. Waddell, *Annals of Augusta County, Virginia* (Staunton, VA: C. R. Caldwell, 1902), 293.

20. Boyd et al., eds., *Papers of Jefferson*, 5:603-4.
21. Ibid., 5:605; H. J. Eckenrode, *The Revolution in Virginia* (Boston and New York: Houghton Mifflin Co., 1916), 248-49; Waddell, *Augusta County*, 294.
22. E.M. Sanchez-Saavedras, ed. *A Guide to Virginia Military Organizations in the American Revolution* (Richmond, VA: Virginia State Library, 1978), 33.
23. General von Steuben to Recruiting Officers, 14 May 1781 and 17 May 1781, New York Historical Society Library, New York, NY.
24. Sanchez-Saavedras, ed. *Guide to Virginia Military Organizations*, 92.
25. Febiger to Col. William Davies, 30 June 1781, *Calendar of Virginia State Papers*, ed. William P. Palmer, 11 vols. (Richmond, VA: Commonwealth of Virginia, 1875-1881), 2:25-26.
26. Ibid., Febiger to Governor Thomas Nelson, 12 August 1781, 2:321-22.
27. Ibid., Febiger to Davies, 12 August 1781, 2:322-23.
28. Ibid.
29. Sanchez-Saavedras, ed., *Guide to Virginia Military Organizations,* 30.
30. Thomas Posey's sibling, Milly Posey, was still a member of the Mount Vernon household at this time, as she had been in April 1781, when the British sloop-of-war *Savage,* anchored in the Potomac offshore, trained its guns on the stately mansion and forced farm manager Lund Washington to send provisions on board. Freeman, *Washington*, 5:282-83; John C. Fitzpatrick, ed., *The Writings of George Washington*, 39 vols. (Washington, DC: U.S. Government Printing Office, 1931-44), 21:385-87, 22:14-15.
31. For a detailed account of events in Virginia in the months leading up to the siege of Yorktown, see: Selby, *Revolution in Virginia*, 286-303.
32. Freeman, *Washington*, 5:333; William A. Crozier, *Virginia County Records—Spotsylvania County, Vol. 1* (New York: Genealogical Publishing Co., 1905), 528; Lyman Chalkley, *Chronicles of the Scotch-Irish Settlement in Virginia*, 3 vols. (Baltimore: Genealogical Publishing Co., 1966), 2:488.
33. Undated entry, MS Memorandum Book of Thomas Posey, Thomas Posey Papers, IHS.
34. George Washington to von Steuben, 23 October 1781, *Writings of Washington*, ed. Fitzpatrick, 23:258.
35. Ibid.
36. Febiger to Davies, 6 November 1781, *Calendar of Virginia State Papers*, ed. Palmer, 2:580-82.
37. Ibid., 2:582-84.
38. Ibid., 11 November 1781, 2:584-85.
39. Ibid., Febiger to Governor Thomas Nelson, 16 November 1781, 2:602-4.
40. Ibid., Febiger to Davies, 18 November 1781, 2:611.
41. Ibid., Virginia Officers' Memorial to Febiger, 17 November 1781, 2:609-11.
42. Ibid.
43. Arthur St. Clair to Washington, 26 November 1781, Jared Sparks, ed., *Correspondence of the American Revolution, Being Letters of Eminent Men to George Washington*, 4 vols. (Boston: Ayer Co. Publishers, 1853), 3:449-51.
44. Washington to Arthur St. Clair, 30 November 1781, *Writings of Washington*, ed. Fitzpatrick, 23:366-67.
45. Ibid., Washington to Febiger, 12 January 1782, 23:442-44.
46. Ibid.

47. Ibid., Washington to Governor Benjamin Harrison, 10 January 1782, 23:436-37.
48. Harrison to Washington, 8 February 1782, *Calendar of Virginia State Papers*, ed. Palmer, 3:145-46.
49. Ibid.; Virginia's fiscal insolvency reached its lowest point in 1782. An act to commutate all tax payments for four months contributed to the state's inability to maintain its Continental troops. Richard R. Beeman, *Patrick Henry: A Biography* (New York: McGraw-Hill, 1974), 118.
50. Harrison to Washington, 8 February 1782, *Calendar of Virginia State Papers*, ed. Palmer, 3:145-46.
51. Christian Febiger to George Washington, 10 February 1782, *The George Washington Papers* (Washington, DC: Library of Congress, 1964, text-fiche), Reel 83. (Hereafter cited as *GW Papers—text-fiche—LC*).
52. Ibid., Thomas Posey to George Washington, 11 February 1782, Reel 83.
53. Ibid.
54. Febiger to Davies, 3 December 1781, *Calendar of Virginia State Papers*, ed. Palmer, 2:635.
55. Febiger to Davies, 21 January 1782, *Calendar of Virginia State Papers*, ed. Palmer 3:44-45.
56. Febiger to Washington, 10 February 1782, *GW Papers—text-fiche—LC*, Reel 83.
57. Febiger to Harrison, 7 February 1782, *Calendar of Virginia State Papers*, ed. Palmer, 3:55.
58. Febiger to Washington, 10 February 1782, *GW Papers—text-fiche—LC,* Reel 83.
59. Ibid., Febiger to Washington, 14 March 1782.
60. Febiger to Harrison, 23 February 1782, *Calendar of Virginia State Papers*, ed. Palmer, 3:73-74.
61. Ibid., Febiger to Davies, 23 February 1782, 3:72.
62. Posey to Febiger, 16 February 1782, *GW Papers—text-fiche—LC*, Reel 83. (Extract enclosed in Febiger to Washington, 14 March 1782.)
63. Ibid., Posey to Febiger, 17 February 1782. A gill of rum (four ounces) was part of the daily ration of the Continental army, but apparently had not been available at Cumberland for some time. Charles Royster, *A Revolutionary People at War: The Continental Army and American Character, 1775-1783* (Chapel Hill, NC: University of North Carolina Press, 1979), 75.
64. Posey to Febiger, 18 February 1782, *GW Papers—text-fiche—LC*, Reel 83. (Extract enclosed in Febiger to Washington, 14 March 1782).
65. Ibid., Febiger to Washington, 14 March 1782; see also: Harold L. Peterson, *The Book of the Continental Soldier* (Harrisburg, PA: Stackpole Books, 1968), 196-97.
66. Posey to Febiger, 22 February 1782, *GW Papers—text-fiche—LC*, Reel 83. (Extract enclosed in Febiger to Washington, 14 March 1782).
67. Ibid., "Weekly Return of the Detachment Comm'd by Lt. Col. Thomas Posey, Prince Edward C. House," 18 February 1782.
68. Posey to Davies, 23 February 1782, *Calendar of Virginia State Papers*, ed. Palmer, 3:71.
69. Ibid., 3:72.

70. Posey to Nathanael Greene, 22 February 1782, Greene Papers, William L. Clements Library, The University of Michigan, Ann Arbor, MI; Posey to Greene, 11 March 1782, Nathanael Greene Papers, William R. Perkins Library, Duke University, Durham, NC; Posey to Greene, 16 March 1782 and 28 March 1782, Clements Library, The University of Michigan, Ann Arbor, MI; Posey to Ichabod Burnet, 30 March 1782, Greene Papers, Perkins Library, Duke University, Durham, NC; Posey to Greene, 1 April 1782, Clements Library, The University of Michigan, Ann Arbor, MI.
71. Greene to Posey, 24 March 1782, Nathanael Greene Papers, William R. Perkins Library, Duke University, Durham, NC.
72. Anthony Wayne to Posey, 4 April 1782, Wayne Papers, HSP, 16:25.
73. Ibid., Posey to Wayne, 2 April 1782, 16:13.
74. Ibid., 5 April 1782, 16:28.
75. Posey to Greene, 9 May 1782, Nathanael Greene Papers, William R. Perkins Library, Duke University, Durham, NC.
76. Ibid., Posey to Greene, 11 May 1782.
77. Harry Emerson Wildes, *Anthony Wayne: Trouble Shooter of the American Revolution* (Westport, CT: Greenwood Press, 1970), 28.
78. Ibid., 284; Thomas Boyd, *Mad Anthony Wayne* (New York and London: Oxford University Press, 1929), 203-6; Charles Janaway Stille, *Major-General Anthony Wayne and the Pennsylvania Line* (Port Washington, NY: Kennikat Press, 1893), 289; Glenn Tucker, *Mad Anthony Wayne and the New Nation* (Harrisburg, PA: Stackpole Books, 1973), 212-15; Nelson, *Wayne*, 174-75.
79. Posey to Wayne, 12 June 1782, Wayne Papers, HSP,17:66.
80. Wayne to Greene, 24 June 1782, *GW Papers—text-fiche—LC*, Reel 85. (Enclosed in Greene to Washington, 11 July 1782.)
81. Henry Lee, *Memoirs of the War in the Southern Department of the United States*, ed. Robert E. Lee (New York: University Publishing Co., 1869 edition, reprint, *The New York Times* and Arno Press, 1969), 555-63.
82. Ibid., 558-59.
83. Ibid.
84. John Hyde Preston, *A Gentleman Rebel: The Exploits of Anthony Wayne* (New York: Farrar & Rinehart, Inc., 1930), 243.
85. Lee, *Memoirs of the War*, ed. Lee, 559-60.
86. Ibid.
87. Ibid.
88. Wayne to Greene, 24 June 1782, *GW Papers—text-fiche—LC*, Reel 85. (Enclosed in Greene to Washington, 11 July 1782.)
89. Ibid.
90. Lee, *Memoirs of the War*, ed. Lee, 558. Alexander Lawrence Posey, (1873-1908), a leading poet of the Creek Indian Nation, is believed to have been a descendant or a distant cousin of Thomas Posey. See: Alexander Lawrence Posey, *Poems of Alexander Lawrence Posey, Creek Indian Bard*, ed. Minnie H. Posey, (Muskogee, OK: Five Civilized Tribes Heritage Foundation, Inc.; 1st revised edition, 1969).
91. Wayne to Posey, 5 August 1782, Wayne Papers, HSP, 18:55.
92. Ibid., Posey to Wayne, 6 August 1782, 18:56.

93. Isaac Wayne to Posey, 10 February 1811; Posey to Isaac Wayne, 13 May 1811 and 10 September 1811, Wayne Papers, Clements Library, The University of Michigan, Ann Arbor, MI.
94. Thomas Posey and Samuel Finley to Anthony Wayne, 30 August 1782, *Papers of the Continental Congress*, Item 152.11-611, National Archives, Washington, DC.
95. Ibid., Wayne to Posey and Finley, 30 August 1782, Item 152.11-615.
96. "Report of the Intention of the Officers of the Virginia Line," Lt. Col. Thomas Posey, 18 September 1782, Thomas Posey Papers, IHS.
97. "A Short Biography," Thomas Posey Papers, IHS.
98. Royster, *A Revolutionary People at War*, 95-96.
99. Elswyth Thane, *The Fighting Quaker: Nathanael Greene* (New York: Amereon, Ltd., 1972), 264-66; Theodore Thayer, *Nathanael Greene: Strategist of the American Revolution* (New York: Twayne Publishers, 1960), 408-409.
100. Febiger to Washington, 10 February 1782, *GW Papers—text-fiche—LC*, Reel 83.
101. Thane, *Greene*, 267; Thayer, *Greene*, 409.
102. Sanchez-Saavedra, ed., *Guide to Virginia Military Organizations*, 33, 53; Berg, *Encyclopedia of Continental Units*, 124.
103. Harold C. Syrett, ed., *The Papers of Alexander Hamilton*, 26 vols. to date (New York and London: Columbia University Press, 1962-), 5:408.
104. Selby, *Revolution in Virginia*, 322-23.
105. Francis B. Heitman, ed., *Historical Register of Officers of the Continental Army, 1775-1783* (Washington, DC: Lowdermilk & Co., 1893), 333-34.
106. Royster, *A Revolutionary People at War*, 244-45.

CHAPTER FIVE

(1783-1793)

". . . we are to loose you, perhaps for ever. . . ."

The months following Thomas Posey's return from the war brought wrenching personal adjustment. As head of the small Fincastle household on Main Street, he confronted the practical problems of supporting and nurturing his reunited family, as well as charting a future course in life for himself. There is no evidence that he sought to revive the saddlery business long dissipated by his wartime absence, or to seek other gainful employment. The retired lieutenant colonel was probably the most renowned war hero not only in his little community, but throughout the western counties of Virginia, and he was not at all the same man who marched his company of fellow-frontiersmen out of Staunton seven years before. Earlier in life, the ruin of Captain John Posey had divested Thomas of his birthright and position among the gentry of Fairfax County, and reduced him to the level of a frontier tradesman. Now, his military service and station had brought about another metamorphosis in his social status.

The structure of the Revolutionary army closely paralleled its traditional European counterpart, whose officer corps was drawn from the moneyed upper class, the manor-born and well-educated younger sons of the powerful and prominent. But there were not enough men of that socio-economic standing available to meet the needs of the Continental line, and many company and field grade officers came directly from colonial farms and workshops. These soldiers of humble origin and limited wealth and education earned their gentility and respectability on the field of battle. Previously only gentlemen could be officers. Now plebeian-born officers *became* gentlemen, acquiring through their position and conduct the respect and stature they had been denied by birth, schooling, or adverse circumstances. The gentrification process was institutionalized and validated by the observance of a strict and traditional code of honor within the officer corps of the American army.[1] Thus it happens that the youthful gentility that Thomas Posey, Saddler, had lost through family misfortune was regained through his own gallant wartime service and leadership. He had emerged from the War of Independence as Thomas Posey, Gentleman.

Hard-won social status did not, however, bring commensurate economic advantage, and Posey's postwar financial resources were alarmingly meager. Many years were to pass before the new nation fully settled accounts with its fighting men for back pay and delinquent subsistence allowances. As partial compensation for their sacrifices in the revolutionary cause, special bounties were awarded them in the form of rights to lay future claim to land in the newly opened frontier territories beyond the Appalachians. On 1 April 1783 Thomas duly applied for and received a land grant warrant for 7,000 acres of such land, based upon his seven years' service and his attained rank of lieutenant colonel.[2] But this was not a liquid or readily disposable asset, although many years later it would provide the basis for removing his family to the western frontier. For the present, Posey found himself an unemployed widower with no immediate means of providing either a livelihood or a proper home environment for his two children.

Within a year, Thomas found the solution to his economic as well as his domestic dilemma, resorting to an old and honorable practice not uncommon in those times for similarly situated Virginia gentlemen—and significantly, a course pursued by both of his role models, Captain John Posey and George Washington. He laid suit to, and won the hand of, an eligible widow of means. On 22 January 1784, Posey married the well-born Mary Alexander Thornton, widow of Major George Thornton, a prominent citizen of the Piedmont area of Virginia. The simple marriage ceremony took place in Fredericksburg, Spotsylvania County, in the Thorntons' home parish church, St. George's, the Reverend Mr. Stephens officiating.[3]

Mary was the eldest daughter of John Alexander, scion of the aristocratic family which founded, and gave its name to, the town of Alexandria, Virginia. She was born, raised, and unusually well-educated at "Salisbury," the Alexander family's comfortable estate in Stafford County. At age seventeen, she had married the equally well-connected George Thornton, whose maternal grandmother, Mildred Washington Gregory, was the sister of George Washington's father, Augustine. At the time of their marriage on 9 October 1773, George Thornton, born at "Rumford" in Stafford County, was already a prominent Fredericksburg businessman and landowner.[4] At the time of his death on 30 April 1781 while on active service in the state militia, Major Thornton was a Delegate in the lower house of the Virginia Assembly.[5] The Thorntons had two sons, George W. and Reuben. Their only daughter, Lucy Frances, was born seven months after her father's death. Due to that circumstance, perhaps, her twelve godparents comprised the most prominent citizens of Fredericksburg, including Mrs. Betsy Lewis and Mrs. Fanny Ball, the sister and niece, respectively, of George Washington.[6]

It is not known how the match was made between Thomas Posey and Mary Alexander Thornton. Possibly he knew some members of the Alexander family from his Fairfax County youth. Philip Alexander had been Captain John Posey's personal attorney in 1769,[7] and Charles Alexander had gone bail for Thomas' younger sibling, Hanson Posey, in 1770.[8] Thomas had no known personal connections in Stafford or Spotsylvania counties, but he may have become casually acquainted with Major Thornton in the 1776 campaign to oust Lord Dunmore from Virginia, or during Posey's military service in that state in 1780 and early 1781. In all likelihood, however, helpful mutual friends initiated and encouraged the courtship process after Thomas' return to civilian life. The 200 miles between Fincastle and Fredericksburg seems not to have been a major obstacle. It is known that Thomas was in the latter city on 6 October 1783 to attend the organizational meeting of the Society of the Cincinnati in the State of Virginia.[9] That visit would have provided a convenient and appropriate occasion to formalize his engagement to Mary Thornton, and to make plans for their wedding the following January.

The proposed union appears to have offered many advantages to the young widow and widower alike, each left alone with small children to raise from their first marriages. One account has it that when Mary consulted a trusted adviser on the suitability of Posey as a prospective husband, she was told that family pride and lineage presented no serious impediment to the match, and that it would be unseemly to reject, if offered, the marriage proposal of so distinguished a Revolutionary officer.[10] In those days, romantic attachment played a lesser role in matrimonial decisions than in the modern era. But based upon contemporaneous descriptions of Mary as a beautiful woman, and Thomas as a strikingly handsome man, it is to be hoped that theirs was as much a love match as a marriage of convenience. Given the prevailing mores of the times, it was, in all likelihood, more than a little of both.

Just three weeks before the wedding ceremony, their happiness was marred by a tragic event—the death, from unknown causes, of Thomas Posey's oldest son, Thomas, on 31 December 1783.[11] Shortly thereafter, nine-year-old John, the only surviving child of Thomas and Martha Mathews Posey, departed with his father from the Shenandoah Valley to join the three Thornton children and their mother in a new Posey household in Spotsylvania County, where the family was to grow and flourish in a secluded rural and largely unsettled wooded setting of Piedmont Virginia.

Major George Thornton and his family had resided within the limits of Fredericksburg itself. One of his other properties was a tract of land located several miles west of the town, lying on a major creek called Wilderness Run, from which the neighborhood took its name—The Wilderness. Thomas and Mary Posey chose to make their new home on this site. They erected a new two-story brick addition to an existing log country house or lodge; the new wing featured a long hallway running from front to back, opening on to porches at each end. Designed, perhaps, after the Washington mansion at Mount Vernon so familiar to Thomas, the larger porch, or portico, was built at the rear of the house, overlooking a beautifully terraced slope extending down to the stream below. Farther downstream, a dam created a small fish-stocked lake, on the shores of which a grist mill was later constructed. A meathouse and another small brick building, (possibly a detached kitchen), were located near the main dwelling. On a nearby hill east of the main building several small wooden cabins housed the family's slaves and servants. The Poseys called their new home "Greenwood." Their nearest neighbors in the sparsely settled area were William and Lucy Gordon Jones, whose home, named "Ellwood," was located some distance upstream along Wilderness Run.[12]

Thomas Posey never acquired legal title to Greenwood, nor to any other realty owned at the time of his death by George Thornton. His wife Mary took the usual widow's dower interest in the estate, but outright title to most of the major properties would pass directly to the three Thornton children as they attained legal age. In the interim, Thomas and Mary had effective fiduciary control of the entire Thornton estate, and on 7 November 1786 they were formally appointed legal guardians of George W., Reuben and Lucy Frances

Thornton, secured by a £5000 bond which their neighbor William Jones signed as their personal surety.[13]

Thomas appears to have had no difficulty settling comfortably into his new lifestyle as a gentleman-planter of post-revolutionary Virginia country society. It was a role in remarkable contrast to his pre-war socio-economic status as a struggling young tradesman in frontier Shenandoah Valley. Farming was now his major interest, although the extent and nature of his arable acres is unknown. A gift sent to him by Daniel Morgan reflects his new mode of life—a large bag of hardy timothy seed. Morgan, Thomas' old Rifle Regiment commander, had prospered from extensive land speculations in the west, and a letter accompanying his gift reflects Posey's own early interest in the expanding new frontier. Thomas was going to make a long "journey over the mountains" in the spring of 1785. He had planned to bring his wife along with him as far as Morgan's Virginia mansion, where she was to remain as a house guest while he went on to examine prospective sites on which to exercise his military warrants. For reasons not clear from Morgan's letter—possibly one of Mary's frequent pregnancies—the trip had to be postponed.[14] But later in the decade, Posey was to make several such exploratory journeys.

During their nineteen years at Greenwood, the Poseys engaged in some limited purchases and sales of real property in Spotsylvania County. From James Frazier and John Minor they acquired an improved five-acre plot just outside Fredericksburg, a segment of a larger estate called "Sligo," which had been a hospital during the war, partially burned, and later restored. Later they sold the property to John Lewis, kinsman to George Washington, for £1250 on 5 September 1794.[15] In 1788 Thomas Posey bought 188 acres of county farmland from William and Sarah Thompson for £1250, but sold it the next year to the Reverend Fontain Maury for a token £2 profit.[16] At the same time, James and Sarah Frazier conveyed Lot No. 7 in Fredericksburg to Posey; its £400 price suggests that this might have been an unimproved lot, a possible future residential or business site.[17] The limited value and scope of these conveyances do not evidence any great wealth or disposable capital. Rather, they establish the financial status of the Thomas Posey family as one of modest means, with income primarily derived from lands under cultivation or lease, perhaps supplemented by revenues from former Thornton business properties, which included a local brewery.

Accordingly, it seems clear that it was not wealth, but rather personal merit, undeniably enhanced by his past military achievements, that soon gained Posey a prominent and respected position in the Spotsylvania community. During most of his residency there, he held the judicial post of magistrate or justice of the peace.[18] His wartime reputation was recognized on 2 March 1786, when Governor Edmund Randolph commissioned Thomas Posey, Esq. as the County Lieutenant of Spotsylvania County—the officer responsible for the recruitment, training and, if necessary, the combat command of all local militia units. This was a position of some responsibility and prominence at a time when the national army had almost ceased to exist, and there were no general or field-grade officers in the cadre of the state militia organization.[19]

When not engaged in his judicial and militia duties, Posey did not choose to isolate himself on his secluded homestead. He was an active member of Masonic Lodge No. 4 in Fredericksburg, the Mother Lodge of George Washington, who had been enrolled in 1752, when freemasonry was still in its infancy in America.[20] Posey was a brother Mason throughout his entire adult life, having been first initiated into the Botetourt Lodge in 1776, just before marching off to war. Three years later, while stationed near Schoharie in upstate New York, he was "passed to a Fellow Craft and raised to the Sublime Degree of a Master" at Union Lodge in Albany.[21] In his future years, after removing to the frontier, he would continue until his death active masonic affiliations, which obviously held a meaningful place in his life.

Through his Lodge associations, military and judicial activities, church and other civic functions, Thomas became well acquainted with most of the leading citizens of Spotsylvania County and Fredericksburg, not the least of whom was a rising young attorney with good political connections, James Monroe. Although little of Posey's personal correspondence from this period has survived, later events confirm that he also continued to maintain close ties with many of his old army friends throughout Virginia, including John Marshall, Henry ("Lighthorse Harry") Lee, and Christian ("Old Denmark") Febiger—and it is known that he was a frequent visitor to Daniel Morgan's splendid estate, "Saratoga."[22] These were particularly warm and cherished friendships which endured for many years. But Thomas also sought out and maintained repeated contact with many other wartime associates through his active role in the Society of the Cincinnati in the State of Virginia—the state branch of a new national patriotic organization composed of Revolutionary officers. The group later developed into a kind of "old-boy" network that was to serve Posey well in the years to come.

The national Society came into existence in the spring of 1783 at the main army encampment outside Newburgh, New York, with

George Washington as its first President-General. It was named for Lucius Quinctius Cincinnatus who, after leaving his humble farm to win a glorious victory as a general of the Roman Republic, rejected all the power, wealth and glory offered to him by a grateful nation and chose to retire to the simple country life of a farmer. The purpose of the Society was to organize those most directly responsible for the attainment of American independence—the officers of the Continental army—to guarantee the continuation of the ideals of the Revolution. The group came under early attack as elitist and aristocratic because it perpetuated its membership through hereditary primogeniture, and adopted an eagle badge and other militaristic symbols. One objective scholar has, however, recently judged that the group sprang solely from the resolute concern of revolutionary soldiers that posterity honor and preserve their achievements, noting that it "neither intended nor attempted to introduce itself and hereditary office-holding into the institutions of government."[23]

Thomas Posey was one of the original founding members of the Virginia branch of the Society of the Cincinnati, attending its organizational meeting at the Town House in Fredericksburg on 6 October 1783. He served on its first Standing Committee (board of directors), which was headed by his old commanding general at Saratoga, General Horatio Gates. In addition to his close friends Morgan, Febiger, Lee and Marshall, other old comrades-in-arms who attended this meeting included Samuel Finley, John Poulson, Alexander Parker and Joseph Scott, (all co-signers with Posey of the Cumberland Officers' Memorial), generals Charles Scott and Samuel Hopkins, who would play key roles in Posey's future career in Kentucky, and future president James Monroe.[24] Thomas esteemed his membership in this Society as one of his most prized possessions, and in his will proudly passed along his "Order of Cincinati" to his oldest son, John.[25]

There is every reason to believe that Thomas and Mary Posey's marriage was happy and harmonious—and certainly it was fruitful. All nine of their children who lived to maturity were born at Greenwood. One by one, their births are recorded in Mary's fine script in the family bible she had begun as a seventeen-year-old bride on the day of her marriage to George Thornton—devoting the first page of entries to that union and its issue, and the succeeding pages to her married life with Thomas Posey. In order of birth, the arrival of these children is set down as: Fayette (24 October 1784), Lloyd (16 June 1786), Thornton Alexander (21 February 1788), William Churchill (13 May 1789), Thomas (29 March 1791), Eliza

Maria (26 August 1792), Alexander (20 September 1794), Washington Adams Glassell (30 January 1799), and Sarah Ann Thornton Taliaferro (20 August 1800). Another son, Addison, was born 13 September 1796, but died less than a year later, on 1 August 1797.[26]

As these infants arrived one by one to join the four older children of their first marriages, the Poseys obviously found it necessary to enlarge Greenwood's physical dimensions and to bolster the staff of household slaves and servants required to maintain the comfortable lifestyle of their Virginia social stratum. Regrettably, there is scant record of the identities or functions of the many individuals who formed a part of their domestic retinue. Together with the labor force needed to operate a farm capable of sustaining such a household, the total establishment clearly became increasingly burdensome to maintain in the uncertain and volatile economy of the times. Over the years, this reality would make ever more attractive the available military land grants and perceived opportunities waiting on the frontier. But it would be nearly two decades before Thomas Posey chose to follow the path eventually taken by so many of the revolutionary generation: to accept the challenges, brave the risks, and pursue the rewards of a new life in the west.

Posey always set his course with one objective dominating all others. He was fiercely determined to give his growing circle of children a better education and greater advantages in life than had been dealt out to him by his own uncertain origin and ill-fated family connections. Greenwood's remote location precluded the childrens' attendance at Fredericksburg's Free School (or later, its fine Academy), so a resident tutor was always an essential member of the Posey household. Some of the succession of young live-in teachers went on to greater things. The most prominent of these, in attendance at Greenwood in 1787-88, was William Wirt, who later rose to serve as a notable U.S. Attorney-General in the administrations of James Monroe and John Quincy Adams.[27] Another was Archibald Alexander, a distant cousin of Mary, who later became a renowned Presbyterian clergyman, writer, and founder of the theological seminary at Princeton University. We are indebted to Dr. Alexander, a faithful diarist, for a delightfully detailed and insightful account of life at Greenwood during the period 1788-1789.[28]

The seventeen-year-old tutor's students (one of whom, he wryly noted, was taller than himself) were John Posey and George and Reuben Thornton, occasionally joined by their younger sister, Lucy Frances Thornton. The older boys were already so advanced in Latin that their instructor was hard-pressed to keep ahead of them.

"His nights were often spent in preparing for the next day's lesson, amidst regrets that he had not made more faithful preparation."[29] The Poseys' small country library at that time included such erudite works as Rollin's *Ancient History* and his sixteen-volume *History of Rome*, as well as Rapin's *History of England* and many books of geography and travel. Significantly, rationalist philosopher John Locke's *Essays* also occupied a prominent place in the library. Alexander described Greenwood's location as "a very retired situation, where a few persons of wealth had valuable estates. Among these, visits were frequent, but few other persons came in to the neighborhood."[30] The Poseys, he stated, "though somewhat decayed in wealth . . . maintained much of the style which belonged to old Virginia families."[31]

During this period, Virginia was in widespread ferment over religion, a topic of much interest and frequent discussion at Greenwood. Both Thomas and Mary had, of course, been born and raised in the Established (Anglican) Church. Captain John Posey had been a longtime vestryman and churchwarden of Fairfax County's Truro Parish, while Mary's first husband, George Thornton, was a member of the vestry of Fredericksburg's St. George's Parish, where the Poseys' own marriage had been solemnized. Most of their social class were at least nominal Anglicans. But dissenters were becoming an increasingly visible and vocal element in Virginia society. In the Shenandoah Valley, where Posey had spent his young manhood, a flood of Scotch-Irish settlers faithful to their Presbyterian tenets had made extensive inroads. A famed "blind preacher," Dr. James Waddel, had ministered to a Presbyterian congregation in Staunton from 1778 to 1785, exerting a strong influence on young Archibald Alexander, who later married Waddel's daughter.[32]

In 1785 the Virginia Assembly finally enacted an historic Statute for Religious Freedom, long sought by freethinkers Thomas Jefferson and James Madison. The new law separated the Established Church from state control and support, and mandated toleration and freedom for other creeds.[33] Once legal sanctions limiting the free exercise of religious expression had been lifted, a massive and irresistible wave of revivalism swept through the Virginia Piedmont, led by a zealous band of evangelical Baptist preachers. Their public meetings, so distinct in style and content from the staid and structured Anglican services, attracted large crowds and won many converts. By 1790, the Baptists had become the most numerous non-establishment sect in Virginia.[34] According to Archibald Alexander, one such ardent Baptist adherent, "an aged

Christian lady, Mrs. Tyler, had found a refuge" in the hospitable household of Thomas and Mary Posey.[35]

One lazy Sunday afternoon, the Poseys had their nearest neighbors, the Joneses, over for dinner at Greenwood. During the meal, Mrs. Tyler apparently gave a vivid description of the intensely intimate and moving experience of being publicly "born again," an event she had often observed at evangelical meetings, and probably had undergone personally. The others listened politely, but after the elderly lady retired from the table, they resumed a more candid discussion of the topic. Mary Posey and her neighbor, Lucy Jones, both defended the validity of the Baptist teaching on this phenomenon, while William Jones scoffed at the whole idea, and "plainly insinuated that religion was a disease of weak and superstitious minds." The mildly skeptical Thomas Posey stated that, while he did not personally believe "in any such miraculous change, he would credit it, if Mrs. Posey should ever profess that she had experienced it."[36]

This revealing vignette strongly indicates that Thomas had moved from his early inherited Anglicanism to the impersonal Deism or natural religion postulated by John Locke and other leading theorists of the new Enlightenment. In this philosophy, reason and logic replaced the revealed orthodoxy of institutional religions, and the only creditable "miracles" were tangible and measurable events susceptible to secular analysis. This was the Age of Reason, and these views were widely held by the intellectual and political leaders of Posey's generation. Interestingly, in their later years, Thomas and Mary Posey, along with many of their children, would become devout members of the Presbyterian church, and he himself became a founding Elder and a regional leader of that faith, as well as an officer in national bible societies.

The keenly observant Dr. Alexander has also left us with a brief but striking description of his Greenwood employers' appearance and personalities. Mary Posey, he stated, "had been a beauty in her youth," and "was now at the age of forty a fine and stately person. She was addicted to the pleasures of society, but generally took the side of religion," and, in that period at least, she "seemed to be vacillating between duty and the world." Thomas Posey, the young tutor wrote succinctly, was "a man of noble appearance and courtly manners."[37] Maturity seemingly had only enhanced Posey's appearance, depicted elsewhere as "tall, athletic, and finely formed, with singularly handsome features, his exterior . . . very prepossessing," with manners harmoniously blending "the bearing of the soldier . . . with the ease of the refined gentleman."[38]

Thomas' deferential attitude at the dinner table toward his wife Mary's views on religion might well have characterized their entire conjugal relationship. Toward the end of his life, Posey would exhort his sons to "be kind, loving, affectionate, to your wives, they are the weaker vessels and require to be treated with great tenderness and affection . . . politeness, affection, prudence, and in conversation avoid of giving the least offence, never hasty or apparently speaking in a way to hurt their feelings."[39] But perhaps Mary Posey herself is the best judge of Thomas' husbandly devotion and character. Referring to one of her grandsons in a later letter to her daughter, she fervently hoped "the Lord grant he may make as good, handsome & useful man as my dear Mr. Posey."[40]

The isolated serenity of Greenwood did not totally insulate its residents from the raging political issues of the historic 1780s. The loose confederation of independent state governments emerging from the War of Independence had proved to be flawed and unworkable. A national constitutional convention in Philadelphia had produced and submitted to the individual states a carefully crafted and balanced new constitution formulating a centralized and strengthened federal government. In June of 1788 a special convention gathered in Richmond to consider its ratification by Virginia. The state was badly split on the issue. The eastern Tidewater and Northern Neck areas largely favored ratification, while popular opinion in the southern and western counties generally was opposed.[41]

In the central Piedmont area, the prevailing sentiment in Spotsylvania County also appears to have weighed against ratification. Significantly, one of its elected delegates was the moderately anti-federalist James Monroe. Thomas Posey, strongly favoring the creation of a cohesive, viable national government as the ultimate and logical goal of the revolutionary struggle, was not chosen to represent the county at the convention. He did, however, attend many, if not most, of its historic sessions, sitting as a keenly interested observer in the crowded gallery of the capital's newly constructed Academy.[42]

The assembly attracted most of Virginia's glittering spectrum of brilliant and influential leaders. Notable exceptions were Thomas Jefferson, then serving in Europe as American Minister to France, and George Washington, who had chaired the national convention, but chose to remain at Mount Vernon while quietly exerting his considerable influence in the cause of ratification. Like the state itself, its most prominent figures were evenly split on the critical issue. The anti-ratification delegates were led by the still-charismatic

Patrick Henry, and included such notables as James Monroe, George Mason, Benjamin Harrison, John Tyler, and Richard Henry Lee. The pro-ratification bloc was ably headed by James Madison, and included the highly regarded incumbent governor Edmund Randolph and the respected lawyer George Wythe, as well as Posey's wartime comrades, John Marshall and Henry Lee.

During his stay in Richmond, Thomas often joined his old friends at the Swan Tavern, the town's leading hostelry, as between formal sessions they discussed the day's events and tomorrow's strategy. The country's future teetered on the outcome of their deliberations. Virginia's acceptance of the new constitution would provide the critical ninth state required to validate its enactment, while rejection could shift momentum away from ratification in other uncommitted states, and also deprive the infant nation of its most populous and geographically pivotal component.[43]

The fiery rhetoric of Patrick Henry nearly carried the day against the new federal charter. Henry, whose constituency lay in the state's western counties, fervently believed that a decentralized national government better served the interests of the Virginians he represented.[44] In what has been called his most eloquent address, the brilliant orator painted in picturesque terms the evils and horrors he predicted would befall citizens under a more powerful national government. His imagery was so real that one transfixed delegate instinctively felt around his own wrists for the iron fetters the speaker direly predicted would soon bind every denizen under the proposed new system.[45] Even so dedicated a believer in the new constitution as Thomas Posey was visibly shaken by the fervid oratory of Patrick Henry. He later confessed to Archibald Alexander—who considered Posey to be "a man of observation and cool judgment"—that after hearing Henry's speech, "he felt himself as fully persuaded that the Constitution if adopted would be our ruin, as of his own existence." Within hours, however, "subsequent reflection restored his former judgment, and his well considered opinion resumed its place."[46]

Fortunately for history, and probably for future generations of Americans, a scant majority of the delegates was also able to shake off the spellbinding effects of Patrick Henry's metaphorical passion. The Virginia Convention of 1788 eventually ratified the new constitution by a vote of eighty-nine to seventy-nine. Within a year, a fledgling new central government, operating under broadened constitutional powers, was functioning in its temporary capital at New York City, with a two-tier federal Congress, an independent judiciary, and as its president, Thomas Posey's old neighbor, George Washington.

As a private citizen, Posey was keenly interested in the new government's handling of national issues. One question of more than casual concern to him was that of whether and how the government should redeem currency notes issued by the Continental authorities during the war. James Madison, the new Congressman from the district including Spotsylvania County, proposed a plan which favored original holders of those notes over later purchasers who had acquired them at greatly discounted rates. In 1790 Edmund Randolph, now Attorney-General in President Washington's cabinet, reported to Madison that Colonel Posey, among other notables with whom he had conferred, reported little or no support for the plan in his area of the state.[47] Soon thereafter, Posey himself wrote to Congressman Madison, seeking advice on how he could avoid speculators in applying to the government for payment of subsistence arrears due him for his service with the Southern Army.[48]

During this same year, Posey was one of twenty former revolutionary officers who attended the annual meeting of the Virginia branch of the Society of the Cincinnati in Richmond. Another of those present was General Charles Scott, who was then representing the County of Kentucky in the Virginia House of Delegates.[49] Scott and Posey were later to serve as fellow generals in the Northwest Expedition of 1793-94, and later still, the two wartime comrades would become close associates in Kentucky government, and eventually rivals for the governorship of that state.

In the spring of 1791, President Washington embarked upon an extensive and historic tour of the southern states. Starting from Mount Vernon, he arrived at "Kenmore," the residence of his sister Mrs. Betty Lewis, near Fredericksburg, on 8 April. The following day and evening, the president was feted in the town itself by a multitude of public officials and citizens. Posey, as commander of county militia and a distinguished veteran of the Revolution, played a prominent part in the elaborate welcoming ceremonies and reception. Later, Washington was the honored guest at a gala public banquet at the Town Hall, in the course of which no less than fifteen toasts were proposed. As was his custom, the president arose at 6:00 the next morning, and was escorted for some miles southward toward Richmond by a large group of mounted leading gentlemen of the town and militia officers, doubtlessly led by County Lieutenant Thomas Posey.[50]

Two months later, on 1 June, while Washington was still on his southern tour, Posey wrote the president an extraordinarily personal and revealing letter. Its tenor strongly suggests that, during the recent festivities in Fredericksburg, the two had discussed, at least briefly, the possibility of a federal government appointment for the younger man. It seems to have been Thomas' intention to deliver the letter personally to Washington as he returned through Spotsylvania County on his way home, but the opportunity to do so apparently did not present itself during the president's brief overnight stop at Betty Lewis' Kenmore on 10 June.[51]

Posey's letter stated candidly that "the estate I am in consists of not more than will barely subsist my wife and myself, three stepchildren who are heirs to the greater part of the estate, and six sons of my own." These circumstances were now impelling him to seek "some eligible means that would enable me to bring up my children in such a manner as could render them worthy members of the community and a credit to their country." Recognizing that "my talents are better calculated for a military than any other line," he was inclined toward "a military appointment in some post on the frontier." But he feared lack of educational facilities in the west: "should I lose the opportunity of giving my children such an education as I could wish . . . I could not forgive myself."[52]

Leaving this dilemma seemingly unresolved, Thomas closed his letter by asking the president to keep him in mind for some opening in government service for which he would be deemed qualified, but which would not deprive his children of the educational advantages they currently enjoyed. He pointed out modestly that, "although my exertions in the service of my country cannot be ranked among many of the most conspicuous, yet I have the consolation to think they have not been the most feeble."[53]

A close and objective study of this letter clearly shows some sort of personal relationship between Posey and Washington apart from and pre-dating their common service in the War of Independence. In its tone and scope, it is more than a somewhat tentative and ambiguous application by an ex-soldier to his former commander for a government job. Rather, it is a personal plea for guidance by a perplexed father to an older and wiser friend and counselor. Growing up next door to Mount Vernon, in the "mad and distracted" household of Captain John Posey, Thomas must have observed time and again Washington's concern for the welfare and education of his friends' offspring—most notably, his regard for the hapless Posey children, Milly and St. Lawrence. Now he himself faced a growing inability to give his own children such an upbringing as would make them "a credit to their country." His forthright recital of this quandary, and the frank revelation of the financial cause of his embarrassment, were intensely personal matters that

Posey would bring only to a man whom he knew from their past associations would care, and care deeply.

Curiously, he neither hand-delivered nor mailed the letter to Washington immediately after it was written. Some impediment (pride, perhaps, or indecision) made him lay it aside for nearly six months. In November, however, he finally did summon up the courage to send the original letter to the president, along with a brief explanation that he had held it up "from a thought that I might be too troublesome, but I trust your goodness will excuse my boldness." In the interim, Posey added, he had become "more & more confirmed, that a change in my mode of life must take place." He was now seeking a specific appointment: a militia position "with a salary annexed." He closed, respectfully, "I will not trespass further upon your patience, but submit to the best that can be done for me."[54] Washington made no immediate response, but events were to show that he did not ignore what he well knew must have been a reluctant and painfully written plea from a man who had been a troubled spectator to the improvident Captain John Posey's shameless and progressive dependency upon his generous Mount Vernon neighbor.

When these letters were written, Posey was not yet aware of a recent disaster in the west that would profoundly affect his family concerns, governmental career, and future on the western frontier. In the Treaty of Paris ending the Revolutionary War, the British had ceded to the United States all its claims to the Indian-occupied lands north of the Ohio River, up to and including a string of forts along the lower Great Lakes, which controlled the lucrative fur trade in the northwest. Reluctant to evacuate these posts, they chose instead to provide arms to the native tribes, encouraging them to violently resist American efforts to open the territory to further settlement and development. In 1790 a force commanded by General Josiah Harmar had been badly mauled by hostile Indians in Ohio. Now, news arrived that on 4 November 1791, a larger army under General Arthur St. Clair had been ambushed and largely destroyed near the main villages of the Miami Indian tribes he had been sent to quell.[55]

The massacre of St. Clair's force convinced President Washington and other government leaders that a new, highly trained regular army must be raised and deployed in the Northwest Territory. Its mission would be either to induce the hostile native American tribes to agree to a durable peace or, failing in that, to strike a decisive military blow against them. In March of 1792 Congress authorized the creation of a special 5,000-man United States Legion, including three new regiments. The president was empowered to appoint up to four brigadier generals, who were to serve under the command of a newly named commander, Major General Anthony Wayne, entrusted with the sole mission of enforcing American hegemony over the territory of the Northwest.[56]

News of these developments, upon reaching Virginia, clearly only whetted Thomas Posey's already-strong inclination to resume his military career. His intentions were now spurred, not only by pressing economic considerations, but by a patriotic soldier's zeal to once again take up arms in his country's behalf. To improve his chances of gaining an appointment, he solicited the assistance of James Monroe, his former Fredericksburg acquaintance, who had since removed to Albemarle County, and was now representing Virginia in the U. S. Senate. Posey's first objective was a colonelcy in one of the newly authorized regiments, and Senator Monroe notified him that his interest in such a commission had been communicated with his strong recommendation to Secretary of War Henry Knox. The senator concluded, "I cannot say how far your wishes will be attended to by the Executive, but can assure you of my best efforts in your behalf. Being satisfied that you ought to be appointed."[57]

It is interesting to note, parenthetically, that Monroe closed his letter to Thomas with warm expressions of special regard to Mary Posey. As a long-time friend of the Thornton family, he had known Mary since George Thornton had first brought her to Fredericksburg as his seventeen-year-old bride. Early in the Revolution, Monroe had served under his close friend, Major John Thornton. Later, from the Pennsylvania encampment of the main American army, Monroe wrote to his former commander with obvious affection and delight that "Your brother George this day made his appearance in camp as fat as a porpoise. He dines with me today. I with you were here, to test the old copper bowl, which is to be filled."[58]

Two other influential Fredericksburg acquaintances of the Poseys wrote directly to the president in support of Thomas' quest for a military command. Colonel Burgess Ball, Washington's close kinsman, detailed Posey's years of residency and wartime recruiting service in western Virginia. He pointed out that he "wou'd be able . . . to raise a capital Regiment in the frontier counties, in most of which he could have great influence." Colonel Ball added, in passing, that Posey planned eventually to live permanently in the west, and also that he had "a large and growing family and but a small fortune."[59]

The respected former general William Weedon, under whose command Thomas had once briefly served in the Virginia Continental line, chose rather to emphasize Posey's unique military qualifications for the upcoming campaign. He reminded Washington that he was "a gentleman that is well acquainted with Indian Warfare," that he was personally familiar with "the Western country, having been once or twice over the Ohio," and that his appointment into the U.S. Legion would be "popular and the duties of the office discharged with prudence, punctuality and firmness."[60]

The recommendations of these reputable friends, although duly noted by Washington, did not immediately produce a field command for Posey. But the president was at this time considering him, among others, for an even higher army staff job: the post of Adjutant-General. He wrote Secretary Knox that "Colo. Posey also (who wants to be employed) might if ready at his pen make a good one, for in other respects (and I do not know that he is deficient in this) he is said to be an excellent Officer."[61] Seven weeks later, with the position still unfilled, the president authorized Knox to name Colonel Ebenezer Sproat on a temporary basis, "provided it is *known* that he is a man of liberal education and correct in his writing; *doubts* of these qualifications in Colo. Posey are the only obstacles to my giving him a preference over any other."[62]

Washington surely must have known, from his personal knowledge and observation of the younger man's upbringing and family circumstances at Rover's Delight, that Thomas Posey's formal education had been as limited as his own—neither man having advanced beyond the secondary school level. But during and after the Revolution, the president had also received several letters from his young former neighbor demonstrating a relatively high degree of literary skill and precise articulation. In any event, whatever uncertainties or doubts Washington might have harbored as to Thomas' intellectual qualifications or writing proficiency must soon have been put to rest. Within days, through the president's nephew Robert Lewis of Fredericksburg, a permanent appointment to the Adjutant-Generalship of the nation's regular army was offered to Posey.

After briefly considering this flattering offer, Thomas gratefully declined the appointment to this high administrative post. He informed Washington on 10 October that "my inclination and interest leads me to a great desire to become an inhabitant of the western Country, which probably may take place in the course of a few years, for which reason I think a more active office would suit me." The more "active office" he now sought was a combat command in the U.S. Legion, where he could serve once again under "Mad Anthony" Wayne, his old commander at Stony Point and Sharon. "If any vacancy in the line of the brigadier-generals should take place, and you think me adequate to the office, I will accept of it, and use my best skill and abilities in the execution thereof."[63] His eyes now firmly fixed on the western frontier as his future home, Posey had in one bold stroke rejected a high staff position in the capital, and raised his sights from a regimental colonelcy to a brigadier's star and a field command in the Northwest expedition.

The president did indeed think Thomas to be "adequate" to the position he now sought. An opening soon arose in the line of authorized general officers of the Legion, and it was filled shortly after Washington's unanimous reelection to a second term in office by the Electoral College on 13 February 1793. Two weeks later, Secretary Knox officially notified Posey that he had been appointed by the president, and confirmed by the United States Senate, as a brigadier general in the regular army. Asked by the secretary to signify his acceptance and indicate his readiness to report for duty, Thomas forwarded the formal notification of his full compliance, effective as of 11 March 1793.[64]

One of the first persons Thomas informed of his appointment was his old wartime comrade Henry Lee, now governor of Virginia. "Lighthorse Harry" responded with a warm congratulatory note tinged with grim foreboding. "I have your letter . . . and find by its contents that we are to loose you, perhaps for ever . . . my feelings partake of joy & grief." Perhaps because he had earlier sought the top Legion command for himself but had been passed over in favor of Anthony Wayne,[65] Lee had grave misgivings about the Pennsylvanian's military abilities. "I fear in all wars a want of sagacity in the leader, but this want is most to be depreciated in an Indian warfare. From this source flow considerations which agitate my breast." Wayne had been one of the most able and effective of Washington's revolutionary generals, but his daring in the planning and vigor in the execution of military actions had created an image of rashness and impetuosity—a veritable "Mad Anthony." Despite his fears, Harry Lee's letter closed with a warmth and eloquence befitting two close friends: "Whatever you may do, or whereever go my prayers for health, honor & prosperity will ever attend you . . . Farewell my friend."[66]

While Thomas busied himself in preparations to take the field, George Washington left the capital, arriving home at Mount Vernon on 2 April. Within three days, newly commissioned Brigadier General Posey arrived there to confer with the president.[67] As far as is known from existing records, this was Thomas' first visit to the lovely old manse since leaving his broken home at nearby Rover's Delight nearly a quarter century earlier to make a life of his own. As he rode up to the small rounded front entrance of Mount Vernon and dismounted, Posey must have been overcome by a flood of memories and emotions, both pleasant and sad. It was here that he had come in better days as a child, with his parents and siblings, to dine, and sometimes to lodge, always warmly welcomed at the front door by the cordial master of the mansion and his kindly consort. It was here, too, that desperation sometimes drove him as a youth seeking aid or counsel during the progressive disintegration of the Posey family circle, and finally as a young man planning to better his fortunes on the frontier. Now, as a middle-aged man with an honorable war record behind him and a large family of his own, he had returned, once again on the brink of a challenging venture into the west, to seek the counsel of the one man he had always revered and respected above all others.

It is unknown if the president or Posey initiated the meeting at Mount Vernon. Washington presumably used the occasion of Thomas' visit to impart to the younger man his own vast experience and knowledge of Indian warfare. Perhaps also, although Anthony Wayne was his personal choice to lead the Legion, he encouraged Posey to act as a restraining influence on the commander's perceived recklessness—that "want of sagacity" so deplored by Henry Lee and other detractors of the doughty Pennsylvania general. What is known is that the president spoke long and earnestly to Thomas of his desire for peaceful resolution of the nation's differences with the native American tribes of the Northwest Territory.[68]

Apart from public business, there was ample time to talk of other, more personal matters. The two old warriors, not unlike soldiers of every age and era, undoubtedly exchanged "war stories," reliving some of their shared military experiences: the frustration of Monmouth, the suffering of Valley Forge, the glory of Stony Point, the exultation of Yorktown. It is likely also that the conversation sometimes turned to reminiscences of the good and bad times experienced by and between the Posey and Washington families in the nearly two decades between Thomas' birth and his departure from Rover's Delight. It would be sheer speculation to suggest that even more intimate subjects could have been brought up. No one will ever know what words might have passed between the two men as they sat alone after dinner on the wide back portico of Mount Vernon, gazing down in the gathering dusk on the broad Potomac River flowing at the foot of the mansion's long, gently sloping hillside.

Less than a week later, back home in Spotsylvania County, Posey received official orders from Secretary Knox to report for duty as soon as possible to General Wayne at Legionville, the new army's main encampment near Pittsburgh.[69] He bade a sad and tender farewell to his weeping wife Mary and the tearful circle of young children clustered around him at Greenwood's outer gate. Thomas Posey, after ten comfortable years as a country squire in the peaceful seclusion of The Wilderness, rode northward alone to renew his old battle with an ancient enemy, but in a new arena—the dark and menacing forests of the Northwest Territory.

NOTES

1. Charles Royster, *A Revolutionary People at War: The Continental Army and American Character, 1775-1783* (Chapel Hill NC: The University of North Carolina Press, 1979), 86-87.
2. Gaius Marcus Brumbaugh, ed., *Revolutionary War Records: Virginia*, 2 vols. (Baltimore: Genealogical Publishing Co., 1967 edition), 1:109.
3. Thornton and Posey Family Bible, The Presbyterian Study Center, Montreat, NC.
4. Ibid.; Donald Jackson and Dorothy Twohig, eds., *The Diaries of George Washington*, 7 vols. (Charlottesville, VA: The University Press of Virginia, 1976-79), 2:166, 175. Mary Alexander, through her mother Lucy Thornton Alexander, was a distant cousin of her first husband. George Brown Goode, *Virginia Cousins* (Harrisonburg, VA: C. J. Carrier Co., 1974), 212-16; Thornton Genealogical Chart, Thornton Family Folder no. 8, George H.S. King Papers, MS. K5823g, Virginia Historical Society Library, Richmond, VA.
5. Goode, *Virginia Cousins*, 213-14.
6. Thornton and Posey Family Bible, The Presbyterian Study Center, Montreat, NC.
7. Jackson and Twohig, eds., *Diaries of Washington*, 2:166.
8. Court Order Book No. 1770, p. 92, Fairfax County Court Archives, Judicial Center, Fairfax County, Fairfax, VA.
9. *Roster of the Society of the Cincinnati* (Washington, DC: The Society of the Cincinnati, 1989), 95, 191.
10. "The Posey Romance," St. Louis (MO) *Daily Globe-Democrat*, 6 November 1898.
11. Lloyd Franklin Posey and Betty Sue Drake Posey, *The Posey Family in America* (Hattiesburg, MS: University of Southern Mississippi Press, 1971), 155.
12. "Greenwood," *WPA of Virginia Historical Inventory, Spotsylvania County, Vol. 1*, 23 December 1936, Central Rappahannock Regional Library, Fredericksburg, VA. Two major battles of the Civil War—Chancellorsville (1863) and The Wilderness (1864)—were fought in the vicinity; both were won by Confederate forces led by General Robert E. Lee, son of Thomas Posey's Revolutionary comrade and friend, Henry ("Lighthorse Harry") Lee.

13. William Armstrong Crozier, ed., *Virginia County Records—Spotsylvania County—1721-1800* (New York: Genealogical Publishing Co., 1905), 79.
14. Daniel Morgan to Thomas Posey, 11 July 1785, Gratz Collection, Historical Society of Pennsylvania, Philadelphia, PA; Don Higginbotham, *Daniel Morgan: Revolutionary Rifleman* (Chapel Hill, NC: The University of North Carolina Press, 1961), 179.
15. Crozier, ed., *Virginia County Records—Spotsylvania*, 472; "Sligo," *WPA of Virginia—Spotsylvania—Vol. 3*, Central Rappahannock Regional Library, Fredericksburg, VA.
16. Crozier, ed., *Virginia County Records—Spotsylvania*, 419, 427.
17. Ibid., 428.
18. "A Short Biography of the Life of Governor Posey," Thomas Posey Papers, Indiana Historical Society Library, Indianapolis, IN (hereafter cited as IHS).
19. MS Certificate of Appointment, 1 March 1787, Thomas Posey Papers, IHS; James Hall, "Memoir of Thomas Posey, Major General and Governor of Indiana," *The Library of American Biography*, ed. Jared Sparks, ser. 2 (Boston: Little, Brown & Co., 1846), 9:389-90.
20. Alvin T. Embry, *History of Fredericksburg, Virginia* (Richmond, VA: Old Dominion Press, 1937), 92.
21. MS Receipt for initiation fee, 1 May 1776; MS Certificate, F. & A.M., 21 January 1779, Union Lodge, Albany, NY; Thomas Posey Papers, IHS.
22. Higginbotham, *Morgan*, 180.
23. Royster, *Revolutionary People at War*, 353-58; Charles Royster, *Light-Horse Harry Lee and the Legacy of the American Revolution* (New York: Alfred A. Knopf, 1981), 95-96.
24. Virginius Dabney, *BiCentennial History and Roster of the Society of the Cincinnati in the State of Virginia, 1783-1983* (Richmond, VA: The Society of the Cincinnati in the State of Virginia, 1983), 7-8, 11, 14, 26, 213.
25. Last will and testament of Thomas Posey, 6 April 1816, Will Record Book A, 96, Knox County Circuit Court, Vincennes, IN.
26. Thornton and Posey Family Bible, The Presbyterian Study Center, Montreat, NC.
27. Ibid.
28. For the full account of Dr. Alexander's year-long sojourn at Greenwood, see: James W. Alexander, *The Life of Archibald Alexander* (New York: Charles Scribner, 1854), 32-47.
29. Ibid., 35.
30. Ibid., 34.
31. Ibid., 35.
32. *Dictionary of American Biography*, 1963 ed., s.v. "Alexander, Archibald," 1:162-63; s.v. "Waddel, James," 10:298-99. At the time, there were already 20 Presbyterian churches in southern Shenandoah Valley to only one Anglican. Robert Mitchell, *Commercialism and the Frontier: Perspectives on the Early Shenandoah Valley* (Charlottesville, VA: University Press of Virginia, 1977), 104-5.
33. Virginius Dabney, *Virginia—The New Dominion* (Garden City, NY: The University Press of Virginia, 1971), 163.

34. Mechal Sobel, *Travelin' On: The Slave Journey to an Afro-Baptist Faith* (Westport, CT: Greenwood Press, 1979), 88-89.
35. Alexander, *Life of Alexander*, 38.
36. Ibid., 41.
37. Ibid., 35.
38. Hall, "Memoir of Thomas Posey," *Library of American Biography*, ed. Sparks, ser. 2, 9:403.
39. Thomas Posey's letter to "My dearly beloved children and grandchildren," 4 February 1814, Thomas Posey Papers, IHS.
40. Mary Posey to Eliza Maria Posey Street, 9 September 1814, Thomas Posey Papers, IHS.
41. Richard A. Beeman, *Patrick Henry: A Biography* (New York: McGraw-Hill, 1974), 145.
42. The Academy was located about a mile from the scene of the public hanging, less than five months before, of Thomas' sibling, John Price Posey. (See Appendix B.)
43. For an excellent account of the Virginia Convention and the roles played by its leaders, see: Catherine Drinker Bowen, *Miracle at Philadelphia*, 2nd ed. (New York: Little, Brown & Co., 1986), 293-305.
44. Henry cited the recent failure of the Jay Treaty with Spain to open navigation along the lower Mississippi River as a prime example of how a strong central government would put the interests of northern states over the western states and territories. Beeman, *Henry*, 135-41.
45. Bowen, *Miracle*, 298.
46. Alexander, *Life of Alexander*, 190-91. See also: Nathaniel Wright Stephenson and Waldo Hilary Dunn, *George Washington* (New York, London, and Toronto: Oxford University Press, 1940), 2:247; William Wirt Henry, *Patrick Henry*, 3 vols. (New York: Charles Scribner's Sons, 1891), 2:358-359.
47. Edmund Randolph to James Madison, 6 March 1790, *The Papers of James Madison*, ed. William T. Hutchinson, 16 vols. to date (Charlottesville, VA: University Press of Virginia, 1962-), 13:92-93; Douglas Southall Freeman, *George Washington: A Biography*, 7 vols. (New York: Charles Scribner's Sons, 1948-57), 6:256.
48. Thomas Posey to James Madison, 5 July 1790, *Madison Papers*, ed. Hutchinson, 13:263-64; see also: Julian P. Boyd et al., eds., *The Papers of Thomas Jefferson*, 22 vols. to date (Princeton, NJ: Princeton University Press, 1950-), 18:615-17.
49. Harry M. Ward, *Charles Scott and the "Spirit of '76"* (Charlottesville, VA: The University Press of Virginia, 1988), 104-5; *Papers of the Society of the Cincinnati in the State of Virginia, 1783-1824* (Richmond, VA: The Society of the Cincinnati in the State of Virginia, minutes, 6-7 October 1790, 38-39.
50. Archibald Henderson, *Washington's Southern Tour—1791* (Boston and New York: Houghton Mifflin Co., 1923), 43-46; Freeman, *Washington*, 6:307-8.
51. Freeman, *Washington*, 6:320-21.
52. Thomas Posey to George Washington, 1 June 1791, *The George Washington Papers* (Washington, DC: Library of Congress, 1964, text-fiche), reel 122 (Hereafter cited as *GW Papers—text-fiche—LC*).

53. Ibid.
54. Ibid., Thomas Posey to George Washington, 20 November 1791.
55. Freeman, *Washington*, 6:288-89. Among the fatalities was Lt. Colonel William Butler of Pennsylvania, Posey's superior in the Rifle Regiment and at Schoharie, and fellow officer at Stony Point and in the Southern Army of 1782.
56. Ibid., 6:340-42.
57. James Monroe to Thomas Posey, 11 March 1792, Thomas Posey Papers, IHS.
58. James Monroe to Major John Thornton, 12 August 1777, quoted in Harry Ammon, *James Monroe: The Quest for National Identity* (New York: McGraw-Hill, 1971), 16.
59. Col. B. Ball to Washington, 16 March 1792, *GW Papers—text-fiche—LC*, reel 122.
60. Ibid., Gen. William Weedon to Washington, 5 June 1792, reel 122.
61. Washington to Secretary of War Henry Knox, 1 August 1792, *The Writings of George Washington*, ed. John C. Fitzpatrick (Washington, DC: U.S. Government Printing Office, 1931-44), 32:103-5.
62. Ibid., 21 September 1792, 32:159-61.
63. Thomas Posey to George Washington, 10 October 1792, *The Papers of George Washington, Presidential Series*, eds. W.W. Abbot and Dorothy Twohig, 2 vols. to date (Charlottesville, VA: The University Press of Virginia, 1987-), unpublished volume.
64. Henry Knox to Thomas Posey, 1 March 1793; MS Certificate, War Department, 2 May 1793; Thomas Posey Papers, IHS.
65. Noel B. Gerson, *Lighthorse Harry* (Garden City, NY: Doubleday, 1966), 176.
66. Henry Lee to Thomas Posey, 12 March 1793, Thomas Posey Papers, IHS.
67. Washington to Knox, 5 April 1793, *Writings of Washington*, ed. Fitzpatrick, 32:407-8.
68. Thomas Posey to Cornplanter and New Arrow, 27 May 1793, Anthony Wayne Papers, Historical Society of Pennsylvania, Philadelphia, PA.
69. Knox to Posey, 10 April 1793, Thomas Posey Papers, IHS.

CHAPTER SIX

(1793-1800)

". . . a most amiable wife and sweet little family of children. . . ."

Brigadier-General Posey paused in the nation's capital of Philadelphia just long enough to purchase necessary personal supplies for a campaign in the field and to visit briefly with his friends in the Virginia congressional delegation. He paid a duty call on Secretary Knox at the War Department, where his 11 March 1793 commission was formally docketed.[1] Then he hurried along to Pittsburgh, and on to the army's winter quarters at Legionville, twenty-two miles west of that city. But he found the huge encampment all but deserted—on 30 April General Anthony Wayne had loaded his entire command aboard a fleet of barges, and embarked down the Ohio River, with Cincinnati as their destination.[2]

In the midst of making arrangements to follow the troops westward, Posey was approached by Chief Cornplanter and other emissaries of the Indian tribes of the northwest. Wayne had conferred with them prior to his departure, but had impatiently broken off further talks after finding them adamant in claiming for their peoples all lands north of the Ohio River. Now, visibly agitated by the army's embarkation, the Indians sought to reopen discussion of the territorial issue with Posey. He tried to soothe their concerns by pointing out that the national government had already sent three high commissioners to Sandusky, deep in Indian country, to make a final effort to negotiate a peaceful settlement of the dispute directly with top tribal chiefs. Pending the outcome of those talks, he assured them, the Legion was under military orders not to undertake any offensive operations. Furthermore, Thomas told the emissaries, President Washington had personally assured him of the administration's strong desire for peace, a sentiment which he personally and wholeheartedly shared:

> Brothers, peace is my great wish, and I expect I shall settle and live somewhere near to you in this western world. I shall always try to do my part towards keeping peace and good order which I wish may be as lasting as the streams and to spread over us like the warmth of the sun.[3]

The expected tedium of Posey's long passage down the river to join Wayne was pleasantly relieved by the company of two fellow-passengers: James Wilkinson, the Legion's designated senior brigadier-general, and his well-born wife, the former Ann Biddle of the Philadelphia Biddles. The convivial Wilkinson could always turn on the charm when it suited his purposes. He had already amassed a remarkable and not altogether admirable public record, and after this campaign he would go on to become one of the most enigmatic and controversial legends in early American history. But Thomas knew him only as a fellow soldier at Saratoga, where he had been General Horatio Gates' trusted aide-de-camp. The two veteran officers would maintain an intermittent and uneasy friendship for another quarter century after their current association in the Legion expedition. As the vessel carrying the two generals and their party neared Cincinnati, Wilkinson sent this note ahead to Wayne:

> I dispatched the barge to announce to you my approach after a long voyage—we expect to land this night, & will have the honor to see you in the morning—we are all in Health and quite fit for duty. Genl. Posey bears you large pacquets from the mountains. He begs his respects to you, in which my Ann very sincerely joins.
>
> Your truly Affectionate Friend and Serv't,
> Ja. Wilkinson[4]

Upon reporting for field duty on 8 June 1793, Brigadier-General Thomas Posey was immediately assigned to command a brigade of two regimental-sized sub-legions, composing one-half of the Legion army. General Wayne warmly welcomed the arrival and presence of his reliable old subordinate of Stony Point and Savannah. He needed all the help he could get in preparing his forces for the impending campaign. After landing his army at Cincinnati, the commander had found the moral climate of the little river port town too corrupt to maintain discipline among his troops. He moved them a few miles away to an isolated encampment he caustically named Hobson's Choice, signifying that it was the lesser of two evils. He was in the midst of implementing an innovative restructuring of his army. Instead of traditional infantry regiments and independent cavalry and artillery units, he divided his troops into four autonomous and self-contained sub-legions, each having its own integrated detachments of light infantry, artillery and mounted dragoons. The new configuration would have been ideal for the full 5,000-man army authorized by Congress, but during the entire Northwest expedition, Wayne's Legion never numbered more than 3,000 regulars, stretched thin among four under-strength sub-legions.[5]

As Posey had told Chief Cornplanter, Wayne was under strict orders to mount no offensive operations against the Indians pending the outcome of the peace commissioners' negotiations with the major tribes at Sandusky. The army busied itself with a rigorous training program initiated at Legionville, and pursued with vigor at Hobson's Choice and a string of fortified outposts north of Cincinnati. Daily exercises in target practice, trail-march discipline, and rigid nighttime security were designed to bring the troops to a high level of combat-readiness. In his training regimen, Wayne drew heavily upon Posey's military expertise and experience in Indian warfare. Thomas had never commanded anything larger than a battalion in the Revolution, but he had served under and learned much from the war's greatest generals—Washington, Lafayette, Greene, and of course, Wayne himself. Just as Posey, the former saddler, had soon developed into a capable company officer, he now moved with seeming ease into the role of brigade commander. But even as he capably executed his assigned military duties, Thomas soon found himself caught up in the middle of a vicious power struggle between Wayne and James Wilkinson who, as the senior brigadier, was second in command of the Legion.

Wilkinson had long coveted the top command of the army and, like Henry Lee, was bitterly disappointed when Wayne was selected to lead the Northwest Legion. From the time of his arrival in Cincinnati, he worked constantly to undermine Wayne's authority and destroy his reputation. As records subsequently revealed, he sent numerous secret dispatches directly to Secretary Knox and key congressional leaders, accusing Wayne of incompetence, drunkenness and cowardice. Within the Legion itself, he covertly fomented unrest among the officers, supporting a clique opposing Wayne, and at the same time harassing any officer under his authority who remained loyal to the Legion commander. Strangely, the usually thin-skinned and irascible Wayne appeared at first to be oblivious to Wilkinson's intrigue, or perhaps he simply chose to ignore it, since in any event he had no power to remove or curb his second-in-command.[6]

James Wilkinson's early career had been spectacular. Already a full colonel at age twenty, he was given the high honor of reporting the victory at Saratoga to the Continental Congress, but he tarried so long along the way that the great news had long preceded his arrival at Philadelphia. His early military luster dimmed when he was linked to the abortive "Conway Cabal" plot to displace George Washington as commander of the Revolutionary army. He later lost a high staff post as Clothier-General of the army when grave irregularities were found in his accounts. Retiring from the army at war's end and moving to the western frontier, he attracted widespread support in Kentucky by vigorously advocating that district's partition from Virginia and its eventual statehood in 1792. During this period he entered into a covert relationship with the Spanish governor of New Orleans, securing a monopoly of trade down the Mississippi River through that port city. In exchange, he promised to foster and encourage an abortive movement in Kentucky and Tennessee to separate those territories (later states) from the Union and annex them to adjacent Spanish possessions. Long after his death, official Spanish archives revealed him to have sworn secret allegiance to Spain, and to have been a longtime paid agent of that foreign power. But historians have never established if Wilkinson, as "Agent No. 13," was actually serious in his purported separatist activities. Some scholars have more plausibly concluded that he simply fabricated the elaborate schemes he reported to the Spanish governor, in order to deceive him into continuing the generous annual stipend he received in shiny gold pieces-of-eight. One of his contemporaries later said of him, that hard drinking was his vice, money his passion, and intrigue his avocation.[7] After reentering the regular army as a ranking brigadier general, he had ample occasion to indulge himself in all three of these profligate pursuits.

Thomas Posey was one of many deceived by the devious Wilkinson. He could, of course, know nothing of the dark side of his fellow general's character, and regarded him only as a worthy revolutionary veteran and a competent military officer, as indeed he usually proved to be. But at Hobson's Choice, Thomas must soon have become acutely uncomfortable with Wilkinson's thinly veiled efforts to undercut another old comrade for whom Posey had the utmost respect: their commander, Anthony Wayne. An early instance of such chicanery occurred when Captain Isaak Guion, an officer in Thomas' brigade who belonged to Wilkinson's coterie, formally petitioned Posey to bring charges of unsoldierly conduct against Captain Edward Butler. Butler, an aide-de-camp and personal protege of General Wayne, was the younger brother of Wayne's closest friend, Colonel Richard Butler, who had been killed during the Indian massacre of St. Clair's army in 1791. Sensing a conspiratorial motive behind Guion's charges, Posey curtly notified him that, since young Butler was Deputy Adjutant and Inspector General of the entire Legion, "your request to have that officer arrested will come more properly under the notice of the commander in chief." Wayne, of course, refused to consider the accusations against Butler, and later disciplined Captain Guion for filing them.[8]

Perhaps it was to curry Posey's favor in future such incidents that, a few days later, Wilkinson sent a friendly invitation to join him at Fort Hamilton, one of the fortified outposts north of Hobson's Choice. "We are here well quartered & living on pork, venison, fish, butter & eggs, with the trimmings, and would be happy could you with propriety participate our Humble fare."[9] It is not known if Thomas chose to join the Wilkinsons in partaking of this tempting menu. But as he became increasingly aware of James Wilkinson's motives, he made every effort to remain aloof from the internecine rivalries those motives inspired among the subordinate officers, while striving to retain the esteem of both his fellow generals. But charges and counter charges mounted among the officers partial to each general. Perhaps some of this activity can be written off as normal military politics, but Wilkinson seems to have stepped over the line. There is strong evidence that he may have tampered with the Legion's tenuous supply system, risking the success and safety of the expedition itself in order to disgrace Wayne in the eyes of the administration and congressional critics in Philadelphia.[10]

The summer months, the traditional and most favorable season for military campaigns, sped by without any word from the peace commissioners in Sandusky as to whether the critical issues with the Indians had been resolved. Failure of the talks would trigger immediate renewed hostilities. This was an outcome that the pugnacious Wayne devoutly desired and for which he had so carefully prepared, but each passing month progressively reduced his prospects of gaining a decisive victory. In the early spring, arrangements had been made to raise 1,500 mounted volunteer reinforcements from Kentucky, which had suffered much from repeated Indian incursions. But as time passed and harvest time approached without orders to mobilize and ride, enthusiasm in that usually militant state began to wane.

The designated commander of the Kentucky volunteers was militia General Charles Scott, a survivor of Harmar's and St. Clair's ill-fated expeditions, and Posey's former Virginia Revolutionary war comrade and friend. On 15 August Scott nervously wrote Thomas from Lexington:

> We have no news but what comes from Head quarters. I can only tell you that the Volunteers are more than Complete & extremely anxious to be called into Service. I tremble for fear that it may be so long Delayed that the fever will be over. For godsakes my friend write me by every opportunity.[11]

But it was not until 11 September that Wayne received the long-awaited word: the peace conference had collapsed. The Northwest tribes, armed and strongly influenced by British advisers from their forts along the lower Great Lakes, continued to insist that the American frontier be rolled back to the south bank of the Ohio River. The truce which had, with some lapses, been observed during the peace parley ended at once, as Indian raiding parties attacked supply trains and outposts throughout the vast territory they claimed as their own. But when Wayne sent out an urgent call for Scott's Kentucky volunteers, only 360 were immediately available; several weeks were required to mobilize and send forward the full complement of 1,500 men. The impatient Wayne, unwilling to wait for all of them to arrive, ordered that his regular units prepare for imminent departure. On 17 September General Posey, acting to fill numerous vacancies among the junior officers in his command, promoted twenty-three young men to the rank of ensign, determining by lottery the order of rank-priority each held to the others.[12] Untimely epidemics of influenza and ague, and inexplicable delays in bringing up needed supplies, caused Wayne to move back by several days his original march date. But on 7 October, with Posey riding at the head of his brigade, the Legion marched out of Hobson's Choice in full battle order, standards flying. Its mission: to seek out and destroy the waiting enemy, and restore American hegemony over the Northwest Territory.[13]

Moving carefully but efficiently along recently widened roads leading through a string of fortified outposts, the Legion progressed fifty miles in only six days. Passing Fort Jefferson, the most advanced position, it plunged into the deep forest beyond. Security measures planned and practiced during the long months of waiting were rigorously applied. Anthony Wayne was determined never again to be victimized by a surprise night attack as at Paoli and Sharon. A shoulder-high breastworks of logs and earth was constructed completely around each night's campsite, well-manned by a strong and vigilant guard. Every step of the advance was observed and noted by well-hidden Indian scouts, who reported to their chiefs that this was one white general who never slept. Well aware of the dangers of ambush along the line of march which had befallen Harmar and St. Clair, Wayne deployed strong dragoon detachments around the front, flanks and rear of his army as it slowly hacked its way through the thickly wooded forest. Night and day, the Legion was subjected to frequent harassing skirmishes, but Wayne was denied the ultimate confrontation with major Indian forces that he had hoped would bring him a decisive victory and complete control of the disputed territory during the 1793 campaign season.[14]

Incredibly, the ongoing strife between the factions of Legion officers loyal to Wayne and Wilkinson did not cease even during this perilous march into the wilderness. The commander had incurred the unrelenting enmity of Major Thomas H. Cushing by passing over him for promotion to a sub-legion command. Cushing, in turn, took up Captain Isaac Guion's old charges against Wayne aide Captain Edward Butler, but these were again summarily dismissed by General Wayne. Next, Captain Robert Mis Campbell, commander of Legion dragoons and a Wayne protege, retaliated against Cushing on 13 October by petitioning General Posey to arrest the major for "interfering with my command of the third troop of dragoons."[15] Thomas, again correctly identifying the complaint as just another salvo in the Wayne-Wilkinson feud, bucked it up to the Legion commander, who predictably ordered Cushing's immediate arrest.[16]

The Legion's advance ground to a halt some distance beyond Fort Jefferson with a breakdown in its supply system. The army's civilian supply contractors consistently failed to move food and other vital stores north along the line of march from Fort Washington, the Legion's supply base at Cincinnati. As winter approached, it became increasingly clear that the Indians were not going to commit their main forces to a showdown battle. The army's secondary objective, destruction of the main villages of the Miami Indian tribes on the Maumee River, would require further stretching of the already overextended supply line. On 31 October, Wayne called a formal council of war, attended by Wilkinson, Posey and Charles

Scott, along with two other Kentucky militia generals, Robert Todd and Thomas Barbee.

Wayne submitted to his fellow general for consideration a detailed plan to construct a strong permanent military installation at the army's present location, to serve as winter quarters and a base for renewed advances in the spring. After a full discussion, all those present verbally approved Wayne's proposal, and later, at his request, submitted their written opinions. Thomas Posey's concurrence cited the inadequacy of food, forage and winter clothing, and an acute shortage of company-grade officers in many units of the army, as the major grounds for his "decided opinion that under the present existing circumstances and situation of the Legion, a *stand* should be made at this place."[17]

The entire army, under close supervision and prodding from its top officers, set to work immediately. It constructed an impregnable stockade enclosing fifty acres of high ground above a small stream, designed with strong bastions at each corner, upon which howitzers were emplaced covering all approaches to the fort. Inside, wooden huts similar to those which sheltered revolutionary soldiers at Valley Forge were built for the rank-and-file. More solid structures were erected for officers' quarters, mess halls, and storage of food, forage, and arms. Standing defiantly in the midst of a hostile wilderness, the new installation was named Fort Greeneville (now Greenville, Ohio), in honor of a man greatly admired by both Wayne and Posey: General Nathanael Greene, former commander of the Southern Army in the Revolution. From the completed fort, strong mounted patrols were regularly sent out into the surrounding countryside to detect any major activity by the Indian enemy. Wayne also sent heavily armed detachments back to Fort Washington, to speed up the dispatch of laggard provision trains along the line of outposts and to escort them safely through Fort Greeneville's sturdy gates.[18]

In early December, with the Legion securely winter-quartered and no prospect of any major military operations until spring, Posey applied to General Wayne for permission to return home to Virginia to visit his family. The commander was at this time in almost constant discomfort from gout and other assorted ailments, frustrated over the prolongation of the campaign, and increasingly paranoid over disloyalty within his officer corps. Although he would sorely miss his trusted Virginia brigadier, he wrote a graceful and extraordinarily personal letter to Thomas granting his requested leave of absence. He stressed how "extremely necessary" Posey's aid and advice had been to him in the past months, and admitted that "friendship may have prevailed over duty" in his decision to approve his departure. Wayne could only "regret the temporary absence of a friend and brother officer with whom I have participated in almost every vicissitude of fortune from the frozen lakes of Canada to the burning sands of Florida."[19]

The embattled commander was clearly sorry that he would not have his old Revolutionary War comrade at his side in Fort Greeneville during the winter. But he perceived that Posey's visit to the east provided an opportunity to present a defense of his command decisions to the administration and congressional critics, as well as to lobby for support in bringing Legion ranks up to full strength:

> I pray you to make a point of impressing every member of Congress with whom you may converse with the absolute necessity of the immediate completion of the Legion, and that you also pay a visit to the seat of government, and wait personally upon the President and Secretary of War, and give them every information, vive voce, that they may wish to receive relative to the situation of the Legion, together with the motives and circumstances which influenced an advance and halt at this place.[20]

Wayne had now plainly become aware of the flood of secret letters and reports reaching the capital castigating his character and military abilities, although he might not have known the identity of all of his critics. He saw in Thomas Posey a loyal and respected general officer, personally known to the president and leading congressional figures, whose testimony might largely negate the criticism which he feared could lead to the loss of his command. Interestingly, Posey's last official act before riding out of Fort Greeneville on 3 December involved one of those secret critics, the disgruntled Major Thomas Cushing. The major's court martial on charges of insubordination was approaching, and he had applied to Thomas to have the trial transferred from Fort Greeneville to Fort Washington, where he obviously felt his prospects for exoneration were brighter. It was Posey's duty to notify Cushing that General Wayne had denied his petition for a change of venue.[21] The major, however, remained in the Legion, and over the next year sent to members of Congress and other influential officials a flood of messages vilifying Wayne, some of which were anonymously published in leading journals.[22]

When Posey reached Fort Washington, he paused to write a warm response to Wayne's "polite, friendly and much esteemed letter" granting him home leave. He stressed that "nothing but business of the most commendable import, added to the extreme anxiety I had to see an amiable wife, and several small children," had induced him to seek a furlough. He assured the commander that he understood the importance of the mission Wayne had entrusted to him, to confer with President Washington, Secretary Knox, and congressional leaders, and he promised that those duties "shall be duly attended to." He would, he said, use all his abilities and influence for the good of the country, the welfare of the army and, particularly, "the support of my commanding officer. I shall make it a point to contradict misrepresentations, and exaggerated accounts, which may be mentioned either before me, or in circulation."[23]

Thomas also took the occasion to give Wayne a warning that he probably had not been prepared to discuss face to face with his commander:

> I am aware that you are not without your enemies who will be ready to lay hold of, and take advantage of every mishap. indeed some whom you hold friendly inclined towards you, I have some reason to believe may endeavor to insinuate and place many of your operations in such a point of view, as to mislead the populace, and prejudice government, but be that as it may truth will ultimately preponderate.[24]

Intrigue was utterly foreign to the nature of Thomas Posey. He nonetheless was the prisoner of his own code of honor and sense of acceptable behavior. Under the obviously painful and delicate circumstances in which he found himself, loyalty and concern for his commanding officer clearly won out over his ties of comradeship with James Wilkinson; although not to the point of expressly identifying him as the hidden enemy Anthony Wayne held to be "friendly inclined."

While at Fort Washington, Posey tried, with some success, to energize the laggard army supply contractors, Elliott and Williams, into speeding late deliveries of provisions to Fort Greeneville and its intermediate outposts. He informed Wayne in a 10 December letter that four boat loads of flour and salt (for curing meat) had just been dispatched up the Miami River, and that 400 hogs and cattle would shortly be herded up the overland trail, protected by a strong mounted escort which had recently arrived at the supply base. Thomas had originally planned to travel east on a pacquet boat upstream along the Ohio River to Pittsburgh. He changed his mind after recently arrived visitors from that city described the painfully slow progress previous vessels, powered only by sail and oarsmen, were making against the strong downstream current. He decided to go directly home by the longer but more reliable (if more dangerous) land route southward through Kentucky and the Cumberland Gap into southwestern Virginia.[25]

Four days later, Posey wrote to General Wayne again, this time from the Legion's cavalry camp ten miles south of Lexington, Kentucky. He reported that the horses and stables there were in reasonably good condition, despite having recurrent problems with the supply contractors. Thomas arranged to be escorted by a seven-man dragoon detachment along the next segment of the Wilderness Road. No solitary traveler could expect to survive marauding gangs of highwaymen or random Indian raiders lurking along the narrow forest trails and remote mountain passes of this historic frontier byway. Thomas Posey was a brave man, but he was not a fool. He intended to send his escorts back to their post if they overtook a larger traveling party along the way.

Thomas also used his letter to alert Wayne to some alarming recent news from the east. There was a possibility that war with Great Britain was imminent, due to that nation's continued impressment of American seamen on the high seas. This was a recurrent problem that would plague the fledgling republic for the next two decades. "The President . . . has directed the minister at the court of London to demand that a reparation should be immediately made and that the American Flag could no longer be insulted with impunity should such daring outrages be any longer practised."[26]

Seven weeks after Posey's departure from Fort Greeneville, General Wayne sent him a long, detailed report describing the Legion's recent operations and adventures. There had been several sharp skirmishes between Indians and Wayne's scouting parties, but no major battles. The most notable event had been the reoccupation by a large American detachment of the tragic site of General St. Clair's 1791 defeat. The troops had interred the mutilated remains of the massacred soldiers which had lain unburied there for over two years, and then erected over their graves a fortified strong point symbolically called Fort Recovery. The new outpost was the closest advance made by the Legion to the main villages of the Miami tribes, and within a short time, a tentative peace overture arrived from some of those tribes. Wayne felt that it was only a ruse "to insiduously gain time, in order to secure their provisions & to remove their women and children from pending destruction." In any event, the skeptical commander observed, "time will soon discover the sincerity or perfidy of their hearts."[27]

General Wayne, having fully briefed Posey on the current status of the Legion, then asked him to hurry back to duty, stating somewhat wistfully,

> In the interior here I am without an officer of rank or experience to aid or advise me. Genl. Wilkinson has been all winter at Jefferson with his Lady whose delicate situation requires his presence. Colo. Hamtramck has gone to Post Vincents—Colo. Strong to Fort Washington & yourself to the Ancient Dominion. I must therefore request you to return the soonest possible.[28]

During the intervening weeks, Thomas had not been idle in promoting the interests of the Legion and its isolated commander. He had arrived safely at his Greenwood home and been joyfully reunited with his wife and children. True to his promise, he then journeyed to Philadelphia to deliver a first-hand report of the army's march and present posture to the president and secretary of war. He also tried to dispel the denunciations of Wayne with which General Wilkinson and other disaffected Legion officers had bombarded the capital. There is every evidence that Posey's efforts were well received. Despite all adverse reports, Washington and Knox, throughout the entire Northwest campaign, never lost their faith and confidence in the Legion commander. Wayne was harshly criticized in a 6 January 1794 debate in the House of Representatives. But that body also voted to increase the pay and ration allowances of the Legionnaires, and to award future land grants to the soldiers whose lives were then on the line in the wilderness of the Northwest Territory.[29]

Posey reported his exertions on behalf of the Legion in a letter to General Wayne dated 20 February: "I have used all the influence I was master of to promote an additional pay and a bounty of lands for the soldiery." He also passed along to the Legion commander the latest news gleaned during his recent sojourn at the seat of government concerning the precarious state of relations between the United States and the two major European powers. "Matters in the affairs of France wears a bright prospect; and Great Britain appears more and more the mortal enemy of America."[30] This would come as no great surprise to Wayne, who was at that very moment eyeball-to-eyeball with a hostile Indian confederation which had been instigated and partially armed by agents of that same unfriendly foreign foe. Those representatives of the Crown, mostly military officers, were operating from the Great Lakes forts they continued to occupy contrary to the express terms of the Treaty of Paris.

Wayne undoubtedly took in stride the news of these foreign provocations, but it is likely that the embattled and lonely old Legion commander was more surprised and dismayed by word in Posey's letter of a personal decision the Virginian had recently made concerning his future in the military:

> Finding it impossible to continue any longer in the Army without rendering a most amiable wife and sweet little family of children extremely miserable I have this day enclosed to the Secretary of War my resignation.[31]

Thomas Posey's devotion to his children is well documented. His 1791 letter seeking a federal appointment from President Washington graphically expressed his determination to give his growing family a proper education.[32] Now, by February of 1794, Thomas and Mary had six children at Greenwood under ten years of age, (and, unknown to him at the time, another on the way). Virtually all of their modest estate was earmarked for distribution to Mary's three older Thornton children, the eldest of whom was now nearing legal age. Death in combat with the Legion, however glorious, would have been a total emotional and financial disaster for his wife and young dependents.

There is no reason to doubt that Thomas deeply loved his family. He was neither ashamed nor deterred by male machismo from frankly telling the hard-bitten and decidedly unsentimental Wayne that he was giving up his coveted commission to spare his "most amiable wife and sweet little family of children" from the misery of his further absence and possible death in battle. This deep familial affection and concern would continue throughout Posey's life. A highly regarded biographer of Washington described Thomas Posey as having been "six feet, two inches high, with light brown hair and blue eyes, and so powerfully built that he killed several men with his own sword in battles."[33] This huge and powerful man, so dangerous and deadly in mortal combat with his enemies, was, in his family relationships, a blue-eyed and fair-haired, but clearly a gentle, giant.

Posey's difficult decision to retire from the army was undoubtedly reinforced by considerations other than his family responsibilities. His old friend, Governor Henry Lee, who earlier had so feared that "we are to loose you, perhaps for ever," hearing now that Thomas was home on leave, had written: "Tell me how you do, whether you return . . . how comes it that so many reports circulate discrediting G. Wayne, especially that his officers are all leaving him."[34] Lee's question underscores the undeniable fact that service under Wayne, even for one staunchly loyal to the Legion commander, had grown increasingly difficult. The general, in constant pain from gout and intestinal ills, his plans for a decisive summer campaign gone awry, and alienated by factionalism among his officers and anonymous attacks in the press, had become unreasonable and almost irrational in dealing with his subordinates. Even the faithful Colonel John Hamtramck, leader of the First Sub-Legion under General Posey, (and eventual successor as commander of his brigade), exclaimed after an undeserved dressing-down from Wayne: "There is no doubt about it, the old man is really mad."[35]

"Mad Anthony" Wayne had never been a man to suffer fools gladly. Early in his military career he had acquired a well-earned reputation as the most profane and prodigious swearer among the general officers of the Revolutionary army. One of his junior officers described an incident in which Wayne, "finding no sentry . . . damned all our souls to hell, and immediately ordered two by night and one by day, which I immediately put in execution—but shall not forget his damns, which he is very apt to bestow upon people; but my great consolation is, that the power thereof is not in his hands, blessed be God for it."[36] During the 1782 Georgia campaign, Wayne had undoubtedly directed some of his choicest "damns" at Lieutenant Colonel Thomas Posey after finding that he had captured twelve Creek "savages" in the aftermath of Chief Guristersigo's attack on the American camp outside Savannah. But the record discloses no evidence of any personal friction or confrontation between Wayne and Posey during the Northwest expedition, and their friendly, almost affectionate, exchange of letters when Thomas left Fort Greeneville strongly argues to the contrary. In all likelihood, Posey was one of the few regular officers in the Legion who managed to retain the beleaguered commander's complete trust, and Thomas' continued respect and admiration for the increasingly fractious Wayne is evident and undeniable.

Back in the quiet serenity of Greenwood, however, Thomas had ample opportunity to give intense and objective consideration to the venomous atmosphere in the Legion's officer corps. He may simply have concluded that the bitter rivalry between Wayne and Wilkinson compromised his own position as third-ranking officer in the command, seriously impairing his ability to lead the brigade for which he was personally responsible. He surely did not fear doing battle with the enemy. On the contrary, there is every evidence in his past and future record of avid eagerness to serve his country in an active combat role. One final circumstance places the motives for resigning his commission in the most honorable and acceptable light. His nineteen-year-old son John was at this very time serving at Fort Greeneville as a cornet (later captain) of dragoons. Only the most compelling and unimpeachable reasons would have kept Thomas from the side of his oldest son in the impending battle for control of the Northwest.[37]

Young Cornet John Posey did indeed ride to glory with the Legion cavalry on 20 August 1794, when General Wayne's forces decisively defeated the Miami Indian tribes at the Battle of Fallen Timbers, near present-day Toledo, Ohio. The dragoons mounted an all-out charge against the enemy's left flank, forcing them to withdraw in disorder, although Captain Robert Mis Campbell, the dragoon commander, was mortally wounded during the attack. General James Wilkinson, to his credit, led his right wing bravely and effectively, while Thomas Posey's old brigade, under Colonel Hamtramck, fought equally well on the left. General Charles Scott's Kentucky mounted volunteers, who had returned home during the winter and been recalled in the spring, executed an encircling movement around the Indians' right flank which hastened their withdrawal from the tree-cluttered battlefield. The commander of the nearby British fort refused to open his gates to give refuge to the fleeing Indians.[38] The victory secured the American frontier and extended its borders for further expansion into the northwest, a movement in which the civilian Thomas Posey was later destined to play a notable part.

Wayne, despite all obstacles and internal disruptions, had conducted a flawlessly prudent and professional expedition, and thus refuted for all time his sobriquet as an impetuous and reckless "Mad Anthony." But even the victory did not end increasingly open attacks upon his character and military skills. When Congress convened in December to award the customary battle honors and commendations, Wayne's name was inexplicably stricken from the congratulatory resolution before its unanimous passage. The bemedaled hero of Stony Point had somehow become the pariah of the Northwest campaign. Shrugging off this incredible slight, Wayne went on to cap his singular contribution to his young country by negotiating the Treaty of Fort Greeneville. Signed on 3 August 1795, it opened up most of Ohio and a large part of Indiana to immediate settlement. After taking peaceful possession of all British-occupied forts in the lower Great Lakes, Wayne began the long journey homeward after nearly four years of continuous service in the west, only to die along the way, at Presque Isle (now Erie, Pennsylvania) on 15 December 1796.[39]

There probably were times when the soldierly instincts embedded in Thomas Posey's soul regretted the circumstances which had precluded his participation in the Battle of Fallen Timbers. After retiring from the army, however, he quickly resumed his active civilian, spousal and paternal roles at Greenwood. Although he had long expressed a desire to relocate to the western frontier, it was to take another full decade to finally complete that monumental undertaking. It was first necessary to shift some resources. Within months of leaving the Legion, the Poseys' property "Sligo," located just outside Fredericksburg, was sold for £1250 to George Washington's kinsman, John Lewis.[40] The old Main Street residence in Fincastle was disposed of a year later.[41] From the proceeds of these sales, Thomas made his first outright purchase of western land, also from John Lewis: two tracts in the Kentucky counties of Jefferson and Shelby, "on Crooke's Run, a branch of Floyd's Fork," at a cost of £1445. Two additional Kentucky tracts were acquired in 1797, and another in 1802.[42]

During the late 1790s, Posey made several trips of varying length to Kentucky to examine these and other prospective home sites, but the family continued to live and multiply at Greenwood until 1802. All nine of Thomas and Mary's children were born there. Along with Mary's three Thornton offspring, they comprised a large and formidable circle around the family dinner table presided over by the courtly retired general and his stately wife. The fold was completed when Thomas' oldest son, Captain John Posey, who remained in the Legion long enough to witness the solemn signing of Anthony Wayne's Treaty of Fort Greeneville, resigned his army commission on 19 October 1795 and returned to Virginia.[43]

While mulling over the homestead options available to him in Kentucky, Thomas heard that a federal land office was soon to be opened to handle settlement in the newly created Northwest Territory. Having become thoroughly familiar with the area during his Legion service, Posey thought that he might qualify for the position. He wrote his congressman, James Madison, asking him to "mention me to the President as a candidate for the appointment." He assured Madison, who was apparently aware of his plans to remove to the west, that "had I any reason to suppose that I could get the appointment I would immediately arrange my business in such a manner as to settle on the Northwest side of the Ohio instead of Kentucky."[44]

Posey, having few real qualifications for the position, did not get the appointment, but this did not signify that he had lost the respect and regard of George Washington. In the following year (1796), he was among several prominent Virginians asked by the president to recommend prospective sites on which to found a planned new state university. Thomas submitted three possible locations, all in the Shenandoah Valley area of his young manhood—Staunton, Fincastle and Lexington. Interestingly, he strongly advised against the selection of a competing site, Charlottesville, a small town which was fortuitously situated near "Monticello," the elegant home of Thomas Jefferson. The eventual founding of the University of Virginia in that location clearly evidences the well-deserved predominance of Jefferson's influence over all others in arriving at the final choice.[45]

Within a few months, Posey was among several retired army officers under consideration by the president for the post of Surveyor General. Washington asked John Marshall for his evaluation of the qualifications of Posey and other Virginians who had been proposed as prospects for the job. The president stressed that the position required a combination of "mathematical knowledge (which should extend beyond common Surveying)," plus "integrity to resist the temptation which opportunities, and an overweening fondness for speculation in Lands, may throw in his way."[46] Washington knew whereof he spoke—from the time he was a seventeen-year-old surveyor, he himself had always demonstrated more than a mild interest in land speculation. As for Thomas Posey, he clearly met every test of character and integrity, but even his good friend Marshall could hardly have suggested that he had the professional qualifications the post demanded, and it properly went elsewhere.

During one of his early land-inspection trips to Kentucky, Posey had spent some time in Frankfort, the state capital, and entered into a partnership there with two local citizens, John Logan and Baker Ewing, to operate a mercantile establishment under the name "Thomas Posey & Co." Apart from his youthful saddlery shop, this appears to have been Thomas' only commercial enterprise. Little is known of the details or nature of this business. In all likelihood, Posey provided all or most of the venture capital, while Logan and Ewing were to be its local operating partners. Somewhat predictably, the budding business failed, probably because of Thomas' prolonged absences from the state. The partnership was formally dissolved on 1 April 1797, and Thomas sent his son John to Frankfort to represent his interests in winding up the affairs of the ill-fated enterprise. All its debtors were publicly notified to settle up their accounts with either John Posey or Baker Ewing.[47]

Perhaps not coincidentally, the floundering of the Kentucky business was occurring while Thomas Posey's time and energies were fully engaged in Virginia by his first venture into major electoral politics. Congressman James Madison had chosen to retire from his seat in the district which encompassed Spotsylvania County, and early in 1797 Thomas announced his candidacy for the vacant post. His subsequent failure to win this high office can best be understood only in the context of the rapidly developing political climate of the United States during the first decade of its existence.

Richard Buel, Jr., has written a penetrating study of the formation and development of America's first party system in the 1790s. The leading figures in the new national government, most of whom had supported the adoption of the federal constitution, literally abhorred the concept of political partyism or factionalism. They were confident that a constitutional republic could best be governed by a single broad popular consensus. Curiously, however, basic differences arose almost immediately over the proper means to be employed in implementing the shining promises of the Revolution. The split is reflected most dramatically in President Washington's first cabinet. Treasury Secretary Alexander Hamilton conceived a bold program to create a central bank, fund the entire national debt, and assume the state governments' Continental obligations. These key measures met with immediate opposition from Secretary of State Thomas Jefferson and his chief congressional ally, James Madison. A deep philosophical division soon arose over many other domestic issues, and was exacerbated by an equally bitter split over the foreign policy of the infant nation. Two coalitions, broadly labeled federalist and republican, emerged. They came into existence on purely ideological issues. Unlike later political parties, they were not originally formed to promote or support the election of individuals or groups to public office.[48]

The Federalists, in general, favored a strong central government with extensive fiscal and tax powers, protective tariffs, maintenance of a national military force, and relatively broader executive over congressional authority. The Republicans were suspicious of centralized power in all its manifestations. They wanted a national government more responsive and accountable to the individual states and the people, enforced through the narrow construction of its constitutional authority. They saw federal fiscal powers as a threat to their agrarian constituency, and a national army as a danger to state autonomy. In foreign affairs, the Republicans, viewing the French Revolution as a continuation of the New World wave of democratic government, favored close diplomatic ties with France, despite that nation's later revolutionary excesses and devolution into military despotism. The Federalists took a more neutral or even-handed stance among the continually warring European powers, thus becoming vulnerable to charges of favoring alliance or reunion with Great Britain—a goal said to be consistent with their perceived aristocratic or monarchical biases. In time, the distrust of some extreme Federalists, including Hamilton, in the durability of popular government partially vindicated republican suspicions of elitism and autocratic tendencies.[49]

President George Washington strove constantly to stand above the evolving partisan strife. His own personal policy decisions appeared to tilt toward a mild federalist persuasion, but in his public speeches and Farewell Address he deplored political party affiliation and expressly warned the nation against "the Spirit of Party."[50] Washington's vice-president, John Adams, who succeeded to the presidency in early 1797, was also considered to be a moderate Federalist, but his vice-president and successor Thomas Jefferson was, of course, the founder and leader of the national republican faction.

By the time of the 1797 Virginia congressional race, these ideological divisions were well-defined and pervasive, if not highly organized. There were strong enclaves of federalist support in the Northern Neck and the Shenandoah Valley, where Thomas Posey had his roots, but overall the state, and particularly his central Piedmont district, was overwhelmingly republican.[51] Significantly, even before the contending political philosophies solidified into formal party organizations or caucuses, Posey was already identified in public perception as espousing fundamentally federalist sentiments. Unlike his two closest Virginia friends, Henry Lee and John Marshall, who were early and lifelong leaders of the federal party, Posey at no time in his life either claimed to be, or admitted to being, a card-carrying Federalist. But as early as 1797, local republican partisans clearly deemed him unacceptable to fill the congressional seat of their temporarily retired leader, James Madison. They threw their backing to Madison's political ally, John Dawson, and he decisively defeated Posey in all four counties of the district.[52] It was the first, but far from the last, occasion that Thomas' deeply felt support for the strong national institutions he had fought so hard to bring into existence would prove to be his political undoing.

With his immediate hopes of elective office in Virginia dashed, Posey revived his interest in Kentucky, and later in 1797 he again visited that rapidly-growing state to lay new groundwork for his long-deferred move to the west. On this trip he also performed a valuable service for his old neighbor and commander, George Washington, who had now retired to his cherished Mount Vernon, but had not lost his keen interest in western land investment. Alexander Spottswood of Spotsylvania County, who handled many business matters for the former president, had asked Posey's assistance, while in Kentucky, in obtaining documentation needed to clarify warrants held by Washington on certain lands lying on Rough Creek. This stream emptied into the Green River, a major tributary of the Ohio in western Kentucky.[53]

A few months later, Washington asked Spottswood to thank General Posey for bringing back from Kentucky the plats and surveys needed to validate title to his Rough Creek land holdings.[54] Two years earlier, Posey had filed military land claims on 1,200 acres in Bourbon County, 2,000 acres in Logan County, and 2,000 acres in Jefferson County, all located in the central region of Kentucky.[55] But interestingly, it was near the Green River in the western area of the state, not far removed from Washington's Rough Creek holdings, that Thomas eventually selected as the site for his new home on the western frontier.

For reasons not clear from surviving correspondence and records, another four years passed before Posey finally moved his family to Kentucky. In the interim, his two youngest children were born, and he received another federal appointment. In 1798 President Adams named him the United States Commissioner for the 11th District of Virginia to oversee an enumeration of slaves and evaluation of property mandated by Congress.[56] Earlier in that year, on 25 January, a happy family event took place, one which must have brought great personal satisfaction to both Thomas and Mary Posey. His oldest son John, and her daughter Lucy Frances Thornton, were married by the Rev. James Stephenson at Fredericksburg's St. George's Parish, the scene of their parents' earlier marriage. The young couple, with the probable assistance of Lucy's Thornton legacy, settled down on a beautiful farm near Lexington in the Shenandoah Valley, not far from where John had lived as a boy while his father was away at war.[57]

Thomas continued to buy and sell small tracts of land in Kentucky. He does not appear to have profited greatly in these early speculations, and the difficulty in obtaining and proving clear title to property in the state may actually have caused him losses, or at least unduly tied up his limited venture capital. In one 1798 transaction, Harry Innes, a federal judge in Frankfort, drew a £300 draft on Posey, presumably covering a debt for the purchase of property, or possibly liquidating obligations of the defunct "Thomas Posey & Co."[58] Innes was, incidentally, the jurist who was later to preside over historic conspiracy charges against former Vice-President Aaron Burr—a drama in which Thomas Posey was to play a role, seemingly minor, but one which severely damaged his future political prospects in Kentucky.

On a broader stage, the series of grave crises between the United States and the two warring European powers, Great Britain and France, continued through the critical decade of the 1790s. Each country, seeking to enforce a sea blockade against the other, committed repeated depredations against American shipping. Posey's friend John Marshall was one of three special commissioners sent to France by President Adams to negotiate the dispute. These emissaries were insulted and humiliated by agents of Talleyrand, the French Foreign Minister, who demanded bribes, loans, and a personal apology from the American president before he would receive them. When reports of this shameful incident—known as the XYZ Affair—reached the United States, a wave of anti-French feeling swept over the country, temporarily reversing the pro-French Republican party's growing strength and political advantage over the federalists.[59]

This revulsion was so strong that, had these events occurred a year earlier, Posey would probably have been elected to Congress from Virginia. But his defeat had not lessened Thomas' intense interest in national affairs. When John Marshall returned from Europe, he wrote Posey a long, analytical letter outlining his own views on American foreign policy. During and after the Revolution, Marshall asserted, the actions of Great Britain and France had been dictated solely by their own national self-interests, rather than any particular concern for the emerging new nation. America, Marshall reasoned, should likewise set its own course on the same principle of enlightened self-interest. It should deal impartially with both of the two major world powers, not, as republicans advocated, view one antagonist (France) as an historical friend and benefactor while treating the other (Britain) as a traditional and implacable enemy. Long-term national interests, the future Chief Justice argued, were not irrevocably or permanently linked by allegiance to any European power.[60] Marshall's pragmatic view, so closely reflecting the policy eloquently recommended to the nation in President George Washington's Farewell Address in 1796,[61] was clearly shared by their fellow Virginian, Thomas Posey.

But sea-borne outrages by both warring countries against American shipping continued. To meet the perceived threat of war with one or the other foreign power, President Adams in 1798 commissioned George Washington a lieutenant general, with authority to organize and command a new national army. The following spring, Secretary of War James McHenry forwarded to General Washington the names of three Spotsylvania militia officers who had been recommended by their local commander, Thomas Posey, for commissions in the new army. One was Thomas Hord, described as "very much wounded and cut to pieces in Burgoyne's defeat"—obviously, one of Posey's old Rifle Regiment comrades who had fought at his side at Saratoga.[62] Thomas himself was prominently mentioned for a high command in the new force; John Marshall recommended him to Washington for a brigadier general's commission. But Posey, fully engrossed in his preparations to remove to the frontier, apparently did not actively seek the appointment, and was not seriously considered by Washington for a military position.[63]

Even as the century drew to a close late in 1799, Posey, after nearly a decade of intermittent planning and commitment to Kentucky as the future home of his family, seemed to be wavering in that choice. His attention had momentarily shifted to the vast area north of the Ohio River recently opened to settlement by the terms of Anthony Wayne's Treaty of Fort Greeneville. On 19 November, the newly constituted legislature of the Northwest Territory took up for consideration,

> A memorial of Thomas Posey, on behalf of himself and several officers and soldiers of the Virginia line . . . praying that an act may be passed authorizing persons holding slaves under the laws of the State in which they acquire that species of property, and removing into this Territory, to bring their slaves with them, under certain restrictions.[64]

When the Northwest Territory was created by the federal Ordinance of 1787, Article VI clearly forbade the buying or selling of slaves within its borders. But left unresolved or subject to interpretation was the legal status of slaves which had been legally acquired in other states, and then brought into the Territory.[65] The issue was of vital economic importance to every slave-owning Virginian contemplating emigration to the frontier. Next to land, slaves composed the bulk of the wealth of such settlers, and the loss of this substantial asset by operation of law or unfavorable construction of the ordinance would have been devastating.

Nowhere in his letters or papers is there any clear expression of Thomas Posey's personal view of the practice of human slavery. The institution itself was the greatest and most damning contradiction of the revolutionary ideal of equality and freedom for all—a concept for which Posey and his contemporaries had risked their lives, honor, and fortunes. But Thomas and his fellow Virginia veterans were the products and lifelong clients of a culture and economy which had its foundations in, and drew its sustenance from, a system of enforced human bondage. This incongruity between principle and practice is logically irreconcilable, although it may not be entirely fair to judge any eighteenth-century man by twentieth-century standards. It is quite likely that Posey, like George Washington, Thomas Jefferson, Patrick Henry and many other enlightened slave-owning Virginians, privately conceded the intrinsic immorality of slavery, but feared that its sudden or forced abolition would create utter chaos and the total collapse of a society they had inherited—the only one they had ever known or could envision.[66]

Later in life Posey would choose to renounce slavery and dispose of all of his personally owned slaves. But this action, admittedly taken more for practical and political than altruistic reasons, cannot be fairly judged as an accurate reflection of his personal philosophy, even though it coincided with a remarkable intensification of religious convictions. In 1799, facing an imminent and fearsome move to the west, he was simply unable to visualize a future for himself and his family without the use and support of the dozens of enslaved domestic and farm workers upon whose skills and backs Greenwood's comfortable existence had been maintained. It was a lifestyle that Posey, at the time, had every intention of pursuing, wherever he settled on the frontier.

When the Northwest Territory legislature failed to act favorably upon his petition to be allowed to bring his work force into the area under authority of law, it only reaffirmed Posey's earlier decision to make Kentucky, a slave state, the future home of his household. For the same reason, many other emigrants from Virginia and other eastern slave states rejected the territories and states of the Northwest as their destination of choice. As a consequence, immigration into that immense area flowed largely from free northern states. This created a growing anti-slavery majority in the region, a demographic reality that would later jeopardize Thomas Posey's political career in the emerging state of Indiana. More importantly, its ultimate effect would be felt in the then-distant great national conflict which would resolve once and for all the deeply troubling issue of slavery.

The momentous and historic century ended on a sad and somber note. On 14 December 1799, 67-year-old George Washington, the "first of men" and preeminent figure of his era, died of a respiratory infection, contracted after a five-hour ride around his beloved farms in snow, sleet, and a cold, steady rain. Four days later, he was interred at Mount Vernon, after a solemn military funeral attended by a multitude of mourners.[67] Although the record is silent, it is reasonable to believe that Thomas Posey, only one day's hard ride away in Spotsylvania County, was in that grieving throng, tearfully honoring the man who had played such a dominant role during the entire fifty years of his own life. It is even possible that Posey marched in the funeral cortege itself. Although not one of the official pallbearers from Alexandria's masonic lodge, as a prominent member of Washington's mother lodge in Fredericksburg, Thomas may have been one of the "Masonic brethern" following immediately behind family members and close associates, as they escorted the fallen master of Mount Vernon to his simple tomb on a slope looking down upon the massive Potomac River below.[68]

NOTES

1. War Department Certificate, docketed 2 May 1793, effective 11 March 1793, Thomas Posey Papers, Indiana Historical Society Library, Indianapolis, IN (hereafter cited as IHS).
2. Harry Emerson Wildes, *Anthony Wayne: Trouble Shooter of the American Revolution*, 2nd ed. (Westport, CT: Greenwood Press, 1969), 381.
3. Thomas Posey to Cornplanter and New Arrow, 27 May 1793, Anthony Wayne Papers, Historical Society of Pennsylvania, Philadelphia, PA (hereafter cited as HSP).
4. James Wilkinson to Anthony Wayne, 7 June 1793, Northwest Territory Collection, IHS.
5. Paul David Nelson, *Anthony Wayne: Soldier of the Early Republic* (Bloomington, IN: Indiana University Press, 1985), 240-42.
6. Ibid., 252-53; Wildes, *Wayne*, 386-87.
7. *Dictionary of American Biography*, 1963 ed., s.v. "Wilkinson, James," 10:222-26. On Wilkinson generally, see: Thomas R. Hay and Morris R. Werner, *The Admirable Trumpter* (New York: Doubleday, 1941); Royal Ornan Shreve, *The Finished Scoundrel* (New York: Bobs-Merrill, 1933); John Edward Weems, *Men Without Countries* (Boston: Houghton Mifflin Co., 1969); James R. Jacobs, *Tarnished Warrior: Major General James Wilkinson* (New York: Ayer Co. Publishers, 1938).
8. Posey to Captain Isaac Guion, 5 July 1793, Wayne Papers, HSP.
9. Wilkinson to Posey, 14 July 1793, Thomas Posey Papers, IHS.
10. Wildes, *Wayne*, 388-90, 401.
11. Charles Scott to Posey, 15 August 1793, Thomas Posey Papers, IHS.

12. Order of B. Genl. Thomas Posey, 17 September 1793, Wayne Papers, HSP.
13. Wildes, *Wayne*, 396-98.
14. Ibid., 398-99; Nelson, *Wayne*, 245-46.
15. Robert Mis Campbell to Posey, 13 October 1793, Wayne Papers, HSP.
16. Wildes, *Wayne*, 390, 402-3; Nelson, *Wayne*, 250.
17. Posey to Wayne, 2 November 1793, Wayne Papers, HSP; Nelson, *Wayne*, 247.
18. Nelson, *Wayne*, 247-48; Wildes, *Wayne*, 399.
19. Wayne to Posey, 5 December 1793, quoted in William Wesley Woolen, "Thomas Posey," *Biographical and Historical Sketches of Early Indiana* (Indianapolis, IN: Hammond & Co., 1883), 24.
20. Ibid.
21. Posey to Cushing, 3 December 1793, Northwest Territory Collection, IHS.
22. Wildes, *Wayne*, 405-7; Nelson, *Wayne*, 250.
23. Posey to Wayne, 8 December 1793, Wayne Papers, HSP.
24. Ibid.
25. Posey to Wayne, 10 December 1793, Wayne Papers, HSP.
26. Idem., 14 December 1793, Wayne Papers, HSP.
27. Wayne to Posey, 21 January 1794, Thomas Posey Papers, IHS.
28. Ibid.
29. Douglas Southall Freeman, *George Washington: A Biography*, 7 vols. (New York: Charles Scribner's Sons,1948-1951), 7:136-37; Wildes, *Wayne*, 407.
30. Posey to Wayne, 20 February 1794, Wayne Papers, HSP.
31. Ibid.
32. Posey to Washington, 1 June 1791, *The George Washington Papers* (Library of Congress: Washington, DC, 1964, text-fiche), reel 122 (Hereafter cited as *GW Papers—text-fiche—LC*).,
33. Rupert Hughes, *George Washington: The Rebel and the Patriot, 1762-1777* (New York: William Morrow & Co., 1927), 655.
34. Henry Lee to Posey, 6 March 1794, Thomas Posey Papers, IHS.
35. Nelson, *Wayne*, 249-50; Wildes, *Wayne*, 402-4. Hamtramck protested bitterly to Wayne when, after taking over Posey's command, he was not promoted to brigadier general. Hamtramck to Wayne, 9 June 1794, Wayne Papers, HSP.
36. Ebenezer Elmer, "Journal Kept During an Expedition to Canada in 1776," 13 January 1777, *Proceedings*, 1st ser. 3(1849): 55, New Jersey Historical Society, Princeton, NJ.
37. *The Kentucky Gazette*, 6:11, (30 November 1793); Francis B. Heitman, *Historical Register and Dictionary of the United States Army, 1789-1903* (Washington, DC: Lowdermilk & Co., 1903; Urbana, IL: University of Illinois Press, 1965), 800; Obituary of Captain John Posey, Thornton and Posey Family Bible, The Presbyterian Study Center, Montreat, NC. General James Wilkinson confirms the presence of Posey's "eldest son" in the Legion camp. Wilkinson to Posey, 14 July 1793, Thomas Posey Papers, IHS.
38. Harry M. Ward, *Charles Scott and the "Spirit of '76"* (Charlottesville, VA: University Press of Virginia, 1988), 140-43.
39. Wildes, *Wayne*, 414-47; Nelson, *Wayne*, 253-83.
40. Deed of 5 September 1794, Thomas and Mary Posey to John Lewis, *Virginia County Records—Spotsylvania County*, ed. William A. Crozier (Baltimore: Genealogical Publishing Co., 1971), 1:472.

41. Robert Douthat Stoner, *A Seedbed of the Republic* (Radford, VA: Commonwealth Press, Inc., 1962), 311-12.
42. MS Indenture Deed, 27 June 1795, John and Mary Lewis to Thomas Posey, Manuscript Collection, Kentucky Historical Society, Louisville, KY; *Early Kentucky Records, Register of the Kentucky Historical Society* (Baltimore: Genealogical Publishing Co., 1984), 57; Willard Rouse Jillson, ed., *Old Kentucky Entries and Deeds* (Baltimore: Genealogical Publishing Co., 1978), 442.
43. Obituary of Captain John Posey, Thornton and Posey Family Bible, The Presbyterian Study Center, Montreat, NC.
44. Thomas Posey to James Madison, 21 November 1795, *The Papers of James Madison*, ed. William T. Hutchinson, 16 vols. to date (Charlottesville, VA: University Press of Virginia, 1962-), 16:131 (Enclosed in Madison to Washington, 25 May 1796, *GW Papers—text-fiche—LC*, reel 122.
45. Posey to Washington, 2 March 1796, *GW Papers—text-fiche—LC*, reel 108.
46. Washington to John Marshall, 15 July 1796, *The Writings of George Washington*, ed. John C. Fitzpatrick, 39 vols. (Washington, DC: U.S. Government Printing Office, 1931-1944), 35:139-41, .
47. *The Kentucky Gazette*, 10:533, (21 June 1797).
48. See generally: Richard Buel, Jr., *Securing the Revolution: Ideology in American Politics, 1789-1815* (Ithaca, NY: Cornell University Press, 1972).
49. Ibid.; Lance Banning, *The Jeffersonian Persuasion: Evolution of a Party Ideology* (Ithaca, NY: Cornell University Press, 1978), 211.
50. Richard Hofstadter, *The Idea of a Party System: The Rise of Legitimate Opposition in the United States, 1780-1840* (Berkeley, CA: University of California Press, 1969), 2, 90-92.
51. Ibid., 117-18; Buel, *Securing the Revolution*, 86.
52. Lawrence Taliaferro to Madison, 4 January 1797, 16:445, Joseph Jones to Madison, 23 March 1797, 16:1286, *Papers of Madison*, ed. Hutchinson.
53. Alexander Spottswood to Washington, 4 November 1797, *GW Papers—text-fiche—LC*, reel 111.
54. Washington to Alexander Spottswood (2), 9 January 1798, *Writings of Washington*, ed. Fitzpatrick, 36:119-21.
55. *Early Kentucky Tax Records* (Baltimore: Genealogical Publishing Co., 1984), 57-58.
56. President John Adams to Thomas Posey, MS Commissions (2), 20 October 1798 and 20 December 1798, Thomas Posey Papers, IHS.
57. Thornton and Posey Family Bible, The Presbyterian Study Center, Montreat, NC.
58. J. Dandridge to Dr. David Stuart, 13 June 1798, Gunther Collection, Washington Family Papers, Chicago Historical Society Library, Chicago, IL.
59. Buel, *Securing the Revolution*, 160-83.
60. John Marshall to Posey (2), 30 January 1799 and 1 February 1799, Thomas Posey Papers, IHS.
61. David Franklin Musto, *George Washington and the Temptations of the Political Life* (Richmond, VA: The Society of the Cincinnati in the State of Virginia, 1983), 29-43.
62. Thomas Posey to James McHenry, 2 May 1799, *GW Papers—text-fiche—LC*, reel 114.

63. Charles T. Cullen, ed., *The Papers of John Marshall*, 6 vols. to date (Chapel Hill, NC: The University of North Carolina Press, 1977-), 4:17-18.
64. Jacob P. Dunn, *Indiana, A Redemption from Slavery* (Boston: AMS Press, 1890), 289; Charles Jay Wilson, "The Negro in Early Ohio," *Ohio Archaelogical and Historical Publications* (Columbus, OH: Ohio Archaelogical and Historical Society, 1930), 34:193.
65. For an incisive analysis of the subject, see: Paul Finkelman, "Slavery and Bondage in the 'Empire of Liberty'," *The Northwest Ordinance: Essays on Its Formulation, Provisions and Legacy*, ed. Frederick D. Williams (East Lansing, MI: Michigan State University Press, 1989), 61-95.
66. Richard R. Beeman, *Patrick Henry: A Biography* (New York: McGraw-Hill, 1974), 96-97.
67. Freeman, *Washington*, 7:620-29.
68. "Washington Entombed," Ulster County (NY) *Gazette*, 4 January 1800.

CHAPTER SEVEN

(1800-1810)

"I was not born to riches or . . . high birth, or great family."

Washington's death removed the last great symbol of non-partisan political leadership. During President Adams' four-year administration, the ruling federalists had unwisely used their fleeting gain in popular sentiment from the XYZ affair to impose the harsh Alien and Sedition Laws, designed to suppress dissent from their policies. These measures only reinforced a widespread perception of absolutist monarchical overtones in Alexander Hamilton's brand of political nationalism, and public opinion swung massively to the Jeffersonians. The 1800 national elections brought the ascendancy of the Republican party, and the start of a 24-year presidential dynasty of Virginia republican leaders Thomas Jefferson, James Madison and James Monroe. The transfer of power from a ruling to an opposition party by peaceful and constitutional means—the first such transition in modern history—happily fulfilled the fundamental purpose and promise of the founding revolutionary generation.

President Jefferson himself, in his first inaugural address, sought to heal the deep residual factional divisions by declaring to the nation that "we are all republicans, we are all federalists," but elsewhere he expressed a more candid and realistic view:

> In every free and deliberating society, there must, from the nature of man, be opposite parties, and violent dissensions

> and discords, and one of these, for the most part, must prevail over the other for a longer or shorter time. Perhaps this party division is necessary to induce each to watch and relate to the people the proceedings of the other.[1]

The Federalist party never regained power nationally, and gradually sank into oblivion as an organized political force. Many of its policies, however, including a national bank, protective tariffs, a standing army, and a stronger executive, were eventually adopted in varying degrees by the succeeding Republican administrations. Furthermore, that most dedicated of federalists, John Marshall, during his long tenure as Chief Justice of the United States Supreme Court, was notably successful in imposing his concept of judicial nationalism on the American constitutional system.[2]

The loss of Washington, his lifelong exemplar, seemingly cut Thomas Posey's strongest tie to Virginia and removed any lingering reluctance he may have had about leaving that state—in the spring of 1802 he moved his entire family and household to Kentucky. There were by then nine children in the Greenwood family circle, ranging from Fayette, age eighteen, to one-year-old Sarah Ann. She alone was left in Virginia, apparently deemed too young or frail to withstand the arduous journey. She was entrusted to the care of Mary Posey's childless younger sister, Mrs. William (Frances Alexander) Fitzhugh, who raised her to adulthood. The two older Thornton boys, both now of legal age, remained in Virginia to assume their father's legacy. On the first leg of their trek, the family paused long enough at the Shenandoah Valley farm of John and Lucy Frances Posey to induce the young couple, themselves the parents of two children under three years of age, to join the venture. The caravan then resumed its slow progress along the 1,000-mile journey, through the Cumberland Gap gateway to the west, and northwesterly on the tortuous Wilderness Trail. Its goal was the central Kentucky town of Lexington, proudly known, because of its urbane and relatively cultured society, as "the Athens of the West."[3]

Posey himself was, of course, an experienced wayfarer, and no stranger to the demands and hardships of frontier travel. Even so, despite all the careful planning and experience of his earlier visits to Kentucky, the sheer physical rigors and difficulties of the trip by a party of this size must have been truly awesome. At least a dozen domestic slaves and servants were required to maintain a household of fourteen family members of Virginia landed gentry. The entourage included Thomas and Mary's personal servants, and several domestic, nursing and kitchen staff. Since a continued agrarian lifestyle in Kentucky was planned, a farm overseer and several groomsmen and artisans would have been numbered in the party, even though most of Greenwood's slave farm laborers remained in Virginia as part of the Thornton estate. Finally, given Posey's firm commitment to the continued schooling of his children, the retinue would almost certainly have included a young resident tutor.

Several sturdy wagons, and some trail-wise wagon drivers, would have had to be engaged to transport all these persons and the Poseys' considerable furniture, clothing and personal possessions. Food, fodder and other necessities would be taken along, to provide for the sizable party's needs between the scattered inns along the way. Even if Thomas was forced to leave behind all but the pick of his cattle, sheep and swine herds, he certainly brought along his best riding horses. An elegant carriage drawn by the Poseys' finest team of carriage horses was probably the conveyance of choice for Mary and the younger children. Under even the best conditions, several weeks would be required to move such a caravan over nearly impassable roads, through a massive mountain range, and across five major rivers and innumerable streams, many undoubtedly swollen by spring rains. The sheer size of the group had the one advantage of discouraging attack by outlaws known to prey upon solitary wayfarers braving the lonely forest glens and remote passes of the old Wilderness Road.

Arriving at last in central Kentucky, the exhausted party paused in Lexington to reprovision and rest from the long journey. Thomas and one or two of his older sons rode on ahead into the western part of the state, to complete arrangements for sheltering the household in the largely unsettled area he had chosen to start a new life. The 1778 Virginia legislature had awarded a huge grant of 200,000 acres of land at the confluence of the Ohio and Green Rivers to the Transylvania Company, headed by Colonel Richard Henderson of North Carolina. It lay undeveloped for a number of years, but in 1797 the company sent its agent, General Samuel Hopkins, to survey the tract, lay out a town, and draw property lines and boundaries for land sales to new settlers. Within a year, the newly created state of Kentucky designated the area as Henderson County. Soon hardy pioneers were trickling in from Virginia and other eastern states to buy and clear acreage, erect rude log cabins, and move their families to the fertile river-bottom country.[4]

Thomas Posey's early interest in Kentucky was probably reinforced during the Northwest expedition by his fellow generals

Charles Scott and James Wilkinson. Samuel Hopkins was yet another of Posey's Revolutionary war comrades, largely Virginians, who formed a kind of support group or network for their associates who ventured out to the frontier seeking to better their fortunes. General Hopkins had been captured with most of the Virginia Continental line when Charleston fell in 1780. But he knew Posey well, and it was almost surely he who assisted in obtaining the surveys and plats validating George Washington's land holdings along nearby Rough Creek during Thomas' visit to Kentucky in 1797. That occasion would have afforded ample opportunity for Hopkins to acquaint his old wartime associate with the attractions of the Transylvania tract. Not long after his return to Virginia, Posey exercised a portion of his 7,000-acre military warrant, earned by his seven years' service in the Revolution, to claim a sizable parcel of rich farmland in Henderson County.[5]

Posey's plot lay midway between the little Ohio River settlement of Red Banks, (soon to be renamed Henderson), and the Green River crossing known as Spottsville, about eighteen miles east of the town. The new family home, sitting on one of the highest of the area's gently rolling hills, afforded a wide vista extending to both nearby rivers, and was appropriately called "Longview." The last leg of the family's long trek from Virginia could not be completed overland. Roads running to western Kentucky from the more populous central areas were little more than widened Indian trails, virtually impassable for heavily-loaded wagons. The family and its possessions were loaded onto a flatboat at Louisville, below the falls of the Ohio, and floated down the river the final one hundred miles. At last, they moored at a weedy landing dominated by the steep clay bluff of Red Banks—in 1802, the lone river settlement between Louisville and the Mississippi. The town, at this time, consisted only of some scattered log houses, and a few stores serving the new settlers beginning to arrive and claim their farm acreage out in the county.[6]

John and Lucy Frances Posey soon left the extended family at Longview to set up their own household. With the proceeds of their Virginia farm and his military land grant earned as a dragoon in Wayne's Legion, they built "Walnut Hill" on a sizable tract in Henderson County twelve miles west of Red Banks, near present-day Corydon. Their brother Fayette married a local girl, Elizabeth Davis, in 1807 and settled on a farm called "Rose Creek" at the junction of the Ohio and Green rivers, not far from Longview. These two eldest sons of Thomas Posey—the only ones who settled permanently in Kentucky—became prosperous farmers, merchants and respected community leaders.[7] Eventually, at least one of Posey's children was to settle and prosper in every frontier state in which he served—fulfilling, by their lives, a pledge made by their father to George Washington in 1791 "to bring up my children in such a manner as could render them worthy members of the community and a credit to their country."[8]

Very little is known of the quality of life the Poseys made for themselves in Kentucky. The first years—clearing and planting the land, raising buildings, organizing a stable household—must have required tremendous effort and dedication, not achieved without considerable hardship. Thomas, who had been through hard times in his youth and rugged living conditions in the army, probably took the primitive new lifestyle in stride. But the privileged Mary Alexander Thornton Posey, who had never known a day's want or serious discomfort in the first forty-six years of her life, must certainly have undergone a traumatic period of adjustment and culture shock. The contrast between the structured, gentrified way of life in Piedmont Virginia and the crude accommodations, scarce amenities, and unmannered inhabitants of the western frontier, was stark and pervasive. The older children also, like Mary, must often have felt a deep sense of loss and isolation from the supportive family and societal network of Spotsylvania County.

Later in life, Mary's letters would reflect a woman of hardy and resilient character, with a resignation to adversity born of strong religious faith. These latent qualities undoubtedly sustained her through the difficult early years of struggle on the very edge of civilization in western Kentucky. Slowly, conditions improved. Affluence always eluded the Poseys, but somehow the raw land was tamed and made to support an establishment of some thirty or more persons, and to provide the means for raising and educating the growing children of the family. This achievement may have been Thomas Posey's primary responsibility, but Mary must be largely credited with having created and maintained some semblance of traditional Virginia values and culture in the midst of a turbulent and volatile frontier society.

One glimpse into the financial pressures felt by Posey in these early years is reflected in letters he wrote from Henderson in 1804. William Lytle of Williamsburg, Ohio, had expressed some interest in buying 1,000 acres of Kentucky land Thomas owned along the Ohio River in Campbell County. He had bought the tract four years earlier for $4,000, probably speculating on an increase in riverfront land values if intermittent government negotiations to open a Mississippi River trade route through Spanish New Orleans were successfully concluded. The acquisition of Louisiana by France, and its subsequent sale to the United States in 1803, finally assured open water passage from Kentucky into the Gulf of Mexico. But Posey was not in a position to hold onto his property long enough to realize the full benefit of these developments. He was willing and anxious to sell the valuable land to Lytle for only $5,000—barely enough to recover his investment and holding expenses.[9]

Unlike his private land investments, Posey's public career took a sudden and unforeseen upturn at this time. Less than two years after settling in Kentucky, he became deeply involved in the new state's stormy and byzantine political arena. Many of the settlers in the Transylvania tract were veterans of the Revolutionary or Northwest Expedition armies, company-grade officers or humble rank-and-filers. In the mass emigration to the frontier in search of a better life, they had applied their military warrants to modest plots of farmland in the fertile area west of Green River.[10] Not surprisingly, they looked for political leadership to one of their own: the distinguished General Thomas Posey, a war hero and a major landholder in the area. In 1804, he was elected to a two-year term of office in the state senate from a district encompassing a large part of the sparsely settled region: Henderson, Livingston, Muhlenburg and Ohio counties.

Considerably more remarkable, if not extraordinary, is the drama that unfolded shortly after Posey, completing the long, difficult horseback ride from his home, arrived in the busy little capital city of Frankfort to attend the first session of the new senate. Five days after formally opening the initial meeting of the legislature, John Caldwell, the recently elected lieutenant governor, died of an "inflammation of the brain." On that same day, 10 November 1804, the senate met and selected Thomas Posey to assume Caldwell's constitutional position as its Speaker and presiding officer.[11] This assemblage contained Kentucky's most able and prominent public figures. It was already split into federalist and republican blocs roughly reflecting national party factionalism. Why would they turn for leadership to this stranger who, after living in the state for only two years, had just been elected to his first public office?

Two major factors in Posey's elevation to the speakership can be identified. Scholars have noted the awe and reverence in which the more storied fighters for American independence were held by the citizens of the emerging frontier states. As these retired warriors, preceded by their military renown, emigrated westward, they were regarded by their fellow settlers as a veritable resource pool of talent, energy and leadership. Even James Wilkinson, with his dubious martial credentials, acquired immediate high public status after arriving in Kentucky in 1784.[12] A more certifiable Revolutionary hero, General Charles Scott, further enhanced his stature in Indian campaigns with Harmar, St. Clair and Wayne, and eventually rose to the governorship in 1808.[13] General Samuel Hopkins, whose impressive Revolutionary credentials included the battles of Trenton, Princeton, Monmouth, Brandywine and Germantown, represented Henderson County in the lower branch of the Kentucky legislature from 1800 to 1806. He succeeded to Posey's state senatorial seat in 1809, and later went on to serve in the federal House of Representatives.[14]

An even more compelling element in Posey's immediate selection to the speakership may have been his fellow senators' perception of him as a member and representative of the dominant gentry leadership of the American nation. Robert H. Wiebe has described how, with independence won, a well-defined class of gentlemen, of whom Washington, Jefferson, Hamilton and Madison were only the most notable figures, led the revolutionary generation into the creation and realization of a national republic. The gentry leaders viewed the structure of civilized society as a natural hierarchy. They claimed, on the strength of their demonstrated virtue or character, the right as a class to lead that society. This form of natural aristocracy or leadership through character, in which the concepts of society, government and character merged and synergized, was widely recognized and accepted by the gentry and non-gentry alike in the early years of the nineteenth century, when the grip of the gentry elite was shaken by the emergence and predominance of local and regional interests, and the general democratization of society and politics.[15]

Posey was perhaps a natural choice for the suddenly vacant post of presiding officer. As a renowned revolutionary freedom-fighter, and the known associate and neighbor of national gentry leaders Washington, Madison and Monroe, he already possessed the esteem and respect of his fellow senators even before taking his first step onto the floor of the Kentucky senate chamber. As a recent arrival, he had not yet formed close ties or become identified with any local leader or political faction. He was not the first, and would not be the last, soldier whose contributions to his country continued on the frontier after the fighting ended in 1782. But with a postwar record of service in four western states, Thomas might, in fact, be regarded as a quintessential member of that special class of revolutionary nation-builders.

General Posey presided over the Kentucky senate for three years. The legislative record discloses little of his conduct or actions as Speaker of this body. That he performed creditably is indicated by his re-appointment to the chair on 4 November 1805, and his formal election by the senate on 23 November of that year to fill John Caldwell's unexpired term of office as lieutenant-governor.[16] In the early spring of 1806, in a bid for even higher office, Thomas chose to relinquish the senate seat he held representing western Kentucky, although continuing to serve as lieutenant governor and ex-officio presiding officer of the upper legislative body. Incumbent Governor Christopher Greenup was constitutionally ineligible to succeed himself. The state's two leading newspapers, the Frankfort *Palladium* and Lexington's *Kentucky Gazette and General Advertiser*, were soon carrying announcements of Posey's candidacy for the state governorship in the 1808 election.[17] At the time, his hopes were high, and his chances of winning the highest state office looked exceedingly good.

Within six months, however, a series of unforeseeable adverse events would intervene to fatally damage Thomas Posey's promising political future in the state of Kentucky. Two young journalists from the east, Joseph M. Street and John Wood, had recently established in Frankfort a weekly journal, *The Western World*. They soon began publishing a barrage of sensational charges against many prominent Kentuckians, accusing them of having engaged in a succession of treasonous acts dating back to the late 1780s while covertly seeking to separate Kentucky from the Union and align it with Spain. Targets of the attacks included United States senators John Brown and John Adair, federal judge Harry Innes, state judge Benjamin Sebastian, and General James Wilkinson, now Governor of Upper Louisiana Territory.

There had, in fact, been some strong separatist sentiment expressed in Kentucky and other frontier areas after the Jay Treaty with the leading European powers failed to open a free trade route down the Ohio and Mississippi rivers through the port of New Orleans. Many frontiersmen regarded this key diplomatic failure, which they felt doomed the entire region to commercial and economic strangulation, as evidence of unconcern by the federal government for western interests. Spanish authorities in the region, in an effort to exploit these feelings of alienation, did seek to sway some frontier leaders toward separation from the United States. But apart from James Wilkinson's posthumously disclosed secret relationship with Spain, there is little or no proof that any of the other principals named by *The Western World* as parties to the alleged "Spanish Conspiracy" allowed their open displeasure with the national government to cross over the line into treasonable or criminal conduct.[18]

Material for the articles printed by Street and Wood is believed to have been fed to the journalists by two leading Federalists in the state. One, Humphrey Marshall, was a first cousin and brother-in-law of Chief Justice John Marshall; the other, also a brother-in-law of the chief justice, was Joseph Hamilton Daviess, the United States Attorney in Frankfort. Their efforts were apparently designed to discredit the popular republican cause in Kentucky, as all of the individuals named in *The Western World's* charges were prominent leaders of that faction.[19] Although never proven, the lurid accusations effectively ended the public careers of some of those named, and tarnished others. But they also created resentment and a powerful backlash against other eminent local figures perceived as Federalists. One of these, much to his own dismay, turned out to be Lieutenant Governor Thomas Posey.

The two national political factions had been vying for public support in Kentucky for many years, and by 1806 a clear majority of citizens had embraced republican policies and principles. As the opposing viewpoint fell into disfavor, aspiring politicians scrambled to shed the unpopular federalist label. After three years in the public arena, Posey was experiencing increasing difficulty in finding a comfortable niche for himself in the political spectrum. As time passed, his identification with the federal administration through his familiarity with republican gentry leaders Jefferson, Madison and Monroe began to lose its aura, while his personal friendships with John Marshall, Henry Lee, and other fervid Federalists became well known. Ambitious local leaders now saw Thomas as a serious rival for political power and influence in state government, and perhaps a threat to their own aspirations for the governorship or other high office. Word began to spread in the central population centers that General Posey's beliefs, far from embodying accepted and politically correct republican precepts, were, in fact, fundamentally federalist.

The acute sensitivity and critical importance of this issue is well illustrated by an amusing account of a banquet-meeting of young men in Frankfort on 4 July 1806—a group euphemistically described in *The Western World* as "the Republican Citizens of this place." But their true political orientation is perhaps better indicated by the formal toasts with which they celebrated the nation's thirtieth Independence Day. Among those so honored were Governor Greenup, ("may he never be succeeded by a Spanish conspirator or traitor to his country"), and Lieutenant-Governor Posey, ("who undauntedly braved the horrors of war, and risked his life for independence—may his fellow citizens continue to appreciate his services, and honor him with their confidence").[20]

Among those listed as present at this gathering of patriotic "Republicans" were journalists Street and Wood, as well as Samuel G. Hopkins, son of General Hopkins, who proposed a toast to "those judges of the Kentucky courts, whose integrity has never been stained by Spanish gold." Also attending was Thomas' son, Thornton A. Posey, but his toast reflected a somewhat different agenda. Thornton's concern was for new settlers who, like the Poseys, had chosen to live west of the Green River: "may the compassion, not the vengeance, of the state be extended towards them."[21] He was referring to another split, superimposed on the republican-federalist antagonism, which had only recently appeared in the Kentucky political maelstrom. It pitted the poor farmers beyond the Green River against an elite clique of merchants and men of wealth in and around the cities of Lexington and Frankfort. By 1806, this central Bluegrass caucus completely dominated state fiscal and tax policy, and young Posey's appeal for fairness and leniency toward the struggling settlers in the west was doomed to fall on deaf ears.[22]

Curiously, the influential Frankfort *Palladium*, a partisan republican weekly, reprinted word-for-word the account of this meeting as originally published by the rival *The Western World.* But it followed this narrative with a disparaging editorial comment that most of those attending the dinner had been "transient young men, (the greater part of whom have not resided in the town twelve months)." The paper then went on to describe "another meeting (consisting of most of the principal inhabitants)," whom it clearly considered to be *real* republicans. This latter group had observed the Fourth of July with a series of more appropriately-republican toasts, including one honoring a public figure conspicuously slighted by the "transient young men"—President Thomas Jefferson ("Long may he remain in the confidence of Republicans").[23]

Thomas Posey, perhaps intentionally, had chosen not to attend either of these two obviously partisan gatherings. Had he been a better politician, he might well have been present at the second dinner, and would certainly have not allowed his son to attend the first. As the summer passed, he sensed a serious erosion in his popular support for the governor's race. Fighting for his political life, on 15 September 1806 he composed a long, emotional letter to a "Frankfort correspondent," which the *Palladium* published verbatim five weeks later. It strongly challenged the reports circulating in central Kentucky "that I am called a Federalist, with an intention to injure me in my election." The same charge, he noted, had once been leveled against him in a Virginia election, (undoubtedly the 1797 congressional race against John Dawson), "with a view to attach the opprobrium of being a violent party man, and attached to what is called the federal party in Congress." Then, as now, such reports were nothing more than "false rumours," disseminated by enemies who would "spare no pains to spread falsehood" to serve their political ends.[24]

In a desperate effort to define his true convictions and differentiate them from his detractors' false allegations, Posey flatly declared that he always had been, and still remained, above party factionalism. He emphasized this stance by expressly and firmly disassociating himself from those national political figures whose extreme public policies and private practices had given the term "Federalist" such a bad name on the frontier—"men strongly attached to monarchy, some to aristocracy; and some to a re-union under the British government."[25] These were all positions which were abhorrent to everything he had fought for in the Revolution, and stood for throughout his life. No man on the frontier was ever more adamantly opposed to monarchy, aristocracy, or reunion with Great Britain than Thomas Posey.

Nonetheless, Posey wanted it clearly understood that he was steadfastly devoted to the new form and system of government he had struggled so hard to help create, whatever label his enemies chose to put on that fundamental loyalty:

> If to have been a strenuous advocate of the present happy constitution of the United States bestows on me the name of Federalist, I confess myself one. If to support the unparalleled and happy constitution entitles me to the name of Federalist, I hope it never will depart from me; for I do hold it one of the most glorious events of my life, that I was in the least productive of its adoption. And tho' attempts have been made to sully, or cast a stain upon my political sentiments in giving me the name of federalist, no person can, with the least shadow of truth, say I am not a republican: for that is a name I equally glory in with that of Federalist, agreeable to the foregoing construction of the term.[26]

The political antecedents of these impassioned assertions were impeccable. George Washington's prescient Farewell Address had solemnly warned against "the baneful effects of the spirit of party,"[27] and that most republican of presidents, Thomas Jefferson, had publicly dismissed party labels as more rhetoric than reality. But Posey was confronted in Kentucky, as he had already encountered in Virginia and would again in Louisiana and Indiana, with an immutable political truth. In politics, as on the nation's highways and byways, any public figure who hews to the "middle of the road" is likely to collide violently with fellow travelers in both the left and right lanes of ideological traffic.

But Thomas struggled mightily to defuse the party label issue, stressing that his quest for the governorship was not encumbered by any pretensions of class or caste—all he had to offer the electorate was his own personal reputation and record. "I was not born to riches or what is vainly called high birth, but a plebian . . . my walk in life has been humble, endeavoring to give as little offence as possible, and to render all the good in my power." Promising only to give the high office to which he aspired all his time, energies and abilities, he closed his letter by assuring his fellow citizens that if they were not inclined to support his candidacy, "their will, in the choice of any other person, will meet my cheerful approbation."[28]

But his implacable political opponents were not appeased. When the state senate reconvened in early November, two of its republican leaders, Green Clay and William M. Bledsoe, rose to contest Posey's right to preside as Speaker, on the ground that he was no longer a member of the senate. This seems clearly to have been a spurious or contrived issue, since under the constitution the speakership was an ex-officio function of the office of lieutenant-governor, which Thomas had not relinquished, and which even his challengers did not deny he lawfully occupied. But the question was hotly debated for two full days, during which Posey, "from motives of delicacy," did not take the presiding officer's chair. Bledsoe, a gifted orator, was particularly ruthless, declaiming that "the continuation of a man in office as a legislator whose time of service (as senator) by the constitution and his election has expired, in his opinion was aristocratic."[29] On 4 November 1806, however, by a vote of 12 to 8, a majority of Posey's former colleagues in the senate upheld his continued status as Speaker of that body.

All the leading journals in the state reported this rhetorical skirmish in great detail. Although he emerged victorious, Thomas was seriously damaged by the mean-spirited and disparaging debate, especially the charges that imputed to him the much-despised elitism of the extreme federalist faction. The affair was, however, quickly overshadowed by succeeding events of high public drama that were destined to prove fatal to Posey's gubernatorial aspirations. Only one day after the senate debate ended, U.S. Attorney Joseph Hamilton Daviess filed in federal judge Harry Innes' Frankfort courtroom a motion to issue a warrant for the arrest of Aaron Burr, recent vice-president of the United States. Daviess' petition charged that Burr was currently engaged in a conspiracy to raise a private army of American citizens for the unlawful purpose of invading and seizing the Spanish province of Mexico from adjacent American territory in Louisiana.

Burr, a brilliant lawyer and charismatic politician, is one of the most fascinating and controversial figures in early American history. In the Revolution he had been a lieutenant colonel and, (briefly), an aide-de-camp to George Washington, later serving under General Horatio Gates at Saratoga. After the war, he practiced law and politics in New York City, rising to the leadership of the state's republican faction, and incurring along the way the bitter personal enmity of Alexander Hamilton, the federalist leader. In the landmark 1800 presidential race, Thomas Jefferson's republicans prevailed over the federalists, but Burr, ostensibly running for vice-president on Jefferson's ticket, contrived to obtain a tie with him in the electoral college vote for the highest office.[30]

Under the federal constitution, the issue went to the House of Representatives, and only after thirty-six ballots was Jefferson narrowly elected president, with Burr then automatically becoming vice-president. While holding this high office Burr engaged in a duel with Hamilton who, after Washington's death late in 1799, had become commander-in-chief of the American army. Burr, a deadly accurate pistol shot, killed the federalist leader on the Jersey shore on 11 July 1804. He fell into immediate disgrace—all his property was seized, and he fled to Georgia to avoid imprisonment after being indicted for murder in New York and New Jersey. Soon, however, he reappeared in Washington City where, as Vice-President, he was immune from arrest on state criminal charges. He resumed all his constitutional duties, including presiding regularly over the U.S. Senate, and surprisingly was, for a time, received into the homes and confidence of President Jefferson and Secretary of State James Madison. They did not, however, support him for reelection in 1804, and by the time his term of office expired early in the following year, he was already busily engaged in laying plans for a bizarre and Kafkaesque adventure on the western frontier.

During the final months of his vice-presidency, Burr had conferred long and often with his old wartime acquaintance and fellow master of intrigue, Brigadier General James Wilkinson who, with Hamilton's death, had again become ranking general of the army. Together, the two schemers conceived a bold plan to raise a private army of American adventurers, invade and conquer Spanish Mexico, and install Burr as its king. As a first step in implementing this blueprint, Burr used his short-lived influence with President Jefferson to secure Wilkinson's appointment as Governor of Upper Louisiana District. The presence of the general and his command at St. Louis, the district's strategically located headquarters on the Mississippi River, was essential in carrying out the master plan. The next step was to raise the funds needed to recruit, arm and train the proposed invading army.

Burr held secret meetings in Philadelphia with the British minister, seeking financial backing for his plan from Great Britain, then at war with Bonapartist Spain. When it became obvious that such aid would not be forthcoming from the wary British, Burr, with Wilkinson acting as intermediary and sponsor, turned brazenly to the Spanish governor of Mexico for financial support. In order to make the project acceptable and attractive to Spain, he altered his original scenario to make it appear that the real objective of his army was to capture the city of New Orleans, newly acquired by the United States in the Louisiana Purchase. He would then use that city's rich bank reserves, manpower, and strategic control of Mississippi River commerce to separate Louisiana, Mississippi, Kentucky and Tennessee from the Union, and create a new nation, ruled by Burr but closely allied with Spain.

Even Wilkinson's gullible Spanish "handlers" would not take this fanciful plan seriously, and denied it their support. But the obsessed Burr would not be deterred. He resourcefully lined up private financial backing, and was soon traveling extensively along the Ohio River, raising recruits and stockpiling arms and supplies for his planned foray down that stream and into the Mississippi toward his chosen target of opportunity. Some of his main American supporters were men of stature who were convinced that the Jefferson administration, in which Burr had until recently been such a major figure, secretly backed his plan to wrest Mexico from the tottering Spanish empire and annex it to the United States. Many of the young adventurers who signed on to the undertaking were further misled by Burr's vague assurances that the first objective of the expedition was to occupy and develop a huge tract of land in Mississippi Territory to which their leader declared he had legal title.

Word of Burr's activities inevitably leaked out. In the fall of 1806 *The Western World* broke the story in its usual flamboyant style, headlining the version of the plan he had tried to sell to Spanish authorities—that the target of his army was New Orleans. But the legal action filed by U.S. Attorney Daviess in Frankfort's federal court was based upon the original plan presented to the British minister. It alleged that Burr, by organizing and arming a private army to invade Spanish Mexico, was violating a federal statute barring ordinary citizens from attacking any foreign power with which the nation was at peace.[31] Most Kentuckians, long anesthetized by *The Western World's* many wild and unproven charges, were inclined to regard that journal's expose of the Burr plot, as well as Daviess' subsequent court action, as just another attempt by diehard federalists to discredit republicanism by attacking the recent Jeffersonian vice-president. As for Judge Harry Innes, a staunch Republican, he himself had long been Daviess' political target, and had been prominent among the notables implicated in *The Western World's* earlier "Spanish Conspiracy" charges. He, understandably, was not particularly sympathetic to Daviess' efforts to take Burr into custody.

Burr was at this time busy raising funds and proselytizing recruits in the nearby Kentucky city of Lexington. As soon as he learned of the charges filed against him, he hurried over to Frankfort, arriving at the capital's leading hostelry, Loves Inn, in the early evening of 7 November. There he conferred with his attorney, Henry Clay, a rising young republican politician who was soon to be named a United States Senator by the Kentucky legislature. Acting upon Clay's advice, several prominent public figures then in the capital were called in to help formulate a defense strategy. One of these notables was, inexplicably, Thomas Posey. Posey's connections to Burr were tenuous at best, but he did know Clay well. His son, Lloyd Posey, was at this time "reading," (i.e. studying) law in Henry Clay's Lexington law office.[32] Thomas had recently done Clay a personal favor by helping one of his clients, Francis T. Brooke, locate and appraise some land holdings in western Kentucky.[33]

By the next morning, Saturday, 8 November, word of Burr's presence had spread throughout the capital. It was evident that public sentiment ran heavily in his favor as he strode through supportive crowds along the cobblestone streets from Loves Inn to the three-story limestone federal courthouse. The former vice-president was flanked by Clay and his associate, John Allen. They were closely followed by two older counselors whose faces were familiar to every citizen of Frankfort—state Representative Samuel Hopkins and Lieutenant Governor Thomas Posey.[34] Entering Judge Innes' crowded courtroom, Burr and his entourage found that the jurist had, upon his own initiative, just dismissed Daviess' motion because it was unsupported by any evidence other than the U.S. Attorney's own deposition. But Burr was eager to defend himself, and would not be denied this ideal public forum. He walked to the front of the courtroom and delivered a fiery oration, eloquently denying the truth of all allegations made against him. Then, shrewdly seizing upon the notoriety of the proceedings to attract supporters to his cause, Burr turned to Judge Innes and demanded that he call a grand jury as soon as possible to hear the prosecutor's case, so that he could be officially exonerated by his peers, rather than through a legal technicality.[35]

The judge was only too willing to oblige. When a grand jury was empaneled the following Wednesday, Daviess was unable to produce any witnesses to support his charges, and the jurymen soon returned to a packed courtroom to report "not a true bill." The scene that followed was vividly described in the *Palladium*: "the disappointment and chagrin of a crowded audience may be conceived, but the ridicule and laughter which followed was universal. The public sentiment which had all along been strongly in favor of Col. Burr now burst forth without disguise."[36]

The prosecutor asked for and received further time to assemble his case, and in early December Aaron Burr was back in Judge Innes' courtroom for another grand jury session. Numerous witnesses were heard, including *Western World* coeditors Street and Wood, but all charges were summarily dismissed. Burr walked out of the courthouse onto the streets of Frankfort to the cheers of hundreds who had flocked to the city from all over Kentucky to shake the hand of the famous visitor. That evening, he was the honored guest at a gala victory ball held in the excited little capital—the last public adulation he would ever know. For even as one toast after another was being raised to the smiling little ex-Vice-President, a small flotilla of his armed followers was speeding down the Ohio River toward a planned rendezvous at the Mississippi with General Wilkinson and his troops, and a joint movement downstream toward New Orleans.[37]

But Burr had met his match in the wily Wilkinson, who always managed to be at least one move ahead of his delusionary co-conspirator. At some point the general, probably alarmed by *The Western World's* disclosures, had decided that Burr's plan was doomed to failure—and that there was advantage to be gained by betraying it. Instead of preparing to meet with Burr at the river junction, Wilkinson now denounced him to the federal government. He sent President Jefferson a deciphered copy of the former vice-president's coded plan of operation, so detailed that it even spelled out the pecking order of the proposed new nation's leaders: "Wilkinson shall be second to Burr only." Even while professing ignorance of Burr's real objective, the general had hurried on down the Mississippi with his troops, loudly proclaiming his determination to defend to the death the city of New Orleans against Burr's pathetic little "army" of sixty men. At the same time, he alerted his Spanish contacts to the "danger" posed to Mexico by the approaching expedition, and demanded $112,000 advance payment to cover expenses he estimated would be required to abort the threatened invasion of their territory.[38]

Jefferson, who from earlier reports had become increasingly uneasy about Burr's activities, put out a general alarm for the arrest of his former vice-president as soon as he received Wilkinson's denunciation. Mississippi Territory militia forces apprehended Burr without resistance, and he was brought back for trial to Richmond, Virginia. Although historians differ on Burr's actual intentions, the treason conspiracy charges brought against him there were founded on the scenario he had outlined to Spanish authorities, rather than his putative designs on Mexico, on which the Kentucky grand jury deliberations were based. The chief prosecution witness at the Richmond trial was James Wilkinson, who himself only narrowly escaped being indicted for his part in the conspiracy. Burr was acquitted on narrow constitutional grounds by Chief Justice John Marshall, the presiding judge at the proceedings. But the would-be King Aaron I of Mexico, now totally disgraced, went on to a life of humiliating exile in Europe, and never again held high public office.[39]

Back in Kentucky, Burr's disillusioned admirers—those who had cheered him most mightily in the streets of Frankfort and most fervently toasted his grand jury victory—now turned with a vengeance on any notable local figures they perceived as friends or supporters of their ruined ex-hero. Sadly, one of those singled out for their rage and displeasure was Thomas Posey. Less than a year after his ill-starred public appearance with Burr at the federal courthouse, Posey quietly announced his withdrawal as a candidate for the governorship, citing poor health.[40]

Thomas certainly had no inkling of Burr's real purpose, whatever it was. With his impressive record and connections in the national government, the former vice-president's claim of secret Jefferson administration backing must have seemed as plausible to Posey as it apparently did to such certifiable patriots (and future presidents) as Tennessee's Andrew Jackson,[41] and Indiana territorial governor

William Henry Harrison,[42]—as well as Burr's own attorney, the astute and prudent statesman Henry Clay.[43] Although the episode created much ill-will and suspicion in the state, and damaged some political careers, no Kentuckian was consciously involved in treasonable activity against the United States.[44] But the question remains, what actually motivated Posey's puzzling gesture of support? Personal friendship was not a factor. While both men served at Saratoga, any contact between the backwoods captain of Virginia riflemen and the polished, Princeton-educated lieutenant colonel from New Jersey must have been casual and fleeting.[45] Concededly, as his relationship with James Wilkinson attests, Posey had an undiscriminating and not altogether rational tolerance and trust, bordering almost on naivete, for any fellow officer who had shared in the dangers and glories of the Revolution. But one must look deeper than wartime comraderie to explain his supportive presence at the side of Aaron Burr on the streets of Frankfort.

It is entirely reasonable to surmise that Posey's purpose was largely political. His cherished posture of non-partisanship had just been openly and unfairly challenged by his relentless political opponents in the state senate. What better way to dispel the undeserved aristocratic/monarchistic stigma of federalism than to show support publicly for the wildly popular Jeffersonian republican leader? The gamble, if indeed it was such, might have been worth the risk. Had Burr turned out to be everything he so convincingly claimed to be, Posey would very likely have been swept into gubernatorial office in 1808. But his well-intentioned misjudgment of character proved to be his political undoing. The irony is further underscored by the fact that, not long after this misguided decision, Posey's oldest daughter, Eliza Maria, married Joseph Montfort Street. Through *The Western World,* Street had been largely instrumental in Burr's exposure and downfall, and thus it was he who inadvertently caused the political demise of his future father-in-law in his adopted state of Kentucky.

As lieutenant-governor, Posey continued to preside over the state senate until its closing session on 29 December 1807. Thereafter, his republican adversaries were finally successful in replacing him with one of their own, Green Clay.[46] In one of his last acts as Speaker, Thomas drafted and delivered to the outgoing governor, Christopher Greenup, the senate's obligatory farewell message. In an obvious reference to the recent Burr case, Posey poured out the harsh feelings he now shared with most Kentuckians toward the disgraced adventurer. He expressed satisfaction that "our freedom is secured, and the ambitious machinations of designing individuals have been rendered abortive." Thomas now clearly recognized what grave danger was posed to the republic he so revered by men such as Burr. He lauded the vigilance exercised by federal authorities when faced with the conspirators' secret plots—a time when "American liberty was to have been sacrificed at the shrine of ambition to answer the purposes of a few discontented and aspiring demagogues."[47] Left unspoken was his own deeply felt chagrin and regret at having been so deceived by one such demagogue.

Posey's address to the governor provides a backdrop to the international conflict upon which the nation was soon to embark. It noted with grim foreboding the continuing attacks upon neutral American shipping by warring foreign nations. "our vessels are searched by the hostile powers of Europe, our property captured and confiscated, our flag insulted and our citizens murdered." In the senate's name, and doubtlessly voicing the overwhelming sentiment of Kentucky and the militantly-nationalist frontier generally, Posey called upon the federal government to make "manifest to the world that our rights as an independent nation are not to be trampled upon with impunity."[48] Thomas' personal support of the nation his generation had brought into existence was unquestioning and unquestionable. He would shortly be called upon to play a part in the impending crisis, but in his more familiar role as a soldier and not, regrettably, as Kentucky's governor.

Posey's withdrawal from the gubernatorial race on 12 January 1808 opened the door to the candidacy of another hero of the War of Independence. General Charles Scott declared on 11 February that he would seek election to the office. Scott was the state's highest-ranking revolutionary officer. He had further enhanced his military credentials with honorable service in three major expeditions against the Indian tribes of the Northwest Territory, including command of the mounted Kentucky volunteers in Anthony Wayne's 1793-1794 Legion. Perhaps even more significantly, he had not previously been active in the state's political cauldron. Although a nominal "republican," he had formed no visible ties with any of the contending factions or cliques. Scott fell heir to much of Thomas Posey's natural constituency: the large numbers of Virginia-born revolutionary officers and soldiers who had used their military land warrants to settle on Kentucky soil. Thomas himself threw his support to Scott, a fellow Virginian and wartime comrade. In the 1808 election, Scott handily defeated two more politically active republican challengers, senate Speaker Green Clay and John Allen, the latter damaged by his role as co-counsel for Aaron Burr in the recent Frankfort court hearings.[49]

The newly elected governor was soon confronted with serious international concerns. Worsening relations with Great Britain and France required an immediate strengthening in American military forces. In accordance with prevailing republican principles, the regular standing army had been allowed to dwindle both in numbers and combat-readiness. Congress ordered a national mobilization of 100,000 militiamen, and assigned Kentucky a quota of 5,005 men. Governor Scott chose Thomas Posey to raise and command the new force, and commissioned him a major general, with standing orders to be prepared to march at a moment's notice. Thomas took his oath of office in Henderson on 3 November 1808, and immediately immersed himself in the recruiting, training and command responsibilities he had effectively discharged in so many past crises.[50]

Although the Kentucky mobilization was largely successful, the national effort uncovered some serious flaws inherent in the militia system. Fortunately, a temporary easing of international tensions in 1809 allowed the disbanding of the partially assembled forces.[51] In his official order discharging the Kentucky units, Governor Scott was lavish in his praise of General Posey. He particularly singled out "the promptitude and zeal with which you undertook and discharged the duties of commander-in-chief . . . You have set an example of military spirit, at the expense of private convenience, which I hope ever to see imitated by the militia of this State when the interests of their country is at stake."[52]

Thomas reply acknowledged and thanked the governor for his kind sentiments. He assured Scott that "I reciprocate with you joyfull sensations, upon the prospect of a happy termination to the affair which led to the late eventful situation of the most sacred concerns of our common country; in the interest of which I hope as long as I have breath, always to have the disposition to embark."[53] Syntax aside, this single sentence accurately expresses the principle of service over self that embodied Posey's core concept of public duty and private responsibility.

It is interesting and particularly noteworthy that old warhorses such as Posey and Scott, who had personally experienced all the horrors of combat, never failed, despite their militant patriotism, to prefer a peaceful solution of international disputes over armed conflict. But on this occasion, their hopes and expectations of a nonviolent resolution of grave foreign provocations proved to be illusory. All too soon, war clouds would again threaten the young nation's tranquility and safety, and afford Thomas other occasions to demonstrate his willingness to again fight for his country.

Meanwhile Posey's son, Thornton, who was also destined to play a conspicuous role in the impending conflict, had embarked upon the career of a professional soldier. Commissioned a captain in the regular army on 3 May 1808, he was serving a tour of recruiting duty in Russellville, Kentucky. Having apparently dipped too deeply into his own funds for expenses and enlistment bonuses, he turned to his father for temporary financial assistance. Before addressing that request, Thomas, a veteran recruiter in his own right, first had a few unsolicited words of wisdom for his son: specifically, that he restrain his recruiting sergeant from making "too free use of your money . . . there are men who spend the money of another much freer than their own."[54]

Captain Thornton Posey clearly needed money more than advice, but Thomas' response to his request for a loan was also only too typically father-like. "I wish it were possible for me to help you; but one solitary dollar is all that I have had by me for several months; & I am dun'd on all quarters for what little I am owing."[55] With due allowance for paternal poor-mouthing, this portrayal of his monetary condition, if it is to be taken literally, reflects a truly alarming and lamentable state of financial affairs for an eminent soldier and distinguished public statesman.

Other Posey children were also experiencing the hardships of adulthood. Eliza Maria, Thomas and Mary's oldest daughter, was seventeen years of age when she married Joseph Montfort Street, the embattled coeditor of the *Western World*, on 9 October 1809. Street had fought and survived several duels arising from his paper's sensational charges against prominent Kentuckians. He finally announced that he would accept no further challenges, but would simply print them in his paper in the order and form they were received. While courageously but unwisely attending the victory ball honoring Aaron Burr in Frankfort after his acquittal in federal court, Street was physically assaulted by some of Burr's supporters. He had to brandish his dagger repeatedly to stave off the attackers, and managed to escape through a window only with the timely assistance of his mulatto manservant. When other adversaries later sought to oust him bodily from another social gathering, his future brother-in-law, Captain Thornton Posey, came to his aid and helped him successfully resist their efforts.[56]

Finally, an enemy fired a pistol shot into Street's chest as he emerged from his Frankfort newspaper office into the public road. His fiancee, Eliza Maria Posey, then a student at the Academy for Young Ladies in Lexington, rushed to his side. Told that he was dying, she insisted that a marriage ceremony be performed immediately. His young wife then slowly nursed Street back to health. But their early married life remained troubled. In the capable hands of Henry Clay, a long-standing lawsuit filed against Street by Judge Harry Innes, seeking damages for libel arising from allegations in *The Western World* of complicity in the "Spanish Conspiracy," culminated in a substantial judgment against the young journalist. To avoid financial ruin, he and his wife were eventually forced to flee Kentucky altogether and settle in Illinois Territory.[57]

In the meantime, however, late in 1809 Street hand-delivered a message from his new father-in-law to Governor Charles Scott. In tone and content, the letter contrasted sharply with the pleasantries the two old campaigners had exchanged only six months before when the Kentucky militia disbanded. It seems that Thomas Posey's son Lloyd, after studying law for four years in the Lexington law firm of Clay & Wickliffe, had removed to the Orleans Territory, (now Louisiana), to set up his own legal practice. Territorial laws required that he provide a certificate of good character from a responsible official of his home state, but Scott had unaccountably ignored several letters Thomas had written to him requesting the document needed by his son to open his practice.

Visibly upset, and making no effort to conceal his annoyance, Posey first reminded the governor that "you are sufficiently acquainted with me to be convinced that I would not be instrumental in bringing you into any difficulties, or embarrassment." In initially contacting him to request the certificate, Thomas continued, he had acted under the conviction that Scott knew his son Lloyd well enough to vouch for the young lawyer; he pointedly made reference to "the respectful manner in which I have heard him speak of you, & the interest he took in your election." But getting no response or acknowledgement, Posey asserted, he was now forced to conclude that the governor was "not sufficiently acquainted with my son's character; or that you have been imposed on by some enemy of his, who has endeavored to make you entertain unfavorable impressions relative to him." Under those circumstances, Thomas scathingly assured Scott, he would not bother him again in the matter, but would turn to "Mr. Henry Clay & other prominent characters in the State" who, he was confident, "will not refuse so reasonable a request."[58]

Despite Governor Scott's seeming indifference to his former comrade and recent militia commander, Posey continued to stand tall in the estimation of another old associate. By 1810, foreign encroachments on American shipping had resumed, and national resentment was beginning to focus on Great Britain. It was widely believed that war with that former enemy was inevitable, and concern mounted on the demonstrated need for a more reliable and durable militia system to meet that contingency. Indiana territorial governor William Henry Harrison, who had served under Wayne and Posey in the Northwest Legion expedition, urged Governor Charles Scott to take the lead in creating a state model for such an organization. Reflecting the respect younger frontier officials held for the veteran officers of the War of Independence, Harrison pointed out that the state of Kentucky was blessed with "an advantage which is scarcely left to any other in the union—of three distinguished revolutionary officers" capable of building and leading the proposed new force. "The exertions of a Scott, a Hopkins, and a Posey might be sufficient to put into operation a system that would soon pervade the continent—a disciplined militia."[59]

Scott's reaction to this suggestion is unknown. In the rapidly approaching national crisis, he might well have called once again upon Posey's military skills and experience, displayed only a year earlier as commander-in-chief of Kentucky militia, which Scott himself had praised so effusively. There is certainly no doubt that Thomas, if called upon, would not have been deterred from accepting the assignment by any personal slight, real or perceived, on the part of the governor. But before the occasion arose, new circumstances intervened. The restless spirit which had sent young Thomas Posey from Fairfax County to the Virginia frontier, and induced the mature man to sacrifice the comforts of Spotsylvania for the hardships of primitive Kentucky, was once again irresistibly spurring the now-aging pioneer toward another adventure on America's expanding border.

Posey, during a visit to Louisiana to assist his son Lloyd establish a home and law practice, had become interested in the fresh opportunities and challenges offered in the new and emerging territory. He bought a tract of land in the south-central Attakapas region, with the apparent intention of developing it into the future home for himself, his wife, and younger children.[60] Thomas' sights were now firmly fixed on Louisiana, but his long-range plans were fated to be aborted by the outbreak of another war, another call to arms, and, incidentally, another involvement with the ubiquitous General James Wilkinson.

NOTES

1. Richard Hofstadter, *The Idea of a Party System: The Rise of Legitimate Opposition in the United States, 1780-1840* (Berkeley, CA: University of California Press, 1969), xi, 115, 152. See generally: Richard Buel, Jr., *Securing the Revolution: Ideology in American Politics, 1789-1815* (Ithaca, NY: Cornell University Press, 1972); Lance Banning, *The Jeffersonian Persuasion: Evolution of a Party Ideology* (Ithaca, NY: Cornell University Press, 1978), 252-74.
2. Hofstadter, *Party System*, 182-88. Many leading eastern institutions remained strongly federalist until after the War of 1812. Joseph Dorfman, *The Economic Mind in American Civilization: 1606-1865*, 5 vols. (New York: Kelley, 1946), 2:504.
3. Obituary of Captain John Posey, Thornton and Posey Family Bible, The Presbyterian Study Center, Montreat, NC.
4. *Dictionary of American Biography*, 1963 ed., s.v. "Hopkins, Samuel," 5:218-19; E.L. Starling, *History of Henderson County, Kentucky*, 2nd ed. (Evansville, IN: Unigraphics, Inc., 1887), 796; Maralea Arnett, *The Annals & Scandals of Henderson County, Ky., (1775-1925)* (Henderson, KY: Audubon Printers, 1976), 5-10; William Steward Lester, *The Transylvania Colony* (Spencer, IN: S. R. Guard Co., 1935), 276.
5. Williard Rouse Jillson, ed., *Old Kentucky Entries and Deeds* (Baltimore: Genealogical Publishing Co., 1978), 355. Posey later got a military warrant for another 833 1/3 acres on 16 September 1807 for his ten months' service as brigadier-general in Wayne's Northwest expedition of 1793-1794. *Virginia Soldiers of 1776*, 3 vols. (Baltimore: Genealogical Publishing Co., 1973), 3:1437.
6. Walter Havighurst, *River to the West* (New York: Putnam, 1970), 151.
7. S.L. Marshall, "General Thomas Posey as Civilian and Politician," 16 January 1934, Posey File, Kentucky Historical Society Library, Frankfort, KY.
8. Thomas Posey to George Washington, 1 June 1791, *The George Washington Papers* (Washington, DC: Library of Congress, 1964, text-fiche), reel 122 (Hereafter cited as *GW Papers—text-fiche—LC).*
9. Posey to William Lytle, 14 January and 30 January 1804, Lytle Papers, Cincinnati Historical Society Library, Cincinnati, OH. Posey still owned this tract in 1809. His Kentucky land holdings then totaled 23,716 acres of unimproved realty in Campbell, Bracken, Hopkins, Ohio and Jefferson counties, plus 1,125 homestead acres in Henderson County. Letter of 9 May 1922, Kentucky State Historical Society to John E. Englehart, Thomas Posey Folder No. 000208, Mt. Vernon Public Library, Mt. Vernon, IN.
10. Thomas D. Clark, *Kentucky: Land of Contrast* (New York, Evanston, and London: Harper & Row, 1968), 99-100.
11. Lexington (KY) *Kentucky Gazette and General Advertiser*, 13 November and 20 November 1804; Letter of 9 May 1922, Kentucky State Historical Society to John E. Inglehart, Thomas Posey Folder No. 000208, Mt. Vernon Public Library, Mt. Vernon, IN.
12. Milton Lomask, *Aaron Burr: The Conspiracy and Years of Exile, 1805-1836* (New York: Farrar, Straus, Giroux, 1982), 16-19.

13. For an excellent recent biography of Scott, see generally: Harry W. Ward, *Charles Scott and the "Spirit of '76"* (Charlottesville, VA: The University Press of Virginia, 1988).
14. *Dictionary of American Biography*, 1963 ed., s.v. "Hopkins, Samuel," 5:218-19.
15. Robert H. Wiebe, *The Opening of American Society* (New York: Alfred A. Knopf, 1984), xi-xv, 3-41.
16. Lewis and Richard H. Collins, *History of Kentucky*, 2 vols. (Covington, KY: Southern History Press, 1874), 1:363; Frankfort (KY) *Palladium*, 26 November 1806.
17. *Kentucky Gazette and General Advertiser*, 1 July 1806; *Palladium*, 26 June 1806. The latter paper noted, "this gentleman has spent several years in the service of his country; and that since the death of the Lieutenant Governor he has ably and satisfactorily discharged the duties of Speaker of the Senate."
18. *Dictionary of American Biography*, 1963 ed., s.v. "Street, Joseph Montfort," 9:136-37. Wilkinson's secret letter of 18 September 1789 to Spanish Governor Estevan Miro solicited bribes ostensibly to sway several Kentucky notables, (including Innes, Brown, and Sebastian), toward separatism, but it is likely that most, if not all, of the $17,700 he sought went into Wilkinson's own pocket. W.R. Shepard, "Documents," *American Historical Review*, 9(1904): 764-65
19. *Dictionary of American Biography*, 1963 ed., s.v. "Marshall, Humphrey," 6:209-310; s.v. "Davies, Joseph Hamilton," 3:80.
20. "From the *Western World*," *Palladium*, 17 July 1806.
21. Ibid.
22. Ward, *Scott*, 157.
23. "From the *Western World*," *Palladium*, 17 July 1806.
24. "Letter from Gen. Posey to a correspondent in Lexington," Paladium, 23 October 1806.
25. Ibid.
26. Ibid.
27. David Franklin Munro, *George Washington and the Temptations of the Political Life* (Richmond, VA: The Society of the Cincinnati in the State of Virginia, 1983), 35-36. One recent study says that Washington believed in and eventually threw his support to Alexander Hamilton's federalist policies. John E. Ferling, *The First of Men: A Life of George Washington* (Knoxville, TN: The University of Tennessee Press, 1988), 417-18.
28. "Letter from Gen. Posey to a correspondent in Lexington," *Palladium*, 26 October 1806.
29. *Palladium*, 6 November 1806; "Debate in the Senate of Kentucky," *Palladium*, 26 November and 27 November 1806.
30. *Dictionary of American Biography,* 1963 ed., s.v. "Burr, Aaron," 2:314-420; For detailed accounts of Burr, see generally: Philip Vail, *The Great American Rascal* (New York: Hawthorne Books, 1973); Lomask, *Burr*.
31. "The United States versus Aaron Burr," *Palladium*, 13 November 1806.
32. Bill of Sale from A. Smith, 3 May 1806, *The Papers of Henry Clay*, ed. James F. Hopkins and Mary W. Hargreaves, 9 vols. to date (Lexington, KY: The University Press of Kentucky, 1959-), 1:234.

33. Ibid., Francis T. Brooke to Henry Clay, 2 June 1804, 1:137-38; 12 December 1804, 1:161-62; 12 December 1805, 1:213-13; 22 February 1806, 1:219-20.
34. Thomas D. Clark, *A History of Kentucky* (New York: Prentice-Hall, 1937), 173-74; William E. Connelley and E.M. Coulter, *History of Kentucky*, 5 vols. (Chicago: American Historical Society, 1924), 1:447.
35. "Communication," *Palladium*, 13 November 1806.
36. Ibid.
37. Lomask, *Burr*, 142-148. For a scholarly legal account of Burr's Kentucky court proceedings, see: Mary K. Bonsteel Tachau, *Federal Courts in the Early Republic: Kentucky, 1789-1816* (Princeton, NJ: Princeton University Press, 1978), 138-44.
38. *Dictionary of American Biography*, 1963 ed., s.v. "Wilkinson, James," 10:222-26; John Edward Weems, *Men Without Countries* (Boston: Houghton Mifflin Co., 1969), 175-87; Thomas R. Hay and Morris R. Werner, *The Admirable Trumpter* (New York: Doubleday, 1941), 265-67; Royal Ornan Shreve, *The Finished Scoundrel* (Indianapolis: Bobs-Merrill, 1933), 160-70.
39. See generally, all works cited in note 38 above.
40. *Kentucky Gazette and General Advertiser*, 12 January 1808.
41. Lomask, *Burr*, 193-94. Despite misgivings, Jackson finalized arrangements to procure two provision-laden boats for Burr and later went to Richmond prepared to testify on Burr's behalf at his treason trial. Robert V. Remini, *The Life of Andrew Jackson* (New York: Harper/Collins, 1988), 55-60.
42. Lomask, *Burr*, 145-46.
43. Ibid.; Clay later openly acknowledged that he had been totally deceived by Burr and was embarrassed by his gullibility. Tachau, *Federal Courts: Kentucky*, 145; Hopkins, ed., *Papers of Clay*, 1:256-57, 271-76, 280-81, 310-11.
44. Clark, *History of Kentucky*, 248. One analytical observer has adjudged that all principals, both pro- and anti-Burr, who were involved in the Kentucky proceedings, have been vindicated by history. Tachau, *Federal Courts: Kentucky*, 145.
45. Burr was closer to Posey's friend Henry Lee; the two attended Princeton together, and Lee, as a Virginia congressman, voted for Burr rather than Jefferson in the deadlocked presidential race of 1800. Charles Royster, *Light-Horse Harry Lee and the Legacy of the American Revolution* (New York: Alfred A. Knopf, 1981), 207.
46. Collins, *History of Kentucky*, 1:363.
47. Message to Governor Christopher Greenup from Thomas Posey, Speaker of the State Senate of Kentucky, November-December 1807, Greenup Papers, Kentucky Department for Libraries and Archives, Frankfort, KY
48. Ibid.
49. Ward, *Scott*, 156-69.
50. Ibid., 171. MS Commission, Governor Charles Scott to Thomas Posey, 28 October 1808, Thomas Posey Papers, Indiana Historical Society Library, Indianapolis, IN (Hereafter cited as IHS).
51. Ward, *Scott*, 179.
52. Scott to Posey, 22 May 1809, quoted in S.L. Marshall, "General Thomas Posey as Civilian and Politician," Posey File, Kentucky Historical Society Library, Frankfort, KY.

53. Posey to Scott, 7 June 1809, *Gunther Collection*, Letter File, Chicago Historical Society Library, Chicago, IL.
54. Thomas Posey to Thornton A. Posey, 28 November 1808, Gratz Collection, Historical Society of Pennsylvania Library, Philadelphia, PA.
55. Ibid.
56. *Dictionary of American Biography*, 1963 ed., s.v. "Street, Joseph Montfort," 9:136-37; Hopkins, ed., *Papers of Clay*, 1:296, 358, 649; William B. Street, "General Joseph M. Street," *Annals of Iowa*, 2:2-3, 3d ser. (Des Moines, IA: Iowa Historical Society, July-October 1895), 82-84; George Wilson, "General Joseph M. Street," *Register of the Kentucky Historical Society* (Frankfort, KY: Kentucky Historical Society, September 1906), 23-24; "The Romantic Career of Gen. Street," Milwaukee (WI) *Sentinel*, 15 May 1907.
57. See generally, all works cited in note 56 above.
58. Posey to Scott, 4 December 1809, Thomas Posey Papers, IHS.
59. Harrison to Scott, 4 April 1810, *Governors' Messages and Letters: Messages and Letters of William Henry Harrison*, ed. Logan Esarey (Indianapolis: Ayer Co. Publishers, 1922), 1:400-17; Ward, *Scott*, 182.
60. "A Short Biography of the Life of Governor Thomas Posey," Thomas Posey Papers, IHS.

CHAPTER EIGHT

(1810-1813)

"I am not . . . above shewing an example to my fellow citizens. . . ."

Thomas Posey was accounted a resident of Kentucky's Henderson County in the federal census of 1810,[1] but the arrival of a new decade found him busily planning a major move to the Territory of Orleans. Posey's nature was intrinsically restive and venturesome, but his decision was based partly upon more practical considerations. The long-planned removal from Virginia to Kentucky had not brought the financial security he envisioned for himself and his family. Farming was, at best, a marginal and precarious existence, and the prospect of further military assignments was highly uncertain. His investments in land had been notably unprofitable—securing and establishing clear legal title to real property in Kentucky was notoriously difficult, and Thomas simply did not have the combination of foresight, patience, canniness and luck that characterized most of the successful land speculators of his day. Public office offered the most promising means of maintaining a comfortable lifestyle, but after the Burr affair his political prospects in Kentucky were not propitious. They had been further diminished by the election of General Charles Scott to the governorship. Two military heroes in one state was one too many, and if he was to improve his public and private fortunes, it was time to move along.

Conversely, the heavy burden of educating his family was gradually lightening with the progressive maturation of most of his older children during their first decade on the frontier. Of the older sons, John and Fayette, (the latter a sometime major in the state militia), were now well-established householders in Henderson County, duly recorded as such in the 1810 census, along with their 21-year old brother William, a merchant.[2] Army captain Thornton Posey had recently been transferred from Kentucky to the garrison at Vincennes, Indiana Territory, where a violent and career-threatening encounter with a fellow officer awaited him. Twenty-five-year-old Lloyd Posey was nurturing a budding law practice in the Opelousas district of Orleans Territory, while holding local appointive offices in St. Mary's Parish and the settlement of LaFourche.[3]

Daughter Eliza Maria Posey Street, her studies at Lexington's Academy for Young Ladies cut short by her early marriage, would soon accompany her duel-scarred, debt-ridden husband across the Ohio River to nearby Shawneetown, Illinois Territory. Sixteen-year-old Alexander, the family scholar, had been put under the tutelage of Dr. John Croghan of Louisville. He would later go on to medical and divinity degrees at the University of Pennsylvania, and a brilliant medical practice. It was undoubtedly these past and continuing educational expenses that contributed to the reduction of Thomas' liquid cash assets in 1808 to the deplorable sum of "but one solitary dollar."[4]

It thus appears that, of Posey's ten children, only 19-year-old Thomas and young Washington, age 11, were still resident members of the family's Henderson County homestead in 1810. (Their youngest sister, Sarah Ann, left in Virginia eight years before, had never joined her Kentucky siblings). The younger Thomas possibly accompanied his father on one or more exploratory trips to Louisiana in 1811 in search of a future family homesite. These journeys, and the contemplated move itself, presented no formidable travel problems. With a convenient water route down the Ohio and Mississippi rivers, and a much smaller household and retinue, the trip would be much faster and infinitely more comfortable than the arduous overland trek across the Appalachians to Kentucky a decade earlier. But there is no evidence that Mary Posey herself ever visited Louisiana. She appears, during this period, to have continued to preside over the family hearth and home at Longview.[5]

Long before the Louisiana Purchase of 1803 brought the lower Mississippi delta and the port of New Orleans under American sovereignty, the area had been a tempting target for a wide and varied array of immigrants. Initially opened to settlement by the French, it was forty years under Spanish rule, then briefly restored to

France before its purchase by the Jefferson administration. Acadian refugees from British Nova Scotia and other early French-speaking settlers—generally called Creoles—made up its largest single ethnic component. But there were also well-defined enclaves of Spanish and German derivation, a growing Anglo-Saxon trickle coming mainly from Tennessee and Kentucky, and a sizable black population, both slave and free, concentrated in and around the capital of New Orleans.[6] So it was indeed a polyglot citizenry that assembled in the historic Cabildo on 20 December 1803 to witness the ceremony at which the United States took formal possession of its new $15,000,000 acquisition. Delegated to represent the American government on the occasion were General James Wilkinson, ranking military commander in the west, and William C. C. Claiborne, then governor of adjacent Mississippi Territory, who was soon to be named territorial governor of the southern part of the Louisiana Purchase, called the Territory of Orleans.[7]

Claiborne, a native Virginian, had gone west and earned his political spurs when, as a Tennessee congressman, he swung that state's delegation to Thomas Jefferson over Aaron Burr in the presidential electoral contest of 1800. Given the territorial governorship as a political reward, he proved to be a competent, conscientious administrator. He worked in close concert with General Wilkinson in the crisis provoked by the perceived threat to New Orleans posed by the advance of Burr's armed force down the Mississippi in early 1807. Wilkinson, not unlike Burr, seems to have had the knack of working harmoniously with scrupulous and honorable men such as Claiborne, often while manipulating them to his own designs. After assuming the governorship of Orleans Territory, Claiborne was at least moderately successful in reconciling the wildly diverse ethnic elements of his constituency. When Louisiana became a state early in 1812, Claiborne ran for the office of governor, and somewhat to his own surprise was elected over a respected native-born Creole, General Jacques Villere.[8]

There is no evidence in the record that James Wilkinson triggered Thomas Posey's interest in Louisiana, or influenced his decision to settle there. Governor Claiborne does not appear to have even met Kentucky's former lieutenant-governor until some time after his first arrival there in late 1810. But it is apparent from later events that Posey soon gained the respect and confidence of the Louisiana governor, and rekindled his sporadic friendship with his old comrade-in-arms, General Wilkinson. During these same early months, largely devoted to exploring the area and settling upon a likely spot to establish a new home for his wife and family, Thomas was more than a little distracted by two major personal crises. One raised the specter of financial ruin from a long-forgotten incident in his Revolutionary War days, and the other brought the apparent disgrace and possible condemnation of one of his sons.

In early 1811 Governor Scott of Kentucky forwarded to Posey in Louisiana a letter from Isaac Wayne, the son and Executor of the last will and testament of the late General Anthony Wayne. Young Wayne informed Thomas that attorneys representing Patrick Crookshank, a British merchant, had filed a legal action in Pennsylvania seeking to recover a judgment for £1,415 from Posey and the Wayne estate. The claim was based upon a 1782 contract entered into in newly liberated Savannah, Georgia, between Crookshank and certain junior officers of Posey's Virginia Battalion for the purchase of supplies and clothing, the terms of which were alleged to have been personally guaranteed by Wayne and Posey. The suit stated that neither the officers who signed the contract nor the state of Virginia (which was responsible for supplying its troops) had delivered to the merchant the quantities of tobacco agreed upon as payment for their purchases, or otherwise settled up for the balance due the British merchant.[9]

The claim, if legally valid and enforceable, would have bankrupted the financially strapped Posey. He must have been stunned by the emergence, after nearly thirty years, of this devastating potential liability, and his response to Wayne reflects his outrage and anger. He confirmed that "a parcel of half-starved & naked officers did purchase of a Mr. Crookshank a merchant that had been left behind by the British army a parcel of goods the amount of which I know not neither was ever furnished with." But Thomas vehemently denied that either he or General Wayne had entered into any agreement with the merchant to guarantee the delivery of tobacco, or to assume any personal obligation for the performance of the contract terms. They had, in fact, expressly refused to do so. Their only involvement was a verbal promise to use whatever influence they had with the state government to redeem the commitments of the junior officers. That he had done, Posey informed Isaac Wayne, by promptly writing Virginia Governor Benjamin Harrison, urging that the state recognize its responsibility for maintaining its ill-supplied fighting men. But Harrison had replied that the then-existing state of war legally precluded the delivery of tobacco or other produce to a British subject either by the state or any of its citizens.[10]

After the war, Posey continued, he had met personally in Richmond with Crookshank, who informed him that the officers had paid a portion of the debt, and were making arrangements to settle the balance. The merchant agreed that Posey and Wayne had carried out their promise to the best of their ability, and that he would not look further to them in the matter. But in any event, Thomas advised the son of his old wartime comrade, if Crookshank pressed his case and imposed any liability on the Wayne estate, Isaac should petition Congress for relief, since the clothing and food had been "absolutely necessary not only to the comfort but to the saving of the lives of many valuable officers & soldiers under our command." It was unthinkable, Posey felt, that the country would not come to the assistance of the Waynes, as it had done in a similar case involving General Nathanael Greene for army supplies purchased in Charleston. "General Wayne had been one of the great instruments in giving the standing which the United States assumed in the ranks of the great nations of the earth." In Thomas' estimation, Wayne deserved to be ranked either second or third behind Washington in the order of top American generals in the War of Independence.[11]

Interestingly, even in a context largely concerned with legal matters, Posey's letter to young Wayne literally brimmed with a sense of generational pride and historical achievement. Thirty years after the war, he had an acute awareness, bordering almost on wonderment, of individual and collective accomplishment in producing a nation which, in his own time, had attained the stature of a world power. As for Crookshank, he apparently did not further pursue his claim against the Waynes and Posey, as Thomas' correspondence makes no further reference to the case. But just as this worrisome threat was waning, he was overtaken by another traumatic event, one more personal and not nearly so easily shrugged off.

In July of 1810 Captain Thornton Posey had marched his company of regular army troops from Kentucky to Vincennes, the historic old capital of Indiana Territory. Within a year, Captain Posey was the garrison commander of Fort Knox, located just outside the town, charged with the duty of countering a growing threat posed to the Wabash River valley settlers by an Indian confederation organized by the warlike Tecumseh.[12] In the interim, unfortunately, bad blood had developed between Thornton and another Kentuckian, Lieutenant Jesse Jennings, the next-ranking company commander stationed at the fort. Their personal differences worsened. Early in June of 1811, Jennings told at least two persons that he intended to kill the captain if he could, and Posey confided to others that he had twice found the lieutenant lurking outside the door of his quarters, with the apparent intent to ambush or assassinate him.[13]

Late in the evening of 23 June, the fort's commissary officer heard two shots ring out. Rushing to the barracks area, he saw Lieutenant Jennings, mortally wounded, stagger out the open door of Captain Posey's quarters and fall dead. The captain at first warned the Commissary away, but later asked him to come in, and related the following account of the tragic event. Detecting Jennings at his door, Posey had called him inside, challenged him, and offered him the choice of two loaded dueling pistols. When the lieutenant refused to make a choice, Thornton thrust one of them into his hand. Jennings, instead of firing, seized Posey by the throat with his free hand, and began to choke him. The captain then fired his own pistol, causing the lieutenant to drop his weapon. But when he did not release his grip on Posey's throat, the captain picked up the fallen pistol and shot Jennings a second time.[14]

With its two ranking officers involved in the shooting, the garrison was in a state of chaos. A few hours after the encounter, Captain Thornton Posey, accompanied by a sergeant of his company, rode out of Fort Knox. He returned to his regimental headquarters at Louisville and placed himself in the custody of his immediate superior officer. Back in Vincennes, the incident was reported to Secretary of War William Eustis by territorial Governor William Henry Harrison, a good friend of Captain Posey's father from their service together in Wayne's Northwest Legion. Governor Harrison expressed the fear that the then-known circumstances, even "if viewed in the most favorable light for the Captain . . . are such as to attach an imputation upon his character which he will never be able to wipe off, if indeed he should escape an ignominious death."[15]

But the governor's dire foreboding, based upon the fragmentary information at his disposal, did not materialize. In the stressful hours before he departed Fort Knox, young Posey had written out and sent directly to the Secretary of War a full account of the encounter, and the circumstances preceding it. This report appears to have satisfied higher military authorities that Thornton had acted in justifiable self-defense in the affair. Although there is no existing record of a formal court martial, he seems to have been fully exonerated by the army from any guilt or punishment. At the time of the shooting incident, Posey's promotion to the rank of major was being processed, and it was eventually approved by Secretary Eustis retroactive to 6 June 1811. As of the same date, he was officially transferred from the Seventh to the Fifth U.S. Infantry Regiment.[16]

In distant Louisiana, Thomas Posey, upon getting first reports of this dark drama, must have agonized for months over Thornton's behavior and fate, before learning of his eventual vindication. In retrospect, the pain and anxiety of those times was to be alleviated by paternal pride in the subsequent military exploits of the only one of his sons who had chosen to follow his father into the honorable profession of arms. Thornton Posey served his country well throughout the War of 1812. He rose to the rank of lieutenant colonel, and after being reassigned to the Seventh Infantry on 30 April 1813, fought with distinction under General Andrew Jackson in the bloody Battle of New Orleans.[17] But sadly, after retiring from the army, he was destined to predecease his father, succumbing to yellow fever contracted while leading a daring invasion of Spanish-held Amelia Island, Florida, under the flag of a legendary Scottish soldier-of-fortune, General Sir Gregor MacGregor.[18]

Thomas' exploratory sojourn in the Territory of Orleans coincided with that entity's transition into statehood. The Union into which Louisiana was officially received as its eighteenth state on 30 April 1812 was a nation poised on the brink of war. Its old enemy, Great Britain, had abandoned all restraint in its desperate worldwide struggle with the Napoleonic powers. It stepped up the practice of stopping American ships on the high seas to search for and impound cargoes it considered contraband, and to forcibly impress into its own naval service any seamen who could not prove their American citizenship. Meanwhile, the British were pursuing their traditional policy of destabilizing the American interior; from their Canadian bases, they continued to incite and arm Indian tribes along the northern and western frontiers of the United States. Finally, strongly pressed by President James Madison, Congress by a narrow margin declared war on 18 June. This drastic action was popularly supported in the southern and western states, but was bitterly opposed by extreme federalist majorities in New England, and some of those states actively obstructed the prosecution of the war effort. "Mr. Madison's War" was openly derided in some areas, and Massachusetts, Connecticut and Rhode Island refused at times to meet federal militia requisitions. At the Hartford Convention of 1814, called by states in the northeast, there was vocal support for the outright secession of New England from the Union, and the making of a separate peace by the region with Great Britain.[19]

Posey had nothing but contempt for those who failed to rally to the support of their country in time of war. In his view, not to step forward in such a crisis would have betrayed everything he had fought for as a soldier in the Revolution. Far from sympathizing with the eastern Federalists whose unwelcome label had proven so politically damaging to him in the past, Thomas was from the outset a vigorous supporter of the nation's resumption of hostilities with its old enemy. News of the war's beginning found him living temporarily in Baton Rouge, the major population center of what had been until recently the western portion of Spanish West Florida. Two years before, American settlers in the area had overthrown Spanish rule, petitioned for annexation to the United States, and been received into Governor Claiborne's Orleans Territory. There is no evidence, however, that Posey had been among the "filibusters" spearheading this uprising, who had been privately encouraged by President Madison, even while he publicly disassociated his government from their actions.[20]

The recently Americanized citizens in the Baton Rouge area were eager to demonstrate their loyalty to their new country, and they found in Thomas Posey the ideal leader around whom to rally. Within weeks after word of the new war arrived in Louisiana, Posey had personally recruited and outfitted, at his own expense, a full company of volunteer soldiers. The offer of the services of himself and his company to the American army for the duration of the conflict was gratefully accepted. On 14 September he was officially commissioned a captain, and authorized "to command a company of volunteers levied by him in the District of Louisiana." On the back of his formal certificate of commission, Thomas hand-wrote:

> I accept of this commission merely to discover that I am not (altho of the rank of Majr. Genl.) above shewing an example to my fellow citizens especially at this critical period the commencement of a second war with the British. TH. POSEY[21]

Posey's mandate was issued, signed and elaborately sealed in red wax by an old associate, General James Wilkinson, then the ranking military commander on the southwest frontier. Two years earlier, his first wife having died, the general had taken a young Creole woman as his bride. Soon thereafter, he had been summoned back to Maryland to stand court-martial on charges related to his role in the Burr conspiracy and recurrent reports of his secret Spanish connections. But the crafty Wilkinson never faced a military court he could not confound. As in all previous courts of inquiry—and as would occur in a later court martial—he was found not guilty on all charges. When the verdict, as dictated by military protocol, was forwarded to President Madison, it was accepted, curtly but meaningfully, "with regret." He had hoped that the court-martial would finally rid the service of the perennially troublesome and politically embarrassing general.[22]

The acquittal automatically restored Wilkinson's status as the ranking brigadier general of the army, and his military command in New Orleans. He set sail immediately for that city, arriving on 9 July 1812 only to learn for the first time that the nation was at war with England. He acted promptly and effectively to prepare that strategic and vulnerable port against attack expected imminently from a British fleet then entering the Gulf of Mexico. A coordinated land offensive from the adjacent borders of Mexico and West Florida—territories of a Spain now allied with the British—was a distinct possibility. To forestall that danger, Wilkinson ably mounted a show of military strength to force the peaceful withdrawal from Mobile of a weak Spanish garrison. At the same time, he dispatched regular army units to reinforce American outposts on the western border of Louisiana.[23]

Because he needed all the help he could get in augmenting the meager forces available to defend the area, General Wilkinson undoubtedly welcomed and encouraged Posey's offer to recruit and equip a volunteer militia company. Perhaps he also perceived, characteristically, that Thomas, in the limited role of a company commander, would pose no threat to his own position as commanding general in the district. As for Posey, his soldierly career had now come full circle from the time, thirty-six years before, when he raised and led his first company of frontier riflemen out of Virginia's Shenandoah Valley. The doughty old campaigner, a lieutenant colonel under Washington, brigadier general under Wayne, and recent major general of Kentucky militia was, at the age of sixty-two years, quite ready and eager to don a captain's insignia and, as at Stony Point, spur his new company of volunteers over the nearest enemy ramparts.

But, probably to his own regret, it was not ordained that "Captain" Posey would ever again seize a spontoon and lead a phalanx of men in another desperate bayonet charge, or slash a path with his sword through another wave of attacking Indian warriors. Early in October, just as he had completed preparations to take the field with his company under Wilkinson's command, he was notified that he had been appointed to serve as one of the first two men to represent the new state of Louisiana in the United States Senate.

The Louisiana General Assembly, pursuant to then-prevailing constitutional law, had recently selected two well-regarded officials, Allan B. Magruder and Jean-Noel Destrehan, as the state's first federal senators. Destrehan, however, submitted his formal resignation on 1 October, before actually taking office. With the state legislature then in adjournment, Governor Claiborne was empowered by law to fill the vacancy with a temporary replacement. Within a week he wrote a letter, directed to "Major General Posey" at Baton Rouge, stating that:

> Confiding in your private and public virtues—Grateful for your past services to your country, & assured of your devotion to the principles of Civil & religious freedom;—Believing also that you highly appreciate the government & union of these States, & that the present eventful Crisis, you will firmly support such measures as the honor, the safety, the Independence of the Nation advise, I take great pleasure, in transmitting you a Commission, by which you are appointed a Senator of the United States.[24]

The governor further noted with regret that the appointment was only temporary and that its continuance was conditional upon legislative approval, but expressed his strong hope that this unavoidable circumstance would not deter Posey from accepting the office. He felt it imperative that Louisiana be fully represented in the federal government at this time of national crisis. Since the Congress was scheduled to reconvene in extraordinary session in the near future, Claiborne emphasized that "it is important that you repair to Washington with all possible dispatch." He closed his letter with "a fervent wish, that my choice may be confirmed by the Legislature of this State."[25]

There is no evidence that Thomas had applied for this high position, and it is unlikely that he even knew of its availability in the short interval between Destrehan's resignation and the date of his appointment. He was undoubtedly pleasantly surprised and honored when it was offered to him. There is some indication, however, that James Wilkinson may have proposed Posey's name to the governor. The general was always on top of any subtle shift in the political winds in the state capital, and he was still in Claiborne's full confidence. Significantly, the official appointment notice and its accompanying certificate of commission did not come to Posey directly from the governor's office. They arrived as enclosures in a personal letter Wilkinson sent to Thomas two days later: "It is with infinite pleasure I send you the enclosed Evidence of your appointment to the Senate of the United States." Strongly implying that he had played a key role in securing the post for Posey, Wilkinson urged him to accept the assignment in spite of its uncertain duration. The general promised further that "I shall be able in cooperation with the Governor, I do verily believe, to assure the ratification of your appointment."[26]

But the artful Wilkinson did not stop with these heartening if nebulous affirmations of support and influence. Assuming the unsolicited role of personal adviser to his old comrade, he assured Posey that even if the state legislature failed to confirm his nomination, "the trip will be important to you." Perhaps he was referring to financial rather than political advantage, as he next made the point that Thomas' mileage allowance for the long trip from Louisiana to Washington would in itself total nearly one thousand dollars. The general was indeed so anxious to send Posey on his way that he even offered to finance the trip himself. If Posey found himself short of ready cash to cover his travel expenses, Wilkinson urged, "treat me like a Brother and draw on me at thirty or forty day's sight for two or three hundred dollars, which you can repay in the City of Washington."[27]

With all the advantages of historical hindsight, the true motivations of James Wilkinson in this incident (and, in fact, throughout his entire public life) remain an impenetrable enigma. He was a man who truly raised rascality to an art form, and seemingly sought self-advantage from every turn of events, favorable or otherwise. He clearly liked and respected Posey, and probably did recommend him to Claiborne for the senatorial vacancy—but even had he not actually done so, he would not have been above claiming credit anyway. As for his real reasons for backing Thomas, it may be charitably hoped that he knew Louisiana would thereby get a worthy representative in the capital. But it must also have crossed his mind that the appointment would remove from the area an experienced and well-regarded general officer, one whom the Madison administration might well have considered as his own replacement as military commander in the region, (as indeed it did later). Better to have Posey in Washington than on some nearby battlefield conspicuously defending Louisiana's borders. Furthermore, Wilkinson knew only too well that he was on very shaky ground with the national authorities. He badly needed a friendly voice and vote in the federal Senate, where, in the haste of war mobilization, coveted major generalships were being parceled out to brigadiers of lower standing and lesser experience than himself.

It may be said, not unfairly, that even when James Wilkinson did the right thing, it nearly always sprang at least in part from the wrong reasons. Perhaps it was just such a paradoxical quirk of reasoning from the complex mind of a "finished scoundrel" that sent Posey to the United States Senate. In any event, the general now assured Thomas, with every display of evident sincerity, that he intended to become his biggest advocate and booster in gaining the confirmation of the state legislature. He pointedly asked that Posey provide him with "a particular memorandum of your Revolutionary Services, the actions in which you were engaged, the rank you held & the date of each operation as well as memory serves—I mean to become your Biographer."[28]

Governor Claiborne, for his part, wasted no time in soliciting support for the ratification and extension of Posey's temporary senatorial appointment. In a letter to Judge Andrew Steele, an influential jurist in Baton Rouge, he expressed hope that all or most of the legislators from Filiciana County, (formerly West Florida), would unite in confirming his choice for the position:

> I have always considered the Soldiers & patriots of Seventy six, as the fathers of our Country, & that their service should never be forgotten by a grateful people.—Of Genl. Posey's private virtues, all who know him can bear testimony, & of his faithful public service every one acquainted with American History must have a knowledge.[29]

Nowhere is there better expressed the esteem, reverence and gratitude felt for the soldiers of the revolutionary generation by most of the people living in the frontier regions. While Kentucky's Charles Scott best exemplifies the phenomenon, new leaders such as Claiborne and Indiana's Harrison, who were too young to have fought in the War of Independence, turned consistently to the dwindling numbers of revolutionary veterans in their areas to fill responsible civil and military posts. Earlier reference has been made to Charles Royster's scholarly thesis that the motivating force driving the "soldiers and patriots of Seventy six" was their consciousness of how future generations would judge their actions.[30] In the development of the western states, the roles meted out to Thomas Posey and his contemporaries by the first postwar generation of leaders appear to validate and honor the revolutionaries' sense of historical accountability and accomplishment. But at this very time, powerful social, economic and political forces were at work that would shortly transform the central hierarchical order of the old gentry leaders into a class-driven, state-dominated democracy.[31]

Posey had, of course, quickly accepted his senatorial appointment and set out for Washington. The less time-consuming sea route from New Orleans was cut off by a British naval blockade, so, accompanied only by his faithful manservant Billy, he rode north from Baton Rouge on horseback, following the long but well-beaten overland route paralleling the Mississippi and Ohio rivers. If he paused in Kentucky to see his wife Mary and his family, the visit must have been very brief, indeed. He reached the capital city on 6 December, "in tolerable good health considering the distance of the journey, considerable rainy weather, high waters, and bad roads."[32] He found upon his arrival that Congress was already sitting, called into emergency session to act upon the many pressing issues raised by a sputtering war effort. On the next morning Thomas Posey, freshly powdered, bewigged and dressed in his best civilian apparel, presented his official credentials to Vice-President George Clinton, the presiding officer of the Senate. He was immediately assigned to, and took his seat at, one of the back desks of that eminent body's small, ornate chamber, as one of Louisiana's first two United States senators.[33]

Despite the advance portents of the impending conflict, the divided nation had been totally unprepared for the war upon which it had embarked. Consistent with prevailing republican ideology, the regular army and navy had been kept small and weak, and the disparate state militia systems were incapable of producing a combat-ready force. With the notable exception of the northwest frontier, the first year of hostilities brought an almost unbroken series of humiliating military setbacks, due in large measure to incompetent field commanders and inept civilian officials. As time and events exposed their inadequacies, they were replaced by others, often of little better ilk. Posey, after taking his seat in the Senate, was promptly immersed in the daily public debate, committee deliberations, and cloakroom bargaining aimed at correcting the personnel, supply and political problems contributing to the lagging war effort.

Only ten days after taking his oath of office Thomas, in a letter to Philip Hickey, (a friendly Louisiana legislator), outlined a long series of emergency military measures being considered by Congress. He mentioned the wholesale changes taking place in President Madison's cabinet, including the resignation of Secretary of War William Eustis. The secretary's duties had been temporarily assumed by Posey's old Virginia senator and Fredericksburg friend, James Monroe, who already held the high post of Secretary of State. If was rumored, Posey told Hickey, that Monroe would soon be named commander-in-chief of the army with the rank of lieutenant general. There was also talk that James Wilkinson would shortly be recalled from Louisiana, promoted to major general, and put in command of one wing of a new army then being readied for a planned major invasion of British Canada.[34]

Meanwhile, Posey had it on the highest authority that he himself was under active consideration by the administration for a major military appointment. In mid-January, he informed his son-in-law, Joseph Street, that,

> Shortly after my arrival here Mr. Monroe asked me if I would accept a command in the army. I told him whenever my country thought proper to call for my services I should always obey the call. He said he was glad to hear it, and wanted me (as he had charge of the War Office) to call frequently and render what services I could in arranging the staff of the army.[35]

Thomas told Street that he was giving every moment he could spare to the army staff duties assigned to him by Secretary Monroe, "but have been so closely engaged in the Senate that I could not devote as much of my time to the War Office as I could have wished."[36] Reading between the lines, one can sense that the old soldier's heart was less in Washington that with the troops facing the British enemy in the field. But even while he was applying all his time and energies to his legislative and military commitments in the capital, Posey was suffering an unexpected personal and political defeat in Louisiana.

Governor Claiborne, to his own great embarrassment, found it necessary to notify Thomas in late January that the state General Assembly had failed to extend his temporary appointment to the Senate. "Attribute not my long silence to a want of friendship or respect, but rather to the mortification I have experienced at the unjust course which the Legislature of Louisiana pursued toward you, & the wish I had, that the information should first reach you thro' another Channel."[37] The governor detailed the complex factors leading to the legislature's ultimate election of James Brown of New Orleans to fill out Jean-Noel Destrehan's unexpired term in the Senate. In the critical voting, Posey had received the unanimous backing of the Creole members. But surprisingly the support he might have expected from his natural constituency of West Florida and other non-Creole areas had been evenly split on the first ballot between Brown and a Baton Rouge attorney, William Fulwar Skipwith, "& on the second Ballot . . . (they) voted to a Man for Brown."[38] There is no evidence whatever in the record of any effort by General James Wilkinson to influence the vote or advance Posey's cause in the legislature.

A few days later, Claiborne continued, Posey's name was again proposed in the legislature as a candidate to succeed the other sitting Louisiana senator, Allan B. Magruder, whose term, by lot, was to expire on 3 March 1813. On this ballot, most (except for a decisive few) of the errant West Florida legislators now voted for Thomas, but he lost the support of all the Creole delegates, who swung behind one of their own, Eligius Fromentin. The Creole nominee was thus narrowly elected to the post. The two or three key members whose votes could have elected Posey to either seat, but who consistently opposed him, later explained their position to the exasperated governor. "They did justice to you as a Man & a Soldier—they acknowledged your integrity & faithful public service—but objected to your want of residence in the State, & to your political Tenets, which they thought were federal."[39] So once again, Thomas Posey's political career had been sidetracked by the misplaced but fatal taint of federalism, as it had been before in Virginia and Kentucky, and would be again in Indiana.

Robert H. Wiebe has commented on how, during the early nineteenth-century swing from the "natural aristocracy" of gentry leadership to a broad-based democratic surge, "the name 'Federalist' became a curse, not for its war record, but for its reputation as an enemy of 'the people.' "[40] But an equally important factor in Posey's rejection by the Louisiana General Assembly may have been what Wiebe calls the "new politics of development" which "infected one state legislature after another and quickly came to dominate their proceedings."[41] As the democratization process grew, local and regional interests took precedence over national concerns, and the new state leaders of developmental politics displaced representatives of the old national gentry hierarchy like Posey. Governor Claiborne had cited Thomas' legislative opponents' objections to his "want of residence in the State," and stated elsewhere the members' complaint "that his family is in Kentucky, & that he has no fixed residence in Lousiana."[42] It is evident that Posey was denied ratification of his senatorial appointment by the perception of a few such state developmental leaders that he was more concerned with national than with emerging local and state issues.

Thomas could do little or nothing about his persistent reputation as a Federalist. There was more than a little truth in the assessment that his fierce nationalism and dedication to old revolutionary ideals and goals tended to overshadow his interest in the popular politics of choice and economic self-determination being ever more widely adopted by a new generation of state leaders. But even before he received news of his defeat in Louisiana, he had already taken time from his heavy Washington responsibilities to correct what he might well have considered an even more serious historical injustice—a blot on his soldierly record and reputation. His longtime friend and comrade, Henry Lee of Virginia, had recently published a monumental memoir tracing the southern campaigns of the Revolutionary War. The book contained a detailed description of the attack by Chief Guristersigo's Creek warriors on General Anthony Wayne's encampment outside Savannah, Georgia, on 24 June 1782. Lee's account of this episode, based largely upon the recollections of one of Posey's captains, Alexander Parker, inaccurately depicted Thomas' personal role in the engagement. Posey, after reading the book, wrote out and sent to Lee his own eyewitness account of the battle. To support his corrected version, he also enclosed a recent letter of concurrence from Parker, now a colonel in the regular army, conceding that "your better memory will state the affair in its true light."[43]

"Lighthorse Harry" Lee shared the intense desire and determination of all his revolutionary peers that history preserve the memory and recognize the enormity of their achievements. He responded warmly to Thomas' desire that the record of his performance in the encounter be corrected. "It will give me great pleasure to comply with your request as no doubt exists in my mind, that I was mistaken in my narrative of that engagement, so far as relates to yourself." The first edition, of course, had already been released, but he promised that "if a second edition of the work should take place," it would definitely redress the injustice done in the first to his wartime associate.[44]

That was good enough for Thomas Posey. Neither he nor Henry Lee lived to see the appearance of a second edition—the two old friends died within a week of one another. But the author's son, General Robert E. Lee, honored his father's promise. When an edited version of the original book was published after the Civil War in 1869, the younger Lee inserted in the new edition Posey's verbatim account of the battle, with the editorial comment: "the veracity of Posey was as unquestioned as his courage, and it is satisfactory to be able to render him justice in his own words."[45]

Posey was undoubtedly disappointed to hear that his congressional career had been cut short by the labyrinthine ethnic and ideological maneuvers of the Louisiana General Assembly. One may well wonder, though, if the old campaigner was quite temperamentally suited to the confined and sedentary daily routine of the U.S.

Senate, or if he found himself personally comfortable with the political intrigues and traditions of that contentious if prestigious body. His letters convey a sense of mild resentment that his senatorial duties had left him so little time to attend to the organizational work in the War Office delegated to him by James Monroe. In a time of war, given a preference, Posey by nature and experience would in all likelihood have gladly exchanged his senatorial toga for a military uniform.

If so, Thomas must have been more than casually interested in a rumor passed along to him by Governor Claiborne from New Orleans. It confirmed reports already circulating in the Senate cloakroom, that General James Wilkinson was soon to be recalled from his Louisiana command and reassigned to the Canadian front. But the governor had heard more, of even greater import to Posey: "It is reported here, that you are called to the Armies with the rank of General, & will command in this quarter; I sincerely wish this may be true."[46]

Only the first part of Claiborne's gossip was true. In May of 1813, Wilkinson, having finally received his long-sought promotion to major general, was ordered back to the east and put in charge of an army with orders to advance into Canada and capture Montreal. The "tarnished warrior," despite his hidden Spanish connections, had always competently performed his military duties in his prior border commands, but away from the Western frontier he proved to be strangely indecisive and ineffective. His Montreal campaign was a complete fiasco, and although in the resultant court martial he once again emerged unscathed, he never received another army command or political appointment.[47]

Wilkinson came to an ignominious end. After publishing his voluminous but highly selective memoirs and papers, he died penniless in the very city he and Aaron Burr had once targeted as the capital of their new empire—Mexico City. Long after his death, the full extent of his longtime collaboration with Spain was disclosed in that nation's secret archives—records in which he was identified as the storied "Agent No. 13." But it has never been proven that he used his Spanish ties to harm vital American interests, or if he maintained them merely to assure the continued payment of his annual stipend of shiny gold Spanish doubloons. Thus ended the curious and contradictory life of a man whom historians might well regard as America's first professional double agent, but who nonetheless played a significant role in the career of Thomas Posey.[48]

The vacated army command in Louisiana eventually went, not to Posey, but to a younger rising star in the military firmament, the fiery Andrew Jackson. From the humblest of births and a brief career as an underage fourteen-year-old soldier in the Revolution, he laboriously forged a legal, political and military career in Tennessee. In the War of 1812, he proved his mettle at the battle of Horseshoe Bend in present-day Alabama, leading a force of army regulars and Tennessee volunteers to a decisive victory over the Creeks. This militant tribe was allied once again with the British in the new conflict, just as it had been when Guristersigo and his brave warriors emerged from the south Georgia swamps to attack Thomas Posey's Virginia battalion outside Savannah. General Jackson, of course, went on to glory as the hero of the Battle of New Orleans, a feat that later took him to the nation's highest office.[49] One may wonder what career path Thomas Posey might have followed had he been given the Louisiana command as Governor Claiborne wished.

But the Madison administration had other plans for Posey. His brief Senate service officially ended on 5 February 1813, when his successor, James Brown, took his seat in Congress' upper house.[50] Thomas' sudden availability for other duties, as luck would have it, came at a time when there was a conspicuous vacancy in the west—the governorship of Indiana Territory, a post for which he was eminently qualified. Some months previous, Governor William Henry Harrison had resigned to accept a commission as brigadier general in command of American regular forces in the northwest frontier area. Harrison's mission was to counter a threat to the lower Great Lakes region posed by a British-Canadian force reinforced by Native American warriors from the many tribes in the area which had chosen to throw in their lot with the enemy.[51]

Posey's departure from Congress had allowed him greater opportunity to perform his staff work at the War Office. He also took advantage of his proximity to Virginia to take a brief trip to that state's central Piedmont region, to visit relatives and friends he had not seen since emigrating to the frontier more than a decade earlier. But within three weeks of his departure from the Senate, Posey's name was presented to that body by President Madison as his nominee to fill the gubernatorial post in Indiana Territory left vacant by General Harrison. On 2 March 1813 Thomas' recent senatorial colleagues formally confirmed him for that office.[52] The territorial post confronted Posey with the most demanding and difficult challenges of his entire public career—challenges that would require all the strength and wisdom gleaned from his past experiences in both military and civil life.

NOTES

1. Lowell M. Volkel, ed., *An Index to the 1810 Federal Census of Kentucky*, 2 vols. (Springfield, IL: Lowell M. Volkel, 1917), 2:55.
2. Ibid.
3. Logan Esarey, ed., *Governors' Messages and Letters: Messages and Letters of William Henry Harrison*, 2 vols. (Indianapolis, IN: Ayer Co. Publishers, 1922), 1:423; Dunbar Rowland, ed., *Official Letter Book of W. C. C. Claiborne, 1801-1816*, 6 vols. (Jackson, MS: AMS Press, 1917), 5:222; *The Territory of Orleans, 1803-1812*, vol 9 of *The Territorial Papers of the United States*, ed. Clarence Edwin Carter (Washington, DC: AMS Press, 1940), 985.
4. Thomas Posey to Thornton A. Posey, 28 November 1808, Gratz Collection, Historical Society of Pennsylvania Library, Philadelphia, PA.
5. Posey witnessed two deeds in Baton Rouge in 1811, on 4 May and 11 December. Alma S. Hammond, ed., *Archives of Spanish West Florida* (New Orleans, LA: Work Projects Administration of Louisiana, 1940), 19:428, 451-52. His autobiography states only that he "removed a part of his family" to Louisiana. "A Short Biography of the Life of Governor Thomas Posey," Thomas Posey Papers, Indiana State Historical Society Library, Indianapolis, IN, (hereafter cited as IHS).
6. Joe Gray Taylor, *Louisiana: A Bicentennial History* (New York: Norton, 1976), 3-41; Edwin Adams Davis, *Louisiana: The Pelican State* (Baton Rouge, LA: Louisiana State University Press, 1959), 4-137; Charles L. Dufour, *Ten Flags in the Wind: The Story of Louisiana* (New York: Harper & Row, 1967), 8-132.
7. Taylor, *Louisiana*, 45-48; Dufour, *Louisiana*, 133-36.
8. *Dictionary of American Biography*, 1963 ed., s.v. "Claiborne, William Charles Coles," 2:115-16; Dufour, *Louisiana*, 135-40.
9. Isaac Wayne to Thomas Posey, 10 February 1811, Wayne Papers, William L. Clements Library, The University of Michigan, Ann Arbor, MI.
10. Ibid., Thomas Posey to Isaac Wayne, 13 May 1811, Wayne Papers.
11. Ibid.
12. Thornton A. Posey to Richard C. Anderson, 14 November 1810, Huntington Library, San Marino, CA.
13. William Henry Harrison to Secretary of War William Eustis, 2 July 1811, *Governors' Messages and Letters*, ed. Esarey, 1:526-28; Holman Hamilton, *Zachary Taylor: Soldier of the Republic*, 2 vols. (Indianapolis, IN: Bobs-Merrill, 1941), 37-38.
14. Harrison to Eustis, 25 June 1811, *Governors' Messages and Letters*, ed. Esarey, 1:525-26. Captain Zachary Taylor was soon ordered to Fort Knox from his Louisville recruiting post and quickly restored order in the demoralized garrison. Florence G. Watts, "Fort Knox: Frontier Outpost on the Wabash, 1787-1816," *Indiana Magazine of History*, 62 (1966): 73-74.
15. Harrison to Eustis, 25 June 1811, *Governors' Messages and Letters*, ed. Esarey, 1:525-26.
16. Francis B. Heitman, *Historical Register and Dictionary of the United States Army, 1789-1903* (Washington, DC: Lowdermilk & Co., 1903; Urbana, IL:

University of Illinois Press, 1965), 800; Holman Hamilton, "The Vincennes Days of Zachary Taylor," *Indiana Magazine of History*, 47(1941): 66.

17. Heitman, *Historical Register*, 800.
18. David Bushnell, ed., *La Republica de las Floridas: Texts and Documents* (Tallahassee, FL : Pan American Institute of Geography and History, 1986), 20-21; T. Frederick Davis, *MacGregor's Invasion of Florida, 1817* (Tallahassee, FL: The Florida Historical Society, 1928), 14-15.
19. Richard Buel, Jr., *Securing the Revolution: Ideology in American Politics, 1789-1815* (Ithaca, NY: Cornell University Press, 1972), 281-85.
20. Robert H. Wiebe, *The Opening of American Society* (New York: Alfred A. Knopf, 1984), 236.
21. MS Certificate of Appointment of Thomas Posey, 14 September 1812, Thomas Posey Papers, IHS.
22. James Edward Weems, *Men Without Countries* (Boston: Houghton Mifflin Co., 1969), 219-22; *Dictionary of American Biography*, 1963 ed., s.v. "Wilkinson, James," 10:222-26; Thomas R. Hay and Morris R. Werner, *The Admirable Trumpter* (New York: Doubleday, 1941), 307; Royal Ornan Shreve, *The Finished Scoundrel* (Indianapolis: Bobs-Merrill, 1933), 270-271; James Ripley Jacobs, *Tarnished Warrior: Major General James Wilkinson* (New York: Macmillan, 1938), 274-84.
23. See generally, all words cited in Endnote 22 above.
24. Claiborne to Thomas Posey, 8 October 1812, *Letter Book of Claiborne*, ed. Rowland, 6:187-88.
25. Ibid.
26. Wilkinson to Posey, 10 October 1812, Thomas Posey Papers, IHS.
27. Ibid.
28. Ibid.
29. Claiborne to Judge Steele, 13 October 1812, *Letter Book of Claiborne*, ed. Rowland, 6:190-91.
30. Charles Royster, *A Revolutionary People at War: The Continental Army and American Character, 1775-1783* (Chapel Hill, NC: The University of North Carolina Press, 1979), 8.
31. Wiebe, *Opening of American Society*, 144-46.
32. Posey to Philip Hickey, 18 December 1812, Philip Hickey Papers, Louisiana and Lower Mississippi Collections, LSU Libraries, Hill Memorial Library, Louisiana State University, Baton Rouge, LA.
33. *Biographical Directory of the American Congress, 1774-1971*, 12th Cong., 2d. sess., 4 March 1811 to 3 March 1813 (Washington, DC: U.S. Government Printing Office, 1971), 81.
34. Posey to Hickey, 18 December 1812, Philip Hickey Papers, Louisiana and Lower Mississippi Collections, LSU Libraries, Hill Memorial Library, Louisiana State University, Baton Rouge, LA.
35. Thomas Posey to Joseph M. Street, 21 January 1813, quoted in "The Posey Romance," St. Louis (MO) *Daily Globe-Democrat*, 6 November 1898.
36. Ibid.
37. Claiborne to Posey, 25 January 1813, *Letter Book of Claiborne*, ed. Rowland, 6:209-211.
38. Ibid.

39. Ibid. See also: Address leaf, Genl. Thos. Posey, Senator of the U. States from Louisiana to Wm. Fulwar Skipwith, near Baton Rouge, Louisiana, Miscellaneous Papers, (Thomas Posey Collection), The New York Public Library, New York, NY.
40. Weibe, *Opening of American Society*, 206.
41. Ibid., 152.
42. Claiborne to Secretary of the Treasury Albert Gallatin, 29 December 1812, *Letter Book of Claiborne*, ed. Rowland, 6:205-6.
43. Alexander Parker to Posey, 22 January 1813, Draper Manuscripts, ser. F, vol. 21, State Historical Society of Wisconsin, Madison, WI.
44. Henry Lee to Posey, 30 January 1813, quoted in "General Thomas Posey," Memoirs of Eminent Persons, *Port Folio* (Philadelphia, PA: Harrison Hall, 1827), from a transcript copy, Thomas Posey File, Henderson County Public Library, Henderson, KY.
45. Henry Lee, *Memoirs of the War in the Southern Department of the United States*, ed. Robert E. Lee (New York: University Publishing Co., 1969), 558-59.
46. Claiborne to Posey, 25 January 1813, *Letter Book of Claiborne*, ed. Rowland, 6:209-11.
47. Weems, *Men Without Countries*, 219-29, 243-53; *Dictionary of American Biography*, s.v. "Wilkinson, James," 10:222-26.
48. See generally, works cited in Endnote 47 above.
49. *Dictionary of American Biography*, 1963 ed., s.v. "Jackson, Andrew," 5:529.
50. *Biographical Directory of the American Congress, 1774-1971*, 81.
51. *Dictionary of American Biography*, 1963 ed., s.v. "Harrison, William Henry," 4:348-51.
52. Ibid.

CHAPTER NINE

(1813-1816)

". . . under your auspices, we have become as one people."

President James Madison submitted Thomas Posey's name to the U. S. Senate on 27 February 1813 as his nominee for the governorship of Indiana Territory. Sometime prior to that date Posey, having been relieved of his Senate duties, had gone to visit his daughter, Sarah Ann, and his Thornton stepsons in the Virginia counties of Spotsylvania and Stafford. Although his general availability for other public office was well known in the capital, he had not specifically applied for the governorship, and was unaware that he had been nominated and confirmed until his return to Washington on 11 March. Awaiting him in his quarters was a letter from Secretary of State James Monroe, enclosing his commission and verifying his appointment for a three-year term beginning 3 March.[1] On the same day that Thomas was confirmed, the Senate also approved the promotion to the rank of major general of two of his former Northwest Expedition comrades, brigadier generals James Wilkinson and William Henry Harrison.[2]

Posey conferred immediately with President Madison, Secretary Monroe, and the newly appointed Secretary of War, John Armstrong. It was clear that the paramount factor in his selection had been his military background and experience in Indian warfare. At this time, settlers in Indiana were being increasingly subjected to random attacks by marauding Indian raiding parties. The territory's normal complement of regular army troops had been depleted by the redeployment of most units to Ohio, where General Harrison was assembling a force for an imminent northward march to the lower Great Lakes region.[3] Posey, as governor, automatically became commander-in-chief of all local militia forces, directly responsible for the defense and security of all the inhabitants of Indiana Territory.

There can be little doubt that Thomas' old personal ties with fellow Virginians Madison and Monroe played a significant part in his selection as governor. But his impressive military qualifications and record of civic leadership were clearly the more dominant considerations. While his appointment seemingly contravened the growing practice of awarding territorial posts to men more closely identified than he with the basic ideological views of the republican administration, he was not perceived in the capital as a die-hard federalist, and his credentials as a fellow gentry leader were unimpeachable. The government officials with whom he conferred after his appointment now directed him to proceed without delay to Indiana to rally its militia and strengthen the defense of the settlements on its western border, which had suffered greatly during the several months the territory had been without a governor.[4]

The new governor was acutely aware that he faced immediate political challenges as difficult, if not as menacing, as his military ones. His predecessor, Harrison, during the last years in office, had grown increasingly unpopular in the territory due to his rigid federalist views and the sometimes autocratic exercise of his nearly absolute gubernatorial powers. Harrison's term of office spanned the ultimate extension of national gentry leadership to the frontier, and the massive growth of a localist, state-centered developmental opposition to the old policies, practices and style of government.[5] Governor Harrison and his small coterie of supporters were derisively called "the Virginia Aristocrats," although not all of them came from that state, and many of his opponents were also Virginia-born.[6]

Slavery was the most divisive and partisan issue of the time in the territory. Article VI of the controlling Northwest Ordinance of 1787 expressly provided that "There shall be neither Slavery nor involuntary Servitude in the said territory."[7] But other provisions of the ordinance cast some ambiguity on this strict prohibitory language, and Harrison's repeated efforts to abolish or subvert its literal interpretation were bitterly resented by an emerging majority of anti-slavery citizens. The local leaders of this movement, openly hostile to the governor, had taken firm control of the territorial legislature, while their acknowledged chief, Jonathan Jennings, was now serving in Washington as the territory's non-voting delegate to Congress. Shortly after Harrison's resignation, the Indiana General Assembly had petitioned Congress not to appoint to the governor's post anyone who favored slavery.[8] When Thomas Posey's name was submitted to the Senate, Jennings actively opposed his confirmation,[9] and the effectiveness of the influential delegate is reflected in the outcome of the roll call ballot. Eighteen senators approved, but eight of the nominee's recent colleagues—all but one of whom represented free northern states—voted nay.[10] Throughout Posey's governorship and even beyond, Jennings would persist as his most powerful and prominent political opponent.

On the slavery question alone, the dominant territorial leaders can hardly be blamed for thinking that the federal government was sending them another Harrison. As a lifelong resident of slave states and himself a known slave-holder, Posey was rightly suspect on this key issue. It was well known that in 1799 he had, on behalf of himself and other Virginia war veterans, unsuccessfully petitioned the old Northwest Territory legislature to be allowed to bring into the region any slaves previously acquired in their home state, without dissolving the legal master-slave relationship.[11] Unless immediate steps were taken to clear the air on this most contentious issue, Posey's effectiveness as governor would be diminished or destroyed even before taking up the duties of his new office.

On the evening before his hasty departure from the capital, and probably acting upon the advice of President Madison and Secretary Monroe, Thomas wrote and dispatched by express mail a definitive letter to John Gibson, the Secretary and acting governor of the territory. He asked Gibson to convey to the leaders and people of Indiana his firm assurances that he had no intention of seeking the repeal or relaxation of the territory's existing prohibition of slavery. "I am as much opposed to slavery as any person whatever . . . (as governor) I am sure I shall never sanction a law for slavery or any modification of it."[12]

As evidence of his good faith on this issue, and to prove that this was not a convenient overnight conversion, Posey informed Gibson that he had already disposed of most of the slaves he still owned—which, incidentally, represented a significant portion of his net worth—either by way of gifts to his children, or by outright emancipation. His last Will, written during his tenure as governor, confirms that he had made pretestamentary distributions of slaves to most of his children, and it also stipulated gifts of two slaves each to three others who had not already been provided for.[13] A later letter to his son Fayette in Henderson contains detailed instructions to finalize the sale of the last of his Kentucky farm hands at the slave market in Shawneetown, Illinois Territory.[14]

Posey never violated this pledge to the people of Indiana. At no time during his governorship did he initiate or support any effort to repeal or modify the existing restrictions on slavery. Nor is there any evidence that he sought, as had his predecessor Harrison, to influence the election of any advocate of slavery to the legislature or other local elective office. He did not oppose the strong ban on slavery embodied in Indiana's first state constitution. He did, however, retain the personal services of Charles and Betsy, two emancipated slaves, under eight-year contracts of indenture—an arrangement which, although perfectly legal and commonplace in Indiana Territory, might arguably be construed as violating the spirit, if not the letter, of his declaration to John Gibson.[15]

Thomas' letter to Gibson also outlined a high-minded vision of the role he proposed to play in public affairs as governor of Indiana:

> I am aware of the party spirit that has prevailed in the Territory. I never was a party man, neither shall I ever undertake to be one. I shall neither meddle or interfere with parties or elections. I shall attend to what is strictly my duty in office, and endeavor to make the people as happy as I am capable, paying strict attention to the general welfare of the Territory.[16]

An Indiana historian has said of Thomas Posey that "he was not much of a politician."[17] It would perhaps be more accurate to describe him as a man who in his public life sought, as did his mentor George Washington before him, to hold himself above party bickering and confrontation. This was his greatest strength as a public servant and, sadly, his greatest vulnerability as a politician. In his aborted race for the governorship of Kentucky, when he was desperately seeking to defend himself against baseless charges of aristocratic or monarchical leanings, Posey had echoed Thomas Jefferson's inaugural declaration that he was both a Republican and a Federalist. Unlike Jefferson, however, Posey was in fact neither—his true ideology can best be described as nationalist, and his political posture as neutral or centrist.

His position on the political spectrum in 1813 can best be illustrated by comparison with some of his fellow Virginians who attended the state's constitutional convention a quarter-century previous. James Madison, leader of the pro-ratification bloc, had moved left with the absent Jefferson and the anti-ratification moderate James Monroe to form the core leadership of the new Republican party. Posey's wartime comrades Henry Lee and John Marshall, with whom he had shared strong pro ratification views, had since moved to the right to align themselves with the policies of Federalist party leader Alexander Hamilton. Even the rabidly anti ratification orator Patrick Henry in his final years joined the extreme federalist faction, which seemed finally to have lost all hope in the successful continuity of democratic self-government.[18]

Thomas Posey, by contrast, never lost faith in the basic revolutionary ideal of the supremacy of public virtue over private self-interest, or in the ability of the new republic to maintain and perpetuate itself through popular or majoritarian politics.[19] His support of such federalist concepts as a strong national government and a permanent, professional regular army was based upon the perceived need to bind the expanding trans-Appalachian region firmly to the Union, and to deter—and if necessary resist—encroachments upon those western territories by the major European powers. But the extreme federalist notion of an elitist or aristocratic ruling class was as repellent to him as it had been to his lifelong political role model, George Washington.

Despite his unwanted and undeserved identification on the frontier with that odious eastern federalist faction, Thomas maintained throughout his public life cordial and supportive relationships with republican leaders Madison and Monroe. This was never more evident than in his unqualified and enthusiastic backing of the federal administration during the War of 1812. But in the bitterly partisan political climate that prevailed in the western region in the post-Washington era, a truly nonpartisan public official such as Posey found it increasingly difficult to avoid identification with one or the other contending faction—and even less likely to achieve success in attaining any office subject to popular electoral vote.

Three days after learning of his appointment to the Indiana post, Thomas hurriedly departed the capital for the west. On his way out of Washington, he dropped off a hasty note at Secretary of War Armstrong's office, asking that all available information on current or planned military supply shipments to his territory be sent forward to his new headquarters at Vincennes.[20] Taking a fast packet boat down the Ohio River from Pittsburgh, he disembarked, "after a very fatiguing journey," at Jeffersonville, Indiana Territory, on 7 April.[21] After a brief rest and a checkup by his personal physician, Dr. John Croghan, across the river in Louisville, he continued downstream to Henderson where he enjoyed a short visit with his wife and family there. Then, crossing the broad Ohio after paying the genial ferryman, Jonathan Edwards, twenty-five cents fare for himself and his horse, Thomas rode northward alone along the old Red Banks Trace, an ancient Indian trail, the final perilous seventy miles to Vincennes. He arrived at the little capital on 4 May, promptly reporting to Secretary Armstrong that small parties of Indian raiders were harassing scattered settlements in the very area through which he had just ridden.[22]

Posey's first six months as governor were totally engaged in installing a massive program to mobilize, train and deploy militia units throughout the vast territory. Fortunately, many warriors from the hostile Indian tribes along the lower Wabash River had followed the militant and able war chief, Tecumseh, north to fight alongside their British allies confronting General Harrison's Northwest army. Thomas' efforts were competently supported by Major Zachary Taylor, heading the small contingent of army regulars left at Fort Knox—the command once held by Posey's son, Thornton. Several special companies of mounted volunteers, called Rangers, were formed to provide a mobile emergency force in more remote areas.[23] Governor Posey's militia, numbering at its peak a staggering 5,000 officers and men, was largely successful in limiting the loss of citizens' lives and property under his jurisdiction.[24] The defeat of the British-Indian army by General Harrison at the Thames River on 5 October 1813—a battle in which Chief Tecumseh lost his life—greatly relieved the further immediate threat of more serious incursions against Hoosier settlers.

But during the countless musters and reviews of militia units throughout the territory, often conducted in freezing drizzle, sleet and snow, Thomas' health suffered grievously.[25] He was now sixty-three years old, considered quite elderly at the time, and he had not enjoyed the benefits of a settled, stable family life since leaving Kentucky to explore Orleans Territory more than three years before. The long, exhausting trips to Louisiana, Washington City, and back to Indiana had taken their toll, and his old Stony Point leg wound, which had never entirely healed, was acting up again. A further minor dislocation occurred in mid-1813 when the territorial capital was moved from the relatively comfortable and cultivated old town of Vincennes to the tiny and primitive, but more centrally located, hamlet of Corydon.[26] Posey was not a well man when he arose before the opening session of the newly convened General Assembly on 6 December 1813 to deliver the first "state of the territory" welcoming address of his gubernatorial term.

The governor's first and greatest oratorical concern was the ongoing but lagging national armed conflict with the British. "The present crisis is awful and big with great events; our land and nation is involved in the common calamity of war." He voiced confidence that "the beneficent Being who has, on a former occasion, bro't us in safety through an arduous struggle" would not now "suffer to be taken from us what he in his great wisdom has tho't proper to confer and bless us with, if we make a wise and virtuous use of his good gifts." Bedeviled all his political life with the Federalist epithet, Posey had no sympathy for the real, radical federalists of the northeast states who had opposed entering the war, and were lending little or no support to President Madison's efforts to win it. There was no question in his mind that "we were forced into the war, every measure consistent with honor" had been tried, only to be contemptuously spurned by the enemy. Accordingly, the old patriot asked rhetorically, "where is the man who is a friend to his country that will not give a helping hand and use his best exertions to preserve and maintain inviolate the just rights of his country? It is to be hoped that there is none such."[27]

Turning only then to strictly territorial concerns, Posey called upon the legislature to correct defects in the militia law exposed during the current mobilization, and to restructure an obsolete court system overwhelmed by rapid increases in population and commerce. He recommended broadening the territory's inadequate road and highway infrastructure, and called for the improvement of the educational system by the greater use of lands allocated by the federal government for the establishment of public schools. The ailing governor concluded his oration by benevolently wishing the assembled legislators "a pleasant session, recommending harmony and dispatch of business."[28]

A week after his appearance before the General Assembly, Posey sent out urgent requests to his son and namesake, Thomas, whom he knew to be in either Henderson or Shawneetown, to join him at once in Corydon. "I wish you to come up immediately upon the rec't of any of my letters. I am anxious you should be near me that you may pay some attention to carrying on my business."[29] The dire need for his son's prompt assistance soon became apparent. Within weeks, the governor's health had so worsened that he was forced to dispatch a formal message to the presidents of both houses of the legislature:

> I wish to communicate to your honorable body that the delicate state of my health will not admit of my longer continuance at this place. I find myself badly situated on account of the

> want of medical aid. My physician is at Louisville, and I have taken all the medicine brought with me . . . Be assured, sir, that nothing but imperious necessity compels me to this step.[30]

Thomas informed the legislators that he would be residing temporarily in Jeffersonville, a small town less than twenty-five miles from Corydon, on the Indiana side of the Ohio River opposite Louisville. He assured them that his secretary, Mr. Prather, would serve as a courier to speed all their official communications to him there, and would return equally promptly with his responses. But the Assembly, acutely sensitized by former Governor Harrison's often autocratic if not disdainful attitude toward the territorial legislators, did not take kindly to Posey's sudden departure from the capital in mid-session. When his letter was read aloud to the upper Council, it angrily passed a resolution—concurred in the following day by the lower House of Representatives—sternly instructing the Assembly's joint committee of enrolled bills not under any circumstances to place any enacted legislative measures into the hands of any person other than the governor himself.[31]

Resentment over the governor's absence was still boiling on 6 January 1814, two days after the General Assembly had completed its deliberations. Under territorial law, the governor had absolute power to approve or veto any measure. The joint committee had been duly dispatched to Jeffersonville with all the enrolled bills passed during the session, but had not yet returned to Corydon with Posey's responses. Nor had his permission to prorogue the legislature been received. More than a little annoyed by the delay, the two houses passed a resolution, stating in part:

> . . . WHEREAS, The expense of near fifty dollars per day doth arise to the people of the Territory by reason of the Legislature being kept in session—-all of which evils and inconveniences doth arise from the Governor leaving the seat of government during the session of the Legislature and going to Jeffersonville, and the Legislature having to send their committee of enrolled bills to that place to lay them before him for his approval and signature. . . .[32]

The Assembly, having duly registered its understandable frustration and ire over the delay in finalizing the session's business so its members could go home, thereupon adjourned on its own motion and dispersed. It authorized its two presiding officers to remain in Corydon to receive and record the governor's report of bills signed or rejected, as well as his formal order of prorogation. The incident did not bode well for future harmonious relations between the executive and legislative branches of government. But happily, it was the first and only instance of any serious friction or disagreement between the territorial legislature and Posey during his entire tenure as governor.

Posey's son Thomas arrived in Jeffersonville on 17 January, to find his father's health failing and his financial affairs in disarray. A Louisville creditor was pressuring him to pay a long-overdue debt, but Posey, seemingly always cash-poor, was unable to comply because of common delays in clearing title to two tracts of Kentucky land he was selling.[33] The governor was also upset over an unexpected hitch in completing the sale of the few remaining Kentucky slaves, mainly field hands, that he had not freed or distributed to his children. The delay, he feared, might make it appear that he was reneging on his earlier pledge to John Gibson to dispose of all his slaves.

Thomas was particularly concerned over the disposition of his faithful old manservant Billy, who had been with him since the Virginia exodus, and who had accompanied him to Louisiana, Washington, and back to Kentucky. He was unable to take Billy to Indiana because of its anti-slavery law, but he wanted him to spend his last years in a good home back in Virginia—if the price was right. Posey gave specific instructions to his son Fayette in Henderson regarding Billy:

> Your bro. Thomas says Mr. Warner Lewis would purchase Billy, if he will and give not less than $500 for him, I wish you to make sale of him to Mr. Lewis . . . I am anxious that as I must part with Billy not having any use for him, that he should get a good master, & I am pretty certain he will find such a one in Mr. Lewis.[34]

Although he was under the immediate care of Dr. Croghan, one of the finest physicians in the area, Posey's condition continued to deteriorate, and he feared that death was near. After long and intense introspection, he sat down at his desk on 4 February to write out a lengthy, thoughtful letter which he addressed to "My dearly beloved children and grandchildren." This was to be his spiritual testament, not only to his immediate descendants, but also to unborn future generations. He spoke of the uncertainty of life, "with the young as well as the aged," noting that he found himself "declining every day, and in all probability unless a speedy and favorable change takes place soon, I shall be no more in this world." He then imparted his deepest personal values, admonishing his descendants to love one another, avoid such dissipations as gambling and drinking, to behave honorably, and shun dishonorable men. "I have had to do with such men. I have been taken in with men that I had the most unbounded confidence in and . . . have been compelled to pay very considerable sums of money to the very great injury of my family, particularly in depriving me of the means of educating my children in that liberal manner which I otherwise would have had it in my power to have done."[35]

The graphic reference to monetary losses suffered through misplaced trust in others may at least partially account for Posey's apparent financial distress during the greater part of his life on the frontier. More moving, however, is his obvious pain and guilt over the resultant inability to provide the finest education available to each of his ten children. It is noteworthy and tragic that the old man, on what he thought was his deathbed, saw himself as a failure, having fallen short in achieving one of his most cherished goals in life.

It is his simple but heartfelt strictures on intimate family life that best reflect Thomas' own caring personal relationship with his wife Mary. He gently exhorted his eight sons to be "kind, loving, affectionate, to your wives, they are the weaker vessels and require to be treated with great tenderness and attention." Both spouses, he urged, should exhibit "politeness, affection, prudence, and in conversations avoid of giving the least offence, never hasty or apparently speaking in a way to hurt feelings." His concept of parental love and responsibility was equally benevolent. "The very best examples should always be shown to children. If they discover neglect, bad treatment or ill-humor practiced by their parents to each other, it naturally . . . produces bad consequences."[36] The image of warm and tender familial relationships in the Posey household, so vividly evoked in these passages, stands in stark contrast to the unstable milieu in which Thomas himself grew to manhood in what George Washington called the "Mad and distracted" family of Captain John Posey of Rover's Delight.[37]

Although Posey's letter to his family was written *causa mortis*—in expectation of imminent death—the end had not yet come for the old soldier. The original document, along with a lengthy autobiography and a sealed letter to his wife, all written at this time, were found among his personal papers after his death more than four years later. Under Dr. Croghan's ministrations Thomas' health improved, and on 4 April a more fit and vigorous governor called the lower house of the territorial General Assembly into special session to redraw obsolete district lines for the election of the upper legislative Council.[38] Thomas was still residing in Jeffersonville, but he prudently took temporary living quarters in Corydon throughout the session. By May, Posey had also drafted and submitted to the Secretary of War a comprehensive plan to reorganize the 5,000 territorial militiamen into conventional regiments, brigades and divisions, with higher officers of corresponding rank. But the urgency of the measure was soon reduced by a temporary decline in Indian raids; the government did not act on the proposal until 1816, and then on a much more modest scale.[39]

Even so, lingering effects of earlier Indian incursions were still being felt by some, as is touchingly illustrated in Indian Agent John Johnston's letter to one disconsolate inhabitant of the territory. The settler's six-year-old son, Peter Huffman, described as being "of fair complexion, and sandy hair," had in an unguarded moment been "taken at the River Ohio, by Saw Omock or the yellow Beaver in the month of March 1813." The kidnapped boy was carried by his Indian captor northward to the St. Joseph River and sold to a French trader, who later delivered him over to a British officer on faraway Mackinac Island.[40] Since he was now out of Johnston's jurisdiction, the distraught father appealed directly to Governor Posey for help. He, in turn, asked the Secretary of War to try to recover the child through military or diplomatic channels. Thomas noted in passing that the color of the lad's hair was actually "of a shade between red and yellow."[41] The record is silent if little tow-headed, freckled-faced Peter was ever returned to the Ohio River cabin of his devastated family.

Most if not all general territorial concerns appear to have been effectively addressed during Posey's administration. A newly elected General Assembly was called into special session by the governor on 15 August 1814 to ratify a restructured court system; within a few weeks Posey appointed a presiding and two assistant judges for each of the three judicial circuits provided by the new legislation. At this session also, three new counties were created in the rapidly developing region. One of these, in the extreme southwest corner of the Territory, was named Posey County, in honor of the incumbent governor. Other legislative action included the chartering of two banks, a petition to Congress to temporarily suspend payments due for federal lands purchased by new settlers, and authorization for a special census—the first step required in the process of attaining statehood. Dueling was outlawed, and as further evidence of cultural progress, by 1814 a theatrical society and two dancing schools were thriving in Vincennes.[42]

The war that had started so indecisively in 1812 ended inconclusively on 24 December 1814 with the signing of the Treaty of Ghent. The news arrived too late to stop the bloody Battle of New Orleans on the following 8 January. Thomas' soldier-son, Lieutenant Colonel Thornton Posey, served valiantly with his Seventh U.S. Infantry Regiment in this decisive American victory, under future president Andrew Jackson. Formal peace treaties with many of the British-allied native tribes on the northwest frontier were not negotiated and signed by General William Henry Harrison until the following September.[43] In the interim, sporadic Indian raids upon small communities and isolated settlers along the western border of Indiana Territory continued unabated. Governor Posey and his able assistant for Indian affairs, Judge Benjamin Parke, acted vigorously to protect these citizens, as well as members of neutral tribes in the area. On 18 February 1815 Thomas reported to then-Secretary of War James Monroe that he had assembled many friendly Native Americans near fortified posts along the frontier, and arranged to feed them, but "the British are using every endeavor to draw them off from us." Nonetheless, he assured the Secretary that "I shall take the necessary steps to be prepared for any invasion of the Indians on the frontiers of this Territory."[44]

This, of course, was the primary mission entrusted to Posey by Monroe and President Madison. To meet the renewed threat, the governor had organized a special force of territorial militia, modeled after the Massachusetts "minutemen" of 1775, "to be held in readiness to march at the shortest notice." These units were backups to detachments of mounted Indiana Rangers and regular army troops posted "at Vincennes, Fort Harrison (near present-day Terre Haute) and the frontiers of the Territory . . . under the command of Major Zachary Taylor of the U.S. Infantry. He is a very attentive officer and will do his duty."[45] But even after the news of the war's end reached the west and the Rangers had been disbanded, occasional Indian raids continued. An exasperated Posey advised the government in late 1815 that "the Indians heretofore hostile, still discover a very inveterate and hostile disposition. I am of opinion nothing satisfactory will take place with them as to a peaceful disposition, until they are humbled."[46]

Thomas continued to reside in Jeffersonville during his entire term of office as governor. He had found the inhabitants and the ambiance of the little community entirely compatible with his gubernatorial lifestyle, while its proximity to his Louisville physician was beneficial to his well-being. Posey was most circumspect, however, in returning to Corydon for the full duration of all General

Assembly sessions meeting in the capital, thus avoiding any recurrence of the friction generated by his initial absence from the seat of government. Indeed, his entire relationship with the legislators appears to have been generally harmonious and mutually respectful. Although the great divide between old style gentry government and the new wave of state developmental leadership continued to exist beneath the surface, there was little if any overt display of the acrimony and party factionalism that marred the final years of the Harrison administration.[47] While the Jennings bloc, increasingly strengthened by postwar immigration, continued to dominate the legislature and territorial politics, Posey, by strict adherence to his pledge of non-intervention in party matters, successfully maintained his neutral stance as governor of the Territory.

In Jeffersonville, Thomas constructed a fine, sixteen-room mansion boasting four chimneys and a covered second-floor porch running the entire length of the building.[48] It was easily the most impressive structure in the little river town. The residence dominated a large raised lot on the corner of Front and Fort streets, and afforded a splendid view of the broad Ohio and the city of Louisville beyond.[49] Posey's son, Thomas, lived in the governor's house during the early years of his father's term, handling some clerical matters of state, along with his own duties as assistant federal tax collector to Colonel Allan D. Thom. The colonel, Posey's aide and adviser, also appears to have resided for some time in the governor's mansion.[50]

Posey held most of his fellow citizens of Jeffersonville in high esteem, but the community seems also to have harbored a few less estimable residents, and was apparently deficient in security or police protection. While in Corydon during one legislative session, Posey wrote to his son Thomas, suggesting that he borrow Colonel Thom's horse and come join him in the capital. But he cautioned that at all times either his manservant Charles, young Thomas, or Thom "should be at home to take care of house & garden. If we are all from home at the same time our garden will be totally destroyed, & perhaps the house plundered."[51]

The younger Thomas Posey turned out to be an interesting man in his own right. Later in his father's gubernatorial term he moved permanently to Corydon, and there, in partnership with Colonel Thom, built an imposing structure that served as a combined residence-office-mercantile building. He became, in time, a prosperous merchant and banker, served as colonel and Adjutant-General of state militia, and held several public offices, including Harrison County's seat in the state House of Representatives. In that position, he appropriately headed the arrangements committee welcoming General Marquis de Lafayette to his father's old Jeffersonville mansion when that revered French patriot made his triumphal tour of America in 1825.[52] Although young Posey never married, he raised or helped educate fourteen orphan children in Corydon, one of whom, Judge Walter Q. Gresham, later a Secretary of State in President Grover Cleveland's cabinet, referred to his foster father as "one of the noblest men God ever made."[53]

In the fall of 1816 the junior Thomas Posey is reputed to have befriended a dirt-poor immigrant from Kentucky named Thomas Lincoln, storing most of the stranger's worldly goods while he staked out a land claim in an adjoining county. Later that year, when the elder Lincoln returned with his family—including seven-year-old Abraham—Posey rented them a wagon and team of horses to carry their possessions to their new home.[54] It was not to be the future great president's last contact with the Poseys. In 1830 young Mr. Lincoln, by now a rising citizen of Decatur, Illinois, delivered his very first public political speech in support of John Francis Posey—General Thomas Posey's grandson—thereby helping young Posey win a seat in the Illinois legislature.[55] Two years later, volunteer Private Abe Lincoln served briefly in the abortive Black Hawk War with Illinois militia General Alexander Posey, Thomas' physician-son.[56]

Mary Posey, Thomas' wife, did not live in Indiana during the first two years of her husband's term of office. Sometime in the summer of 1813, while the governor was busily engaged in organizing the militia throughout the territory, she returned to Virginia to visit her Thornton sons and her youngest daughter, Sarah Ann, whom she had not seen in eleven years. Mary's traveling companion was her granddaughter, Mary Harrison Posey, oldest daughter of John and Lucy Frances Posey. At this time, Mary's oldest son George and his wife, Mary Randolph, parents of three, were living at "Rumford," the Thorntons' ancestral estate in Chestervillle, Stafford County. His brother Reuben and wife Ann Maria Washington, (grandniece of George), with two sons, had taken over Greenwood, the Poseys' old home in The Wilderness, Spotsylvania County. Mary Posey was a prolific correspondent, and some of her letters from Virginia have fortunately survived, yielding many insightful glimpses into her character and personality, as well as the state of Piedmont society in the Old Dominion during the War of 1812.[57]

During her extended two-year stay in Virginia, Mary appears to have shuttled among the two Thornton households and her

Alexander siblings in King George County. Her letters, written in a precise and literate script reflecting her excellent education, are filled with endearing news and gossip of family members and friends. Her many fond references to her numerous grandchildren in Virginia and the west establish her as the most loving of grandmothers. Her anxious concerns over reports of Thomas' near-fatal illness in early 1814 are tempered by eloquent expressions of her own deep and abiding religious faith. Mary, furthermore, was not averse to imparting her own frontier-fostered doctrinal convictions on any Virginia kin she perceived as errant in their ways—at least those whose minds she adjudged as being receptive to her message, or, as Mary phrased it, "if they are rational."[58]

Sometimes the news was bad. She reported that "old Mamma Phillis," an aged slave who had apparently been the young Posey children's beloved nursemaid at Greenwood, was not well, and after a lingering illness, "died extremely hard."[59] But Mary's young daughter, Sarah Ann, she stated proudly, was "a fine girl and very handsome. She is much like her Father. She sais Kentucky will never see her."[60] In responding to her daughter Eliza Maria's boast that her ailing husband, "dr. Mr. Street," had recently put on considerable weight, Mary Posey, in a rare display of self-deprecatory joviality, commented: "if your good Man fattens so fast he will be a match for me when I return."[61]

The ongoing war struck dangerously close to central Virginia during Mary's long visit there. "My dr. Maria the British have burnt several of the Public buildings in Washington. The bridge across the Potomac is burnt and part of Alexandria. They have given a very general Alarm to our Sect."[62] The enemy had, in fact, at one of the lowest points in American history, landed 4,000 troops off Chesapeake Bay, marched upon and occupied Washington almost unopposed, and defiled and burned the president's mansion, the Capitol, and other government buildings. Had Thomas Posey's tenure in the U.S. Senate not been cut short, the proud old revolutionary might have been forced to be an agonized and helpless eyewitness to this humiliating spectacle. In nearby Spotsylvania County Mary Posey, getting this distressing and alarming news, echoed the anguish and wartime prayer of every mother with a soldier-son in harm's way: "I fear & dread this melancholy War, but have we not a good God?"[63]

During Mary's extended sojourn in Virginia, the Poseys disposed of Longview, their Kentucky residence in Henderson County. Thomas' long absences, his Indiana position, and the sale of most of the family's slaves, had made impractical its further maintenance and operation. Proceeds from the sale of the property were needed to help pay for the building of the impressive governor's residence in Jeffersonville, where Mary would live after her return to the west. Of the three youngest Posey sons remaining in the Kentucky household, the younger Thomas had already joined his father in Indiana, while Alexander was matriculating at the University of Pennsylvania. Young Washington went to live with his sister and brother-in-law, the Joseph Streets, in nearby Shawneetown, Illinois Territory. There, he would in time grow up to become a prominent local merchant and banker. Their mother Mary, returning at last from her long visit in the east, arrived at Jeffersonville on 16 November 1815, only to find her husband Thomas again in poor health—partially disabled and confined to his bed with a recurrent infection in the leg wound he had sustained at Stony Point.[64]

The governor's continued illness caused him to miss, for the first time, the opening session of the territorial legislature's regular annual meeting in Corydon on 4 December. Posey's welcoming address was read to the General Assembly by his aide, Colonel Thom. It noted with pleasure the fact that, during the past year, "a bloody war has been terminated by an honorable peace," emphasizing the special blessings that the cessation of hostilities brought to Indiana Territory:

> In no section of the union is there more cause for rejoicing at the restoration of peace than in this territory. A cruel and bloodthirsty enemy, who border on our frontier, and whose mode of warfare is the indiscriminate slaughter of the infants, the aged, and the helpless part of the community, have agreed to bury the tomahawk, and once more live with us in the bonds of friendship.[65]

Significantly, Posey's prepared address focused upon the arrival of new immigrants who were already flocking into the region, no longer deterred by the threat of attack by the "cruel and bloodthirsty enemy," and perhaps anticipating that some of that enemy's traditional hunting grounds would soon be opened to white settlement. The population increase dominated his recommendations for major capital improvements: expansion of roads and highways, and further betterment in the system of public education. Possibly drawing upon his personal experiences in migrating from Virginia to Kentucky, Posey called the legislators' attention to the financial plight of the newest settlers, asking for measures to temporarily relieve the heavy land tax burden imposed upon them by existing law. "Most of them have removed from a great distance, at a considerable expense. They have to encounter many difficulties in opening their farms for cultivation, before they can derive a support, much more a profit from them." The governor also called particular attention to a momentous civic milestone that would soon be reached by Indiana Territory. He noted that "the emigration which is rapidly populating our fertile land" would soon "enable us to be admitted into the political family of the union as an independent state."[66] That landmark event was to come even sooner than Posey himself imagined or, perhaps, wished.

Thomas' message to the General Assembly was well received. The statehood process was actually well underway, and many lawmakers, anticipating a speedy passage to that goal, felt that this was to be their last meeting as a territorial legislature. They accordingly wished to extend a special gesture of regard to their ailing governor. On 26 December the lower House of Representatives sent a delegation of two prominent members to Jeffersonville to deliver a formal written expression of "the sentiments of esteem and respect which they feel towards your Excellency":

> . . . they cannot refrain from declaring their perfect approbation of your official conduct as Governor of this Territory. During your administration, Sir, many then existing evils have been remedied; and we particularly admire the calm, dispassionate, impartial conduct of your administration, which has produced the salutary effect of quieting the violence of party spirit, harmonizing the interests as well as the feelings of the different parts of the Territory; and under your auspices, we have become as one people.[67]

This was precisely the kind of governor Posey had pledged to the people that he would be when he accepted the position. He had won over legislators who from the first had viewed his appointment with suspicion and hostility, and reacted with anger and open resentment when he absented himself from the capital during their first meeting of his incumbency. The lawmakers' unqualified acclaim evidences beyond question his success in not only rising above, but in significantly reducing, the paralyzing partisanship which had so deeply divided the Territory before his arrival in Indiana. Regrettably, this period of political tranquility would soon be shattered by the reemergence of the violent "party spirit" so deplored in the Assembly's commendatory address. But this should not be allowed to obscure or detract from the undeniable accomplishments of Posey's administration. The legislators themselves attest with eloquence and obvious sincerity their approval of the even-handed, noncontroversial territorial executive Posey had proved himself to be.

Thomas responded with grace and gratitude to the legislature's message. He stated that "the approbation of so respectable a body, relative to my administration, will make an impression upon my mind that can only be eradicated by a dissolution of my existence in this life." Furthermore, he assured the lawmakers that "while life remains . . . you shall always find me devoted to render the citizens of our Territory all the faithful services which are committed to my charge."[68]

Posey was undoubtedly personally touched by the gesture, but it is also undeniable that, career-wise, this unsolicited and unequivocal legislative testimonial could not have come at a better time. His first term of office was due to expire in about two months, and he enclosed a copy of the Assembly's message in his letter of 25 January 1816 to Secretary of State James Monroe requesting reappointment. Thomas was well aware that momentum to accelerate the process leading to statehood was rapidly building, and that the attainment of that status would automatically end his tenure as territorial governor.[69] He himself had, in fact, officially approved and signed the General Assembly's formal Memorial of 11 December 1815 to Congress petitioning for statehood, and his recent welcoming address to the legislature clearly indicates that he did not personally oppose that ultimate goal. But in his private letter to Secretary Monroe, Posey expressed serious reservations about the ability of the citizens of the territory to bear the financial burdens that statehood would immediately impose upon them. "I wish the people were well prepared for the measure, but I may say with propriety that at least two thirds, or three fourths are not able to contribute but very little, if anything to the support of a state."[70]

There was widespread popular desire within the Territory to join the union, but Posey's concerns over its inhabitants' fiscal unpreparedness for statehood were shared by many of his contemporaries,[71] and they have been fully documented in later scholarly studies.[72] In essence, the new legal status would immediately shift the federal government's two-thirds' share of governmental expenses entirely onto the shoulders of the new state's taxpayers.[73] The recent war had devastated the area's finances and trade, and tax revenues had dropped alarmingly—when Governor Posey took office, the net balance in the territorial treasury was only $2.57.[74] Extensive militia and Ranger service had decimated the manpower resources of the region's labor-intensive agricultural economy.

Newly arrived settlers, far from increasing the tax base, found themselves unable to meet even their federal land payments—and Posey's plea in his recent welcoming address for a moratorium or moderation in state and local land taxes speaks for itself.

Indiana's transition from territory to state would undeniably impose crushing new financial burdens on its already struggling citizens. In his letter to Secretary Monroe, Posey would have been wise to confine his qualms over imminent statehood to his well-founded economic arguments. But he chose to add another, more controversial reason to question the territory's readiness to assume the reins of self-government. "There is also a very great scarcity of talents or men of such information as are necessary to fill the respective stations, and offices of government."[75] Subsequent events were to demonstrate that his doubts on this point were totally unwarranted. Within six months, the best and brightest minds in the territory would meet in Corydon to fashion a functional and durable state constitution, and there would prove to be no noticeable dearth of men of ability, integrity and vision to fill the governmental offices it created.

Some respected commentators have understandably attributed Posey's expressed doubts of Indiana's readiness for immediate statehood solely to a self-serving desire to prolong his own tenure as territorial governor.[76] To contend that this consideration never entered his mind would be to deny that Thomas Posey was only human. But it is only fair to point out that traces of self-interest seem to be equally discernable in the actions of those territorial leaders who were in the forefront of the statehood stampede. The eagerness of Jonathan Jennings and his close associates to take over the major governmental offices of the new state is well documented, and has been authoritatively cited as a major factor in their tendency to publicly downplay the obvious economic hardships statehood would inflict upon the citizenry.[77] In the final analysis, however, Thomas' clearly patronizing assessment of the civic abilities of these aspiring office-holders would not serve him well politically in the momentous months to come.

Thomas' own financial condition was seemingly not much better than most of his fellow citizens of Indiana, and his letter to Monroe seeking extension of his term included a revealing personal plea. "Were I not needy, and in some degree thinking myself entitled to a claim of some attention (however small) from my country, I would not ask the favor."[78] It was unlikely that gentry leaders James Madison and James Monroe would forsake the plight of this veteran soldier and fellow-Virginian. Posey's past reputed federalist sympathies had not deterred them from initially awarding him this political plum normally reserved for deserving republican party supporters. But neither personal ties nor political considerations predominated in the administration's current decision. Soon after his letter arrived in the capital city, Posey's commission of reappointment, signed by Madison and attested by Monroe, was on its way to the governor's mansion in Jeffersonville.[79] His three years of solid performance in the post, his diligence in thwarting the Indian menace, and his "calm, dispassionate, impartial conduct" so esteemed and lauded by a once hostile territorial legislature, were surely the principal bases for the prompt renewal of his term of office in 1816.

But Indiana's rush to statehood was swift and inexorable. The General Assembly's Memorial to Congress sought authority to call a constitutional convention empowered to formulate and implement a state government. The prospect offered many appealing benefits. Citizens would thereby gain the right to elect their own executive and judicial officers, while their chosen legislative representatives could then pass laws free from the absolute veto power of the appointed territorial governor. The people would also acquire a vote and a voice in national affairs. The ambitious and talented local leaders of developmental politics had much to gain. Although partisanship had been largely muted during Posey's administration, beckoning statehood status now offered the dominant anti-slavery, anti-Harrison legislative faction a long-sought opportunity to take control of the executive and judicial branches, and pursue the many elective offices previously subject to gubernatorial appointment.

Jonathan Jennings, the acknowledged leader of the majority bloc, was still the Territory's congressional delegate in Washington. He deftly steered the Assembly's statehood Memorial through Congress, a majority of whose members were eager to add another free state to the union, and the key Enabling Act was approved on 19 April. Pursuant to its provisions, a state constitutional convention met in Corydon on 10 June, and promptly elected Jennings as its president, and William Hendricks, a close Jennings associate, as its secretary. The convention quickly produced a well-crafted, broadly democratic and strongly anti-slavery constitution, and set a 5 August election date to fill the newly created state offices.[80]

There was a spirited five-week campaign for the state governorship between Jonathan Jennings and Thomas Posey. They traveled throughout the vast area, appearing at log rollings, militia musters, and camp meetings. They addressed any available gathering of eligible voters—limited at the time to white male taxpayers over age

21 with at least one year's residency. As was the custom of the times, the few existing Indiana newspapers printed many letters extolling the virtues and supporting the views of the two candidates. They provide a rich flavor of early nineteenth-century political campaigning on the western frontier. One unidentified correspondent fulsomely praised,

> . . . the venerable & respectable THOMAS POSEY . . . call to mind the services he has rendered, the many high and important offices he has held, creditably to himself, and beneficially to his country.—-Remember the great experience he has acquired from the extended period of his political life; the judgment he possesses unimpaired by age, & heightened by long and constant exercise; the confidence which he merits, and the faithfulness on which you can rely; remember all these things, & I conjure you in the name of all you hold dear, elect him for your governor.[81]

The popular Jennings was undoubtedly a crowd pleaser during the campaign, but Posey also must have cut an impressive figure on the hustings, standing tall in his carefully preserved general's uniform resplendently adorned with the gold epaulettes presented to him by Mrs. Christian Febiger after the storming of Stony Point. Advancing age and infirmity must certainly have diminished the imposing physical attributes of his younger years, when he was described as "tall, athletic and finely formed." But he surely still retained "the stately and gallant bearing of a soldier"—the characteristic ramrod-stiff posture of the professional military man. Time may indeed have eroded or softened the "high, fine and prominent" features of his still "remarkably handsome" face. Perhaps those features no longer "assumed the sternness of command" with quite the force or authority displayed when he led his brigade of Wayne's Legionnaires into the menacing forests of the Northwest Territory.[82]

But all the old fire, spirit and intelligence still shone out of those "fine blue eyes." As he stood facing many a noisy and boisterous gathering of Hoosier citizens, a respectful silence must have descended at the sight of that "calm and benevolent expression which pervaded the whole countenance, that at once attracted the admiration and won the affections of the beholder."[83] Not even the most vocal Jennings supporter could fail to be struck by the speaker's "noble appearance and courtly manners" so vividly recalled by Archibald Alexander, the young Greenwood tutor.[84] The quality of Posey's oratorical delivery is unknown, but the voice that shouted out the watchword over the din and clamor of Stony Point, and rallied his soldiers fleeing in the darkness from Guristersigo's fierce Creek warriors, must have still retained some resonance and power.

Although candidate Posey made a valiant effort, the result was probably a foregone conclusion. He appears to have largely surmounted the old taint of federalistic tendencies. But the campaign revived the factional emotions he had striven to neutralize during his governorship, and the electorate was inescapably polarized along the political and geographical lines drawn during the contentious years of the long Harrison administration. Jennings' base of support came mainly from the more populous eastern counties, while the central areas were fairly evenly balanced, with a slight advantage to Jennings. Posey's natural constituency lay in the older western communities which had been his predecessor's bailiwick. It was that unsought and unwelcome, but pervasive, identification with the old Harrison "Virginia Aristocrats"—reinforced by Thomas' own state of origin and stigma as a former slave owner—that ultimately proved fatal to his hopes.[85]

Other issues played a significant but subordinate part in the final outcome. Thomas' earlier conservative and negative views on the territory's fiscal readiness for statehood contrasted unfavorably with Jennings' high-visibility leadership role, both in Washington and Corydon, as the principal architect of a cause that enjoyed overwhelming popular support. As in Louisiana, Posey's relatively short period of residency in the state might have been a factor. Another issue, never addressed directly but raised inferentially in the published newspaper letters, and possibly spread in word-of-mouth electioneering, was Thomas' age and physical infirmities. It was well known that he had had two major illnesses during his first three-year term of office.

In any event, when all the county tallies had slowly trickled in from throughout the state's vast expanses, Posey emerged with a respectable showing in the vote totals, but Jennings prevailed by the decisive margin of 5,211 to 3,934.[86] The landmark election assured that the transition from territorial to state government was to be complete and clear-cut, with new local leadership replacing the old gentry-based system of statecraft. As governor of Indiana Territory, Thomas had done his best to "make the people as happy as I am capable."[87] But this losing race was not destined to be his last political hurrah, and it did not mark the end of his long career of service to "the people."

NOTES

1. James Monroe to Thomas Posey, 11 March 1813, Thomas Posey Papers, Indiana Historical Society Library, Indianapolis, IN (hereafter cited as IHS); Posey to John Gibson, 13 March 1813, William H. English Collection, IHS.
2. Logan Esarey, ed., *Governors' Messages and Letters: Messages and Letters of William Henry Harrison*, 2 vols. (Indianapolis: Ayer Co. Publishers, 1922), 2:377.
3. K. Jack Bauer, *Zachary Taylor: Soldier, Planter, Statesman of the Old Southwest* (Baton Rouge, LA: Louisiana State University Press, 1985), 13-17.
4. Posey to Gibson, 13 March 1813, William H. English Collection, IHS.
5. See generally: Robert H. Wiebe, *The Opening of American Society* (New York: Alfred A. Knopf, 1984).
6. John D. Barnhart, "The Southern Influence in the Formation of Indiana," *Indiana Magazine of History*, 33(1937): 261-62 (hereafter cited as *IMH*).
7. Frederick D. Williams, ed., *The Northwest Ordinance: Essays on Its Formulation, Provisions and Legacy* (East Lansing, MI: Michigan State University Press, 1989), 127.
8. John D. Barnhart and Dorothy L. Riker, *Indiana to 1816: The Colonial Period* (Indianapolis: Indiana Historical Bureau and Indiana Historical Society, 1971), 417n.15.
9. Posey to Gibson, 13 March 1813, William H. English Collection, IHS.
10. Esarey, ed., *Governors' Messages and Letters*, 2:377n.1.
11. Charles Jay Wilson, "The Negro in Early Ohio," *Ohio Archaeological and Historical Publications* (Columbus, OH: Ohio Archaeological and Historical Society, 1930), 34:193.
12. Posey to Gibson, 13 March 1813, William H. English Collection, IHS.
13. Last Will and Testament of Thomas Posey, Will Record Book A, p. 96, Office of the Circuit Court Clerk, Knox County, Vincennes, IN.
14. Thomas Posey to Fayette Posey, 17 January 1814, Thomas Posey Papers, IHS. The 1809 Tax Lists for Henderson County, KY, indicate that there were 19 slaves kept at Longview, Posey's Kentucky homestead, shortly before he emigrated to Louisiana. Kentucky State Historical Society to John E. Inglehart, 9 May 1922, Thomas Posey Folder No. 000208, Mt. Vernon (IN) Public Library, Mt. Vernon, IN.
15. Bill of Sale, 17 April 1818, Lasselle Collection, Indiana State Library, Indiana Division, Indianapolis, IN, reproduced in *IMH*, 5 (1909): 27.
16. Posey to Gibson, 12 March 1813, William H. English Collection, IHS.
17. Jacob P. Dunn, *Indiana, A Redemption from Slavery* (Boston: AMS Press, 1890), 418.
18. Richard R. Beeman, *Patrick Henry: A Biography* (New York: McGraw-Hill, 1974), 184-92.
19. Charles Royster, *A Revolutionary People at War: The Continental Army and American Character, 1775-1783* (Chapel Hill, NC: The University of North Carolina Press, 1979), 319-20, 341.
20. Posey to Secretary of War, 14 March 1813, *Governors' Messages and Letters*, ed. Esarey, 2:385.

21. Ibid., Posey to Secretary of War, 4 May 1813, 2:377; Barnhart and Riker, *Indiana to 1816*, 363n.49, 405.
22. Posey to Secretary of War, 4 May 1813, *Governors' Messages and Letters*, ed. Esarey, 2:377.
23. Bauer, *Zachary Taylor*, 20.
24. Posey to Secretary of War, 17 February 1814, *Governors' Messages and Letters*, ed. Esarey, 2:630.
25. Thomas Posey's letter to "My dearly beloved children and grandchildren," 4 February 1814, Thomas Posey Papers, IHS.
26. Christopher B. Coleman, "Restoration of the Capital at Corydon," *IMH*, 30(1934): 255-56.
27. Governor Posey's Message to Assembly, 6 December 1813, *Governors' Messages and Letters*, ed. Esarey, 2:607-9. Posey's old friend Henry Lee, a diehard Federalist, bitterly opposed entry into the War of 1812. Charles Royster, *Light-Horse Harry Lee and the Legacy of the American Revolution* (New York: Alfred A. Knopf, 1981), 50.
28. Governor Posey's Message to Assembly, 6 December 1813, *Governors' Messages and Letters*, ed. Esarey, 2:607-9.
29. Governor Posey to Thomas Posey (the younger), 13 December 1813, Gratz Collection, Historical Society of Pennsylvania, Philadelphia, PA.
30. Posey to Indiana Legislative Council, 27 December 1813, *Governors' Messages and Letters*, ed. Esarey, 2:612.
31. Vincennes (IN) *Western Sun*, 19 February 1814.
32. William Wesley Woolen, "Thomas Posey," *Biographical and Historical Sketches of Early Indiana* (Indianapolis, IN: Hammond & Co., 1883), 26.
33. Thomas Posey to R.E. Anderson, Jr., 30 November 1813, Huntington Library, San Marino, CA.
34. Thomas Posey to Fayette Posey, 17 January 1814, Thomas Posey Papers, IHS.
35. Thomas Posey's letter to "My dearly beloved children and grandchildren," 4 February 1814, Thomas Posey Papers, IHS.
36. Ibid. In an admonitory postscript, Thomas solemnly warned his descendants to "have as little to do with lawsuits as possible. Law is very precarious and subject to be turned and twisted by cunning and designing men, and very little dependence to be placed in the most of lawyers."
37. Washington to Hector Ross, 9 October 1769, *The Writings of George Washington*, 39 vols., ed. John C. Fitzpatrick (Washington, DC: U.S. Government Printing Office, 1931-44), 2:525-27.
38. Proclamation of Thomas Posey, 4 April 1814, *Governors' Messages and Letters*, ed. Esarey, 2:642-43; "Proclamation," Vincennes (IN) *Western Sun*, 16 April 1814.
39. Posey to Secretary of War, 12 May 1814, *Governors' Messages and Letters*, ed. Esarey, 2:648-49; Barnhart and Riker, *Indiana to 1816*, 418.
40. John Johnston to Huffman, 12 April 1814, *Governors' Messages and Letters*, ed. Esarey, 2:643.
41. Ibid., Posey to Secretary of War, 23 June 1814, 2:655.
42. Barnhart and Riker, *Indiana to 1816*, 422-28; Vincennes *Western Sun*, 23 July 1814.

43. Barnhart and Riker, *Indiana to 1816*, 409-11.
44. Posey to Secretary of War, 18 February 1815, *Governors' Messages and Letters*, ed. Esarey, 2:688-89..
45. Ibid., Posey to Secretary of War, 21 February 1815, 2:689.
46. Ibid., Posey to Secretary of War, 12 November 1815, 2:698; Posey to William H. Crawford, Acting Secretary of War, 3 August 1815, Jacob Brown Collection, Massachusetts Historical Society Library, Boston, MA.
47. Jacob P. Dunn, *Indiana and Indianians*, 5 vols. (Chicago: The American Historical Society, 1919), 1:284-85.
48. William H. English, *Conquest of the Northwest, 1778-1783* (Indianapolis: Ayer Co. Publishers, 1895), 2:862-65.
49. Capt. L. C. Baird, "General Lafayette in Indiana," *IMH*, 2(1906): 195.
50. Governor Posey to Thomas Posey (the younger), 13 December 1813, Gratz Collection, Historical Society of Pennsylvania, Philadelphia, PA. Thom was appointed Collector of Internal Revenue in December, 1813. Barnhart and Riker, *Indiana to 1816*, 434n.52.
51. Governor Posey to Thomas Posey (the younger), 22 August 1814, Dreer Collection (Soldiers of the Revolution), Historical Society of Pennsylvania, Philadelphia, PA.
52. Charles N. Thompson, "General La Fayette in Indiana," *IMH*, 34 (1928): 71-72.
53. "The Posey Romance," St. Louis (MO) *Daily Globe-Democrat*, 6 November 1898; Robert M. Taylor, Jr., ed., *Indiana: A New Historical Guide* (Indianapolis: Indiana University Press, 1989), 17.
54. Carl Sandburg, *Abraham Lincoln: The Prairie Years* (New York: Harcourt, Brace & Co., 1926), 18-19; Merrill Moore, "Indiana in 1816," *IMH*, 11 (1916): 278; James R. Holliday, "Early History of Harrison County, Ind." (Ph.D Diss. University of Louisville, Louisville, KY, 1932), 13-14. This story is discounted in Louis A. Warren, *Lincoln's Youth: Indiana Years, Seven to Twenty-One, 1816-1830* (Westport, CT: Greenwood Press, 1959).
55. Ralph Geoffrey Newman, ed., *Abraham Lincoln: His Story in his Own Words* (Garden City, NY: Doubleday, 1975), 20.
56. R. Carlyle Buley, *The Old Northwest: Pioneer Period, 1815-1840*, 2 vols. (Bloomington, IN: Indiana University Press, 1950), 2:72-77; Cecil Eby, *"That Disgraceful Affair": The Black Hawk War* (New York: Norton, 1973), 195-96.
57. Mary Posey to William C. Posey, 28 December 1813, 20 April 1814, 8 July 1814, Letters of Mrs. Thomas Posey, SC 1756, Illinois State Historical Library, Springfield, IL (hereafter cited as ISHL); Mary Posey to Eliza Maria Street, 9 September 1814, Thomas Posey Papers, IHS.
58. Mary Posey to William C. Posey, 28 December 1813, Letters of Mrs. Thomas Posey, ISHL.
59. Ibid., 20 April 1814, 8 July 1814.
60. Ibid., 8 July 1814. Many years later, Sarah Anne did emigrate to Henderson, Kentucky with her husband, William Beverley.
61. Mary Posey to Eliza Maria Street, 8 September 1814, Thomas Posey Papers, IHS.
62. Ibid.
63. Mary Posey to William C. Posey, 8 July 1814, Letters of Mrs. Thomas Posey, ISHL.

64. Ibid., 8 December 1815.
65. Thomas Posey to General Assembly, 4 December 1815, *Governors' Messages and Letters*, ed. Esarey, 2:698-700.
66. Ibid.
67. Ibid., General Assembly to Governor Posey, 26 December 1815, 2:710-11.
68. Ibid., Governor's Reply to General Assembly, 26 December 1815, 2:711-12.
69. Ibid., "The probability is that we shall shortly take a stand as a state, and add one more brilliant star to the Union of our beloved country." The 1815 special census had established that the population of the territory then exceeded the 60,000 threshold required to qualify for statehood. Barnhart and Riker, *Indiana to 1816*, 427.
70. Posey to James Monroe, 25 January 1816, *Governors' Messages and Letters*, ed. Esarey, 2:710.
71. Two letters from "A Farmer of Knox County" raised the issue, (Vincennes [IN] *Western Sun*, 20 April 1816 and 20 July 1816), as well as an insightful letter from "Republican," (Vincennes [IN] *Western Sun*, 1 June 1816).
72. See generally: Donald P. Carmody, "Fiscal Objections to Statehood in Indiana," *IMH*, 42(1946): 311-21.
73. James H. Madison, *The Indiana Way: A State History* (Bloomington and Indianapolis, IN: Indiana University Press, 1986), 50; Barnhart and Riker, *Indiana to 1816*, 432-33; see generally: Donald F. Carmody, "Indiana Territorial Expenditures, 1800-1816," *IMH*, 34(1943): 237-62.
74. Barnhart and Riker, *Indiana to 1816*, 425.
75. Posey to James Monroe, 25 January 1816, *Governors' Messages and Letters*, ed. Esarey, 2:710.
76. Barnhart and Riker, *Indiana to 1816*, 430; Donald F. Carmody, "Statehood Achieved," in *The Hoosier State: Readings in Indiana History: Indiana Prehistory to 1880*, ed. Ralph D. Gray (Bloomington, IN: Indiana University Press, 1980), 146.
77. Madison, *Indiana Way*, 50; Carmody, "Fiscal Objections," *IMH*, 42(1946): 318; "Journal of the Convention of the Indiana Territory, 1816," *IMH*, 61(1965): 80-81.
78. Posey to James Monroe, 25 January 1816, *Governors' Messages and Letters*, ed. Esarey, 2:715.
79. MS Certificate of Appointment as Governor of Indiana Territory, 15 February 1816, Thomas Posey Papers, IHS.
80. For excellent and detailed accounts of the events and circumstances leading up to the attainment of Indiana statehood, see: Madison, *Indiana Way*, 50-54; Barnhart and Riker, *Indiana to 1816*, 412-64.
81. Vincennes (IN) *Western Sun*, 20 July 1816. This single issue carried ten full columns of letters devoted to the approaching election for various state and local offices.
82. Quoted passages are from "General Thomas Posey," Memoirs of Eminent Persons, *Port Folio* (Philadelphia: Harrison Hall, 1827). From unpaginated transcript copy, Thomas Posey File, Henderson County Public Library, Henderson, KY; quoted verbatim in "The Posey Romance," St. Louis (MO) *Daily Globe-Democrat*, 6 November 1898.
83. See generally, sources cited in note 82.

84. James W. Alexander, *Life of Archibald Alexander* (New York: Charles Scribner, 1854), 35.
85. Barnhart, "The Southern Influence," *IMH*, 33(1937): 263-65; Dunn, *Indiana: Redemption from Slavery*, 417-18. One respected scholar downplays the importance of the slavery issue in the 1816 election. Logan Esarey, "Pioneer Politics in Indiana," *IMH*, 13(1917): 100.
86. Madison, *Indiana Way*, 53-54, 131-32; Barnhart and Riker, *Indiana to 1816*, 464. For example, Posey carried western Knox County 571 to 174, but lost eastern Jackson County to Jennings 22 to 124. Vincennes (IN) *Western Sun*, 17 August 1816, 24 August 1816.
87. Posey to John Gibson, 13 March 1813, William H. English Collection, IHS.

CHAPTER TEN

(1816-1818)

". . . he knew him and gave him his hand."

Thomas Posey had emerged penniless at age nineteen from his Rover's Delight family. He had not acquired great wealth in either of his two marriages, in his military and public careers, or in private commercial enterprises or property investments. The last decade of his life was plagued with considerable indebtedness, quite likely arising from earlier financial losses he said he had sustained "by being security or performing other acts of friendship" for duplicitous or irresponsible men.[1] The fast-approaching date of Indiana's formal entry into the Union meant the end of Posey's $2,000 annual salary as territorial governor, upon which he relied to support himself, his wife, and remaining dependent children.[2] He had pled hardship in applying to Secretary of State James Monroe for reappointment to the position that he fully realized would end with the coming of statehood. He had accordingly also asked the administration to consider him for another post "should a new territory be laid off, or should anything occur in creating an office; or should any vacancy take place the office of which I might be thought adequate to perform the duties of."[3] Now, having been defeated for the state governorship, Posey was confronted, at the advanced age of sixty-six years, with the imminent end of his principal means of livelihood.

But he had still other resources to offer his country. After the end of the War of 1812, Thomas had demonstrated great aptitude in dealing with the Indian tribes, both friendly and hostile, whose lands were in or bordering upon Indiana Territory.[4] Throughout his life, he had fought many campaigns against the Native

Americans—the Shawnees at Point Pleasant, the Iroquois of upstate New York, the Creeks in Georgia, and the Miami tribes of the upper Northwest. General Anthony Wayne, like most of his contemporaries, had displayed nothing but contempt and hatred toward what he called the "savages," showing no mercy to the prisoners taken at Savannah. But Posey had emerged from all these fierce and deadly encounters with a certain respect for his Indian foes, and an understanding—if not approval—of their culture and values. These were rare qualities in those unenlightened times, qualities the administration particularly needed in the autumn of 1816 when, more than a year after the war's end, formal peace treaties and territorial issues with many of the Indian tribes of the western borders remained to be negotiated and resolved.

Within weeks of his election loss to Jonathan Jennings, Thomas applied to Secretary of War William H. Crawford for the then-vacant position of United States Agent for Indian Affairs to the tribes of the lower Wabash River country of Indiana and Illinois. His selection to that post was speedily recommended by the Secretary, and approved by President James Madison.[5] Although the office later lost prestige and standing, it was at the time considered a major governmental appointment. Since each Native American tribe had the legal status of an independent nation, the Indian Agency was tantamount to a ministry to a number of small, autonomous countries. Formal treaties entered into by the Agent with each tribe had to be constitutionally approved by the United States Senate.

Secretary Crawford sent Thomas his first major assignment on 12 September. He was to negotiate a land purchase agreement with the Wea and other Indian tribes whose villages and traditional hunting grounds lay along the White River, a meandering tributary of the Wabash in southwestern Indiana. The government was under pressure from immigrants pouring into the area from the east to open portions of these lands to white settlement. Co-commissioners named to assist Posey in the treaty negotiations were Judge Benjamin Parke, who had been the governor's aide in earlier territorial Indian affairs, and Fidelio C. Sharpe, a lawyer and member of the Kentucky state Senate from Livingstone County. Parke's assistance was particularly welcome. He had earlier concluded a preliminary peace pact with the Wea and Kickapoo tribes on 4 June 1816, although the federal Senate did not formally ratify that treaty until 23 December.[6]

Thomas acknowledged receipt of his appointment and first assignment on 29 September.[7] He promptly set about employing and organizing a staff to assist him in carrying out his new duties. Before leaving his Jeffersonville mansion for the west on 10 October, he submitted to Secretary of State James Monroe a list of employees, including three interpreters, an express rider, and a "gun smith at Ft. Harrison for the Indians." In setting out the compensation to be paid by the Indian Department for each employee, he claimed no additional payment for himself while continuing to draw his $2,000 annual salary as outgoing territorial governor.[8] Posey retained the nominal gubernatorial post until Governor-elect Jonathan Jennings took his oath of office as the first chief executive of the new state of Indiana on 7 November 1816. But his time and energies during these last months were largely devoted to his new duties as Indian Agent, which required his constant presence along the lower Wabash River. This meant another enforced separation from his wife Mary, and a return to the familiar surroundings of his first months in the governorship.

He engaged spartan living quarters for himself on the second floor above Hyacinth Lasselle's Inn in old Vincennes. There he brought his official papers and files, an extensive library of books, and many of his most prized personal possessions. According to his will, these included a pair of ivory-handled, silver-inlaid pistols taken from a British officer at Stony Point as a token of surrender; another pair of brass-barreled dueling pistols; a gold watch; and two elegant canes, one mounted with a large molded gold head, the other armed with a hidden, spring-operated sword blade. There is no evidence that Thomas ever had occasion to proffer the dueling pistols to any challenger on the field of honor, or to trip the trigger of his sword-tipped cane in anger against any antagonist.

Posey's indentured manservant Charles accompanied him to Vincennes, but Mary Posey remained at the Jeffersonville residence for a few weeks, and then embarked down the Ohio River to the homes of her children in Henderson County, Kentucky. She seems not to have ever returned to Indiana after her husband's term as territorial governor expired in November. Curiously, one can search in vain for any reference to the politically momentous events of the summer of 1816 in Mary's letters of the period to her son William—events in which her husband was playing such a pivotal role. Although William, now a merchant in the central Kentucky town of Winchester, might be expected to hang on every word concerning these critical months in his father's political career, Mary strangely displays little or no interest in public affairs. Her only reference to the history-making state constitutional convention was the oblique comment, "Your dr. Papa is very harty and gone to

Corydon,"[9] and her letters are totally silent on the subsequent five-week campaign for the state governorship.

But Mary Posey's family letters do provide a wealth of detail and personal insight into the happenings—many mundane, some tragic—within her widespread matriarchal circle. Within a year of her return from Virginia, Mary's son Reuben Thornton and his wife Ann Maria Washington Thornton had both died, and their two orphaned sons had been adopted by the Poseys' old friend of their Greenwood years, Lucy Gordon Jones of neighboring Ellwood. On a happier note, Thomas and Mary's youngest child, fifteen-year-old Sarah Ann, said to have inherited her father's handsome features, had married a well-born scion of King George County, William Beverley, a descendant of the landed proprietor of sprawling Augusta County. Thornton Posey, recently retired from the military with the rank of lieutenant colonel, was on an extended visit in Virginia's Fairfax County with his close friend and army comrade, Fayette Washington. Back in Kentucky, John Posey had temporarily left his Henderson County farm and moved into town to handle his brother Fayette's interests in the local mercantile firm of Ingram & Posey, while Fayette was off visiting their lawyer brother Lloyd in Louisiana.[10]

Thomas Posey himself, just before his departure to Vincennes, had been ordained a founding Elder of Jeffersonville's new Union Presbyterian Church. Indeed, Mary had also found that community very congenial: "There is a good deal of sociability in our little village."[11] The longtime and now-retired Secretary of Indiana Territory, John Gibson, along with his wife, were also residents of Jeffersonville and members of the local Presbyterian congregation. The new church, which also served the nearby village of New Albany, had been organized by the Reverend James McGready, a zealous and peripatetic missionary. The cleric had already come to know Mary and Thomas Posey well while earlier establishing the first Presbyterian church in Henderson. The Poseys' sons, John and Fayette, were the founding Elders of that community of worshipers.[12]

Anticipating that his new duties as Indian Agent would keep her husband in Vincennes indefinitely, Mary had her son, Thomas, escort her to join her Henderson kinfolk. The normally swift voyage down the Ohio was unpleasant: "the winds were against us and we did not get their for 9 days." After a five-week visit with the John and Fayette Posey families, she traveled on "in an elegant carriage" to the Joseph Streets in Shawneetown, a journey involving a forty-mile overland trip and an Ohio River crossing. Her granddaughter

Mary Harrison Posey and a maid accompanied her, and they were escorted on horseback by her youngest son, Washington Posey. Her account of the harrowing passage vividly depicts the period's hazards of land travel:

> The first day we got to Mr. Powel's, it commenced raining & we were all the next day getting to Morganfield. Highland Bridge is a dreadful one and six miles from their unfortunately we got stall'd in a creek for 2 hours & Mary, myself and our maid had to ride out of the creek behind Washington and then the Horses were so frightened they would not pull the empty carriage. Washington . . . pursuaded the driver to put his horse in and he got out. I never saw worse roads.[13]

But by Christmas of 1816, Mary was safely settled in for the winter in the imposing hilltop home of her daughter and son-in-law, and anxiously "looking out for Mr. Posey, he wrote Maria word he wou'd be here soon."[14] The young but observant Archibald Alexander, resident tutor to the Posey children at Greenwood, had described the Mary Posey of a quarter-century earlier as "a fine and stately person"—and through all the years of hardship and adversity on the rustic frontier, a fine and stately person she remained. Mary, always the grande dame, clung to the Virginia traditions and practices of her patrician upbringing, as confirmed in one early account:

> Mrs. Posey was, to the day of her death, as punctillious and ceremonious as any great lady, and regularly every morning each of her numerous descendants in the house had to go and bid her good morning, and inquire the state of her health, or she would be offended.[15]

Thomas Posey, before finding himself free to join his family for Christmas in the Streets' Westwood home, had been diligently negotiating a land treaty with the Weas, Kickapoos and Potatwatomies, three of the Native American tribes under his jurisdiction. The parley process traditionally required the advance distribution of gifts to the tribes' principal chiefs, and Secretary of War Crawford had dispatched the necessary goods from Washington late in September.[16] Posey reported to Crawford that, after arriving in Vincennes, he and Judge Parke had met privately with some of the chiefs, and were now proceeding northward to Fort Harrison, (outside present-day Terre Haute), where the formal treaty talks were to take place. But there was a problem. The chiefs' gifts, which were being transported down the Ohio and up the Wabash rivers, had not yet arrived in Vincennes, and Thomas was worried. "The water is so extremely low that the Indian annuities and presents have not yet reached this place . . . the goods are all safe, but the boat cannot progress for want of water. I must use some method by small craft or waggoning to get them on. The treaty will hold on the eleventh next month."[17]

The government had directed Posey and his co-commissioners to purchase as much land as possible from the three tribes, offering in exchange an increase in the annual subsidy or annuity already being paid to each tribe pursuant to prior treaties. The precise terms of the new agreement were to be discussed and negotiated at the upcoming parley. The goods to be presented before the conference were not payments for land, but were courtesies born of long tribal custom and tradition. If not extended, the chiefs would be offended and put in an unfavorable mood for the ensuing bargaining.

Thomas had a particularly good relationship with the Wea chiefs with whom he had conferred in Vincennes. As governor, he had had earlier dealings with them, after which they had honored him with the Indian name Weactonan—loosely translated, the father or friend of the Wea. Posey confided to Secretary Crawford that the Wea chiefs "appear to be in a pretty good humor, we have met and conversed several times sometimes upon the business of the land, but very litely upon that subject, whenever it is mentioned it comes from themselves. We dont wish to say much upon that subject until they receive their annuities and presents." From his past experience, Thomas knew that the presentation of the gifts, which had an estimated value of $3,200, was all-important. He stressed that "the success of the Treaty very much depends upon a speedy distribution of the annuities and presents."[18]

The scheduled 11 November parley accordingly had to be put off until the delayed arrival of the goods at Fort Harrison, and their distribution among the chiefs of all three tribes.[19] But eleven days later, Thomas Posey arose before an expectant and attentive audience of 760 Indian chiefs and warriors, assembled and seated in order of tribal status along the banks of the Wabash River just outside the fort, and delivered a stirring oration:

> My children: I am happy to meet with you this day, and to have this opportunity to open my mind and speak to you. Unstop your ears, open your eyes, look, hear and consider well what your father Weactonan is going to say to you, let it sink

> deep into your hearts, and if you approve of my advice you should follow it. . . .[20]

Posey then advanced the view that the tribes faced a crisis, pointing out that wild game had been pursued almost to extinction on their traditional hunting grounds. He pleaded with the tribesmen to renounce war and plunder, abandon their nomadic ways, settle into permanent villages, cultivate crops, raise livestock, learn the "useful arts," and teach their children to read and write. The American president, Thomas stated, was prepared to assist them in making this admittedly difficult transition. The government would "send tradesmen to show you how to build houses and make necessary furniture, to make ploughs, axes, hoes and every kind of useful tool; you will have men sent to shew you how to cultivate your fields . . . you will have oxen, carts, sleds, and harness of every kind usefull for you, and you will have women sent to teach your women how to spin, weave and make your clothing."[21] If the tribes were willing to accept the services offered in moving to a stable, agrarian way of life, Posey stated, they should confer among themselves and decide what areas of their old hunting grounds they were willing to cede over to the government in return. The exact terms of the agreement would then be negotiated in detail and finalized in later conferences between himself and the principal chiefs.

As the old soldier stood looking down into the bronzed faces of the hundreds of native Americans seated before him along the Wabash, he must have realized that his life had come full circle from the terrifying day, forty-two years before, when he stood with his back to another river, the Ohio, and fought for his life against the attacking Shawnees at Point Pleasant. Throughout the intervening years, on other battlefields across the breadth of the nation's frontiers, he had met his tribal antagonists again and again in mortal combat. The memory of each of those engagements was as vivid and real to him as the warriors he was facing today. Now, even as those conflicts flashed across his mind, he made a uniquely personal plea for a common and mutual cessation of ancient enmities:

> I have grown old in the service of my country. I have served as a war chief in time of war and have served in time of peace. I have seen and experienced a great deal of the transactions between man and man, and can give you good advice. The time has come that men are wiser, more enlightened, have greater experience and know more the great spirit than formerly.[22]

In one of the great defining moments of his life, Thomas Posey had in his heart finally made his peace with the historic Indian foe. Seeing in himself one of those men who had gained greater wisdom and enlightenment from the bloody encounters of the past, he looked for reciprocal rationality and understanding among the warriors facing him now. He closed his oration with a fervent prayer, appealing to their common God "that the great Spirit may take you into his holy keeping, and guide you unto all truth and do not forget what Weactonan has said to you, he will always do what the great Spirit may enable him to do for your good. You have given me the name of Weactonan, I think it an honorable name, and shall hand it down to my children. I now shake hands with you. . . ."[23]

A long, respectful silence followed Posey's address. Then, one by one, the principal chiefs of each tribe arose and delivered their responses, most of which were positive, to his oration. By agreement the assembly then dispersed, with the understanding that the critical issues raised at the parley would be taken back to all the people of the three tribes for full consideration. It was further agreed that an answer would be delivered to the Indian Agent at his Vincennes headquarters sometime in the coming spring.

In the hindsight of the American government's later shameful treatment of Native American peoples, some may regard Posey's proposals as a cynical forerunner of the blatant exploitation and manipulation by which many succeeding Indian Agents betrayed the tribes under their charge. But that judgment would be an unfair and unwarranted derogation of the personal good faith of the decent man who addressed the assembled warriors on this November day in 1816. Thomas truly believed, rightly or wrongly, that the lifestyle he offered the Indians represented their only hope of permanent peaceful coexistence with the proliferating numbers of white settlers flocking to the frontier. Continuation of the mutually cruel and merciless war of attrition being waged between the two races could end only in the extermination of the outnumbered and outgunned Native Americans. Thus, Thomas saw his plan as the only alternative to genocide, and unlike many of his contemporaries, he recoiled in horror from that outcome.

The record itself documents his sincerity. Posey, in his zeal to advance his vision of a settled, agrarian way of life for the frontier tribes, went well beyond his actual authority as President Madison's envoy in offering them the technical support they would need "to go into a State of civilization." But in his subsequent official report he vigorously defended his proposals and urged their adoption by the administration, assuring Secretary Crawford that

"I would not by any means have the thought that I would do anything contrary to the sentiments of government."[24] To their credit, his superiors in Washington acceded to his recommendations, and early the next year Posey successfully negotiated the specific terms of land agreements with the Wea and Kickapoo tribes—but not, apparently, with the Potawatomie.[25] The final treaty document with the Weas was not formally signed until after Thomas' death, on 2 October 1818, with Governor Jonathan Jennings, Judge Benjamin Parke and Lewis Cass acting as co-commissioners for the national government.[26]

During the remainder of his eighteen months as Indian Agent, Posey divided his time between the historic old Wabash community of Vincennes, and the brand new Ohio River settlement of Shawneetown. His wife remained in the latter area, understandably preferring to reign as matriarch in the comfortable Street household over notably less pretentious surroundings in Thomas' cramped rooms above Lasselles' noisy inn and tavern. Joseph and Eliza Maria Street's gracious "Westwood" was located on a high bluff two miles west of a former Shawnee Indian tribal village and burial ground. The federal government had laid out the town in 1810 as its chosen site for a postal center and land office serving the unsettled areas of the northwest. Despite the fact that its placement on the flood plain of the Ohio River subjected it to periodic flooding, the town grew rapidly, became the county seat of Gallatin County in 1812, and soon developed into the leading banking and commercial hub of the area.[27]

It was also in 1812, three years after his marriage to Eliza Maria Posey, that the embattled young journalist and lawyer, Joseph Montfort Street, had removed his family and possessions from Kentucky to Shawneetown, apparently to avoid the loss of all his property through legal process. Federal judge Harry Innes had filed a libel action alleging that his character had been defamed in Street's paper, *The Western World*, by charges of corruption and treasonable conduct arising out of the so-called "Spanish conspiracy." When a substantial judgment for money damages was entered in the case against Street personally, he vainly sought to protect his property from legal execution by conveying to his brother-in-law, John Posey, six thousand acres of land, six slaves, four horses, two cows, and household furniture—all to be held in trust for Eliza Maria Street.[28] But the Streets were forced to flee Kentucky when further court action by Innes' able attorney, Henry Clay, threatened to penetrate the legal inviolability of the trust property.

The move to Shawneetown proved to be a felicitous one. Wisely eschewing journalism, Joseph Street soon became a leading citizen of the town, holding many local public offices, and rising to the rank of brigadier general in the Illinois state militia. His notable public career reached its pinnacle in the last decades of his life when, serving as a controversial but courageous U.S. Agent for Indian Affairs in Wisconsin and Iowa, he became a staunch and fearless defender of tribal treaty rights. In the face of fierce local opposition, he pioneered in establishing schools for Indian children. His wife, Eliza Maria, conducted classes in sewing and weaving for young Indian girls, thus personally fulfilling the promise made by her father in the Wabash River treaty conference of 1816 to provide Native Americans with instruction in the "useful arts."[29]

In the later years of his Indian Agency, General Street incurred the enmity of influential political and economic interests, including the powerful American Fur Company, which bitterly resented his efforts to thwart their repeated violations of Indian land and mineral rights. Ironically, one of his strongest advocates in Washington was Senator Henry Clay—the same Clay who defended Aaron Burr against Street's charges of treason, and who later, as attorney for Judge Harry Innes, hounded the young journalist out of Kentucky.[30] Street's enemies brought strong pressure on the federal government to remove him from office. But President Andrew Jackson who, as a young lawyer, had ridden with Street on the Kentucky-Tennessee judicial circuit, refused to dismiss him from his post, saying: "I know General Street is a Whig, but he is an honest man and as long as I am president he shall be Indian Agent."[31] Chief Black Hawk, whose peaceful surrender after his ill-fated incursion into Illinois in 1832 was negotiated by Street, later wrote of him: "I have always heard that he was a good man, and a good father—and made no promises that he did not fulfill."[32]

The same could well be said of Indian Agent Thomas Posey. Through 1817 and into the next year, he operated his agency with integrity and distinction from his private chambers above Lasselle's Inn in Vincennes. During his residency there, he very likely spent many a convivial evening hour at the local Masonic Lodge No. 15, which had been founded in 1813 by George Washington Johnson. Many prominent Hoosiers, including Posey's main political rival, Governor Jonathan Jennings, were brother Masons.[33] Although there is no evidence that he led a profligate lifestyle, the modest annual salary of $800 the government paid its Indian Agents appears to have been inadequate to cover all of Thomas' living expenses.[34] He found it necessary to incur additional indebtedness which, after his death, had to be satisfied by the judicially ordered sale of his fine Jeffersonville house.[35]

To the extent that any individual's personal library reflects his or her interests and intellectual level, it is obvious that Thomas had come a long way from the young man of "tolerable english education" whose first adult occupation on the Virginia frontier was that of a humble saddler's apprentice. Among the volumes he might have perused during the many lonely hours spent in his Vincennes chambers were the complete works of Shakespeare, Plutarch's *Lives,* Reid's *Essays,* Hume's *History of England,* a five-volume *Life of Washington,* (probably the work written by his old friend John Marshall), the writings of Alexander Pope, Hunter's *Studies of Nature,* Brown's *Estimate of Manners,* and an eighteen-volume encyclopedia. But none of these scholarly works was as well-worn and frayed by frequent usage as Posey's personal *Holy Bible.*[36]

Unlike his earlier years as the agnostic and skeptical country gentleman presiding over his Sunday dinner table at Greenwood—depicted by tutor Archibald Alexander as seemingly lukewarm in religious fervor—Posey in his later years was a devout and active churchman. His public addresses continued to reflect the abstract Deism of so many prominent men of his time, but Thomas' private writings and personal practices had become thoroughly parochial and Presbyterian. Many passages of his testamentary letter to his children and grandchildren could have been transposed verbatim into a pious sermon from the pulpit. Four of its paragraphs fully extolled the benefits of bible study: "There is more information derived in having a perfect knowledge of its historical parts, its precepts and rules of practice for the government of man and its divine instructions, than all other books written. You can not be too familiar with its contents."[37]

The source and strength of Posey's religious conversion can be traced to his family's move to the frontier in 1802, during the full flowering of the Great Revival, which originated two years earlier in Kentucky and spread throughout the west until it subsided in 1805. Great crowds flocked to camp meetings conducted by eloquent western revivalists, principally Baptists, Methodists and Presbyterians, and returned home to establish their own local congregations, some of which functioned for years before acquiring resident ministers.[38] The instrument of transmutation for Thomas and Mary Posey was a charismatic Presbyterian preacher then toiling in the spiritual vineyards of Henderson County—the Reverend James McGready. His influence within their family was pervasive. Mary Posey's letters contain many glowing references to the character and preaching prowess of the itinerant missionary, and numerous second and third generation Poseys who were exposed to his exhortations became staunch adherents of the Presbyterian creed.[39]

During Thomas' governorship in Indiana, McGready visited Jeffersonville at the Poseys' invitation and was their houseguest while he preached to the local community and oversaw the creation of the new Union church.[40] One of Posey's duties as a founding Elder of that church would have been to conduct services in the absence of a traveling preacher or a full-time pastor.[41] Thomas became a lay leader in his new faith, representing the Presbyterian Church of Indiana at a general convocation in nearby Louisville, as well as a later synod in Kentucky held in October of 1817.[42] At various times in the last years of his life, he served as president and vice-president of the American Bible Society.[43] This group, dedicated to the widespread distribution of the scriptures, was one of several national inter-denominational organizations comprising what was called the Benevolent Empire, aimed at corralling the stream of new settlers flooding the frontier.[44]

Posey's personal involvement in church affairs is typified by a letter he wrote to Presbyterian ecclesiastical authorities early in 1817 in support of a local clergyman—not of his own congregation—who had been suspended from his ministry for doctrinal errors:

> From the personal acquaintance as well as a knowledge of the general character of the Rev'd John Todd, I do not hesitate to say that I think his religious & moral reputation is in my opinion unimpeachable. And could the differences that has taken place with respect to an explanation of some Scriptural passages be maturely investigated, & explain'd I think a reconciliation might take place & Mr. Todd restored to his ministerial functions again.[45]

Deeply concerned with the serious shortage of ordained ministers in the region, Thomas emphasized to the church leaders the "great deal of good among our fellowmen in this part of the country" the defrocked cleric could accomplish if reinstated. But respectful, as always, of higher authority, he emphasized that "from my personal acquaintance I have of Mr. Todd's amiable disposition, piety and desire to promote the welfare of our church I could wish his suspension were removed, was it construed with the views of the General Assembly & general plan of salvation."[46] Posey's careful endorsement apparently carried considerable weight with the church—the erring Reverend Mr. Todd was soon reinstated, and faithfully ministered to his Presbyterian congregation in nearby Charlestown from 1817 to 1824.[47]

Mary Posey's family letters invariably exhibit equally steadfast religious convictions. That strong faith was again severely tested in early 1817 when she received word of the death, from unstated causes, of her other Thornton son, George, at age forty-one. As in the earlier loss of Reuben Thornton, time, distance and travel constraints made her return to Virginia impractical on these sad occasions. But she did arrange to have her son Thomas, who was then traveling in the east on business, call upon the bereaved widow, Mary, at Rumford, the Thornton family home. He later escorted her and her three children to join her Randolph kindred in Richmond.[48]

In June of 1817 General Thomas Posey took a break from his Indian agency duties and private churchly commitments to celebrate a happy occasion and reunion. His old Kentucky friend Henry Clay, now Speaker of the U. S. House of Representatives and a prominent national political figure, visited Vincennes, where he was honored at a gala public dinner. Posey was selected to preside over the festivities, and he delivered the assembled company's first toast to the guest of honor: "Henry Clay, he now possesses, may he long enjoy, the respect of Europe, the honors of his country, and the affections of the west." Clay arose amidst the cheers of the audience to deliver an eloquent response. He first paid tribute to the soldiers of the revolutionary generation, movingly recalling their struggles and sacrifices in the war, "in which you, Mr. President, bore a gallant part." The eminent Speaker down-played his recent diplomatic mission as head of the American delegation which had ended the War of 1812 by negotiating and signing the Treaty of Ghent. Finally, after expressing his great admiration for the pioneering spirit and stalwart citizens of southwestern Indiana, he raised a glass to a toast of his own: "Prosperity to the country of the Wabash!"[49]

It may well have been this exhilarating taste of public attention and adulation, notably missing from his life since leaving the governorship, that induced Posey to re-enter the seductive arena of electoral politics, the source of so many past disappointments. In the approaching election of August, 1817, the incumbent William Hendricks was running to retain his seat as Indiana's first congressman in the national House of Representatives. Hendricks, along with Governor Jonathan Jennings and U.S. Senator James Noble, now composed the dominant triumvirate of the ruling party in state political affairs. In the previous year's first statehood races, he had soundly defeated Thomas' close friend, Allan D. Thom, for the congressional office. Now, a year later, Hendricks was an odds-on favorite to return to Congress. His only declared opponent, Reuben W. Nelson, coeditor of the weekly Corydon *Indiana Herald*, was not widely known, and even worse, was closely identified with the old Harrison pro-slavery faction.[50]

On 9 July, less than four weeks before the scheduled election date, Posey sent a short letter, addressed "To the People of Indiana," to the state's leading journals:

> I have been solicited by a number of my friends to come forward as a candidate for your suffrages for the fifteenth Congress. I am well aware that it is a late period, but as I have ever held it a sacred duty to do every thing in my power for the public good, I have yielded to the wishes of my friends, in consenting to serve, if elected. A long life devoted to public business, renders it I presume, unnecessary for me to make many professions to you—all I will say is, that if you think proper to elect me your representative, my best exertions shall be used to render every service in my power, both to this state, and the United States.[51]

What was the moving force behind this hasty and ill-advised decision? It is likely that a few leaders of the old Harrison faction, in a desperate move to block Hendricks' re-election, had engineered Posey's belated and reluctant entry into the race—a conclusion reinforced by the simultaneous withdrawal of editor Nelson from the contest. Hendricks himself alleged as much after the election. "About the first of August Governor Posey became a candidate. And how was he taken up? Was it by the people, by his own wishes, or by a caucus? By the latter, it may be said without fear of contradiction, a caucus at Vincennes, at which but very few attended."[52]

Hendricks' charges are borne out by the immediate editorial endorsement of Posey's candidacy by the Vincennes *Western Sun*, the congressman's long-time bitter foe:

> With pleasure we announce Gov. Posey as a candidate . . . When we reflect that that venerable man belonged to that family who purchased the inestimable right, which he now offers to be favored with——we cannot believe that there are any who are so lost to the noble passion of gratitude . . . as not to rally round this remaining patriot.[53]

The editorial played strongly on Thomas' political identity as one of the few living survivors of the revolutionary generation of freedom fighters. It spoke movingly of "those who have faced the foe during the day, and reposed upon the mossy couch at night." After extolling Posey's "political services" and "private reputation," the editor concluded with the effusive rhetorical question, "who then among us will oppose his election? None but the ambitious—the selfish—the ungrateful—or those who know nothing of the qualifications of the man."[54]

As in the prior year's race for governor, the congressional contest was less about issues, qualifications or personalities than the continued power struggle between the remnant of the old Harrison conservatives in the Wabash counties, and the Jennings republicans in the state's populous eastern areas.[55] Slavery was no longer a dominant or visible issue. It had been categorically banned by the new state constitution, with only a few peripheral questions remaining to be judicially resolved—notably, clarification of the status of indentured servants bound under contracts legally entered into prior to the adoption of the constitution.[56] Both candidates were well known. Talent-wise, one historian describes Hendricks as "a man of fair ability, a hard worker who attended to the interests of his constituents, and cultivated the newspapers and the soldiers."[57]

Posey's late entry into the race allowed him few opportunities to travel throughout the state, or to appear personally at citizens' assemblies. There was very little time for the race to generate the customary outpouring of letters of support for the candidates in the weekly journals. One of the few such letters to appear before election day reflects a negative personal issue that Hendricks' supporters might have been raising by word-of-mouth around the state:

> The governor's health which for several years since he has been amongst us has been bad, is now happily restored . . . when he was before the people last year, reports were but too successfully propagated by his enemies, that his great age and infirmities disqualified him from discharging the duties of the office for which he was then a candidate.[58]

This letter from one of Posey's supporters suggests that his health and age might have been a major factor in his defeat for the governorship in 1816. The writer, identifying himself simply as "A Voter," in a thinly-veiled effort to link Thomas to national gentry leaders, pointed out that Posey was only slightly older than the last and current American presidents, James Madison and James Monroe. He protested, perhaps too much, that "Gov. Posey is in full possession of his mental as well as physical powers," and expressed the fervent hope that at the polls "we shall all rally around this gallant old soldier, this excellent citizen, this venerable Patriot!"[59] Two additional letters supporting Thomas appeared in the *Western Sun* just before election day—one expressing the politically pragmatic view that "at Washington city general POSEY is as well known as he is here, and what man could effect for us, he can."[60]

One of Thomas' pockets of public support was, appropriately enough, Posey County, located in the extreme southwest corner of the state. It was populated largely by a closely knit colony of members of The Harmonie Society, a unique cult of religious zealots which, led by the dynamic George Rapp, had emigrated from Germany to Pennsylvania in 1803. The sect considered itself God's chosen people, and its adherents, in preparing for an expected imminent second coming of Christ, had renounced private ownership of property for a communal, celibate lifestyle. Upon conferring with Posey in Jeffersonville in September of 1814, Father Rapp was warmly encouraged by the governor to move his followers westward to Indiana Territory. Soon thereafter, the society purchased 25,000 acres of rich farmland along the Wabash River in Posey County, and within a few years had built up a thriving agricultural and light manufacturing community around the town of Harmony. During the short 1817 congressional race, Thomas spent four days campaigning among the Rappites, and was rewarded for his efforts by a 453 to 121 plurality in the county when the votes were cast on 4 August 1817.[61]

Unfortunately, Posey's support among his friends in The Harmonie Society was not typical of electoral demographics elsewhere in Indiana. The old pre-statehood political and regional divisions which had helped deny him the governorship continued to work against him. The congressional race was, furthermore, the classic confrontation between a younger, state-oriented and democratized politician, and the aged representative of a rapidly disappearing generation of gentry leaders personifying, to many, a dying culture of privilege and property. The next national census would find 88 percent of white male Americans to be under 45 years of age; a discerning scholar has commented that the recently inaugurated President James Monroe, "in powdered wig and buckled breeches . . . entered office with political values as obsolete as his dress."[62] Posey's career had been built on his connections with such national figures as Washington, Madison and Monroe, but the coattails of gentry leadership had turned into an electoral albatross. Hendricks' margin of victory was an overwhelming 5,693 to 3,778.[63] The outcome dealt a final blow to the old soldier's hopes of ever gaining a statewide elective post in Indiana, and he never again ran for public office. Sadly, Thomas Posey had become a living political anachronism in his own time.

Hendricks, although harboring well-founded suspicions that his political enemies had used Posey to front their hostility toward him, seemingly bore little personal rancor toward his defeated opponent. Weeks after the election, when the Corydon *Indiana Herald* continued its bitter attacks upon his character and reputation, the congressman published a lengthy defense of his integrity and record in the more editorially friendly Madison *Indiana Republican.* He stoutly maintained that, "against Gov. Posey I have not a word to say. His character both public and private, as far as I know, I admire—I early formed a favorable opinion of him, and that opinion I have not yet changed." But Hendricks went even further. His respect for Posey was so great, he declared somewhat improbably, that had he not already held the congressional seat at issue, he would have voluntarily withdrawn from the race when Thomas announced his candidacy:

> But my situation was a different one. Governor Posey was brought forward by my avowed and inveterate enemies . . . He suffered himself to be taken up if report be true, contrary to his wishes and certainly contrary to his interests, for he had and still has a situation much more lucrative and better suited to his age and infirmities.[64]

Admittedly, Thomas' duties in Vincennes were less physically and mentally stressful than would have been a seat in Washington's House of Representatives, but the modest $800 annual salary of an Indian Agent could hardly be called lucrative. The agency did, however, bring with it a certain importance and prestige, as the connecting link between two vastly disparate and irreconcilable cultures struggling to survive within the same confined area. An interesting insight into Thomas Posey's public persona as Indian Agent is provided in a documented incident occurring during the short congressional campaign. A visitor from the east, Thomas Dean, who had come to Indiana with the avowed mission of bettering the lot of some of its Native Americans, was informed upon arriving in Vincennes,

> . . . that former Gov. Posey & present Gov. Jennings were now in town—Gov. Posey is the present agent for Indian affairs, therefore I thought it advisable to have an interview with them . . . We then proceeded to Governor Posey's, according to appointment, which was at 10 o'clock. We met him and found him an agreeable old gentleman, as I before thought him to be. We had some conversations on our subject. . . .[65]

After a later meeting with Jennings, Dean happened to run into the "agreeable old gentleman" again as Thomas strode into the busy little Vincennes post office, perhaps supporting his bad leg on his gold-headed or sword-tipped cane. "We had some conversations on Gov. Jennings' sentiments as to our business, & he wished that his communications might be kept confidential, what had passed between us heretofore as it relates to our business with the Governor."[66] One can only speculate on why Posey sought to protect the content of his discussions with Dean. Perhaps he wished to keep any possible disagreement between himself and the governor on Indian matters out of the ongoing congressional contest with Jennings' close political ally, William Hendricks. The Native American inhabitants of Indiana were, of course, barred from voting in the election—but Thomas' humane measures for their support and education were undoubtedly controversial among some elements of the eligible voters, and indeed might have contributed to his defeat later that summer.

But the election outcome was not to be the most devastating loss Posey was to suffer in 1817. During the campaign, his wife Mary had summered in Henderson with the John and Fayette Posey households. Thomas joined her there early in October for a rare reunion with their lawyer-son Lloyd, who had come north to purchase and transport twenty-six slaves to a newly-acquired farm in Louisiana. Mary planned to spend the approaching winter with the Street family in Shawneetown, and on this trip it was Thomas himself who escorted her there along the familiar but rugged overland route. They arrived late and weary at Westwood, after unaccountably getting lost along the way. Then, with just two days' rest, Thomas had to hurry back to Vincennes after getting word that his indentured manservant Charles had suddenly eloped, spiriting his bride away on one of Posey's carriage horses.[67] Thus, Thomas and Mary were separated and unable to turn to each other for comfort when distressing news of one of their children began to trickle in from the east.

Mary's letters of this period to her son William, usually full of happy family chitchat and gossip, began to reflect growing concern and foreboding over the fortunes of another of her sons. Recently retired army lieutenant colonel Thornton Posey had signed on to a very perilous venture off the southeast coast of the United States. "We have had very late letters from my dr. Thornton Posey, he directs from Fernadina Emily Island, his health is good, but alas my dr. William my heart often akes for him."[68] Two weeks later, she notes with relief, "my dr. T.A.P. has left Amely Island for which I am thankful"[69]; another week later, "McGregor and my dr. Thornton have left Amely Island, I hope we shall see him shortly."[70] But sometime in the next month, tragic news had arrived. "Oh my dr. William 'tis impossible to describe my feelings when I heard of the death of my dr. beloved Thornton, but I try to be resigned to the will of the Lord."[71]

Amelia Island, present site of Fernadina, Florida, was part of Spanish East Florida. It was situated off the estuary of the St. Mary's River, a stream marking the lower boundary of Georgia, then the nation's southernmost state. The island's pivotal location had made it the major port of entry for illegal smuggling of slaves into the country since their further importation had been outlawed as of 1 January 1808. Many Americans, including high government officials, viewed the strategic island as the key to the ultimate acquisition of all of East Florida from the weak Spanish empire. In 1812 it had been the target of a successful clandestine seizure by American irregulars. The motley group was commanded by former Georgia governor George Mathews, onetime Staunton innkeeper and, incidentally, the uncle of Thomas Posey's first wife, Martha. General Mathews was compelled to withdraw from the island when, after vigorous diplomatic protests by the Spanish government, President Madison and Secretary of State Monroe withdrew their covert support of the operation.[72]

On 29 June 1817 about fifty-five lightly armed men led by Thornton Posey waded ashore from rowboats onto Amelia Island, and advanced through waist-deep swamps toward a Spanish fort held by an alert and tensely waiting seventy-man garrison poised to fire a salvo from their dozen sixteen-pound cannons. The landing party moved forward in groups of two or three men, making it appear that they were only the advance element of a larger invading force. Although they could have been wiped out with one broadside, not a shot was fired. When Colonel Posey, drawn sword in hand, walked up to the gate of the fort and demanded its capitulation, the Spanish commander struck his flag and offered his own sword in surrender. Posey then took ceremonial possession of the fort, raising a banner of white emblazoned with the green cross of St. George, the personal flag of General Sir Gregor MacGregor.[73]

MacGregor, a legendary Scottish soldier of fortune whose origin and knighthood were equally suspect, had fought as a British army captain in the Napoleonic wars. He later attained his generalship as a capable commander in Simon Bolivar's revolutionary army in Venezuela. Early in 1817, he came to the United States with a daring plan to invade and conquer Spanish East Florida, with the avowed purpose of establishing there an independent nation friendly to American interests.[74] He obtained some private financial support in Philadelphia and New York, and was successful in recruiting for the undertaking a small number of free-spirited adventurers, mostly discharged veterans of the War of 1812. In some unknown way, MacGregor prevailed upon Thornton Posey to embrace his cause, and commissioned him a full colonel and second-in-command of the quixotic enterprise.

The venture caught the imagination of the American public, and all the Indiana weeklies carried full and glowing reports of the audacious invasion. The Vincennes *Western Sun* printed extensive excerpts from Thornton's letter of 10 July to his father: "I have drawn the sword once more, & am now engaged as second to the commander in chief, in the conquest of the Floridas."[75] The Madison *Indiana Republican* reproduced the full text of MacGregor's stirring "Proclamation of the Liberating Army," which heralded "a great and glorious cause, against a government which has trampled on all the natural and asserted rights which descend from God to man."[76] But Thornton Posey's later report of 27 July, captioned "Extract of a letter from an officer in the Patriot army," included some potentially ominous foreboding. It mentioned illness starting to spread among several officers of the expedition, noting that "it . . . is very sickly here."[77] A 16 August dispatch from Charleston revealed that a spy had discovered and reported to the Spanish governor of East Florida the small numbers actually comprising MacGregor's force, and noted that the governor was in the process of organizing a massive expedition to drive the "Patriot army" from Amelia Island.[78]

The enterprise was in serious trouble. Despite his initial success in seizing the Spanish fort and occupying the island, MacGregor's anonymous American backers failed to send forward the promised reinforcements and supplies he needed to land on the mainland and pursue his conquest of East Florida. It was later made clear that, far from any desire to promulgate the natural and asserted rights of man, their only interest had been to open Amelia Island's port to slave-running and privateering. When the large Spanish force dispatched from Saint Augustine arrived on the shoreline opposite the island and threatened to overwhelm MacGregor's malaria-decimated troops, it was obvious that his mission was doomed to failure. At a council of war held on 3 September, Colonel Thornton Posey and most of the other American officers resigned their commissions and left Amelia Island.[79]

MacGregor sailed off to the Bahamas to pursue, (unsuccessfully, as it turned out), other efforts to conquer and rule Florida. Posey did not follow him, choosing instead to return directly to the United States. It was to be his last passage. Either on Amelia Island, or aboard ship shortly after his departure, Thornton contracted the deadly yellow fever, a dreaded plague then running rampant in Charleston and other southern ports. He had written his mother of his departure, but when Mary Posey spoke on 29 October of her high hopes of soon again seeing her "dr. Thornton," he had already died in Wilmington, North Carolina, on 17 September 1817, at the young age of twenty-nine.[80]

The *Western Sun* carried a full and emotional account of his death. "The gallant THORNTON POSEY . . . a Col. in the Patriot Army under gen. McGregor breathed his last at Wilmington, N.C. on Wednesday week. He reached that harbour in a vessel from Amelia Island, in company with the gallant friend who shared the toils of the expedition. He had symtoms of the billious fever when he embarked. . . . Much of the success which attended the expedition," the *Western Sun* continued, "was owing to Posey's exertions." But when he realized that "a bold military expedition was about to degenerate into a privateering system, he and his Virginia friend threw up their commissions and bade adieu to Amelia Island. He has now sunk into the grave . . . but over its silent sod is poured the sigh of every man who puts a value upon gallantry, generosity and noble daring."[81]

Although two of Thomas Posey's sons of his first marriage had died in their childhood, Thornton's death was the first among his adult children. The sudden and unexpected loss of his warrior-son, whose personal bravery and military exploits were a source of special pride to the old soldier, must have dealt a severe blow to the heart and soul of the already ailing general, as he sat alone in his cluttered Vincennes chambers. For Mary Posey, of course, Thornton was the third of her sons to die in his young manhood within three years—all suddenly stricken by virulent diseases in distant locations without even the comfort of their mother's farewell embrace. From Westwood, separated from her husband and perhaps fearing the further loss of other of her far flung children, Mary could only commiserate by letter with another son: "I lament my dear William the distance which separates us now, but hope we shall spend a long Eternity in singing praises to our sweet Jesus forever and ever. This life is but short at best. . . ."[82]

Thomas and Mary Posey had not recently maintained the close and intimate relationship that characterized the earlier years of their married life. Since he left Kentucky in 1810 to explore Louisiana as a new homesite, they had enjoyed only one year of sustained cohabitation: the final year of Posey's territorial governorship. Mary had stayed in Kentucky during Thomas' brief term in the U.S. Senate, and her long visit in Virginia spanned the first two years of his Indiana tenure. Thereafter, she resided with one or another of her children in Illinois and Kentucky while Thomas worked out of his Vincennes quarters, with only occasional conjugal visits to his wife. This may perhaps have been due more to a natural and evolving diversion of interests than to any estrangement or diminution of affection between them. The difficulties and responsibilities of Thomas' last public offices appear to have increasingly absorbed his time and energies, while Mary's letters depict a woman deeply engrossed in the lives and well-being of her children and grandchildren, with no interest whatever in public affairs. Whether by choice or economic necessity, Thomas in his final years appears to have put his career ahead of his connubial role—no longer quite the doting husband who gave up a prized field command and general's commission to avoid "rendering a most amiable wife and sweet little family of children extremely miserable."[83]

Still, Mary does not appear to have been unhappy with her lot. In the months that followed Thornton Posey's tragic death, the life she described as "but short at best" seemed to go on as usual, although Thomas' remaining time proved to be short indeed. She found some comfort within the Street household with the timely arrival of yet another "sweet babe," a granddaughter, in the growing Westwood family.[84] Her letters glow with reports of other family members. Lloyd Posey had returned home to Louisiana, there to find awaiting him another son born during his visit to Kentucky. His brother Alexander continued the studies at the University of Pennsylvania that were to lead to an illustrious medical career, while young Washington Posey was in Indiana admiring the fine residence and mercantile structure his brother Thomas had recently completed in Corydon in partnership with Colonel Thom. John, Fayette and William Posey were well established in Kentucky as merchants, farmers and heads of growing families, and young Sarah Ann was settled into a comfortable marriage in the patrician Beverley family in Virginia. Both Thomas and Mary could view with satisfaction and pardonable pride the maturation and prospects of their large and scattered family of children, while doubtlessly contemplating with delight an ever-widening circle of grandchildren.

Posey spent most of his last fall and winter attending to his duties as Indian Agent in and around Vincennes—tasks ranging from prosaic to bizarre. A case falling in the latter category occurred when he was called upon to mediate a potentially major ethnic disturbance arising from an incident at Fort Harrison. It appears that a dispute over ownership of a horse arose between a white youth and one of an band of visiting Indians. A man named Smith, intervening in the scuffle on the youth's behalf, received for his pains a knife wound to the body. Another Indian seized the knife and fled, but was pursued by a crowd of bystanders, joined by a Captain Hamilton, a garrison officer who happened to be in the vicinity. The captain, catching up to the running Indian and thinking that he was Smith's assailant, "knocked him over and gave him some heavy blows, which were considered mortal." The crowd, upon learning of their mistake, then gave chase to the first Indian, who sought to escape on the disputed horse. But "the Indian refusing to stop was shot by Capt. Hamilton and soon expired." Thomas, as Indian Agent, was asked to defuse the ensuing ugly confrontation between the visiting Native Americans and the local populace. The newspaper account of the episode concluded: "We are happy to state that thro' the exertions of Gen. Posey, the affair was amicably adjusted and the remaining Indians departed professing perfect satisfaction."[85]

Clearly, the diverse ethnic groups then sharing the Wabash country maintained at best only a fragile and uneasy relationship. But most such interactions were less violent and more easily "adjusted." In early January of 1818 Posey forwarded to Secretary of War John C. Calhoun a claim from Dr. J. L. McCullough for "goods stolen out of his store by some of the Kickapoo tribe of Indians." Such losses were apparently reimbursable by the United States "agreeable to the custom heretofore observed by government."[86] No major treaty negotiations were underway, and these routine Agency matters were in all likelihood not so onerous during the winter months as to prevent Thomas from venturing as far east as Jeffersonville to check out his property there. His itinerary would certainly have provided for a stopover in Corydon to admire his son Thomas' new home, and perhaps allowed time for a social evening with his masonic brethren at the newly formed Pisgah Lodge in the little capital city.[87] In personality and bearing Posey was naturally reserved and dignified, but his lifelong affiliation with freemasonry demonstrates that he sought out and enjoyed social interaction, and among those he regarded as brothers, friends or equals he proved to be an affable and agreeable companion.

Thomas' last known written message is a rather poignant note sent from his Vincennes chambers to John L. Baker, a Rappite merchant friend in the town of Harmony:

> Will you be so obliging as to let me have one or two pounds of carded merino wool, or yarn, which would be preferable? It is to knit me some socks, for I am badly off, & the common kind of socks dont answer me, they being coarse and not long enough . . . give it to the post rider who will take it to Shawneetown to Mrs. Posey to knit for me, & I will pay you for it when I come down. Have it done up in a snug little package & derected to Mrs. Posey near Shawneetown.[88]

A pair of long woolen socks, knitted by Mary for her "dear Mr. Posey," would indeed have served him well on a cold, drizzly day in early March, as Thomas stood on the open deck of a small vessel taking him down the Wabash River toward the Ohio and over to Shawneetown. It was to be the last of many passages he had made along that dark, winding but lovely tree-lined stream. As the flatboat glided swiftly downstream through cold spray and mist, past the county that bore his name, the old general caught a severe cold. Already afflicted when he arrived in Shawneetown, within eight days he had developed pleurisy, and then a fatal typhus fever. The best doctors in the area were called in, but none offered any hope after examining him, and he died on 19 March 1818. At his bedside were gathered his sorrowing wife, and those of his beloved children and grandchildren who lived nearby or could be summoned from Kentucky and Indiana as death approached.

Within days of his passing, Mary Posey, still feeling an almost inexpressible sadness, sent to one of her absent sons a graphic description of Thomas' last hours:

> My dear William, I have to communicate a very melancholy piece of news, your dear Papa is no more, on the night of 19th he resigned his soul to his heavenly Father . . . His piety, patience and fortitude baffles all description, the pain of his body was great, yet he never complained. Really my dr. William my heart akes so I can hardly hold my pen . . . My dr. Fayette arrived a few hours before he died, he knew him & gave him his hand. Happy circumstances, he retained his

> senses till the very last moment . . . The corpse was the happiest adult I ever looked at . . . The remnant of my days shall be, to try to be prepared to follow him.[89]

In a later response to her son William's grieving but consoling reply to this sad news, Mary summed up in a few words the essence and meaning of her husband's life work: "Yes, my dear, your dear Papa has fought the good fight and finished his course, and has rec'd his crown of glory."[90] .

Thomas was laid to rest in his daughter's rose garden at Westwood, near the crest of a high bluff overlooking the great Ohio River, whose majesty rivals that of another mighty stream, the Potomac in Virginia, along the shores of which he had been born sixty-eight eventful years before.

NOTES

1. Thomas Posey's letter to "My dearly beloved children and grandchildren," 4 February 1814, Thomas Posey Papers, Indiana Historical Society Library, Indianapolis, IN (hereafter cited as IHS).
2. John D. Barnhart and Dorothy L. Riker, *Indiana to 1816: The Colonial Period* (Indianapolis: Indiana Historical Bureau and Indiana Historical Society, 1971), 432.
3. Thomas Posey to James Monroe, 25 January 1816, *Governors' Messages and Letters: Messages and Letters of William Henry Harrison*, ed. Logan Esarey, 2 vols. (Indianapolis: Ayer Co. Publishers, 1922), 2:715.
4. Ibid., Posey to Secretary of War, 12 November 1815, 2:698.
5. Crawford to James Madison, *Calendar of the Correspondence of James Madison,* Bulletin of the Bureau of Rolls and Library of the Department of State, no. 4, March 1894 (Washington, DC: U.S. Government Printing Office, 1894), 229.
6. Clarence Edwin Carter, ed., *The Territory of Indiana 1810-1816, Vol. 8 of The Territorial Papers of the United States*, (Washington, DC: AMS Press, 1939), 418n.55, 420n.57.
7. Posey to Crawford, 29 September 1816, *Governors' Messages and Letters*, ed. Esarey, 2:732.
8. Governor Posey to the Secretary of State, 10 October 1816, *Territorial Papers,* ed. Carter, 444.
9. Mary Posey to William C. Posey, 15 June 1816, Letters of Mrs. Thomas Posey, SC 1756, Illinois State Historical Library, Springfield, IL (hereafter cited as ISHL).
10. Ibid., Mary Posey to William C. Posey, 4 April 1816.
11. Ibid.
12. Mary Scribner Davis Collins, "New Albany, with a Short Sketch of the Scribner Family," *Indiana Magazine of History*, 17(1921): 229, (hereafter

cited as IMH); Rev. J.W. Barnard, "Sketch of Early Presbyterian Church in Indiana," *IMH*, 21(1925): 306; Rev. W. Brant Hall, *First Presbyterian Church* (Henderson, KY: First Presbyterian Church, 1960), 3-4.
13. Mary Posey to William C. Posey, 26 December 1816, Letters of Mrs. Thomas Posey, SC 1756, ISHL.
14. Ibid.
15. "The Son of Washington," St. Louis (MO) *Daily Globe-Democrat*, 21 April 1886.
16. Posey to Crawford, 29 September 1816, *Governors' Messages and Letters*, ed. Esarey, 2:732.
17. Ibid., 24 October 1816, 2:732-33
18. Ibid.
19. Ibid., 21 November 1816, 2:733-34.
20. Ibid., A Speech Delivered by Governor Posey Agent for Indian Affairs, 22 November 1816, 2:739-42.
21. Ibid.
22. Ibid.
23. Ibid. Interestingly, one of the chiefs at the treaty assembly was Yellow Beaver, the Indian who had abducted six-year-old Peter Huffman, he with the hair "of a shade between red and yellow," from his family along the Ohio River in March 1813. (See Chapter Nine.)
24. Ibid., Posey to Crawford, 6 December 1816, 2:738-39.
25. Barnhart and Riker, *Indiana to 1816*, 411n.73.
26. Charles J. Kappler, ed., *Indian Affairs: Laws and Treaties*, 5 vols. (Washington, DC: AMS Press, 1904), 169-70.
27. Local legend has it that in 1827 the town's leading bankers, among them Thomas Posey's youngest son, Washington Posey, rejected as too speculative a loan application from builders developing an obscure little northern settlement called Chicago. Undated pamphlet of Gallatin County Historical Society, Shawneetown Public Library, New Shawneetown, IL.
28. *Dictionary of American Biography*, 1963 ed., s.v. "Street, Joseph Montfort," 9:136-37.
29. Ibid.; "The Romantic Career of Gen. Street," Milwaukee (WI) *Sentinel*, 16 May 1907; Bruce E. Mahan, *Old Fort Crawford and the Frontier* (Iowa City, IA: State Historical Society of Iowa, 1926), 141-216.
30. Joseph M. Street to Henry Clay, 11 January 1827, *The Papers of Henry Clay*, eds. James F. Hopkins and Mary W. Hargreaves, 9 vols. to date (Lexington, KY: University Press of Kentucky, 1959-), 1:45-47.
31. Ida M. Street, "Joseph M. Street's Last Fight with the Fur Traders," *Annals of Iowa* (Des Moines, IA: State Historical Society of Iowa, 1929), 31.
32. Donald Jackson, ed., *Black Hawk: An Autobiography* (Urbana, IL: University of Illinois Press, 1964), 149, 149n.130.
33. "Masonic Notice," Vincennes (IN) *Western Sun*, 23 December 1813, 21 December 1816; George R. Wilson, "General Washington Johnston," *IMH*, 20(1924): 151.
34. Posey to Secretary of War, 10 December 1816, *Governors' Messages and Letters*, ed. Esarey, 2:742-43.
35. Affidavit and Indenture, 14 September 1819, Deed Book 19, 290. Office of the Clerk of the Circuit Court, Clark County, Jeffersonville, IN.

36. Inventory and Appraisement of Estate of Thomas Posey at Vincennes (filed with Posey's last will and testament), Will Record Book A, 96, Office of the Clerk of the Circuit Court, Knox County, Vincennes, IN.
37. Thomas Posey's letter to "My dearly beloved children and grandchildren," 4 February 1814, Thomas Posey Papers, IHS.
38. Robert H. Wiebe, *The Opening of American Society* (New York: Alfred A. Knopf, 1984), 157-58; Ruth H. Bloch, "Battling Infidelity, Heathenism, and Licentiousness: New England Missions on the Post-Revolutionary Frontier, 1792-1805," in *The Northwest Ordinance: Essays on Its Formulation, Provisions and Legacy*, ed. Frederick D. Williams (East Lansing, MI: Michigan State University Press, 1989), 53.
39. Hall, *First Presbyterian Church*, 2.
40. Mary Posey to William C. Posey, 8 December 1815 and 4 April 1816, Letters of Mrs. Thomas Posey, SC 1756, ISHL.
41. Ibid., 4 April 1816.
42. MS Certificate of Appointment, 24 September 1817, Thomas Posey Papers, IHS.
43. Ibid., John T. Romeyne to Thomas Posey, 5 June 1816.
44. Wiebe, *Opening of American Society*, 230-31.
45. Thomas Posey's Endorsement of Rev. John Todd, 6 April 1817, Gratz Collection, Case 4, Box 22, Historical Society of Pennsylvania, Philadelphia, PA.
46. Ibid.
47. Barnard, "Sketch of Early Presbyterian Church in Indiana," *IMH*, 21(1925): 306.
48. Mary Posey to William C. Posey, 4 October 1817, Letters of Mrs. Thomas Posey, SC 1756, ISHL.
49. Toast and Reply at Public Dinner, 4 June 1817, *Papers of Henry Clay*, ed. Hopkins, 2:353-55; Vincennes (IN) *Western Sun*, 7 June 1817.
50. R. Carlyle Buley, *The Old Northwest: Pioneer Period, 1815-1840*, 2 vols. (Bloomington, IN: University of Indiana Press, 1950), 2:12.
51. "To the People of Indiana," Madison (IN) *Indiana Republican*, 19 July 1817.
52. Ibid., "Fellow-citizens of Indiana," 16 September 1817.
53. Vincennes (IN) *Western Sun*, 12 July 1817.
54. Ibid.
55. James H. Madison, *The Indiana Way: A State History* (Bloomington and Indianapolis, IN: Indiana University Press, 1986), 131-33.
56. Ibid., 53-54; Barnhart and Riker, *Indiana to 1816*, 458-59; Jacob Platt Dunn, "Slavery in the Indiana Territory," in *The Hoosier State: Readings in Indiana History: Indiana Prehistory to 1880*, ed. Ralph D. Gray (Bloomington, IN: Indiana University Press, 1980), 104-8.
57. Buley, *The Old Northwest*, 2:12n.35.
58. Vincennes (IN) *Western Sun*, 12 July 1817.
59. Ibid.
60. Ibid., "To the free and independent voters of the state of Indiana," 26 July 1817.
61. Karl J. R. Arndt, ed., *A Documentary History of the Indiana Decade of the Harmony Society, Vol. 1* (Indianapolis: Indiana University Press, 1975), 48,

373; Barnhart and Riker, *Indiana to 1816*, 436; Madison, *Indiana Way*, 116-17.

62. Wiebe, *Opening of American Society*, 200, 213n.
63. Arndt, ed., *Documentary History*, 373.
64. "Fellow-citizens of Indiana," Madison (IN) *Indiana Republican*, 16 September 1817; Nina Kathleen Reid, "Sketches of Early Indiana Senators—(III) William Hendricks," *IMH*, 9(1913): 170.
65. John Candee Dean, ed., *Journal of Thomas Dean: A Voyage to Indiana in 1817*, 6:2 (Indianapolis: Indiana Historical Society, 1919), 300-305.
66. Ibid.
67. Mary Posey to William C. Posey, 4 October 1817, 20 October 1817, 29 November 1817, Letters of Mrs. Thomas Posey, SC 1756, IHSL.
68. Ibid., 4 October 1817.
69. Ibid., 20 October 1817.
70. Mary Posey to Eliza Maria Street, 27 October 1817, Thomas Posey Papers, IHS.
71. Mary Posey to William C. Posey, 29 November 1817, Letters of Mrs. Thomas Posey, SC 1756, IHSL.
72. *Dictionary of American Biography*, 1963 ed. s.v. "Mathews, George," 6:403-4.
73. David Bushnell, ed., *Republica de las Floridas: Texts and Documents* (Tallahassee, FL: Pan American Institute of Geography and History, 1986), 20-21.
74. Ibid.; T. Frederick Davis, *MacGregor's Invasion of Florida, 1817* (Tallahassee, FL: The Florida Historical Society, 1928), 14-15; John Griffin, ed., *Narrative of a Voyage to the Spanish Main in the Ship "Two Friends"* (Gainesville, FL: University Presses of Florida, 1978), 85-101.
75. "Extract of a letter from an officer holding a high command in the Army of Genl. McGregor, to a very respectable correspondent in this Borough, dated St. Fernadina, July 10, 1817," Vincennes (IN) *Western Sun*, 30 August 1817.
76. "Proclamation of the Liberating Army," Madison (IN) *Indiana Republican*, 16 August 1817.
77. "Extract of a letter from an officer in the Patriot army dated Fernadina July 17," Vincennes (IN) *Western Sun*, 6 September 1817.
78. Ibid., "Latest from Amelia," 27 September 1817.
79. Bushnell, ed., *La Republica de las Floridas*, 27-28; "News from Amelia," Madison (IN) *Indiana Republican*, 10 October 1817.
80. "Obituary," Charleston (SC) *Courier*, 26 September 1817.
81. "From the Enquirer of Friday," Vincennes (IN) *Western Sun*, 25 October 1817.
82. Mary Posey to William C. Posey, 29 November 1817, Letters of Mrs. Thomas Posey, SC 1756, IHSL.
83. Thomas Posey to Anthony Wayne, 20 February 1794, Anthony Wayne Papers, Historical Society of Pennsylvania, Philadelphia, PA.
84. Mary Posey to William C. Posey, 29 November 1817, Letters of Mrs. Thomas Posey, SC 1756, IHSL. William C. Posey in later years was a moving founder and original trustee of Illinois College, Jacksonville, IL, the first institution of higher learning founded in the state of Illinois. Charles Henry Rammelkamp, *Illinois College: A Centennial History, 1829-1929* (Princeton, NJ: Princeton University Press, 1928), 36, 39.

85. "Affray at Fort Harrison," Vincennes (IN) *Western Sun*, 6 September 1817.
86. Thomas Posey to John C. Calhoun, 3 January 1818, Boston Public Library, Boston, MA.
87. After Posey's death, the members of Pisgah Lodge marched in a group to the Corydon courthouse to hear a formal eulogy, and the Lodge resolved to wear mourning for 30 days. Funeral oration of John Dunbar, Pisgah Lodge, Corydon, Indiana, 9 April 1818, Thomas Posey Papers, IHS.
88. Thomas Posey to John L. Baker, 15 January 1818, *Documentary History*, ed. Arndt, 448.
89. Mary Posey to William C. Posey, 27 March 1818, Letters of Mrs. Thomas Posey, SC 1756, IHSL. Mary Posey survived her husband by nineteen years, dying on 18 May 1837 in her 81st year at the Walnut Springs home of Captain John and Lucy Frances Posey in Henderson County, KY. "Though death came suddenly upon her, it did not find her unprepared, but willing to meet the summons; her faith bearing her triumphantly over all its terrors." Obituary, Thornton and Posey Bible, The Presbyterian Study Center, Montreat, NC.
90. Mary Posey to William C. Posey, 30 April 1818, Letters of Mrs. Thomas Posey, SC 1756, IHSL. Coincidentally, Posey's Revolutionary War comrade and lifelong close friend, Henry Lee, survived him by only six days, dying at General Nathanael Greene's estate at Cumberland Island, GA (just north of Amelia Island, FL) on 25 March 1818. Charles Royster, *Light-Horse Harry Lee and the Legacy of the American Revolution* (New York: Alfred A. Knopf, 1981).

APPENDIX A

". . . being in Company with her revives my former Passion for your Low Land Beauty. . . ."

During his lifetime Thomas Posey made no claim of, or reference to, descent from George Washington or kinship to the Washington family, nor did Posey's children publicly entertain any such pretensions after his death in 1818.[1] It was more than half a century thereafter that the first allegation of a filial relationship between Posey and Washington appeared in public print. In 1871 the Cincinnati *Daily Commercial*, a leading Ohio journal with some seemingly muckraking proclivities, published a feature article written by an unnamed Indianapolis correspondent, headlined: "Was Geo. Washington a Father?" In commenting upon an oil portrait of territorial Governor Thomas Posey recently unveiled in Indiana's Statehouse, the correspondent stated, "none who are acquainted with the evidence . . . doubts the assertion that Posey was the son of George Washington."[2] Without ever providing the nature or sources of the supposed "evidence," the writer related the story of a couple named Posey who were tenants on Washington's Mount Vernon estate. Sometime after the husband's death in 1754, the widow bore a son, allegedly fathered by the then-unmarried Washington. By this account, the support and maintenance of the child, named Thomas Posey, was provided by the squire of Mount Vernon. After growing to manhood, the article related, Thomas served on his putative father's military staff in the Revolution, and thereafter received many political favors from President

Washington, including appointment to the governorship of Indiana Territory.[3]

The article's appearance understandably created a furor in the Midwest; it was widely copied in other papers, and the Indianapolis *Sentinel* branded it "sensational." The *Daily Commercial* dispatched another reporter to Indiana to investigate its first correspondent's allegations. His follow-up story summarized interviews with numerous informants who, although unnamed, were said to be citizens of "age, experience, eminent Position in society and worth of character." They confirmed that a belief in the Washington paternity of Governor Posey "was a tradition a long time ago with the generation that has passed away . . . and was then often conversed about at the social gatherings of the old-time lawyers, when riding the rounds of the circuit, at log-rollings and at the farmhouse firesides."[4]

A decade after the appearance of these two articles a respected Indiana historian and biographer, William Wesley Woolen, observed that "the Cincinnati *Commercial* started the story that Governor Posey was a natural son of George Washington, but the romance did not take root."[5] Woolen, with the scholar's instinctive aversion to undocumented scandal, probably hoped that the subject raised in the two *Daily Commercial* articles would never re-surface. But by the mid-1880s it was abundantly clear that the rural Hoosier folklore first exposed by the Ohio paper was far more deeply rooted than originally reported, and that it extended well beyond the borders of Indiana. In 1886 the St. Louis (MO) *Daily Globe-Democrat,* in an article captioned "The Son of Washington," found the same belief alive and well in the southern Illinois town of Shawneetown, the burial place of Thomas Posey. "All Shawneetown believes this tradition, and those who have lived in the ancient city longest have the strongest faith. They got the story from their parents who lived in Shawneetown before them, and there has never been any doubt about the truth of it."[6]

The Missouri paper's correspondent, identified only as "WBS," had interviewed, among other Shawneetownsmen, an old physician whose early practice had included several of Thomas Posey's descendants in the town. The doctor based his own firm belief in the story on information reluctantly disclosed by the ladies of the family, (it was never discussed with or by the men), and the strong resemblance one of Posey's sons bore to pictures of Washington.[7] This article again presented no proofs to support its premise, but it clearly corroborates the existence of an oral tradition in the region that may have extended back to Thomas Posey's own lifetime. It particularly emphasized a detailed physical description of Posey published shortly after his death in a biographical sketch, from which "WBS" speculates: "between the lines one may read that the resemblance of Posey to Washington was very striking, but the writer of 1824 makes no mention of it."[8]

Ten days later, the St. Louis paper ran a story following up its original article, featuring an interview by another correspondent with a great-grandson of Thomas Posey—a Lexington, Missouri banker named George Wilson. Wilson categorically denied any intra-family knowledge of the alleged Washington-Posey paternal relationship. He attributed the reported Shawneetown tradition to confusion over the actual kinship, through marriage, of some local Posey descendants to the Washington family. Himself a trained artist, he pinpointed many dissimilarities in facial features as rendered in portraits of Washington and Posey. Further, Wilson had been informed by Colonel John A. Washington, a grand-nephew of George, that he had investigated at least a dozen similar claims of alleged direct descent from the great president, and had found all of them to be total fabrications. Of Thomas Posey himself, Wilson insisted that "the hand of as good and brave a man as he would never have penned the words claiming 'respectable parentage' had his birth been illegitimate."[9] But curiously this same George Wilson, two decades later, would re-emerge as not only a firm believer in, but a resourceful contributor to, the Washington-Posey paternity legend.

In the meantime, the story continued to surface elsewhere in the Midwest. An early county history of Indiana's Posey County, which had been created and named in honor of Thomas Posey during his tenure as territorial governor, stated: "Tradition tells us that he was a son of George Washington, born out of wedlock, and several circumstances seem to indicate the probability of such a story being true."[10] The "circumstances" cited by the county history's nameless author include the alleged close physical resemblance between the two men, and an undocumented incident in which Washington supposedly intervened to forestall a duel between Posey and an unidentified adversary.[11] Perhaps coincidentally, but arguably supportive of Posey's perceived early connections to Washington, a small Ohio River settlement in the county called McFaddin's Bluff was renamed Mount Vernon during Thomas Posey's governorship—it became the county seat in 1825.[12]

Wisconsin soon joined Ohio, Indiana, Illinois and Missouri as feeding grounds for the paternity folklore. In 1907 a prominent Milwaukee daily, the *Sentinel,* in an article featuring General Joseph M. Street, Posey's son-in-law, identified Street's wife as

"Eliza Maria, daughter of Gen. Thomas Posey, a natural son of George Washington, one of the most faithful and meritorious officers of the Revolution."[13]

Commentators with more scholarly credentials than newspaper feature article writers also began to take notice of these reports, not always skeptically. A respected historian of the early Northwest, William H. English, referred to Posey in one of his works as "a man who acted well his part in both war and peace, and about whose life lingers much interesting romance, which will probably never be fully unveiled."[14] Dr. George Brown Goode, a Hoosier-born director of the Smithsonian Institution, reportedly drafted an unpublished essay entitled "Reasons For Believing That General Thomas Posey Was The Son Of George Washington." The paper was said to have been widely circulated among scholars and historical researchers in Washington, D.C., but no copy can be found at this time.[15]

The St. Louis *Daily Globe-Democrat*'s correspondent, "WBS," reentered the arena in 1898 with a lengthy, four-part series of articles, propounding a wide-ranging set of hypotheses supporting the claimed filial relationship between Posey and George Washington. Datelined Washington, D.C., the well-researched articles appear to have drawn heavily on Dr. Goode's private thesis. They also reflect extensive examination of then- unpublished original Washington manuscripts kept in the Library of Congress, as well as direct access to Posey's personal papers held by his family. For the first time, the close relationship between George Washington and his nearby Mount Vernon neighbor, Captain John Posey, was carefully scrutinized. The writer assumed that Thomas Posey was raised in the captain's household, but propounded a theory that he was not born a Posey, but was later placed in that family as the illegitimate child of Washington and "a member of one of the most distinguished families of Virginia . . . the social and family equal of George Washington in all respects. The mystery of Thomas Posey's birth was not created and preserved to shield Washington. But the inspiration for the concealment came from the intense desire of friends to protect the mother and her family."[16]

Among the many arguments advanced in the *Daily Globe-Democrat* articles to support their author's conclusions are the similarity of the two principals' characters, personal habits, handwriting, and military abilities. They also allege a close physical resemblance, based upon a James Peale ivory miniature portrait of Posey allegedly displaying many Washingtonian facial features, including a rare "jimber jaw"—in which the lower teeth close in front of the upper. "WBS" also read some significance into an early biographer's comment following a minutely detailed contemporary description of Posey's physical characteristics: "We should not allude to a subject so apparently unimportant, if it was not that the personal appearance of the distinguished gentleman, both as to form and feature, was so attractive as to be a subject of general remark wherever he was known."[17]

In 1905, the once-skeptical Missourian, George Wilson, reappeared in public print as a devout believer in the legend. To support his remarkable conversion, he came prepared with a complete scenario of the genetic relationship between Washington and Posey, including the name of the well-bred but unfortunate young woman who allegedly bore Washington's child—Elizabeth Lloyd. His views were outlined in an extensive personal interview carried by the Indianapolis *News,* datelined Vincennes, Indiana. The article asserted that Wilson had

> . . . found in the archives of the old courthouse here what he regards as conclusive proof that General Posey was the son of George Washington . . . Mr. Wilson has brought together all the facts obtainable, developing the beautiful story of Washington and his first love, Elizabeth Lloyd. They were betrothed, but family objections ran rampant on both sides, because young George Washington was without means . . . His heart was almost broken when the word passed over Fairfax county, Virginia, that Elizabeth Lloyd was dead.[18]

In Wilson's narrative, the infant Thomas received his surname and upbringing from a Huguenot widow Posey, "a woman of culture and well fitted to care for and teach a motherless boy . . . after he grew to maturer years Washington paid for his broader learning in a school. And the school register gave him the name of Thomas Posey." In Thomas' young manhood on the Virginia frontier, "he was frequently visited by Washington, who manifested great interest in his affairs. Their love for each other was easily apparent and the same love ties remained unbroken throughout the years." During the Revolution, Washington "did not lose sight of Posey. He was the magnet that drew the younger soldier upward from the ranks . . . in 1778 Posey was commissioned a major by General Washington, under whose eye he had been in all the battles in which he had taken part." According to Wilson, Washington's closeness to Posey continued long after the war. "In the hours of peace he found hours, weeks and months of pleasure in company with him." The older man even arranged to have the noted portraitist, James Peale, "paint a miniature on ivory of Posey, which he presented to him." That miniature had come into Wilson's possession, and was reproduced in the *News* article, along with a similar miniature portrait of Washington himself, also attributed to James Peale. [19]

Regrettably, George Wilson died not long after this interview, without ever having published his complete findings and sources. Very little of what he related with such confidence and detail to the *News* interviewer can be verified from presently existing records. Any evidence or documentation corroborating the key role played by Elizabeth Lloyd in the lives of Washington and Posey—or indeed establishing her very existence—appears to have died with Mr. Wilson. The only "proof" cited in the interview to support his romantic vision was the discovery of Thomas Posey's last will and testament in the Knox County archives. It disclosed that one of his children was called Lloyd—"a name that set all Virginia talking when he was born," according to Wilson. Additionally, the first name of Posey's oldest daughter was Eliza, arguably honoring the paternal grandmother Wilson identified as Elizabeth Lloyd.[20]

Whatever it might have lacked in historical documentation, Wilson's particular version of the Washington-Posey legend was credible enough to receive widespread and respectable acceptance in the years that followed, and its influence has lingered down to modern times. An earlier edition of the authoritative *National Cyclopaedia of American Biography*, in a biographical sketch of Thomas Posey, stated only that "little is known of his origin."[21] But in a revised edition of 1906, one year after Wilson's interview appeared, the sketch now asserted: "his mother was Elizabeth Lloyd, of a family of high social standing, but except that little is known of his origin. He is said to have been the natural son of George Washington."[22]

Other published works citing Posey's alleged filial ties to Washington—expressed either directly or inferentially by identifying his mother as Elizabeth Lloyd—include: Clift's *Governors of Kentucky, 1792-1942,* Allen's *Legends & Lore of Southern Illinois,* Walker's *Revolutionary Soldiers Buried in Illinois,* Peat's *Portraits and Painters of the Governors of Indiana, 1800-1943,* and McMullen and Walker's *Biographical Directory of Territorial Governors.* Even the scholarly editors of *The Papers of Henry Clay,* in a biographical footnote, refer to Thomas Posey as "reputedly the natural son of George Washington."[23]

By the 1920s, the Washington-Posey story was so pandemic that several prominent scholars felt obliged to address the issue. One of the most respected of these was John C. Fitzpatrick, director of the

Library of Congress Manuscript Division and a leading Washington expert of his day. He wrote an article for *Scribner's Magazine* explicitly aimed at demolishing that report, as well as other similar legends then current. Fitzpatrick felt passionately that all stories attributing bastard children to George Washington wrongfully sullied the character and good name of that revered leader. But perhaps because he viewed it as the most plausible or pervasive, the Thomas Posey scenario was his most serious concern, and drew his greatest condemnation and scorn. "This charge rests upon such counts as the intimacy which existed between the family at Mount Vernon and the one to which the child belonged; the assumption, by Washington, of a part if not all of the expense of the boy's education; a claimed physical resemblance, and some apocryphal recollections . . . one insinuating reconteur interprets Washington's trip to Barbados with his brother Lawrence, as necessary because of this unwelcomed paternity."[24]

Fitzpatrick did not question the closeness of the master of Mount Vernon to his next door neighbors, the Captain John Posey family. Furthermore, without citing any sources, he readily accepted that Thomas was a member of that family, and that his education was underwritten at least in part by Washington. The eminent scholar's case was based largely upon his detailed recital of documented contributions made by Washington to the schooling of the sons of several other of his close friends. He then delivered this stinging denouement:

> If every child whose education was assisted by Washington were to be stigmatized, in consequence, as his natural offspring, the distinction of being the Father of His Country might take on a new meaning. But one particular lad has been selected from the many on account of an alleged physical resemblance, and in this we encounter the quintessence of inexcusable credulity. Wise shaking of heads appears at this point; old ladies and old men have remembered this and that; all of the familiar stage effects are present, and all of them, as usual, are worthless as proof.[25]

Fitzpatrick next turned to a discussion of some of the "worthless" proofs advanced to support the Washington-Posey hypothesis. He questioned the authenticity and minimized the significance of the Peale miniature portrait of Posey. He expertly demonstrated that a letter from Washington to Posey, claimed to bear the greeting "My dear Son," actually read "My dear Sir." To spare Thomas Posey needless notoriety, the article carefully withheld his name, saying only that "it is that of a worthy man, a firm patriot, and an officer of the Continental Army, with an honorable record both during and after the war."[26]

In a later, revised version of his article, Fitzpatrick attributed the entire Posey paternity story to a recently exposed illegitimate birth arising from an affair between George Washington's cousin and farm manager, Lund Washington, and an unnamed housekeeper at Mount Vernon. He failed, however, to note that the latter incident occurred a full twenty years after Thomas Posey's birth, and that it did not become public knowledge until many decades after the Washington-Posey story was common gossip at every Hoosier fireside and had been made the topic of newspaper feature articles throughout the Midwest.[27] In his later biography of Washington, Dr. Fitzpatrick, while serving as chief editor of the monumental 39-volume *Writings of George Washington*, confronted the issue one final time. Now emphasizing the well-documented fact that not one but several children of Captain John Posey had been befriended by the benevolent squire of Mount Vernon, he wryly commented: "George Washington can hardly be made responsible for the paternity of the entire Posey family."[28]

Another highly regarded scholar, Rupert Hughes, was a leading exponent of the "realism" school of historical biography, which sought to counter the over-idealized and romanticized literary treatment that had been commonly accorded to public heroes prior to his time. But realist Hughes would have no part of the Washington-Posey legend. A lengthy appendix in one volume of his landmark work on the life and character of George Washington is devoted to Captain John Posey and his Rover's Delight family. It vigorously supports Fitzpatrick's utter rejection of Thomas Posey's reputed Washington parentage:

> This might be the last of (John) Posey except for a tradition that will not down. Captain John had a son, Thomas, who is described as having been six feet two inches high, with light brown hair and blue eyes, and so powerfully built that he killed several men with his own sword in battles.
>
> This striking resemblance to Washington and the closeness of the families are doubtless to blame for the persistent fable that he was the natural son of Washington . . . A discussion of such a story seems to be justified by the fact that it is whispered everywhere.[29]

In analyzing the story, Hughes assumed, as had Fitzpatrick, that Martha Price Harrison Posey, wife of Captain John Posey, was Thomas' natural mother. He thus argued that it was "hardly probable" that the two neighboring families would have remained so close socially through the years if Washington had actually fathered one of Martha Posey's children during her marriage to the captain. But Hughes' premise is flawed. There is every reason to believe that Thomas Posey was born before Captain John's marriage to the widow Harrison. Only two weeks before his known birth date in 1750, she is identified in court records as "Martha Harrison, widow and relict of George Harrison."[30] There is even some doubt that Captain Posey himself was residing in Virginia on the date in question. A native Marylander, his first recorded presence in Fairfax County was in 1751, a year after Thomas' birth, and the first confirmed data of his marriage to Martha Harrison is her signature as "Martha Posey" on a deed dated 17 June 1752.[31]

An alternate but equally speculative scenario is suggested by the chronological sequence—that Thomas might have been the out-of-wedlock child of the widow Harrison. That circumstance would validate Hughes' point, to the extent that the subsequent close social relationship between the two families would rule out Washington as the child's father. But neither Hughes nor Fitzpatrick, in their published comments on this issue, considered the possibility that Thomas Posey might have been born of the elusive Elizabeth Lloyd, or another nameless mother who died in or shortly after childbirth, and was later taken into the Posey household as an adopted or foster child. That contingency, of course, would eliminate neither Washington nor any other of his contemporaries as the boy's father, but would add significance to the later extraordinary liberality of Mount Vernon's squire to Captain John Posey and his family.

Nathaniel Wright Stephenson and Waldo Hilary Dunn, scholarly authors of another Washington biography, extolled the efforts of Fitzpatrick and Hughes "in exploding the fiction that the younger Posey was Washington's natural son."[32] A lesser-known biographer, Louis Martin Sears, noted in passing that Washington was so generous to one of Captain Posey's sons that "gossip raised its forked tongue." But, he said, Washington's reputation was saved because it was known that he had been equally beneficent to the sons of several other friends.[33] Finally, a respected historical essayist, Dixon Wecter, after detailing Washington's human side by documenting his delight in dancing, flirting, card-playing, horse racing and similar frivolities, condemned as a "canard" the rumor that he had been forced to flee to Barbados because he was "in trouble," and that "in his absence a neighbor girl bore his child, a boy whose surname was Posey."[34]

A reputable and meticulous genealogical researcher and author, James Wade Emison, Jr., of Vincennes, Indiana, spent literally months exhaustively examining original archives in Fairfax County and elsewhere in Virginia, in an admitted effort to conclusively disprove the Washington-Posey paternity tradition. But he himself finally came to believe in its authenticity, and to accept the Elizabeth Lloyd scenario.[35] Perhaps in deference to Posey's own claim of "respectable parentage," Emison revised his final family ancestral listings to indicate that there had been an arranged marriage of convenience between Elizabeth Lloyd and Captain John Posey prior to the birth of Thomas Posey. He also moved forward the assumed date of the captain's marriage to the widow Martha Price Harrison to "*circa* 1752," two full years after Thomas' birth date.[36]

There appears to be nothing in known historical fact to definitively exclude the possibility that George Washington begot Thomas Posey. His 9 July 1750 date of birth pre-supposes that he was conceived sometime between October and December of the prior year. Throughout that critical span, while Lawrence Washington, George's older half-brother and de facto guardian, was absent from their Mount Vernon home on a visit to England, seventeen- year-old George was busily pursuing his newly attained profession as a licensed public surveyor. His documented itinerary for the interval in question included a ten-day trip to frontier Frederick County in early November to survey some of the vast holdings of Lord Fairfax, who had lately taken up personal residence in that remote area.[37]

Washington's field book or journal from this period contains copies of several letters, some possibly only exercises in writing composition, but all nonetheless clearly reflecting the emotions and mindset of a very love-smitten young man. In one, he declares that "was my affections disengaged I might perhaps form some pleasures in conversations of an agreeable young Lady . . . in the same house with me, but as thats only nourishment to my former Affa(ir) for by often seeing her brings the Other into my remembrance." But for her frequent presence as a reminder, "I might in some measure eliviate my sorrows by burrying the other in the grave of Oblevion."[38] In another letter, also written in the sparsely settled western frontier, George again mentions the "very agreeable Young Lady Lives in the same house," lamenting "but as thats only adding Fuel to fire it makes me the more uneasy for by often and unavoidably being in Company with her revives my former Passion for your Low Land Beauty."[39] The Tidewater region of eastern Virginia was then called the low land, and the fabled "Low Land Beauty" of young Washington's anguished obsession has never been positively identified by historians or biographers.[40] In the poignant if fanciful Washington-Posey scenario propounded a century ago by banker George Wilson, the Low Land Beauty was Washington's first tragic sweetheart—the lovely but doomed Elizabeth Lloyd.

On 9 July 1750, the date of Thomas Posey's birth, young George had returned to the Virginia lowlands, and was residing at Mount Vernon under the aegis of his brother Lawrence, who had in the interim returned from England. The two Washington brothers, however, did not embark upon their long visit to Barbados until 28 September 1751, more than a year after Posey was born.[41]

George Washington's later marriage to Martha Custis, a young widow who had borne several children by her first husband, was childless. This circumstance is the principal basis for a widespread belief that the adult Washington was incapable of generating offspring—the assumption being that he was probably rendered sterile by the smallpox he is known to have contracted during his Barbados sojourn. That hypothesis obviously would not rule out a possible product of some youthful indiscretion occurring prior to 1751. But there is incontrovertible evidence that, in his twilight years, Washington himself firmly believed that he was still fully capable of fathering children. Writing to his nephew in 1786, Washington discussed various ramifications of a remarriage if his wife, Martha, happened to predecease him. He dismissed the likelihood of issue from any such second marriage—not because of any incapacity on his part, but due to the probable mature age of any future wife. "For whilst I retain the reasoning facilities I shall never marry a girl," declared the sage and sensible-minded 54-year-old squire, "and it is not probable that I should have children by a woman of an age suitable to my own, should I be disposed to enter into a second marriage."[42]

The absolute conviction of Washington's assumption that he was still capable of fathering children properly raises a question as to the possible basis of his unqualified self- assurance. What event or experience in his past life could have been so conclusive as to totally negate the irrefutable reality of an intervening twenty-seven-year barren marriage to a demonstrably fecund woman? The ease and artlessness with which he so off-handedly expressed the certitude of his own fertility goes well beyond the mere disregard or denial of any presumed smallpox-induced sterility. In digging deeper for its source, there is no answer more plausible, however conjectural it might well be, than that Washington was speaking in the certain knowledge of having once sired an illegitimate child.

But scholarly analysis properly rejects such rationalization, and positive evidence of a biological link between George Washington and Thomas Posey is admittedly meager, anecdotal and totally circumstantial. Apart from any real or perceived physical resemblance, the two men did appear to possess some common traits of personality and character—integrity, perseverance of purpose, a deliberate and disciplined command over emotion. But many of Posey's contemporaries also had these qualities, as well as the lifelong dedication to the revolutionary ideal that he shared with Washington. Both men demonstrated exceptional personal bravery and coolness amidst the horrors of combat, and both displayed distinguished leadership in public affairs, although on obviously widely different levels of governmental service. Both men died at the same age, of similar causes.

The paternity hypothesis is inferentially supported by a documented twenty-five-year record of extraordinary and seemingly inexplicable generosity extended by the squire of Mount Vernon to the family of his convivial but improvident neighbor, Captain John Posey. Conversely, the theory of an intimate or genetic tie to Thomas Posey is challenged by the glaring absence during that same period of any evidence that he himself was personally the direct recipient of any of Washington's beneficence—and the fact that he was never even mentioned in any of Washington's writings, as replete as they are with references to all the other members of his family.

Proponents of the paternity thesis might attribute this void in the written record to a contrived conspiracy of silence, imposed by common consent to shield the truth from the scandalhungry society of colonial Virginia. Skeptics, on the other hand, would ascribe it to some less historically momentous blemish or shame in the birthright of Thomas Posey, arising from some unacceptable indiscretion on the part of Martha Harrison or Captain John Posey himself. There is always the possibility, however remote, and contrary to the overwhelming consensus of Washington scholars, that Thomas was never actually a member of the Rover's Delight household, but might have been born and raised in some obscure and long-forgotten Posey family far removed from the well-documented brood of Captain John Posey. The puzzling silence might, finally, be due simply to the capricious whim of random happenstance, with no historical significance or relevance whatever to the Washington-Posey enigma.

In the final analysis, when weighing an issue of such delicacy and importance as the intimate character and reputation of the admirable and justly revered Washington, the burden of proof falls inexorably upon the proponents of the alleged paternal relationship. Decades of fireside gossip, followed by a century of published speculation and conjecture, have not only failed to find a "smoking gun," but clearly have not produced the preponderance of evidence reasonably required to sustain that inescapable burden of proof. But since that same long, convoluted and imperfect process has also not yielded any solid evidence conclusively eliminating or rebutting the possibility that the legend was indeed true, those who choose to do so may perhaps be forgiven if they continue to believe that Thomas Posey was really the son of George Washington.

NOTES

1. For a detailed analysis of the Washington-Posey paternity issue, see generally: John Thornton Posey, "Governor Thomas Posey: The Son of George Washington?" *Indiana Magazine of History*, 86 (March 1990), 28-49.
2. "Was Geo. Washington a Father?" Cincinnati (OH) *Daily Commercial*, 28 March 1871.
3. Ibid. Posey never served on Washington's staff. He was appointed governor of Indiana Territory by President James Madison in 1813, 13 years after the death of Washington.
4. "The Paternity of Governor Posey of Indiana: A Man Who Looked Wonderfully Like George Washington," Cincinnati *Daily Commercial*, 10 April 1871.
5. William Wesley Woolen, *Biographical and Historical Sketches of Early Indiana* (Indianapolis, IN: Ayer Co. Publishers, 1883), 28.
6. "The Son of Washington—Shawneetown's Remarkable Tradition and What It Rests Upon—The Secret of Gen. Thos. Posey's Parentage—His Striking Personal Appearance and Wonderful Career—A Story Which the Early Biographers Ignored," St. Louis (MO) *Daily Globe-Democrat*, 11 April 1886.
7. Ibid.
8. Ibid.
9. "The Son of Washington—Investigating the Tradition Regarding Gen. Thomas Posey's Paternity—The Poseys and the Washingtons—The Pride of Colonial Days—Interview with Gen. Posey's Great Grandson," St. Louis *Daily Globe-Democrat*, 21 April 1886.
10. *History of Posey County, Indiana*, (Chicago: Goodspeed Publishing Co., 1886), 329-30.
11. Ibid. The second point may refer to the dispute between Posey and General Anthony Wayne over battle honors after the assault on Stony Point in 1779. There are some indications that General Washington might have intervened to resolve the issue between the two officers. (See Chapter Three.)

12. Ibid., 377; See also: W.P. Leonard, *History and Directory of Posey County* (Evansville, IN: A. C. Isaacs, 1882), 54.
13. "The Romantic Career of General Joseph M. Street," Milwaukee (WI) *Sentinel*, 15 May 1807,
14. William H. English, *Conquest of the Country Northwest of the River Ohio, 1778-1783,* 2 vols. (Indianapolis: Ayer Co. Publishers, 1896), 2:865.
15. "Washington's Love Affair," St. Louis *Daily Globe-Democrat*, 9 October 1898.
16. "Washington and Posey," St. Louis *Daily Globe-Democrat*, 23 October 1898; see also: "Thomas Posey, Gentleman," 25 September 1898 and "The Posey Romance," 6 November 1898.
17. James E. Hall, "Memoir of Thomas Posey, Major General and Governor of Indiana," in *Library of American Biography*, ed. Jared Sparks, ser. 2 (Boston: Little, Brown & Co., 1846), 9:403.
18. "General Posey, Son of Washington: Conclusion After Search of Records," Indianapolis *News*, 25 February 1905. Elizabeth Lloyd is not mentioned in any published biography of George Washington.
19. Ibid. The original Peale ivory miniature of Thomas Posey is on display at the Museum, Anderson House, The Society of the Cincinnati, Washington, DC.
20. Ibid.
21. *The National Cyclopaedia of American Biography,* (New York: James T. White & Co.,1896), 6:323.
22. *The National Cyclopaedia of American Biography,* (New York: James T. White & Co., 1906), 13:265.
23. G. Glenn Clift, *Governors of Kentucky, 1792-1942* (Louisville, KY: Kentucky Historical Society, 1942), 148-52; John W. Allen, *Legends & Lore of Southern Illinois* (Carbondale, IL: Southern Illinois University Press, 1963), 5-6; Harriet J. Walker, *Revolutionary Soldiers Buried in Illinois* (Baltimore: Genealogical Publishing Co., 1917), 44-45; Wilbur D. Peat, *Portraits and Painters of the Governors of Indiana, 1800-1943,* eds. Diane Gail Lazarus and Lana Ruegamer (Indianapolis: Indiana Historical Society and Indianapolis Museum of Art, 1978), 14:393-94; Thomas A. McMullen and David Walker, *Biographical Directory of American Territorial Governors* (Westport, CT: Greenwood Press, 1984), 152; *The Papers of Henry Clay*, ed. James F. Hopkins and Mary W. Hargreaves, 9 vols. to date (Lexington, KY: The University Press of Kentucky, 1959-), 1:138n.
24. John C. Fitzpatrick, "The George Washington Scandals," *Scribner's Magazine*, 81 (April 1927), 393-94.
25. Ibid.
26. Ibid.
27. John C. Fitzpatrick, *The George Washington Scandals* (Alexandria, VA: *Scribner's Magazine*, 1929), 5.
28. John C. Fitzpatrick, *George Washington Himself* (Indianapolis: Bobs-Merrill, 1933), 155.
29. Rupert Hughes, *George Washington: The Rebel and the Patriot, 1762-1771* (New York: William Morrow & Co.,1927), 651-56.
30. Court Order Book 1749, 78-79, Fairfax County (VA) Court Archives, Judicial Center, Fairfax County, Fairfax, VA.

31. Philip Slaughter, *History of Truro Parish in Virginia*, ed. Edward L. Goodwin (Philadelphia: Geo. W. Jacobs & Co., 1908), 28-29; *The Papers of George Washington, Colonial Series*, eds. W.W. Abbot and Dorothy Twohig, 6 vols. to date (Charlottesville, VA: The University Press of Virginia, 1982-), 1:51-52.
32. Nathaniel Wright Stephenson and Waldo Hilary Dunn, *George Washington*, 2 vols. (New York, London, and Toronto: Oxford University Press, 1932), 1:70.
33. Louis Martin Sears, *George Washington* (New York: Thomas Y. Crowell Co., 1932), 70.
34. Dixon Wecter, "President Washington and Parsons Weems," *George Washington: A Profile*, ed. James Morton Smith (New York: Charles Scribner's Sons, 1969), 21.
35. James Wade Emison, Jr. to James Edwin Cox, Chicago, IL, 27 February 1957. A carbon copy of Mr. Emison's letter is in the possession of his family in Vincennes, IN.
36. James Wade Emison, Jr., *The Emison Families: Final Supplement* (Vincennes, IN: James Wade Emison, Jr., 1969), 220.
37. Douglas Southall Freeman, *George Washington: A Biography*, 7 vols. (New York: Charles Scribner's Sons, 1948-1857), 1:234-41.
38. Letter to John, 1749-1750, *Papers of Washington, Colonial Series*, eds. Abbot and Twohig, 1:42, .
39. Ibid., Letter to Robin, 1:40-41.
40. Ibid., 1:41n.2.
41. Freeman, *Washington*, 1:235-48.
42. John C. Fitzpatrick, ed., *The Writings of George Washington*, 39 vols. (Washington, DC: U.S. Government Printing Office, 1931-1944), 29:29. On this issue, Dr. Freeman comments: "Needless to say, this letter indicates clearly that Washington did not think his failure to beget children by Martha was due to sterility on his part." Freeman, *Washington*, 6:63n.

APPENDIX B

"The unfortunate and most unhappy John Price Posey. . . ."

The year 1769 had been one of disaster for Captain John Posey. While his numerous creditors were rapidly tightening their legal tentacles around his estate in Virginia, he sought financial redemption in Maryland by marriage to Elizabeth Adair, whom he cheerfully advertised to the world as "a person . . . of large fortune."[1] But the lady stubbornly resisted all his efforts to gain access to that fortune, and when he returned to his hapless children and deteriorating household at Rover's Delight, he was soon imprisoned for non-payment of debt. Upon his release, although drinking heavily and fighting publicly with his new wife, he was forced to face up to reality. He put up the bulk of his property and estate for sale at a public auction, which left him stripped of all his possessions other than an empty house and a narrow tract of riverfront land containing his ferry landing. The year ended with Elizabeth Adair Posey's sudden death, and the departure to the frontier of his oldest boy, Thomas, to make his own way in life. (See Chapter One.)

Although proceeds from the auction sale had been sufficient to discharge nearly all of the captain's indebtedness to his largest creditor and benefactor, George Washington, very little was realized to apply to his many other pressing obligations. Legal action by these creditors in Fairfax County resulted in his being again briefly jailed for debt in the spring of 1770.[2] Shortly after his release, he returned to Maryland to settle the estate of his late wife Elizabeth, and thus to acquire in death what he had failed to obtain in her lifetime. But his premarital expectations of her "large fortune" proved to be largely illusory, as the claims filed against her estate in probate court exceeded her assets. His Administrator's bond was declared forfeit, and the five slaves formerly owned by Elizabeth, which he had put up as security on his bond, were sold. But the bondsman purchased the slaves at a price Posey protested was far below their market value, leaving a deficit still remaining in the estate, and the captain was committed to debtors' prison in Queenstown. He could have escaped imprisonment by accepting the bondman's offer of £90 for Negro Jack, an accomplished manservant loaned by Washington to Posey after he was forced to sell all his own slaves. But Captain John refused to betray the trust of his longtime friend, and he sent Negro Jack back to Mount Vernon, assuring Washington that "I have all my Life acted honest and is determined to doe so, Lett me suffer ever so much."[3]

Pouring out all his troubles in a letter written to Washington from his prison cell in Queenstown, he passed along another interesting piece of information to the squire of Mount Vernon. All of his current financial problems could have been solved months ago, he confided, had he seized an opportunity to marry an "old widow woman of this County," whose wealth was more than sufficient to clear all his debts and assure him a comfortable old age. The widow was willing, and he himself was favorably inclined toward the match, despite the fact that "she is as thick as she is high—And gits drunk at least three or foure (times) a weak—which is Disagreeable to me." The captain, himself no slouch as a tippler, could perhaps overlook that flaw—but another characteristic proved fatal to the charms of his intended bride. It was the widow's "Viliant Sperrit when Drunk," which reminded him all too vividly of the last Mrs. Posey, that finally impelled him to reject the marriage and choose imprisonment over a debt-free life of ease. "I beleave I shu'd Run all Resk's—if my last wife had been (an) Even temper'd woman, but her Sperrit, has Given me such (a) Shock—that I am afraid to Run the Resk Again, When I see the object before my Ey(e)s (it) is Disagreeable."[4]

The bemused Washington, reading this passage in his comfortable study, and probably thanking his Deity for the demure and gentle personality of his own wife Martha, was not unsympathetic to Posey's plight. He promptly dispatched the captain's son, John Price Posey, to Maryland with the £12 needed to gain his father's release from prison.[5] But Captain Posey may later have bitterly regretted his cavalier rejection of the "old widow woman." For the next three years, he appears sporadically as a sometime houseguest at Mount Vernon, first to sell Washington his last remaining assets, the six-acre tract with Rover's Delight and the ferry,[6] and then his military grant of 3,000 acres of western land, earned by his service in the French and Indian War.[7] Later, penniless, he returns as a pathetic destitute, taking money Washington doled out to him ostensibly as loans, but realistically written off in his ledger as "Charity to Capt. Posey."[8]

Captain John's last letter to Washington reveals a man broken at last in spirit as well as in fortune. "You have granted me many Favors since I have been Acquainted with you—I am now Reduc'd Very Low—And Advanc'd in years—I have noe Person in the world to Apply to, for Assistance—and Really am not Able to work."[9] When he left Mount Vernon for the last time on 7 April 1774, carrying a final £12 gratuity, Washington wrote in his diary, "Captn. Posey went away after dinner."[10] His old friend and fox-hunting companion is never mentioned again in Washington's writings, and he disappears from recorded history after that date.

There is no question but that George Washington played a dominant role in the life of Captain John Posey. Somewhat less clear is to what extent, if any, the master of Mount Vernon might have been influenced by his close observation of, and involvement in, his neighbor's downfall. In the art of handling business affairs there was little, if anything, the profligate Posey could have taught the inherently prudent Washington who, at age seventeen, was already wisely investing his lucrative surveyor's fees in western lands.[11] Mount Vernon's huge and intricate agrarian community dwarfed the modest farming, fishery and ferry operations at Rover's Delight. In a period of great instability in the agricultural economy, when many freeholders were being forced to sell out,[12] perhaps there were some useful lessons to be learned—or mistakes to be avoided—from Posey's unwise land management, careless handling of money, and unbridled use and abuse of credit. In a few commercial transactions, Washington did rely upon the captain's greater knowledge of business practices in Maryland, and his personal connections there.[13] But as time went on, Washington's anguished letters make it abundantly clear that Posey's deteriorating finances were putting an increasingly serious drain on his own resources, not to mention his patience, as the captain blithely went on his way to his own ruin ignoring his patron's sage advice and counsel.[14]

The personal relationship between the two neighbors can be more accurately appraised. Whatever distress Washington felt over their financial dealings, he clearly enjoyed Posey's company and friendship. Captain John has been aptly described as a man who was "ever ready to postpone labor for a hunt or a frolic, or a long session over wine."[15] These were qualities perhaps appreciated and certainly encouraged, if not exploited, by Washington during his frequent social visits to Rover's Delight. It may well be that Washington liked being in Posey's company because at such times he could relax and indulge himself in those latent but usually suppressed weaknesses that he privately envied in his less-disciplined friend. As for the captain, he was always there for Washington when he needed another scarlet-coated hunter to ride with the baying foxhounds assembled outside Mount Vernon's front entrance.[16] Some commentators see Posey as merely an amusing companion or even a kind of court jester to his reserved and sober-sided neighbor.[17] But a deeper and more meaningful bond linked these two dissimilar men. Washington never failed his struggling friend in time of need, and even when the impoverished captain was reduced to taking handouts Mount Vernon's worthy squire discreetly wrote off to charity, Posey was always treated with the same respect and dignity accorded any other associate of his rank and station.

George Washington proved to be a generous benefactor, not only to the father, but to several of Posey's children. The captain's household collapsed after the 1769 public auction had denuded Rover's Delight. Soon thereafter Amelia ("Milly") Posey, the only girl in the family, found a warm and lasting refuge with the Washingtons at Mount Vernon. They enrolled her in the classes held by the itinerant dancing master Francis Christian, along with Martha Washington's daughter, Martha Parke ("Patsy") Custis.[18] The two girls, who were about the same age, later displayed their well-drilled mastery of the minuet and country dances at a grand ball in the ballroom above Gadsby's Tavern in Alexandria, staying overnight with the Washingtons in their elegant town house on nearby Cameron Street.[19] Doubtlessly the highlight of that exciting evening for little Milly was a graceful turn or two around the crowded ballroom floor on the strong arm of the towering squire of Mount Vernon, who himself loved to dance. Even after Patsy Custis' tragic death from epilepsy, Milly Posey continued to live for many years at her benefactor's gracious home, as the companion and protege of the kindly Martha Washington, devastated by the sudden loss of her young and only daughter.

There is ample evidence that the Washingtons came to regard Milly as a member of their extended family. During some of the darkest days of the Revolutionary War, the commander-in-chief was not too preoccupied to send fond regards to Milly Posey in letters written home to his wife and, later, to his farm manager Lund Washington.[20] The last such reference was in 1781—twelve years after Milly came to live at Mount Vernon—at which time she was about twenty-five years old.[21] Thereafter, she seems to disappear from the Washington household; she may have married, rejoined her aging father or another Posey sibling, or possibly died at that early age. Even jaded historians regard her with affection. One scholarly Washington biographer refers to her as "charming little Milly Posey"[22]; another, as a "lovely young woman"[23]; and a third expressed pleasure that Milly, who was so unfortunate in her own family connections, "saw life a little" in the comfortable and socially well-connected Washington family.[24]

A considerably less felicitous experience awaited Milly's younger brother, St. Lawrence Posey, who accompanied his father back to Maryland after the public auction at Rover's Delight. Enrolled in the Free School of Queen Annes County, he showed early promise in his studies, earning the praise of Mr. Cowden, the schoolmaster, as a fine boy and a fast learner. Captain Posey had some of his own clothes cut down to properly outfit St. Lawrence for his classes, but the bright young scholar's education was rudely interrupted when his father was seized and sent to debtors' prison.[25] A kind-hearted city merchant, Francis Baker, came across St. Lawrence wandering homeless and half-starved in the streets of Queenstown, took him into his home, and sent him back to the Free School with his own children.

After Captain John, with Washington's help, was released from prison, he chose to leave his son in Baker's home while he returned to Virginia. But within weeks, one William Minor, a local innkeeper, appeared at the merchant's door with a written order from Captain Posey to turn the boy over to him. Minor then proceeded to put St. Lawrence to work as a bartender in his public house. Baker, by now aware of George Washington's keen interest in the Posey family, appealed to him for assistance, informing him that "for his Age when he went to Mr. Miner there was not his match for writing, any Merchant would gladly have such an Assistant . . . But seeing the innocence of the Boy, I could not think of giving him a Tavern Education."[26]

Washington, who could seldom resist a plea to help a young person, generously agreed to pay for a year's schooling and living expenses at Baker's house. He entrusted his written offer to Captain Posey, who inexcusably mislaid Washington's letter and delayed delivering or forwarding it to Francis Baker. Thus, it was more than three months before the hapless boy was rescued from the unsavory environment of Minor's Tavern and returned to Baker's household to resume his formal education.[27] Washington's solicitude for young St. Lawrence persisted, and as late as 5 November 1774 he was continuing to pay for his board and schooling.[28] But nothing is known of the boy's life or fortunes after that date. Years later, William Minor dunned Washington for the expense of supporting St. Lawrence during his brief employment as a tavern bartender, but the righteous squire of Mount Vernon indignantly refused this brazen request, pointing out that his prior offer of support had been conditioned upon the boy's attendance at school.[29]

Very little is known of another Posey sibling, Hanson. His name appears only infrequently in Washington's ledgers and letters, and but once in the diaries as a visitor at Mount Vernon.[30] In September of 1770, when one of his father's long absences in Maryland had deprived him of parental supervision, he was arrested in Fairfax County for brawling. He was released only after posting a £100 security bond, on which Charles Alexander served as a surety, guaranteeing for a year and a day his good behavior toward his antagonist, one John O'Daniel.[31] The fight might well have arisen out of a political argument—a few months earlier, Hanson was one of many Fairfax citizens who had signed a controversial Non-Importation Agreement in which they pledged to boycott all British-made goods.[32]

By 1775, Hanson Posey had migrated across the Blue Ridge mountains into Frederick County in the northern Shenandoah Valley, and was signatory to a citizens petition addressed to the Fourth Convention of colonial Virginia. It protested a delinquency in payments contracted by the colony for goods and services the petitioners had provided in what is commonly called Lord Dunmore's War, the expedition organized by British governor Dunmore against a Shawnee-led Indian confederation in the Ohio River valley.[33] It was this venture that gave Hanson's sibling, Thomas Posey, his first taste of combat as Commissary- General in the brigade of frontiersmen formed from the southern Shenendoah counties. (See Chapter One). But nothing further is known of Hanson Posey—neither he nor his brothers John Price or St. Lawrence are recorded as having served in the military during the Revolutionary War.

There may have been another Posey sibling in the Rover's Delight family although, like Thomas, he is not mentioned in any writings or records of the period. During the Revolution a William Posey fought as a rank-and-file soldier in the same 3rd and 7th Virginia infantry regiments of the Continental line in which Thomas Posey served as an officer.[34] A later, well-researched genealogical study identifies this William as the youngest son of Captain John and Martha Posey, and the brother of Thomas Posey. By this account,

William Posey settled after the war near Valley Forge in Pennsylvania, married well, and raised a family. There he is said to have eventually brought his aged father, described as "broken in health as well as in fortune," to spend his last years.[35] If this report is correct, it appears that Captain John Posey, the flawed and restless "rover" of Rover's Delight, found peace at last under a simple headstone marked "J.P.," alongside his son William in the tranquil country cemetery of Brownback's Church, East Coventry, West Chester, Pennsylvania.

There remains to be told the story of John Price Posey, whose ultimate fate, unlike that of his siblings Milly, St. Lawrence and Hanson, is only too well documented. Born *circa* 1752, he received a good basic education, and was possibly his father's favorite—a framed oil portrait of John Price Posey was among valuables seized in 1770 by creditors of Captain John Posey.[36] One of his boyhood friends and playmates was George Washington's stepson, John Parke ("Jacky") Custis, who was about the same age, and grew up at Mount Vernon, the great estate abutting the Poseys' property. After the death of his mother and the public sale of most of his father's possessions, Washington sponsored his first employment in Thomas Lawson's iron and flour business at Neabsco Creek in nearby Prince William County.[37] There, with his prior experience in his father's fishery and ferry operations, young Posey appears to have developed further useful commercial and management skills as Lawson's assistant.

Despite his father's ruin, John Price continued to maintain cordial relations with the Washingtons. He was an occasional dinner guest at Mount Vernon, lodged overnight there at least twice, and performed some small services for the family from time to time.[38] His modest financial circumstances do not seem to have hampered his reascent to the gentry status. In 1776 he was listed as "John Price Posey, Gentleman" in testifying for his employer, Lawson, when the merchant was charged in a Prince William court with violating wartime embargo laws by conducting his flour and iron ore trade in the neighboring colony of Maryland.[39]

While still a small child, Posey's friend Jacky Custis had inherited from his late father several large farms along the Patumkey River near Richmond. As the boy's guardian, George Washington controlled these properties until young Custis attained his majority. Since Washington also owned several farms of his own in the same area, he employed his own local agent, James Hill, to manage the Custis properties as well. When Jacky Custis reached legal age and took over control of his estate in 1778, he dispensed with Hill's services. Custis appears to have held John Price Posey in high esteem, and he proceeded to install his boyhood friend as his agent and the manager of all his inherited farm properties in New Kent County.[40]

Early the following year, taking a few precious moments from his pressing duties as commander-in-chief of the Continental army, General Washington sent Posey a written request to confer with James Hill and settle any accounts or balances then found to be outstanding between the Custis and Washington properties.[41] Posey's reply, clearly reflecting the respect he owed a revolutionary leader and former generous patron, assured the general that "it would give me singular pleasure in doing anything to serve you." He stated that he had already had preliminary meetings with Hill, and that when the two managers reached a final agreement, he would promptly remit directly to Washington any monetary balance which might be found to be due him from the Custis farms.[42] But during the next several years, while Washington's military responsibilities distracted him from his usual close scrutiny of his business affairs, he apparently received no further reports from either Posey or Hill.

After moving to New Kent County, John Price Posey had acquired growing stature and influence. He was commissioned a judicial magistrate, and later sat as a Justice on the County Court. At the apex of his career, he was elected a Delegate to the lower house of the Virginia state General Assembly. He represented the county in the legislature during the turbulent years 1780-1781, which saw devastating enemy incursions into the state as well as the decisive victory of American-French forces at Yorktown. Sometime during his period of rising fortunes, he entered into a financially and socially advantageous marriage with Anne Kidley Chamberlayne, a sister of Colonel William Chamberlayne of Poplar Creek, one of the leading citizens of the community. The union produced at least two children.[43]

Posey's downfall appears to have begun, or at least to have been foreshadowed, by the sudden death on 5 November 1781 of his employer, Jacky Custis, from camp fever, soon after the British surrender at Yorktown. Washington, pre-occupied with his military duties, asked his brother-in-law, Judge Bartholomew Dandridge, to accept appointment as Administrator of the estate of young Custis, his nephew. But even at this early date, the general seems to have received some damning information about John Price Posey. He warned in his letter to the judge that "the estate was badly involved because of a manager's thievery."[44]

Dandridge's reports to Washington soon began to corroborate this suspicion, as they detailed serious problems in resolving Custis' financial affairs. "Mr. Posey has been so engaged that he has not had leisure to render me any account of the Estate. . . Mr. Posey has informed me that he has no money in his hands."[45] Washington replied that he had earlier formed a bad opinion of Posey after meeting with him to discuss the details of his arrangements with his deceased stepson.[46] Now, acting upon the judge's reports of apparent irregularities in the handling of Jacky Custis' properties, Washington wrote a scathing letter to John Price Posey, its tone far more ominous and threatening than anything he had ever directed against his father, the improvident Captain John Posey:

> Sir: With a mixture of surprize, concern and even horror; have I heard of your treatment of the deceased Mr. Custis; in the abuse, and misapplication of the Estate which he had committed, with much confidence I am sure, and I believe personal regard, to your management.[47]

The general then proceeded to demand in no uncertain terms that Posey submit a full and complete accounting to Dandridge, together with full payment of any balance due the Custis estate. Otherwise, he promised grimly, his stepson's heirs, (presumably including himself), would "pursue you to the end of the earth . . . let the trouble and cost of doing it be what it may." Then Washington, relapsing into his former role as John Price Posey's patron and his father's longtime friend, continued: "as a Man therefore who wishes for your own sake as well as that of an injurd family to see you act properly, I advise, and warn you the consequences of a contrary conduct."[48]

The record contains no reply to this scorching rebuke, but it does not seem to have moved Posey to modify his inexplicable behavior pattern. In Washington's next letter to Dandridge he warned that "in Posey you have to deal with a most consummate villain . . . he should be removed from his present Stewardship as soon as it can be done with any degree of propriety."[49] Dandridge, in the meantime, had petitioned the governor of Virginia to revoke Posey's commission as magistrate, but he declined to do so, acting on the opinion of his Council of State that such unilateral executive action would violate the state constitution's guarantee of an independent judiciary.[50] The Council was chaired by John Marshall, wartime comrade and friend of John Price Posey's sibling, Thomas Posey, but its decision was consistent with Marshall's later constitutional philosophy as Chief Justice of the U.S. Supreme Court.

Dandridge increasingly shared Washington's negative view of the Custis farm manager:

> Posey has fully answered your predictions of him, he has long since lost all sense of shame, and altho I was guarded against him, yet I could not prevent even with much trouble of his injuring the Estate greatly in many respects. I am still pursuing such methods as I can to bring him to justice, but his cunning is considerable and his villainy more than I can describe or you can conceive.[51]

This harsh assessment of Posey seems to be borne out by a continuation of his self-destructive conduct. In October of 1784 he was twice brought before the General Court of Richmond on criminal charges. On 13 October he was fined £25 for breaking into a Custis "close" (enclosure) and driving away a cow.[52] Two weeks later he was back before the court, charged with "diverse gross misdemeanors" in mismanaging the Custis estate, was found guilty, and fined £200.[53] The last conviction cost Posey his commission as magistrate through impeachment for cause by the state legislature.[54] In March of 1786 Posey was convicted in Northampton County of fraud when he destroyed "in a passion" an arbitration bond he had filed with the court as security for obligations owed to Dandridge as Administrator of the Custis estate.[55]

It was not long thereafter that George Washington learned that he had an even more personal grievance against John Price Posey than depredations committed on his stepson's estate. After the war, he had discharged his former overseer, James Hill, and made repeated demands upon him for an accounting of his stewardship in managing Washington's properties.[56] He was stunned in September of 1786 when Hill finally informed him that he had long ago turned over to John Price Posey all monies and records relating to the Washington farms, as well as cash he had collected from various of Washington's debtors in the area.[57] The outrage felt by Mount Vernon's squire at this news is palpably reflected in a letter he wrote to David Stuart, a friend in Richmond:

> Pray what is become of that Superlative Villain Posey? It has been reported here that he is run off to Georgia. By a letter I have just received from Mr. Hill, I find that the whole produce of my Estate below from the year 1774 together with the monies which Hill received from others on my acct. has got into that abandoned wretchs hands, not one shilling of which I presume, will ever be got out of them.[58]

Washington regained his composure after learning that Posey had not fled to Georgia, but was still to be found in New Kent County. Suspecting perhaps that Hill was not being entirely truthful, and that he might be using the already-disgraced Posey as a convenient scapegoat for his own malfeasance, he wrote to both former managers on 12 January 1787. To Hill, he denied ever instructing or authorizing him to turn over to Posey any of his own money, produce or records, and challenged him to prove otherwise.[59] To Posey, he cited Hill's claim "that the accounts had been settled years ago with you, and not only the produce of that Estate paid into your hands, but that other considerable sums of money which he collected for me . . . had gone this way also." He called upon Posey to respond to Hill's allegations, and if they were correct, to produce and turn over everything he had received from Hill.[60]

John Price Posey fired back an immediate and indignant denial of all of Hill's charges, "which would have been hurtful to the feelings of almost any Man . . . but I am happy in this Instance I doubt not I can satisfy you that I have not act'd with that injustice to you as you so Pointedly have charged me with." He insisted that there had been no settlement such as Hill had claimed, and he denied receiving from him any of Washington's money or property. Finally, he asked Washington's permission to come up to Mount Vernon and vindicate his good name, again professing concern lest the man who had been his family's repeated and generous benefactor judge him unfairly:

> . . . for I will not suffer Mr. Hill or any other man to injure my reputation, particularly to you, Sir—that I ever wish'd to please, and grateful that has receiv'd the favors I have done from you—cou'd not have thought of Deceiving.[61]

There is no record that Washington ever met with the son of his old friend and neighbor, or that Hill's new charges against John Price Posey were either established or disproved. This may be because Posey was soon caught up in an even more grave and deadly course of events. Early in June of 1787 he, for unknown reasons, attacked the Sheriff of New Kent County, Robert B. Armistead. Being unable to post bail, he was sentenced to one month's confinement in the County Prison.[62] On the night of 12 July Posey, with the assistance of a laborer named Thomas Green broke out of his jail cell and made his escape. Instead of fleeing the area, Posey returned to the prison three nights later with Green and two slaves, Hercules and Sawney, and set fire to the building. Riding up the public road from the burning structure, the four men passed the County Clerk's office. According to Green's later deposition, John Price Posey shouted "thar was another Damn'd object that must be destroyed, too, and Damn'd himself if that should not go." Whereupon the clerk's office, containing all the vital public archives of the county, including land deeds, mortgages and court records, was also burned to the ground.[63]

Posey's motivations in this bizarre foray have been authoritatively linked to widespread public unrest arising from a severe economic depression afflicting Virginia in 1786-1787. Small farmers were particularly hard hit by the lowering of market prices for their produce. They had accumulated crushing indebtedness to wealthy landowners in quitclaim rents, and to merchants for goods purchased in anticipation of crop proceeds.[64] Many were in default on the state "certificate tax" levied on lands and lots, free males, slaves, horses, cattle, carriages, billiard tables and ordinary licenses.[65] In several counties, farmers assembled spontaneously to block court foreclosure actions brought by creditors and tax authorities, or to prevent local sheriffs from executing on judgments issued by the courts in such proceedings.

A few months previous, a similar but more organized agrarian uprising, led by Daniel Shays, had occurred in Massachusetts. Although Shays Rebellion was forcibly put down, it set an example for populist resistance in other states with comparable economic problems.[66] In Virginia's Greenbrier County, 300 protesters assembled and signed an agreement to "stand together" in opposing court-ordered seizures for debts or taxes. Their leader, Adonijah ("Black") Matthews, who was suspected of having brought the idea with him from New England, was arrested when he tried to disrupt foreclosures in the county court.[67] Sheriffs in Henry County and elsewhere reported that they feared mob violence if they attempted to collect delinquent taxes. Judges were similarly intimidated—four thousand unheard foreclosure suits had piled up in the General Court of Petersburg, and a mysterious but suspect fire destroyed court records in King William County.[68]

Posey's contemporaries immediately connected his burning of two public buildings in New Kent County to the same populist unrest. A Richmond friend of James Madison informed him that "we have got the burner of one prison & a Mr. Posey of N. Kent, deposited in the gaol of this city."[69] The influential aristocrat Richard Henry Lee informed his cousin Richard Lee that "the Magistrates of New Kent soon found out Price Posey & sent him in chains to Richmond to be tried for his life." Complaining of "the riots and mobbish proceedings in Virginia," R. H. Lee deplored the recent theft of public records from his own Westmoreland County, and assured his cousin that he had contributed to "a public purse . . . made up by the good men of the County, and a large reward offered for discovering the offender."[70]

While there is no evidence to support a direct linkage with rural uprisings elsewhere in Virginia, it may be assumed that the natural sympathies of John Price Posey, a former farm manager, would in such violent class confrontations weigh against wealthy land owners and merchants, and the courts and sheriffs enforcing their vested interests. In his recent past he had been a gentleman, a judicial officer and a respected delegate to the state legislature, but he had been stripped of all offices and honors, and subjected to criminal process as a common thief and embezzler. Without knowing if his fight with Sheriff Armistead arose from personal or ideological grievances, it cannot be determined if Posey's assault upon the County Prison might not have been simply an act of personal frustration and mindless retribution. But his subsequent firing of the County Clerks's office could more plausibly be interpreted as a symbolic individual gesture of defiance on behalf of the hard-pressed farmers of Posey's acquaintance against the Establishment and the legal mechanisms of debt and tax collection it controlled.

Whatever his purposes, Posey was soon identified as the ringleader of the offenders by Thomas Green, who turned state's evidence when the four miscreants were arrested a few hours after the ruined shells of the two public buildings smoldered out. He was arraigned in the County Court, where he had once sat as a respected magistrate, and was tried before the General Court of Richmond, which on 1 October found him guilty of arson, a capital offense. The verdict was sustained in December by nine of the ten justices sitting on the Virginia Supreme Court of Appeals.[71] Presiding Justice Peter Lyons' emotional reading of the appeal court's final judgment drew tears from most of those present in the courtroom. When Posey was asked why sentence of death should not be pronounced upon him, he was at first too overcome to speak, but then, choked with tears, he confessed his guilt, declared deep remorse for his crime, and begged the court for mercy, expressing his hope that "through the merits of his Savior, to obtain a pardon for the sins of his past life."[72]

It is to be fervently hoped that forgiveness was ultimately granted by the Higher Authority to which he appealed. It was certainly not forthcoming from the judges, who promptly sentenced John Price Posey to be hanged on 18 January 1788. The two slaves, Sawney and Hercules, who had earlier been tried and sentenced to death in the County Court, were pardoned and returned to the custody of their owner, Colonel William Chamberlayne, Posey's brother-in-law.[73] There is no knowledge of what, if any, punishment was meted out to the informant Green for his part in the escapade.

On 9 January the most notorious prisoner in the Great Gaol of Richmond asked its warden to transmit to Governor Edmund Randolph this short, plaintive note:

> The unfortunate and most unhappy John Price Posey begs that a further indulgence of a few days could be allowed him—Hopeful that it would be attended with giving further releif to the peace of mind that your unfortunate petitioner is now in search of.[74]

The governor mercifully granted a week's stay of execution. In the absence of any supporting evidence, it may be at least surmised and certainly hoped that during these last days Thomas Posey, then a respected country squire living only one full day's canter away in Spotsylvania County, arrived in Richmond to give what little comfort he could to the doomed sibling and companion of happier youthful days at Rover's Delight.

"The unfortunate and most unhappy John Price Posey" was publicly hanged on the gallows in Richmond on 25 January 1788. His body was buried in an unmarked grave somewhere in New Kent County, probably at or near his home at Mount Airy.[75] The Virginia General Assembly, in which he had sat for one term as an elected Delegate, later restored to Posey's widow, Anne Kidley Chamberlayne Posey, all of his real and personal property, which under then-existing law forfeited to the state in capital cases. In taking this humanitarian action, the Assembly cited the sufferings the family had already undergone, and the fact that most of the property involved had been acquired by Posey through his marriage.[76]

Thus ended in tragedy and disgrace the baffling life of John Price Posey, a man who, like Thomas Posey, appeared to have surmounted the disadvantages and constraints caused by his family's financial and social ruin. His decline and fall parallels to some extent the tragic path of his father, and stands in startling contrast to the continued success and noteworthy career of Thomas Posey. The two young men, though probably of differing biological origins, had emerged from the same household and were subject to identical environmental influences. But John Price, for whatever reasons, seemingly underwent a complete reversal of character, and fell back into a pattern of disreputable and anti-social behavior that ultimately took him to the public gallows.

NOTES

1. "The two following being paid for as Advertisements, we insert them as such," *The Maryland Gazette*, no. 1238, 1 June 1769.
2. Donald Jackson and Dorothy Twohig, eds., *The Diaries of George Washington*, 7 vols. (Charlottesville, VA: The University Press of Virginia, 1976-79), 2:236.
3. John Posey to Washington, 25 May 1771, *Letters to Washington and Accompanying Papers*, ed. Stanislaus M. Hamilton, 5 vols. (Boston and New York: Houghton Mifflin Co., 1898-1902), 4:63-66.
4. Ibid.
5. *Ledger A of George Washington*, 3 vols. (Boston: Massachusetts Historical Society, 1922), 3:256. Repository: The Newberry Library, Chicago, IL.
6. Jackson and Twohig, eds., *Diaries of Washington*, 3:113.
7. Ibid., 3:137; Rupert Hughes, *George Washington: The Rebel and the Patriot, 1762-1777* (New York: William Morrow & Co., 1927), 134.
8. Jackson and Twohig, *Diaries of Washington*, 3:197.
9. John Posey to Washington, 9 August 1773, *Letters to Washington*, ed. Hamilton, 4:245-46.
10. Jackson and Twohig, eds., *Diaries of Washington*, 3:244.
11. Douglas Southall Freeman, *George Washington—A Biography*, 7 vols. (New York: Charles Scribner's Sons, 1948-57), 1:237-40; James Thomas Flexner, *George Washington: The Forge of Experience, 1732-1775* (Boston: Little, Brown & Co., 1965), 44-45.
12. Freeman, *Washington*, 3:234n.33; Washington to John Posey, 24 June 1767, John C. Fitzpatrick, ed., *The Writings of George Washington*, 39 vols. (Washington, DC: U.S. Government Printing Office, 1931-44), 2:455-60.
13. Charles W. Stetson, *Washington and His Neighbors* (Richmond, VA: Garrett & Massie, 1956), 140; Hughes, *Washington*, 110; Jackson and Twohig, eds., *Diaries of Washington*, 1:211.
14. Freeman, *Washington*, 3:100, 184-85, 191-92.
15. Flexner, *Washington*, 252.
16. Ibid.; Freeman, *Washington*, 3:196; Stetson, *Washington*, 139.
17. Nathaniel Wright Stephenson and Waldo Hilary Dunn, *George Washington*, 3 vols. (New York, London, and Toronto: Oxford University Press, 1940), 1:269-70.
18. Washington's *Ledger A*, 314; Elswyth Thane, *Potomac Squire* (Mount Vernon, VA: Mount Vernon Ladies Association, 1953), 107.
19. Jackson and Twohig, eds., *Diaries of Washington*, 3:119.
20. George Washington to Martha Washington, 18 June 1775, *The Papers of George Washington, Revolutionary War Series*, eds. W.W. Abbot and Dorothy Twohig, 3 vols. to date (Charlottesville, VA: The University Press of Virginia, 1982-), 1:3-5, 6 n.8; Stetson, *Washington*, 143-44, 301; Hughes, *Washington*, 655.
21. George Washington to Lund Washington, 30 April 1781, *Writings of Washington*, ed. Fitzpatrick, 22:14-15.
22. John C. Fitzpatrick, *George Washington Himself* (Indianapolis: Bobs-Merrill, 1933), 155.
23. Stetson, *Washington*, 144.
24. Thane, *Potomac Squire*, 83.

25. John Posey to Washington, 25 May 1771, *Letters to Washington*, ed. Hamilton, 4:63-66.
26. Ibid., Francis Baker to Washington, 15 December 1772, 4:169-70.
27. Ibid., John Posey to Washington, 25 May 1771, 4:63-66.
28. Ibid., Francis Baker to Washington, 26 March 1774, 4:363, 363n.1.
29. Washington to William Minor, 27 May 1785 and 16 June 1785, *Writings of Washington*, ed. Fitzpatrick, 28:154-55, 165-66.
30. Jackson and Twohig, eds., *Diaries of Washington*, 3:227.
31. Court order of 19 September 1770, Court Order Book 1770, 92, Fairfax County Court Archives, Judicial Center, Fairfax County, Fairfax, VA.
32. Articles of Association, 22 June 1770, *Calendar of Washington Documents, Library of Congress*, ed. Herbert Friedewold (Washington, DC: Library of Congress, 1901), 276.
33. Robert L. Scribner and Brent Tarter, eds., *Revolutionary Virginia: The Road to Independence* (Charlottesville, VA: The University Press of Virginia, 1970), 5:72-73.
34. John H. Gwathney, *Historical Register of Virginians in the Revolution* (Richmond, VA: Genealogical Publishing Co., 1938), 634; H.J. Eckenrode, *Revolutionary Soldiers of Virginia* (Richmond, VA: Virginia State Library and Archives, 1912), 276.
35. Wilfred Jordan, ed., *Colonial and Revolutionary Families (Pennsylvania)*, part 2, 4 vols. (New York: Genealogical Publishing Co., 1932), 4:494-97.
36. Court order of 21 November 1770, Court Order Book 1770, 140, Fairfax County Court Archives, Judicial Center, Fairfax County, Fairfax, VA.
37. Jackson and Twohig, eds., *Diaries of Washington*, 3:6.
38. Ibid., 3:7, 34, 76, 77, 197, 243, 304.
39. Robert Scribner and Brent Tarter, eds., *Revolutionary Virginia: The Road of Independence—Vol. 7*, part 1, 42-43.
40. Rind's *Virginia Gazette*, 16 October 1778.
41. Washington to John Price Posey, 23 April 1779, *Writings of Washington*, ed. Fitzpatrick, 14:433.
42. John Price Posey to Washington, 3 June 1779, *The George Washington Papers* (Washington, DC: Library of Congress, 1964, text-fiche), reel 59 (Hereafter cited as *GW Papers—text-fiche—LC*.)
43. Malcolm H. Harris, *Old New Kent County*, 2 vols.(West Point, VA: Malcolm Hart Harris, 1977), 1:99.
44. Freeman, *Washington*, 5:401-2, 402n.53.
45. Bartholomew Dandridge to Washington, 20 March 1782, *GW Papers—text-fiche—LC*, reel 83.
46. Washington to Bartholomew Dandridge, 25 June 1782, *Writings of Washington*, ed. Fitzpatrick, 24:386-87.
47. Ibid., Washington to John Price Posey, 7 August 1782, 24:485-87.
48. Ibid.
49. Ibid., Washington to Bartholomew Dandridge, 18 December 1782, 24:443-44.
50. Council of State Opinion, 20 February 1783, *The Papers of John Marshall*, 4 vols. to date, ed. Charles T. Cullen (Chapel Hill, NC: The University of North Carolina Press, 1977-), 1:96-97.
51. Bartholomew Dandridge to Washington, 13 March 1784, *GW Papers—text-fiche—LC,* reel 94.

52. William P. Palmer, ed., *Calendar of Virginia State Papers*, 11 vols. (Richmond, VA: Commonwealth of Virginia, 1875-1881), 3:616.
53. Ibid., 3:620.
54. William T. Hutchinson, ed., *The Papers of James Madison*, 15 vols. to date (Charlottesville, VA: The University Press of Virginia, 1962-), 5:347n.5.
55. Palmer, ed., *Calendar of Virginia State Papers*, 4:95
56. Washington to James Hill, 29 August 1786, *Writings of Washington*, ed. Fitzpatrick, 28:527-28.
57. James Hill to Washington, 24 September 1786, *GW Papers—text-fiche—LC,* reel 96.
58. Washington to David Stuart, 19 November 1786, *Writings of Washington*, ed. Fitzpatrick, 29:75-77.
59. Ibid., 29:144-46.
60. Ibid., 29:143-44.
61. John Price Posey to Washington, 27 January 1787, *GW Papers—text-fiche—LC,* reel 96.
62. Palmer, ed., *Calendar of Virginia State Papers*, 4:321.
63. Ibid., 329-30.
64. Henry Mayer, *A Son of Thunder: Patrick Henry and the American Republic* (New York and Toronto: F. Watts, 1986), 382-83.
65. James McClurg to James Madison, 22 August 1787, *Papers of Madison*, ed. Hutchinson, 10:155n.1.
66. Freeman, *Washington*, 6:72-73; Richard Maxwell Brown, "Back Country Rebellions and the Homestead Ethic in America, 1740-1799," in *Tradition, Conflict and Modernization: Perspectives on the American Revolution*, eds. Richard Maxwell Brown and Don Fehrenbacher (New York, San Francisco, and London: Academic Press, 1977), 73-99.
67. James McClurg to James Madison, 22 August 1787, *Papers of Madison*, ed. Hutchinson, 10:154-56; Mayer, *Son of Thunder*, 382-83.
68. Mayer, *Son of Thunder*, 383.
69. James McClurg to James Madison, 22 August 1787, *Papers of Madison*, ed. Hutchinson, 10:155.
70. Richard Henry Lee to Richard Lee, 13 September 1787, *The Letters of Richard Henry Lee*, ed. James Curtis Ballagh, 2 vols. (New York: University Publishing Co., 1916), 2:436-37.
71. James McClurg to James Madison, 22 August 1787, *Papers of Madison*, ed. Hutchinson, 10:155-56 156n.4.
72. Ibid.
73. Palmer, ed., *Calendar of Virginia State Papers*, 4:329, 367.
74. Ibid., 5:225.
75. Harris, *Old New Kent County*, 1:98.
76. Ibid.; Act of General Assembly, 9 December 1788, Chap. 35, William Waller Hening, ed., *The Statutes at Large: Being a Collection of All the Laws of Virginia. . .* (Richmond: Commonwealth of Virginia, 1819-23), 12: 692.

SELECT BIBLIOGRAPHY

Manuscript Sources

This work draws liberally upon all known primary sources pertaining to its protagonist. The forty-four original manuscripts and documents in the Thomas Posey Papers held by the Indiana Historical Society Library at Indianapolis, Indiana constitute the most extensive collection dedicated solely to General Posey. The William H. English and Northwest Territory collections held by that same depository contain additional valuable material.

The Illinois State Historical Library at Springfield, Illinois holds, in its Special Collection No. 1756, thirty-one autograph family letters of Mrs. Thomas (Mary Alexander Thornton) Posey spanning the period 1813 to 1829, which are cited frequently in the final two chapters of this book.

Manuscripts directly relating to Thomas Posey, held by twenty other depositories, were reviewed in researching this work. The most numerous of these were found in the Anthony Wayne Papers and the Gratz and Dreer collections held by the Historical Society of Pennsylvania Library, Philadelphia, Pennsylvania. Additionally, one or more original documents from each of the following depositories was considered in the preparation of the Posey biography:

Boston Public Library, Boston, MA (General collections).

Chicago Historical Society Library, Chicago, IL (Gunther Collection, Washington Family Papers).

Cincinnati Historical Society Library, Cincinnati, OH (Lytle Papers).

Henderson County Public Library, Henderson, KY (Thomas Posey File).

Hill Memorial Library, Louisiana State University, Baton Rouge, LA (Philip Hickey Papers, Louisiana and Lower Mississippi Collections)

The Huntington Library, San Marino, CA (General collections).

Indiana State Library, Indiana Division, Indianapolis, IN (Lasselle Collection).

Kentucky Department for Libraries and Archives, Frankfort, KY (Greenup Papers).

Kentucky Historical Society Library, Louisville, KY (Manuscript Collection).

Massachusetts Historical Society Library, Boston, MA (Jacob Brown Collection).

Mt. Vernon Public Library, Mt. Vernon, IN (Thomas Posey Folder No. 000208).

New York Historical Society Library, New York, NY (General collections).

New York Public Library, New York, NY (Meyers Collection No. 1013 and Miscellaneous Papers—Thomas Posey Collection).

The Presbyterian Study Center, Montreat, NC (Thornton and Posey Bible).

Shawneetown Public Library, New Shawneetown, IL (Gallatin County Historical Society File).

State Historical Society of Wisconsin, Madison, WI (Draper Manuscripts).

Virginia Historical Society Library, Richmond, VA (Thornton Family Folders, George H. S. King Papers).

William L. Clements Library, University of Michigan, Ann Arbor, MI (Greene Papers).

William R. Perkins Library, Duke University, Durham, NC (Nathanael Greene Papers).

Not listed in this select bibliography are two general categories of source material widely utilized in the narrative:

1. Daily newspapers and weekly news journals.
2. Original county and local public records, including ledger books containing wills, deeds, court orders, and other legal documents.

The specific references to these sources are cited and fully identified and described in the corresponding notes.

Published Sources

Abbot, W. W. and Dorothy Twohig, eds. *The Papers of George Washington,* Colonial Series, 7 vols. to date; Revolutionary Series, 3 vols. to date; Presidential Series, 2 vols. to date. Charlottesville, VA: The University Press of Virginia, 1982- .

Alexander, James W. *The Life of Archibald Alexander.* New York: C. Scribner, 1854.

Bibliography

Allen, John W. *Legends and Lore of Southern Illinois.* Carbondale, IL: Southern Illinois University Press, 1963

Ammon, Harry. *James Monroe: The Quest for National Identity.* New York: McGraw-Hill, 1971.

Arndt, Karl J. R., ed. *A Documentary History of the Indiana Decade of the Harmony Society*, Vol. 1. Indianapolis: Indiana University Press, 1975.

Arnett, Maralea. *The Annals and Scandals of Henderson County, KY, (1775-1925).* Henderson, KY: Audubon Printers, 1976.

Baird, Capt. L. C. "General Lafayette in Indiana." *Indiana Magazine of History* 2 (1906): 193-197.

Ballagh, James Curtis, ed. *The Letters of Richard Henry Lee.* 2 vols. New York: Da Capo, 1916.

Banning, Lance. *The Jeffersonian Persuasion: Evolution of a Party Ideology.* Ithaca, NY: Cornell University Press, 1978.

Barnard, Rev. J. W. "Sketch of Early Presbyterian Church in Indiana." *Indiana Magazine of History* 21 (1925): 304-308.

Barnhart, John D. "The Southern Influence in the Formation of Indiana." *Indiana Magazine of History* 33 (1937): 24-65.

Barnhart, John D. and Dorothy L. Riker. *Indiana to 1816: The Colonial Period.* Indianapolis: Indiana Historical Bureau and Indiana Historical Society, 1971.

Bauer, K. Jack. *Zachary Taylor: Soldier, Planter, Statesman of the Old Southwest.* Baton Rouge, LA: Louisiana State University Press, 1985.

Beeman, Richard E. *Patrick Henry: A Biography.* New York: McGraw-Hill, 1974.

Berg, Fred Anderson, ed. *Encyclopedia of Continental Army Units.* Harrisburg, PA: Stackpose Books, 1974.

Biographical Directory of the American Congress, 1774-1971. Washington: U.S. Government Printing Office, 1971.

Bloch, Ruth H. "Battling Infidelity, Heathenism, and Licentiousness: New England Missions on the Post-Revolutionary Frontier, 1792-1805." In *The Northwest Ordinance: Essays on Its Formulation, Provisions and Legacy,* edited by Frederick D. Williams, 39-60, East Lansing, MI: Michigan State University Press, 1989.

Bowen, Catherine Drinker. *Miracle at Philadelphia.* New York: Little, Brown & Co., 1986 edition.

Boyd, Julian P. et al, eds. *The Papers of Thomas Jefferson.* 24 vols. to date. Princeton, NJ: Princeton University Press, 1950- .

Boyd, Thomas. *Mad Anthony Wayne.* New York and London: Oxford University Press, 1929.

Brown, Richard Maxwell. "Back Country Rebellions and the Homestead Ethic in America, 1740-1799." In *Tradition, Conflict and Modernization: Perspectives on the American Revolution,* edited by Richard Maxwell Brown and Don Fehrenbacher. New York, San Francisco and London: Academic Press, 1977.

Brumbaugh, Gaius Marcus, ed. *Revolutionary War Records: Virginia.* Baltimore: Genealogical Publishing Co., 1936; 1967 edition.

Buel, Richard, Jr. *Securing the Revolution: Ideology in American Politics, 1789-1815.* Ithaca, NY: Cornell University Press, 1972.

Buley, R. Carlyle. The Old Northwest: Pioneer Period, 1815-1840. 2 vols. Bloomington, IN: Indiana University Press, 1950.

Bushnell, David, ed. *La Republica de las Florides: Texts and Documents.* Tallahassee, FL: Pan American Institute of Geography and History, 1986.

Callahan, North. *Daniel Morgan: Ranger of the Revolution.* New York: Holt, Rinehart & Winston, 1961.

Campbell, Charles. *History of the Colony and Ancient Dominion of Virginia.* Philadelphia: Lippincott, 1860.

Carmody, Donald P. "Indiana Territorial Expenditures, 1800-1816." *Indiana Magazine of History* 34 (1943): 237-62.

Carmody, Donald P. "Fiscal Objections to Statehood in Indiana." *Indiana Magazine of History* 42 (1946): 311-321.

Carmody, Donald P. "Statehood Achieved." *In The Hoosier State: Readings in Indiana History: Indiana Prehistory to 1880,* edited by Ralph D. Gray. Bloomington, IN: Indiana University Press, 1980.

Carter, Clarence Edwin, ed. *The Territory of Indiana, 1810-1816,*vol. 8 of *The Territorial Papers of the United States.* Washington: AMS Press, 1939.

Carter, Clarence Edwin, ed. *The Territory of Orleans, 1803-1812,* vol. 9 of *The Territorial Papers of the United States.* Washington: AMS Press, 1940.

Chalkley, Lyman. *Cronicles of the Scotch-Irish Settlement in Virginia.* 3 vols. Baltimore: Genealogical Publishing Co., 1966.

Chalkley, Lyman, ed. *Records of Augusta County, Virginia, 1745-1800.* 3 vols. Baltimore: Genealogical Publishing Co., 1966.

Clark, Murtie Jane. *Colonial Sodiers of the South, 1732-1774.* Baltimore: Genealogical Publishing Co., 1986.

Clark, Thomas D. *A History of Kentucky.* New York: Prentice-Hall, 1937.

Clark, Thomas D. *Kentucky: Land of Contrast.* New York, Evanston and London: Harper & Row, 1968.

Clem, Gladys B. *It Happened Around Staunton in Virginia.* Berryville, VA: Gladys B. Clem, 1964.

Clift, G. Glenn. *Governors of Kentucky, 1792-1942.* Louisville, KY: Kentucky Historical Society, 1942.

Coleman, Christopher E. "George Washington and the West." *Indiana Magazine of History* 28 (1932): 157-61.

Coleman, Christopher E. "Restoration of the Capital at Corydon." *Indiana Magazine of History* 30 (1934): 255-56.

Collins, Lewis and Richard H. *History of Kentucky.* 2 vols. Covington, KY: Southern History Press, 1874.

Collins, Mary Scribner Lewis. "New Albany, with a Short Sketch of the Scribner Family." *Indiana Magazine of History* 17 (1921): 227-31.

Commanger, Henry Steele and Richard B. Morris, eds. *The Spirit of Seventy-Six.* New York: Harper & Row, 1958.

Connelley, William E. and E. M. Coulter. *History of Kentucky.* New York: Prentice-Hall, 1937.

Crozier, William A., ed. *Virginia Colonial Militia, 1651-1776.* Baltimore: Genealogical Publishing Co.,1954.

Crozier, William A., ed. *Virginia County Records: Spotsylvania County, Vol. 1, 1721-1800,* New York: Genealogical Publishing Co., 1905, Reprint 1971.

Crozier, William A., ed. *Virginia County Records: Early Virginia Marriages, Vol. 4,* Richmond: Genealogical Publishing Co., 1986 edition.

Cullen, Charles T., ed. *The Papers of John Marshall.* 6 vols. to date. Chapel Hill, NC: The University of North Carolina Press, 1974-

Dabney, Virginius. *Virginia—The New Dominion.* Garden City, NY: University Press of Virginia, 1971.

Dabney, Virginius. *BiCentennial History and Roster of The Society of the Cincinnati in the State of Virginia, 1783-1983.* Richmond: The Society of the Cincinnati in the State of Virginia, 1983.

Davis, Edwin Adams. *Louisiana: The Pelican State.* Baton Rouge, LA: Louisiana State University Press, 1959.

Davis, T. Frederick. *MacGregor's Invasion of Florida, 1817.* Tallahasee, FL: The Florida Historical Society, 1928.

Dean, John Candee, ed. *Journal of Thomas Dean: A Voyage to Indiana in 1817.* Indianapolis: Indiana Historical Society, 1919.

Dictionary of American Biography, 10 vols. New York: Chales Scribner's Sons, 1963 edition.

Dorfman, Joseph. *The Economic Mind in American Civilization: 1606-1865.* 5 vols. New York: Kelley, 1946.

Dufor, Charles L. *Ten Flags in the Wind: The Story of Louisiana.* New York: Harper and Row, 1967.

Dunn, Jacob P. *Indiana, A Redemption from Slavery.* Boston: AMS Press, 1890.

Dunn, Jacob P. *Indiana and Indianians.* 5 vols. Chicago: American Historical Society, 1919.

Dunn, Jacob P. "Slavery in the Indiana Territory." In *The Hoosier State: Readings in Indiana History: Indiana Prehistory to 1880*, edited by Ralph D. Gray. Bloomington, IN: Indiana University Press, 1980.

Early Kentucky Records: Register of the Kentucky Historical Society. Baltimore: Genealogical Publishing Co., 1978.

Early Kentucky Tax Records. Baltimore: Genealogical Publishing Co., 1984.

Eby, Cecil. *"That Disgraceful Affair": The Black Hawk War.* New York: Norton, 1973.

Eckenrode, H. J. *List of Revolutionary Soldiers in Virginia.* Richmond: Virginia State Library and Archives, 1912.

Eckenrode, H. J. *The Revolution in Virginia.* Boston and New York: Houghton Mifflin Co., 1916.

Eckert, Allan W. *The Wilderness War.* Boston and Toronto: Little, Brown & Co., 1978.

Elmer, Ebenezer. "Journal Kept During an Expedition to Canada in 1776." *Proceedings of the New Jersey Historical Society*, 1st ser. 3 (1849): 55.

Embry, Alvin T. *History of Fredericksburg, Virginia.* Richmond: Old Dominion Press, 1937.

Emison, James Wade, Jr. *The Emison Families—Final Supplement*. Vincennes, IN: James Ward Emison, Jr., 1969.

English, William H. *Conquest of the Country Northwest of the River Ohio, 1778-1783*. 2 vols. Indianapolis: Ayer Co. Publishers, 1895.

Esarey, Logan. "Pioneer Politics in Indiana." *Indiana Magazine of History* 13 (1917): 99-129.

Esarey, Logan, ed. *Governors' Messages and Letters: Messages and Letters of William Henry Harrison.* 2 vols. Indianapolis: Ayer Co. Publishers, 1922.

Ferling, John E. *The First of Men: A Life of George Washington.* Knoxville, TN: University of Tennessee Press, 1988.

Finkelman, Paul. "Slavery and Bondage in the 'Empire of Liberty.'" In *The Northwest Ordinance: Essays on Its Formulation, Provisions and Legacy*, edited by Frederick D. Williams, 61-95. East Lansing, MI: Michigan State University Press, 1989.

Fitzpatrick, John C. "The George Washington Scandals." *Scribner's Magazine* 81 (1927): 389-95.

Fitzpatrick, John C. *The George Washington Scandals.* Alexandria, VA: Scribner's Magazine, 1929.

Fitzpatrick, John C. *George Washington Himself.* Indianapolis: Bobs-Merrill, 1933.

Fitzpatrick, John C., ed. *The Diaries of George Washington.* 4 vols. Boston and New York: Houghton Mifflin Co., 1925.

Fitzpatrick, John C., ed. *The Writings of George Washington.* 39 vols. Washington: U.S. Government Printing Office, 1931-1944.

Flexner, James Thomas. *George Washington: The Forge of Experience, 1732-1775.* Boston: Little, Brown & Co., 1965.

Freeman, Douglas Southall. *George Washington: A Biography.* 7 vols. New York: Charles Scribner's Sons, 1948-1957.

"General Thomas Posey." *Port Folio.* Philadelphia: Harrison Hall, 1827. Thompson, Charles M. "General Lafayette in Indiana." *Indiana Magazine of History* 14 (1928): 71-72.

Gerson, Noel B. *Lighthorse Harry.* Garden City, NY: Doubleday, 1966.

Goode, George B. *Virginia Cousins.* Harrisonburg, VA: C. J. Carrier Co., 1974.

Griffin, John, ed. *Narrative of a Voyage to the Spanish Main in the Ship "Two Friends."* Gainesville, FL: University Presses of Florida, 1978.

Gwathney, John H. *Historical Register of Virginians in the Revolution.* Richmond: Genealogical Publishing Co., 1938.

Hall, James E. "Memoir of Thomas Posey, Major General and Governor of Indiana." In *The Library of American Biography*, 2nd ser., edited by Jared Sparks. Boston: Little, Brown & Co., 1846.

Hall, Rev. W. Brant. *First Presbyterian Church.* Henderson, KY: First Presbyterian Church, 1960.

Hamilton, Holman. "The Vincennes Days of Zachary Taylor." *Indiana Magazine of History* 47 (1941): 66.

Hamilton, Holman. Zachary Taylor: *Soldier of the Republic.* 2 vols. Indianapolis: Bobs-Merril, 1941.

Hamilton, Stanislaus M., ed. *Letters to Washington and Accompanying Papers.* 5 vols. Boston and New York: Houghton Mifflin Co., 1898-1902.

Hammond, Alma S., ed. *Survey of Federal Archives in Louisiana: Archives of Spanish West Florida.* New Orleans: WPA of Louisiana, 1940.

Harris, Malcolm H. *Old New Kent County.* 2 vols. West Point, VA: Malcolm Hart Harris, 1977.

Havighurst, Walter. *River to the West.* New York: Putnam, 1970.

Hay, Thomas R. and Morris R. Werner. *The Admirable Trumpter.* New York: Doubleday, 1941.

Heitman, Francis B. *Historical Register of Officers of the Continental Army, 1775-1783.* Washington: Lowdermilk & Co., 1893.

Heitman, Francis B. *Historical Register and Dictionary of the United States Army, 1789-1903.* Washington: Lowdermilk & Co., 1903; reprint, Urbana, IL: University of Illinois Press, 1965.

Henderson, Archibald. *Washington's Southern Tour—1791.* Boston and New York: Houghton Mifflin Co., 1923.

Hening, William Waller, ed. *The Statutes at Large: Being a Collection of all the Laws of Virginia. . . .*, 13 vols. Richmond: Commonwealth of Virginia, 1819-1823.

Henry, William Wirt. *Patrick Henry.* 3 vols. New York: Charles Scribner's Sons, 1891.

Higginbotham, Don. *Daniel Morgan: Revolutionary Rifleman.* Chapel Hill, NC: University of North Carolina Press, 1961.

History of Posey County, Indiana. Chicago: Goodspeed Publishing Co., 1886.

Hofstader, Richard. *The Idea of a Party System: The Rise of Legitimate Opposition in the United States, 1780-1840.* Berkeley, CA: University of California Press, 1969.

Holliday, James R. "Early History of Harrison County, Ind." Ph. D. diss., University of Louisville, Louisville, KY, 1932.

Hopkins, James F. and Mary W. Hargreaves, eds. *The Papers of Henry Clay.* 9 vols. to date. Lexington, KY: The University Press of Kentucky, 1959- .

Hughes, Rupert. *George Washington: The Rebel and the Patriot, 1762-1777.* New York: William Morrow & Co., 1927.

Hutchinson, William T., ed. *The Papers of James Madison.* 17 vols. to date. Charlottesville, VA: The University Press of Virginia, 1962- .

Irving, Washington. *The Life of Washington.* 5 vols. New York: G. P. Putnam, 1859.

Jackson, Donald, ed. *Black Hawk: An Autobiography.* Urbana, IL: University of Illinois Press, 1964.

Jackson, Donald, and Dorothy Twohig, eds. *The Diaries of George Washington.* 7 vols. Charlottesville, VA: The University Press of Virginia, 1976-1979.

Jacobs, James R. *Tarnished Warrior: Major General James Wilkinson.* New York: Ayer Co. Publishers, 1938.

Jillson, Willard Rouse, ed. *Old Kentucky Entries and Deeds.* Baltimore: Genealogical Publishing Co., 1978.

Johnston, Henry P. *The Storming of Stony Point on the Hudson, Midnight, July 15, 1779.* New York: Da Capo Press, 1900; reprint, 1971.

Jordan, Wilfred, ed. *Colonial and Revolutionary Families (Pennsylvania)*, new ser., part 2. 4 vols. New York: Genealogical Publishing Co., 1932.

Kappler, Charles J., ed. *Indian Affairs: Laws and Treaties.* 5 vols. Washington: AMS Press, 1904.

Kegley, F. B. *Virginia Frontier.* Roanoke, VA: Southwest Historical Society, 1938.

Lancaster, Bruce. *From Lexington to Liberty*, Garden City, NY: Doubleday, 1955.

Ledger A of George Washington, 3 vols. Boston: Massachusetts Historical Society, 1922.

Lee, Henry. *Memoirs of the War in the Southern Department of the United States.* Edited by Robert E. Lee. New York: University Publishing Co., 1869 edition; *The New York Times* and Arno Press, 1969 edition.

Leonard, W. P. *History and Directory of Posey County.* Evansville, IN: A. C. Isaacs, 1882.

Lester, William Stewart. *The Transylvania Colony.* Spencer, IN: S. R. Guard Co., 1935.

Lewis, Virgil A. *History of the Battle of Point Pleasant.* Charleston, WV: N.p. 1909.

Library of Congress. *Calendar of Washington Documents*, edited by Herbert Friedewold. Washington: U.S. Government Printing Office, 1901.

Library of Congress. *The George Washington Papers.* 124 reels. Washington: Library of Congress, 1964. Microfilm.

Lomask, Milton. *Aaron Burr: The Conspiracy and Years of Exile, 1805-1836.* New York: Farrar, Straus, Giroux, 1982.

Madison, James H. *The Indiana Way: A State History.* Bloomington and Indianapolis, IN: Indiana University Press, 1986.

Mahan, Bruce E. *Old Fort Crawford and the Frontier.* Iowa City, IA: State Historical Society of Iowa, 1926.

Marshall, John. *The Life of George Washington.* 5 vols. Philadelphia: AMS Press, 1832 edition.

Marshall, S. L. "General Thomas Posey as Civilian and Politician." Posey File, Frankfort, KY: Kentucky Historical Society Library, 1934.

Mayer, Henry. A Son of Thunder: *Patrick Henry and the American Republic.* New York and Toronto: F. Watts, 1986.

McMullen, Thomas A., and David Walker. *Biographical Directory of American Territorial Governors.* Westport, CT: Greenwood Press, 1984.

Mitchell, Robert. *Commercialism and the Frontier: Perspectives on the Early Shenandoah Valley*. Charlottesville, VA: The University Press of Virginia, 1977.

Moore, Merrill. "Indiana in 1816." *Indiana Magazine of History* 11 (1916): 275-81.

Musto, David Franklin. *George Washington and the Temptations of the Political Life*. Richmond: The Society of the Cincinnati in the State of Virginia, 1988.

National Archives. *Papers of the Continental Congress*. Item 152.11-611.

National Cyclopaedia of American Biography. New York: James T. White & Co., 1896 and 1906 editions.

Nelson, Paul David. *Anthony Wayne: Soldier of the Early Republic*. Bloomington, IN: Indiana University Press, 1985.

Nettles, Curtis P. "Washington on the Eve of the Revolution," in *George Washington: A Profile*, edited by James Morton Smith. New York: Hill and Wang, 1969.

Newman, Ralph Geoffrey, ed. *Abraham Lincoln: His Story in His Own Words*. Garden City, NY: Doubleday, 1975.

Palmer, William P., ed. Calendar of Virginia State Papers, 3 vols., Richmond: Commonwealth of Virginia, 1875-1883.

Pancake, John S. *This Destructive War: The British Campaign in the Carolinas, 1780-1782*. Tuscaloosa, AL: The University of Alabama Press, 1985.

Papers of The Society of the Cincinnati in the State of Virginia, 1783-1824. Richmond: The Society of the Cincinnati in the State of Virgina, 1938.

Peat, Wilbur D. *Portraits and Painters of the Governors of Indiana, 1800-1978*. Edited by Diane Gail Lazarus and Lana Ruegamer. Indianapolis: Indiana Historical Society and Indianapolis Museum of Art, 1978 edition.

Peterson, Harold L. *The Book of the Continental Soldier*. Harrisburg, PA: Stackpole Books, 1968.

Peyton, J. Lewis. *History of Augusta County, Va.*, 2nd ed. Bridgewater, VA: Heritage Books, 1953.

Posey, Alexander Lawrence. *Poems of Alexander Lawrence Posey, Creek Indian Bard*. Edited by Minnie H. Posey. Muskogee, OK: Five Civilized Tribes Heritage Foundation, Inc., First Revised Edition, 1969.

Posey, John Thornton. "Governor Thomas Posey: The Son of George Washington?" *Indiana Magazine of History* 86 (1990): 28-49.

Posey, Lloyd Franklin, and Betty Sue Drake Posey. *The Posey Family in America*. Hattiesburg, MS: University of Southern Mississippi Press, 1971.

Preston, John Hyde. *A Gentleman Rebel: The Exploits of Anthony Wayne*. New York: Farrar & Rinehart, Inc., 1930.

Rammelkamp, Charles Henry. *Illinois College: A Centennial History, 1829-1929*. Princeton, NJ: Princeton University Press, 1928.

Remini, Robert V. *The Life of Andrew Jackson*. New York: Harper/Collins, 1988.

Roster of The Society of the Cincinnati. Washington: The Society of the Cincinnati, 1989.

Rowland, Dunbar, ed. *Official Letter Book of W. C. C. Claiborne, 1801-1816*. 6 bols. Jackson, MS: AMS Press, 1917.

Royster, Charles. *A Revolutionary People at War: The Continental Army and American Character, 1775-1783*. Chapel Hill, NC: The University of North Carolina Press, 1979.

Royster, Charles. *Light-Horse Harry Lee and the Legacy of the American Revolution*. New York: Alfred A Knopf, 1981.

Sanchez-Saavedras, E. M., ed. *A Guide to Virginia Military Organizations in the American Revolution*. Richmond: Virginia State Library, 1978.

Sandburg, Carl. *Abraham Lincoln: The Prairie Years*. New York: Harcourt, Brace, 1926.

Schwartz, Barry. *George Washington: The Making of an American Symbol*. New York and London: Free Press/Macmillan, 1987.

Scribner, Robert L., and Brent Tarter, eds. *Revolutionary Virginia: The Road to Independence,* Vol. 6, *The Time for Decision, 1776: A Documentary Record.* Charlottesville, VA: The University Press of Virginia, 1983.

Sears, Louis Martin. *George Washington.* New York: Thomas Y. Crowell Co., 1932.

Selby, John E. *The Revolution in Virginia, 1775-1783*. Williamsburg, VA: The Colonial Williamsburg Foundation, 1988.

Shreve, Royal Ornan. *The Finished Scoundrel*. Indianapolis: Bobs-Merrill, 1933.

Shepard, W. R. "Document." *American Historical Review* 9 (1904): 764-65.

Showman, Richard K., ed. *The Papers of Nathanael Greene.* 4 vols. to date. Chapel Hill, NC: The University of North Carolina Press, 1986- .

Simpson-Poffenbarger, Livia Nye. *The Battle of Point Pleasant.* Point Pleasant, WV: The State Gazette, 1909.

Slaughter, Rev. Philip. *The History of Truro Parish in Virginia.* Edited by Edward L. Goodwin. Philadelphia: George W. Jacobs & Co., 1908 edition.

Sobel, Mechal. *Travelin' On: The Slave Journey to an Afro-Baptist Faith.* Westport, CT: Greenwood Press, 1979.

Sparks, Jared, ed. *Correspondence of the American Revolution, Being Letters of Eminent Men to George Washington.* 4 vols. Boston: Ayer Publishers, 1853.

Starling, E. L. *History of Henderson County, Kentucky.* Evansville, IN: Unigraphics, Inc., 1965 edition.

Stephenson, Nathaniel Wright, and Walso Hilary Dunn. *George Washington.* 2 vols. New York, London & Toronto: Oxford University Press, 1940.

Stetson, Charles W. *Washington and His Neighbors.* Richmond, VA: Garrett & Massie, 1956.

Stille, Charles Janway. *Major-General Anthony Wayne and the Pennsylvania Line.* Port Washington, NY: Kennikat Press, 1893.

Stoner, Robert Douthat. *A Seed Bed of the Republic.* Radford, VA: Commonwealth Press, Inc., 1962.

Street, Ida M. "Joseph M. Street's Last Fight with the Fur Traders." Iowa Historical Department, *Annals of Iowa,* 3rd ser., vol. 37, no. 2 (October, 1929): 105-148.

Street, William B. "General Joseph M. Street." Iowa Historical Department, *Annals of Iowa,* 3rd ser., vol. 2, nos. 2-3 (July-October, 1895): 82-84.

Syrett, Harold C., ed. *The Papers of Alexander Hamilton,* vol. 4, 26 vols. to date. New York and London: Columbia University Press, 1962- .

Tachau, Mary K. Bonsteel. *Federal Courts in the Early Republic: Kentucky, 1789-1816.* Princeton, NJ: Princeton University Press, 1978.

Taylor, Joe Gray. *Louisiana: A Bicentennial History.* New York: Norton, 1976.

Taylor, Robert M., Errol Wayne Stevens, Mary Ann Ponder, and Paul Brockman, eds. *Indiana: A New Historical Guide.* Indianapolis: Indiana Historical Society, 1989.

Thane, Elswyth. *Potomac Squire.* Mount Vernon, VA: Mount Vernon Ladies Association, 1953.

Thane, Elswyth. *The Fighting Quaker: Nathanael Greene.* New York: Amereon, Ltd., 1972.

Thayer, Theodore. *Nathanael Greene: Strategist of the American Revolution.* New York: Twayne Publishers, 1960.

Toner, J. M., ed. *Diary of Col. George Washington.* Washington: American Historical Society, 1892.

Tucker, Glenn. *Mad Anthony Wayne and the New Nation.* Harrisburg, PA: Stackpole Books, 1973.

Twaites, Reuben G., et al, eds. *Documentary History of Dunmore's War.* Madison, WI: Heritage Books, 1905.

U.S. Department of State. *Calendar of the Correspondence of James Madison,* Bulletin of the Bureau of Rolls and Library, no. 4 (March, 1894). Washington: U.S. Government Printing Office, 1894.

Vail, Philip. *The Great American Rascal: The Turbulent Life of Aaron Burr.* New York: Hawthorne Books, 1973.

Van Dyke, Paul. *George Washington: The Son of His Country.* New York and London: Charles Scribner's Sons, 1931.

Virginia Historical Society Collections, new ser., vol. 9. Richmond: Virginia Historical Society, 1891.

Virginia Soldiers of 1776. 3 vols. Baltimore: Genealogical Publishing Co., 1973.

Volkel, Lowell, M., ed. *An Index to the 1810 Federal Census of Kentucky.* 2 vols. Springfield, IL: Lowell M. Volkel, 1971.

Waddell, Joseph A. *Annals of Augusta County, Virginia.* Staunton, VA: C. R. Caldwell, 1902.

Walker, Harriet J. *Revolutionary Soldiers Buried in Illinois.* Baltimore: Genealogical Publishing, Co., 1967.

Ward, Harry M. *Charles Scott and the "Spirit of '76."* Charlottesville, VA: The University Press of Virginia, 1988.

Warren, Louis A. *Lincoln's Youth: Indiana Years, Seven to Twenty-One, 1816-1830.* Westport, CT: Greenwood Press, 1959.

Watts, Florence G. "Fort Knox: Outpost on the Wabash, 1787-1816." *Indiana Magazine of History* 62 (1966): 73-74.

Wecter, Dixon. "President Washington and Pastor Weems." In *George Washington: A Profile,* edited by James Morton Smith. New York: Charles Scribner's Sons, 1969.

Weems, John Edward. *Men Without Countries.* Boston: Houghton Mifflin Co., 1969.

Wiebe, Robert H. *The Opening of American Society.* New York: Alfred A. Knopf, 1984.

Wildes, Harry Emerson. *Anthony Wayne—Trouble Shooter of the American Revolution.* Westport, CT: Greenwood Press, 1970.

Willcox, William B. *Portrait of a General: Sir Henry Clinton in the War of Independence.* New York: Alfred A. Knopf, 1964.

Wilson, Charles Jay. "The Negro in Early Ohio." *Ohio Archaelogical and Historical Publications* 34 (1930): 191-95.

Wilson, George R. "General Washington Johnston." *Indiana Magazine of History* 20 (1924): 150-51.

Wilstach, Paul. *Mount Vernon: Washington's Home and the Nation's Shrine.* New York: Doubleday, 1916.

Woolen, William Wesley. "Thomas Posey." *Biographical and Historical Sketches of Early Indiana.* Indianapolis: Hammond & Co., 1883.

WPA of Virginia Historical Inventory, Spotsylvania County. Fredericksburg, VA: WPA of Virginia, 1936.

Index

E

F

G

H

T

General Thomas Posey: Son of the American Revolution

Production Editor: Constance M. Hill
Design and Production: Michael J. Brooks

Text composed in 10/11.5 New Century Schoolbook

Printed by Thomson-Shore, Inc.
on 55# Huron Natural (recycled)

Smyth Sewn in Roxite A Linen